SAM BRACKEN

LIGHTNING BUGS

and other
RECONNAISSANCE DRONES

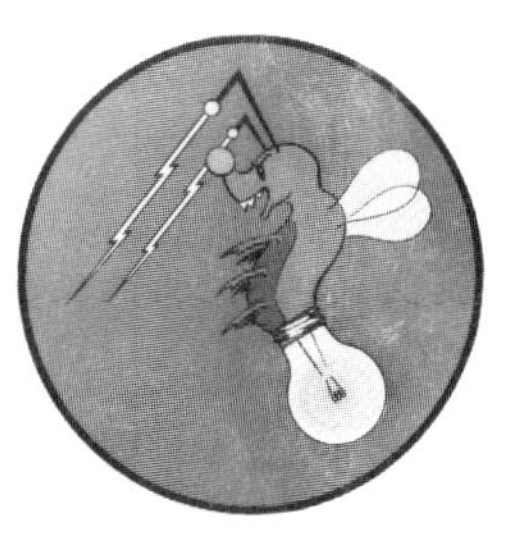

LIGHTNING BUGS

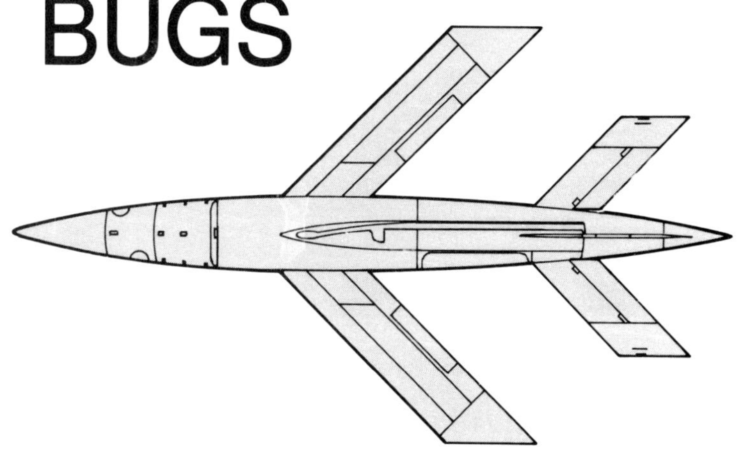

and other RECONNAISSANCE DRONES

by

WILLIAM WAGNER

in cooperation with

AERO PUBLISHERS, INC.

Library of Congress Cataloging in Publication Data

Wagner, William, 1909-
Lightning Bugs and other Reconnaissance Drones.

Includes index.
1. Drone aircraft—United States—History.
2. Reconnaissance aircraft—United States—History.
I. Title.
UG1242.D7W33 1981 358.4'5'0973
ISBN 0-8168-6654-6 (Aero)

International Standard Book Number 0-8168-6654-6
Library of Congress Card Number 81-71064

Published by Armed Forces Journal International
in cooperation with
Aero Publishers, Inc.
329 West Aviation Road, Fallbrook, CA 92028

PRINTED AND BOUND IN THE UNITED STATES OF AMERICA

To those dedicated military and civilian personnel whose can-do spirit made possible the success of unmanned reconnaissance.

APPRECIATION

Like the Lightning Bug reconnaissance drones, this book about their exploits and the skill of their operators, is the work of many people.

But, to pick out a few individuals —

Bill Rutherford, Teledyne, Inc. Vice President, who gave the book project a new breath of life after the manuscript had lain dormant for eight years.

Bob Schwanhausser — and friend Ben Schemmer of Armed Forces Journal — who shared our belief that the record of unmanned reconnaissance should be preserved.

Jo Ann Weaver who transcribed the dozens of interviews and steered me to Red Smith and others whose contributions would not otherwise have been noted.

Dale Weaver and other Ryan recce 'types' like Ed Sly, Gene Motter, Ed Christian, Bill Berry, et al, who made the program go.

And the Air Force 'types' — Lloyd Ryan, Andy Corra, Vic Rudd, Dan Emrich, Fred Yochim, Bill Forehand . . . and countless others.

Dave Gossett, in particular among photographers, especially for his overseas coverage at Bien Hoa, Osan and U-Tapao.

And Al Saiget for the fine quality of the prints which came from his photo lab.

Col. John Dale of SAC who got the birds flying right in Southeast Asia and years later shepherded the manuscript through the clearance maze.

Claude Ryan, my associate for 44 years (rather, I have been his), founder of Ryan Aeronautical Company, who tasked me in 1964 to maintain a narrative account of Ryan's role in unmanned reconnaissance.

And, of course, many friends in the graphic arts who actually got this book on the press — typists, photographers, typesetters, artists, printers.

For the author there is a great deal of satisfaction in researching, writing, illustrating and editing a book such as this. But, there is no way to adequately thank all who have contributed to this work. Yet, those who are aware of the help and encouragement they have given realize that I am eternally grateful to them.

William Wagner

December 1981
San Diego, California

FOREWORD

In the mid-1930s, when England's prospect of standing against the growing Nazi threat looked almost hopeless, a few men of vision developed radar and the Ultra code-breaking computer. Historians now generally agree that those two inventions turned the tide of World War II. Radar let England win the Battle of Britain; at El Alemain two years later, Ultra helped England change an unrelenting torrent of German victories in Europe, Russia and North Africa into hope for her beleagured Allies.

Remotely piloted vehicles (or "RPVs," as they are now known) have yet to alter man's destiny that profoundly. But they may, in our life time. Dr. Edward Teller, father of nuclear weaponry, told a small group of reporters in mid-1981 that, in his opinion, "The unmanned vehicle today is a technology akin to the importance of radars and computers in 1935."[a]

Dr. Teller's remark went unreported except in a small trade newsletter, as did an even more important opinion he voiced in a formal speech that day: "The development of unmanned systems . . . presents the only possibility for the United States to close the military gap between ourselves and the Soviet Union in the foreseeable future."

This book is the story of the men who spawned RPV technology; men who overcame years of bureaucratic inertia and scores of doubting Thomases to turn a controversial concept into operational reality and prove its value in war as well as in crisis and peace. Their idea was simple: to take the cockpit out of the airplane so the pilot could "fly" an unmanned intelligence-gathering mission whose flight path could either be preprogrammed or varied by remote control — at far lesser risk of life, cost, and political repercussion than manned overflight of heavily-defended hostile territory.

Their story begins late in 1959, three and a half years after the United States began overflying Russia in high-altitude U-2 spy planes. Foresighted Air Force officers, concerned about the political fallout that inevitably would develop if the pilot of a U-2 came down in enemy territory, started work on adapting a simple target drone for photographic reconnaissance. Within eight months of their first meeting on the problem, Francis Gary Powers was shot down over Russia on May Day, 1960. In the aftermath, a long-awaited Paris summit meeting was scuttled, and President Eisenhower felt forced to announce that he was ordering the offensive U-2 flights discontinued.

This was at a time when the nation's first spy satellite would not become operational for another 18 months, when work on the higher flying and faster Mach 3 SR-71 had just begun (it would not fly for another three and a half years.) It was also an election year when charges of a "missile gap" inflamed the 1960 Presidential campaign and dominated each day's headlines. At the very time that the "Cold War" reached new heights, the United States had lost its main source of intelligence behind the Iron and Bamboo Curtains.

Not surprisingly, work on an unmanned reconnaissance system that could penetrate hostile territory and bring back precise photographic intelligence began to get serious attention. That work intensified when, two months to the day after Francis Gary Powers was captured in Russia, an RB-47 bomber on an electronic ferret mission over the Barents Sea between Norway and Russia was shot down and two of its five crewmen taken prisoner in the Soviet Union.

Eight days later, the era of remotely piloted vehicles was born under the code name "Red

Wagon," when the United States Air Force awarded a modest $200,000, but highly classified contract to Ryan Aeronautical Company for a flight test demonstration showing how its target drones could be adapted for unmanned, remotely guided photographic surveillance missions. That contract, incidentally, was a harbinger of today's exotic "Stealth" aircraft technology, for one of the factors the Air Force asked Ryan to evaluate was how much it could reduce the drone's radar cross section (without a major redesign) to make it more survivable over heavily defended intelligence targets.

In another sense, that early work on RPVs was also the origin of today's cruise missile, the wonder weapon that then Defense Secretary Harold Brown prophesied in 1980 would "revolutionize warfare."[b] But ironically, as Bill Wagner tells you in the story ahead, that was the same Harold Brown who, when he was the Pentagon's chief weapons architect in 1960, overruled his own boss and abruptly cancelled the nation's first RPV program just as "Red Wagon" was getting underway.

Brown's unilateral blow slowed the program up almost a year and a half. Two months earlier, the Assistant Secretary of the Air Force for Research and Development, Dr. Courtland Perkins, had almost killed it outright when he told the program's action officer that his work was "a waste of time" and ordered him to stop the program. But Perkins never translated that directive into a written memo, and Air Force officers simply decided to ignore it.

Those two early blows were just the first of many potentially fatal setbacks from which the RPV program would reel, but eventually recover, in the two decades following Powers being shot down. Less than two years later, Brown was no doubt anxious to forget his earlier stop-work order when the Cuban missile crisis made the need for unmanned reconnaissance systems brutally apparent.

On October 27th, 1962, the day that President John Kennedy demanded that Russia dismantle its missile bases and remove its nuclear warheads from Cuba, Russian missiles there shot down a U-2, killing its pilot. The Cuban missile crisis was at its very peak. Kennedy needed photographic confirmation that Russia had removed the missiles, or proof that it had refused to do so. When it was found that only two U-2s were immediately available to continue the Cuban overflights, the intelligence community scrambled frantically to see whether or not Ryan's pilotless reconnaissance planes could do the job. (Bill Wagner's account of those weird days, understated though it is, borders on the hilarious, a script worthy of Peter Sellers trying to lead the world away from Armageddon.)

But, due in large part to the 16 month delay caused by Harold Brown's 1960 stop-work order, only two of the Ryan RPVs had been built, and their operational testing had not been completed. Luckily, the Cuban missile crisis soon abated. But the "near miss" gave America's RPV program a badly needed impetus, and by August of 1964, when North Vietnamese and U.S. ships clashed in the dark of night in the Tonkin Gulf, Ryan's RPVs were ready for wartime service.

In the next eight years, during a period when over 5,000 Americans lost their lives in Southeast Asia because their airplanes were shot down or crashed due to malfunctions at a crucial moment, over 3,000 unmanned RPV missions were flown over North Vietnam, China, Laos and elsewhere. With each such mission, new needs and new uses evolved for the program, first renamed "Lightning Bug" and later "Buffalo Hunter." The 1960 Ryan Firebee target drone grew into over 20 RPV configurations, from the 13-foot wing span 147-A recce jet to the 82-foot wing span YQM-98A "Compass Cope," with an increasing variety of payloads for photographic and then electronic intelligence and covert psychological warfare missions.

In a period when 90% of the Americans who became prisoners of war were downed pilots or crewmen, RPVs returned precision intelligence deep from hostile territory without risking the men "flying" the recce drones to possible death or capture. They flew their missions at a fraction of the cost of manned reconnaissance aircraft, whether measured in dollars, lives, or political risk (as in the flights over mainland China).

RPVs were used to collect targeting data for the "Rolling Thunder" bombing campaign over North Vietnam; to help locate prisoner of war camps so American planes would not inadvertently bomb our own airmen — and to plan their rescues (indeed, it was an RPV photo that finally confirmed the existence and location of the Son Tay prison 21 miles west of Hanoi from which the U.S. tried to free its prisoners in a dramatic 1970 raid); to provide bomb damage assessments after attacks on heavily defended targets, to drop propaganda leaflets intended to demoralize North Vietnamese citizenry, and to ferret out electronic intelligence on the Soviet air defense systems protecting North Vietnam. The typical RPV flew 10 such missions before it was finally shot down or failed.

Still, the RPVs in Vietnam represented a meagerly funded new technology: some banked at the wrong instant and returned with photos of blank horizons instead of POW camps; others simply went off course. Yet some of the RPVs' most valuable discoveries were unexpected bonuses resulting from just such malfunctions. In one case, an errant RPV detected a long-suspected but hitherto unlocated huge North Vietnamese fuel depot in the suburbs of Hanoi.[c]

Behind those missions is the story of a small band of gung-ho, can-do Air Force officers and industry technicians, told here largely from the viewpoint of Ryan, the contractor behind the key programs in this narrative. Working under near-clandestine security restrictions, often in combat or near-combat conditions, unable to tell their wives (and sometimes, their bosses) what they were doing or where they were going, they custom tailored a new technology to give America a small but vital edge in a new kind of war.

In the forefront of this story are such men as Air Force Lt. Col. Lloyd Ryan (who, it turns out, discovered only years into the program that he was a very distant relative of the company chairman, Ryan's founder, T. Claude Ryan, whom his "Big Safari," quick-reaction, highly-classified contracting procedures were driving prematurely bald as Ryan figuratively tore his hair out wondering if or when a new project would ever be paid for).

Central to the story is a Ryan engineer named Bob Schwanhausser, who thought his aeronautical career was in jeopardy when first assigned to Ryan's closely-held RPV project, but who has since made a career of overcoming bureaucratic inertia and technical problems to make it work. At overseas locations, the suspense and boredom and terror of day-to-day operations was borne by such men as Col. Bill Forehand, Col. John Des Portes, Col. John Dale — and Ryan's Dale Weaver, a "tech rep" who drew no combat or flight pay but flew countless missions in his RPV's C-130 launch planes, and camera expert Ed Christian, who often risked his life to get a precious photo package back from his returning reconnaissance birds. Too many others held key roles to be mentioned in this brief foreword, but Bill Wagner unveils their full roles in the pages ahead.

As you read this book, many will wonder why you haven't heard more about America's RPV programs before this — and where they stand today. You haven't read more before because until now the story behind them has been too closely held for military and corporate policy and security reasons. For two decades, Bill Wagner has squirreled away notes and memos and vignettes he's overheard about "Red Wagon" and "Lightning Bug" and "Buffalo Hunter" and many other such programs.

He finished his first draft of this story in the early 1970s, but when Pentagon officials read the manuscript, they politely suggested that its publication be postponed indefinitely. By the time "Security Review" would have finished censoring the story, Wagner learned, there wouldn't be much left worth printing. It was not until 1981 that Wagner was able to get the necessary blessings to tell the full story.

That lack of public visibility about what RPVs have done in the past two decades, and what they might do in the future, is a key reason they are not being exploited more by today's military planners. A 1981 report by the General Accounting Office recognized the problem when it spoke of the "apathy" and "unawareness" that characterize the Pentagon's current view of remotely piloted vehicles. GAO noted that because the "missions flown by the RPVs in Southeast Asia were for the most part classified . . . not very many people, including military, were aware of the role they played."

Sheer institutional bias is another reason that RPVs have been in a state of operational limbo since the Vietnam war wound down. During a decade when stunning technical advances in micro-electronics, jam-resistant and secure data links, miniaturized sensors, and all-weather guidance, control and recovery systems have removed the major technological barriers to exploiting unmanned vehicles for what otherwise would be high-risk missions by piloted aircraft — at a time when similar advances in air defense technology have increased the risk of overflying hostile terrain — the Pentagon's enthusiasm for RPVs has languished.

As this book comes off the press, not one U.S. remotely piloted vehicle is operational; indeed, the *only* "RPV" that Teledyne Ryan Aeronautical now has in production is its original Firebee target drone!

The bias behind this hiatus is hard to document. But logic makes one note that within the U.S. Air Force, Navy and Marine Corps, the use of RPVs comes under the purview of aviators. Because RPVs compete with airplanes for funds (even though they are designed to complement, not replace manned missions), any pilot who recommends buying an RPV instead of an airplane may be goring his own future.

RPVs are not "career enhancing," and "flying" them from a "cockpit" far removed from the smoke of battle is a drab occupation compared to the combat environment to which a fighter pilot's adrenalin is conditioned to respond. As Dr. Edward Teller put it in 1981, "The Air Force is built around fliers — and unmanned vehicles put fliers out of business. And that is a serious problem." Or, as the GAO summarized, "RPVs seem to suffer from the attitude of the users and not from technological drawbacks or infeasible systems."

The "problem" Teller described is so serious that the Air Force, Navy and Marine Corps do not even have a single significant research and development program for exploiting the use of RPVs in the future. Only the Army has one. (In the Army, RPVs have been put under the operational purview of artillerymen, not aviators.) Called "Aquila," the Army program is really for a mini-RPV that started out in 1974 as a surveillance and reconnaissance system, but which, because of the dramatic potential it showed in early field tests, has since been developed into a precise target acquisition system to direct artillery fire using laser-designators to give precision-guided artillery rounds a "first-round" hit capability. Thus, RPVs are dormant in the other Services at the very stage when they have finally matured to the point that cannoneers can shoot at targets instead of real estate.

(Aquila was to be readied for operational use by late 1985, but on the very day these words were drafted, the Pentagon announced to Congress that it would have to delay fielding Aquila until 1988 as a fallout of the budget adjustments stemming from President Reagan's $13-billion reduction of his original budget goals for rebuilding America's armed forces. Ironically, this happened only 24 hours after the Army had announced the winner of a major new program for a piloted target acquisition aircraft.)

Yet RPVs have proved their value in combat many times since their last flight in Southeast Asia. During the 1973 Yom Kippur War, Israel used scores of so-called "harrassment" drones, after its Air Force suffered unacceptable losses to Egyptian air defenses opposite the Suez Canal, to saturate the enemy air defense system, deplete its missile supply, and screen fighter-bombers as the Egyptian batteries were trying to reload.

In mid-1981, when Syria deployed SA-6 air defense missiles in Lebanon's Bakaa Valley and brought a new dimension of escalation to the perennial Middle East crisis, Israel flew some of its Teledyne Ryan Aeronautical RPVs over the SA-6 sites to draw Syrian fire. In quick succession, a series of drones were shot down — thus proving exactly what Israel wanted the world to know: the Syrian missiles were a new and very deadly threat. The RPVs even permitted Israel to offer photographic evidence of that: while unmanned reconnaissance "aircraft" preoccupied Syrian gunners, a higher-flying reconnaissance aircraft safely took photos of the batteries actually firing (and confirmed for Israeli intelligence the frequencies on which Syrian radars were operating).

Ironically, while the U.S. interest in RPVs is at a lull, Soviet military literature makes increasingly frequent mention of their potential payoff. Recent articles cite their "low reflection surfaces, low level of infrared emissions, and relatively low cost" to tout their value "when equipped with electronic jammers to screen a salvo of friendly missiles," as "decoy targets," in the "conduct of electronic warfare operations at sea," and even to "tow equipment simulating the radar and infrared signatures of ships."[d]

Like Harold Brown's and Courtland Perkins' early setbacks to America's RPV effort, bureaucracy and bias have probably done more to shoot down progress in this new technology than all of the enemy fire ever directed at unmanned vehicles. Thus, Bill Wagner's history also provides a fascinating, rare, and in-depth insight into the jeopardy that large institutions pose to small bands of creative men working to exploit unconventional ideas.

RPVs may have met their enemy. Could it be us?

November 18, 1981
Washington, D.C.

Benjamin F. Schemmer
Editor
Armed Forces Journal International

[a]*Author's notes from a press conference with Dr. Teller on July 21, 1981, Washington, D.C.*

[b]*Business Week, August 11, 1980.*

[c]*"DoD's Use of Remotely Piloted Vehicle Technology Offers Opportunities for Saving Lives and Dollars," Report by the Comptroller General of the United States, April 3, 1981.*

[d]*"Fly in the Sky Report," by William Ruhe,* **Seapower,** *July 1981.*

CONTENTS

1

COMPROMISE

MOSCOW, MAY 1, 1960

Already Communist party leaders were assembling inside the Kremlin for the traditional May Day parade in Red Square. Shortly they would be reviewing Soviet military preparedness from atop Lenin's tomb.

Then the word flashed in from distant Sverdlovsk.

An American plane had been shot down 1200 miles inside Russia! Cruising at a reported 68,000 feet altitude on a 3800-mile overflight of the Soviet heartland, pilot Francis Gary Powers' U-2 'spy plane' was damaged by a missile. Powers had parachuted safely and been captured uninjured.

Even now a civil transport plane carrying the captured American pilot was en route to Moscow.

Startling as the news was, it should have come as no great surprise to Nikita Khrushchev. Only three weeks before, Russian radar had tracked the overflight of another U-2. Then, too, nearly five years earlier Khruschchev had sat down in Geneva at the Four Power parley with President Dwight D. Eisenhower, France's Edgar Faure and Britain's Sir Anthony Eden. There, on July 21, 1955, the American president had sought agreement for his 'open skies' plan of mutual aerial surveillance as a deterrent to surprise attack, and to reduce tension among the great powers.

But Khrushchev had then been unwilling to permit the Free World to look over the Iron Curtain and no agreement was reached. No doubt he felt the Eisenhower proposal was largely an American attempt to pinpoint Russian targets for U.S. long-range bombers. Since that meeting, Russian insistence on its superiority in missile development following "Sputnik-1" on October 4, 1957 had been virtually an open invitation to the United States to try and find out what the Russians were up to.

The United States knew it was appallingly weak in its intelligence of the U.S.S.R. and had little basis for shaping its own deterrent force. Thus, the secret U-2 flights had been going on for years. In the late '40s and early '50s there had been several not very productive unmanned high-altitude balloon flights, guided by prevailing winds, over Russia, and in mid-1955 a giant radar at Diyarbakir, Turkey, near the Black Sea had been tracking Russian missile launches from Kapustin Yar.

So, while the word from Sverdlovsk was indeed disturbing, it was hardly a great surprise to Khrushchev.

Five years earlier, Eisenhower had been dealing from strength in proposing his 'open skies' policy. The new, long range Lockheed U-2 reconnaissance plane, authorized in 1954, and developed by famed designer Clarence L. (Kelly) Johnson in his secret 'skunk works', would be making its first flight within a matter of weeks. If Russia agreed to overflights, then the United States would have its 'glider with a jet engine' ready to conduct open aerial surveillance. If Khrushchev was unwilling to go along, the U-2 would start covert high-altitude operations above the range of Russian anti-aircraft and missiles.

U-2 DESIGNER AND PILOT — *Kelly Johnson's 'glider with a jet engine' made it possible for Francis Gary Powers, right, to overfly Russia on fatal spy mission.*

Lockheed Aircraft Corp.

Within months after the unsuccessful Geneva summit, U-2s began conducting overflights and peripheral surveillance for the USAF-CIA-NASA combine out of countries friendly to the United States — from Giebelstadt in Germany; Atsugi, Japan; from Taiwan; Adana, Turkey; Peshawar in Pakistan — and others.

A new ICBM test site for long range Russian missiles had been discovered at Tyuratam near the Aral Sea in mid-1957 by a U-2 flying out of Pakistan.

To prepare the President with an updated estimate of Soviet missile strength before the Paris summit, the first U-2 photo flight in some months was flown over southern Russia out of Pakistan on April 9, 1960. A further evaluation was requested in a few weeks when more data might be available on construction progress at suspected ICBM sites.

Francis Gary Powers took off on this fateful mission at 6:26 a.m. on the morning of May 1 on a course planned to take him over the Tyuratam missile test facility.

There had been no physical interference with the U-2 flights in the four years of their operation from Turkey and Pakistan until the Russian missile finally reached out and caught Powers on May Day.

Many in the United States felt the May 1960 overflight of Russia was badly timed, with a new Big Four summit conference due to take place in Paris in little more than two weeks.

Then, with Powers knocked out of the sky, there began a series of bizarre explanations and 'cover' stories, followed by a bombshell from Khrushchev.

Knowing only that Powers had not arrived in Bodo, Norway, as scheduled, U.S. officials in Adana, Turkey, announced in a cover story on May 2 that a plane of the National Aeronautics and Space Administration was missing on a routine weather reconnaissance flight.

Three days later, Khrushchev offered some clarification. Appearing before the Supreme Soviet, he stated he was "duty bound to report on the aggressive acts directed in the last few weeks by the United States of America against the Soviet Union."

He then told how on April 9 a U.S. plane had violated Soviet air space and went 'unpunished.' He added that when a second violation occurred on May 1, the U.S. jet plane — which bore 'no identification signs' — was shot down at his direction.

In Washington, NASA said that the plane, then missing four days, had been a single-place jet U-2 which was on a high-altitude weather research flight. It said the pilot, later identified as Lockheed civilian employee Francis Gary Powers, 30, reported he was having trouble with his oxygen equipment and implied he had strayed off course over Turkey and had drifted into Russia by mistake.

Next the State Department's spokesman told reporters there had been no deliberate attempt to violate Soviet air space.

But on May 7, in a second speech before the Supreme Soviet, Premier Khrushchev sprang his trap. He said the pilot was "alive and kicking" in Moscow, had confessed he was on a spy flight across the heart of Russia from Pakistan to Norway, and had been downed over a thousand miles inside Russia.

Khrushchev branded the U.S. version of the flight a "complete lie" and said he had withheld details in his original announcement to see what kind of 'fabrication' the State Department would issue. He warned that "Turkey, Pakistan and Norway should become aware that they are participants in this hostile act."

The Premier had scored a damaging propaganda blow against the U.S.

OVER SVERDLOVSK, a Russian missile *reached out and caught Powers on a flight from Peshawar in Pakistan to Bodo, Norway.*

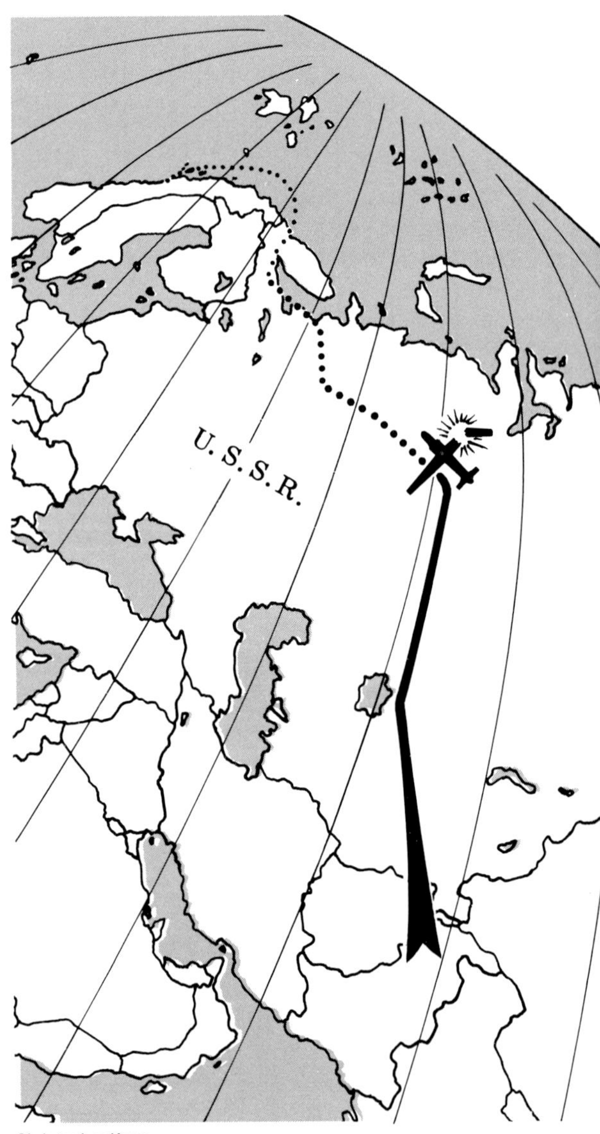

Christopher Kane

HIGH-FLYING U-2 reconnaissance plane, *recently developed, was proposed by President Eisenhower in 1955 to implement his 'open skies' plan of mutual aerial surveillance as a deterrent to surprise attack, and to reduce tension.*

Lockheed Aircraft Corp.

The State Department then officially acknowledged that the U-2 was on a surveillance mission while "endeavoring to obtain information now concealed behind the Iron Curtain." It then went on to say that "it is in relation to the danger of surprise attack that planes of the type of the unarmed civilian U-2 aircraft have made flight along the frontiers of the Free World for the past four years." And, finally, President Eisenhower shouldered all the blame, stating that he had personally approved the flights but only because they were vital to U.S. security due to Soviet secrecy.

Eisenhower flew to Paris, but Khrushchev refused to hold the scheduled parley unless there was a personal apology and promise by the President to punish those responsible for the espionage. The President rejected the vehement demands of Khrushchev, and was backed up by British Prime Minister Harold Macmillan and French President Charles de Gaulle. However, Eisenhower assured the Russian leader that U.S. intelligence flights had been suspended "and are not to be resumed." Actually CIA Director Allen W. Dulles had already cancelled the intelligence-gathering flights as Russian defenses had caught up to the extent that survivability was seriously impaired.

Eisenhower had been scheduled to go to Moscow in June to return the Khrushchev visit to the U.S. the previous September. Khrushchev cancelled the invitation and sabotaged the summit meeting.

Observers speculated that Khrushchev's fury stemmed mainly from the fact Powers' U-2 flight revealed the prior weakness of Soviet interceptor and anti-aircraft missile defenses, and their present lack of a similar reconnaissance capability. To have earlier accused the U.S. of overflights, although they were well aware of them, would have been to admit an inability to defend the Soviet Union against U.S. planes.

"All the News That's Fit to Print"

The New York Times.

LATE CITY EDITION

NEW YORK, SUNDAY, MAY 8, 1960

TWENTY-FIVE CENTS

U. S. CONCEDES FLIGHT OVER SOVIET, DEFENDS SEARCH FOR INTELLIGENCE; RUSSIANS HOLD DOWNED PILOT AS SPY

JOHNSON ARRIVES IN WEST VIRGINIA AS CLIMAX NEARS

Texan Declines to Choose Between Humphrey and Kennedy in Primary

VOTE DRIVES WINDING UP

City of Clarksburg Invaded by Politicians, High School Bands and Rotarians

Nixon Shifts Tactics To Combat Kennedy

N.A.A.C.P. TO FIGHT CURBS AT BEACHES

Plans 'Wade-In' Campaign at Tax-Maintained Resorts From Jersey to Texas

LONDON TROUBLED

Fears That U.S. Stance for Summit Parley Will Be Injured

By DREW MIDDLETON

'CONFESSION' CITED

Khrushchev Charges Jet Was 1,200 Miles From the Border

ACTION EXPLAINED

Officials Say Danger of Surprise Attack Forces Watch

By JAMES RESTON

VOROSHILOV QUITS AS CHIEF OF STATE

Brezhnev, Khrushchev Aide, Rising in Party Councils, Succeeds Marshal, 79

By MAX FRANKEL

Underground Atom Blasts Set by U.S. to Aid Detection

INTELLIGENCE ACTS ADMITTED BY U.S.

Both Soviet and American Efforts in Field Cited in Statement on Plane

ON EISENHOWER'S RETURN from Paris he addressed the nation by radio and television, renewing his five-year-old offer of an 'open skies' agreement with the Soviet Union. He volunteered to donate U.S. reconnaissance aircraft for any such scheme set up by the United Nations.

After making this offer, the President displayed a photo of part of the Naval Air Station, San Diego, taken from an altitude of 70,000 feet to illustrate the detail which cameras could pick up and how effective international air surveillance could be.

Eisenhower went on to explain the "imperative necessity" of reconnaissance flights and his own "grave responsibility" for continuously gathering intelligence by all possible means, including espionage, to safeguard against surprise attack. He cited the attack on Pearl Harbor as an example of what had to be avoided in the future. And he again deplored the "distasteful but vital necessity" of espionage.

Having promised to discontinue the offensive U-2 flights, the United States found itself facing a critical void in its knowledge of what missile and bomber preparations were under way in Russia. And it came at a most inopportune time for the country had lost its main source of authentic intelligence information when the peril of the missile gap seemed the greatest.

Long-range U.S. planning had dictated the need for some follow-on to the U-2 and this was to come in the form of photographic reconnaissance satellites. Work on such a project had begun in 1956.

Thus from the May 1960 downing of Powers' U-2, only 18 months were to lapse before the first photographic inventory of Soviet missile sites along the Trans-Siberian Railroad was obtained by early satellite and missile observation system (SAMOS) vehicles.

Meanwhile, on July 1, only two months after the Powers incident, a Russian MiG shot down another U.S. plane, an RB-47, on a 'ferret' mission over the

NAVAL AIR STATION, San Diego, from 70,000 feet. *President Eisenhower released this photo after Powers' U-2 was downed to illustrate how effective international air surveillance could be as part of his 'open skies' proposal.*

Wide World Photos

radio and
erial photo

of North Island, taken at 70,000 feet over San Diego Bay looking south. Photo shows "land" and "take-off" markings on runways, seaplane ramp at bottom, and the carrier pier at middle left.

13-MILE RANGE

U.S. Navy

FOURTEEN YEARS LATER this oblique photo *from high altitude shows detail of Naval Air Station, North Island, top; Lindbergh Field, right; and downtown San Diego with its network of freeways.*

Barents Sea off Norway and Russia where it was seeking data on Soviet radar signals.

Russia claimed the plane, piloted by Major Willard G. Palm and Capt. Bruce Olmstead with Capt. John McKone as navigator was over Soviet territory. The United States said the plane was 50 miles off the coast over international waters when shot down. The U.S.S.R. refused an impartial check, vetoing a United Nations resolution for an investigation.

Olmstead and McKone had parachuted at sea, were captured and kept prisoner for seven months. Palm kept the plane in the air for 20 minutes after being hit by cannon fire so as to also give three electronic specialists a chance to bail out, but their bodies were never found. Palm went down with his plane, his body later being returned by the Russians.

The U-2 and RB-47 incidents ended all prospect for East-West agreement and the Cold War took on a new, more ominous tone. All the more reason why the U.S. need for intelligence information behind the Iron and Bamboo curtains grew rather than diminished.

2

PROMISE

THE PENTAGON, SEPTEMBER, 1959

"You know, Lloyd, with the recon activity we've got going now, someone had better be giving some thought to the problem we're going to have if and when a U-2 pilot comes down in unfriendly territory."

Col. Harold L. Wood, Chief of the Reconnaissance Division, Directorate of Operations, Headquarters, U.S. Air Force, was speaking.

On the other end of the conversation was his deputy, Lt. Col. Lloyd M. Ryan.

"You're sure right about that, Woody. And it's not just an Air Force problem either, now that the CIA is operating overflights with the U-2s."

Being operations people they knew full well that one of these days a U-2 would surely be shot down.

There, in the basement of the Pentagon with their staffs, were the two action officers responsible for the Air Force role in reconnaissance including developing aircraft for photo and electronic intelligence collection.

No one was mentioning it openly then, but plans were already under way for a new supersonic jet reconnaissance plane, carrying a crew of two. The SR-71 (YF-12) was being designed by Lockheed's Kelly Johnson to go higher, faster and farther than any other recce bird. Still it, too, would have the problems inherent in a man-carrying vehicle.

One of the experts in the recce business who had access to Colonel Ryan's office was Raymond A. Ballweg, Jr., Vice-President of Hycon Manufacturing Company, whose cameras were in the U-2. [Ballweg is now a Vice-President (International) of Teledyne, Inc.]

Ray's boss was Trevor Gardner, Hycon President, who several years earlier had completed a tour of duty as Assistant Secretary of the Air Force for Research and Development. While in the service, Colonel Ballweg had been Gardner's executive officer responsible for handling liaison between Richard M. Bissell, Jr., of the CIA and the Air Force regarding development of the U-2. Gardner had been a key figure in manned reconnaissance, but held a dim view of pilotless planes for the job.

Colonel Hal Wood

Beside the U-2, there were two other recce programs then in the works. Bell at Buffalo had a twin-engine airplane that was in the mock-up stage. The Glenn L. Martin Company had done a conversion of a B-57 — the D Model — which had received high priority treatment.

A few weeks after Colonels Lloyd Ryan and Hal Wood had expressed their concern about manned aircraft, Ballweg dropped in for a chat with his 'customer.'

Ray Ballweg

The conversation drifted onto the subject Ryan and Wood had discussed three weeks earlier. What about the risks of the pilot in manned recon aircraft?

"Hell, Lloyd, why don't you have us install a camera in a jet target drone?" suggested Ballweg. "No reason it can't be programmed to do the recon job for you and bring back pictures."

"Our response, Hal Wood's and mine," Lloyd recalled later, "was, 'what drone?'

"We didn't know anything about drones. The state-of-the-art in recon at that time was RF-101s, RB-47s and U-2s. Except for the U-2, there hadn't been an airplane built just for reconnaissance since World War II."

Then Ballweg mentioned there was an outfit on the west coast, Ryan Aeronautical Company, that was building a jet-powered target drone, the "Firebee", that might do the job.

"I know some of the Ryan types," Ballweg volunteered. "They've got a Firebee briefing coming up in a couple of weeks. That bird's proven to be a pretty stable aerial platform — just what you need when flying a camera. Why don't you drop in and take advantage of the opportunity to get up to speed on jet drones?"

Lt. Colonel Ryan thought the idea had merit even though he knew little about the drone's builder. [Years later he was to discover that he and T. Claude Ryan, founder of Ryan Aeronautical Company, had the same 'Aunt Viola.' And, by an odd coincidence, there was another Col. Lloyd Ryan, middle initial F., then assigned at the Pentagon, who was a nephew of Claude Ryan's.]

"I honestly didn't know anything about the Firebee," Lloyd Ryan said later.

"The last drone I knew anything about was the QB-17 propeller-driven job used in A-bomb tests at Eniwetok and I'd heard vaguely about some six-jet QB-47s down at Eglin Field used in weapons testing. But not being in Air Defense I had no reason to know anything about the target drones then being used in training to sharpen the skills of pilots and anti-aircraft crews.

"Ryan Aeronautical's Bill Orr was giving a briefing to some people in the Pentagon several weeks later and we invited ourselves to attend. We sat in and listened to the briefing about the new Q-2C Firebee, but there was no reference to its ability to fill the recon role. I wasn't even introduced; just sitting in the back of the room listening.

"There was no follow-up by the Ryan company and I didn't want to seem too eager, so decided to let the matter rest for a while.

"It was after that I made a phone call out to San Diego and said I would like to talk to somebody about a role, other than training, for the Firebee, but for security reasons I wasn't able to tell more at the time to stimulate their interest. Somehow nothing

EARLY SUPPORTERS of reconnaissance potential *of basic Ryan Firebee target drone were Mickey McDaniel, left, and T. Claude Ryan, company founder-president, right, shown here with engineering vice-president Bruce Smith and early XQ-2.*

U.S. Air Force

came of that call either."

Actually neither Ryan nor the Air Force had been asleep at the switch. Years earlier, in April 1955, the Department of Defense had permitted Ryan to release the information that "the Firebee jet target drone has potential tactical applications and could be used as a guided missile or for reconnaissance."

Continuing, the Ryan news release stated:

> For tactical reconnaissance, a Firebee could be equipped with aerial cameras, radar, reconofax and television installations to transmit intelligence information to operational headquarters. As a tactical reconnaissance vehicle, it could be catapulted from the ground, vectored over the proposed target areas, and brought back for parachute recovery of the plane and its intelligence data without risking the loss of an expensive plane or an irreplaceable flight crew. For long-range reconnaissance, its scope could be extended by air launching from a 'mother' plane.

But although the potential of drone reconnaissance was being considered, no active program had been undertaken to bring that potential to fruition.

Obviously in 1959 there was still some convincing to be done at both Ryan and Hycon. Ballweg finally got Trevor Gardner to give an okay for Hycon to get started on the program; then Ray ran into initial trouble convincing Ryan, builder of the vehicle necessary to carry the camera. The only real supporter Ray found at Ryan was M. M. (Mickey) McDaniel, one of its first drone technicians and strongest proponents. Ray and Mickey finally put together an agreement for full cooperation between Hycon and Ryan.

Later Lloyd Ryan got on the phone to San Diego again and this time talked to Edward G. Uhl, recently hired by Ryan as Vice President-Technical Administration. Uhl had come from the Glenn L. Martin Company where as Vice President of Engineering he was active with Martin's camera-carrying RB-57 high-altitude manned reconnaissance aircraft operated by the "Black Knights" of the newly formed 4080th Strategic Reconnaissance Wing.

"Things at last began to fall in place," Colonel Ryan recalls.

BY THE HOLIDAY SEASON 1959, it was obvious that management at Ryan at last more fully understood the long-range potential of drone reconnaissance. With a verbal green light from the Air Force to push the concept, but without assurance of eventually receiving a contract, Ryan established a 'secure' group, approved to deal with classified information, to start an unsolicited proposal effort.

January 21, 1960, Robert R. (Swany) Schwanhausser, was advanced by Ryan management from group engineer to Project Engineer for Reconnaissance Drones. He owed his new job to his impatience and rebellious nature.

An aeronautical engineering graduate of M.I.T., Schwanhausser had been the Air Force's Q-2 Firebee target drone project engineer at Holloman Air Force Base in New Mexico. When Lt. Schwanhausser completed his tour of duty he applied to Ryan for an engineering job, but instead was plucked off by Continental Aviation and Engineering Corp. (CAE) to become project engineer on the American version of the French "Marbore" jet engine which, as the J69, was to power the Ryan Firebee target drone.

Don Doerr

AT PLOTTING BOARD watching flight *of Firebee on test range at Holloman Air Force Base are Lieut. R. R. Schwanhausser, left at controls, and Ryan technician.*

Four months later Swany bailed out of CAE at Detroit and landed on the Ryan payroll at Dayton, Ohio, home of Wright-Patterson Air Force Base and the Air Materiel Command.

"The Q-2C Firebee drone was just starting in production," Schwanhausser recalled, "and Ryan had run into a tremendous set of problems, so what they needed was someone to put out the damn fires. Of course, I didn't realize that until I got to Dayton.

"After 18 months there, and as soon as our son was born, I told the company I was either going to work for them in San Diego or sign on with another company. By then, I'd learned a hell of a lot more about the Air Force, especially procurement, but I felt I was then just a communications link between the plant and the customer at Dayton.

Don Doerr

TWO KEY OFFICERS in Ryan Firebee project *at Air Force base in New Mexico were Lieut. Bob Schwanhausser, project officer, right, and Lieut. Wayne Kuncle, pilot of jet chase plane from which running account of target plane performance is radioed.*

"So we moved out to San Diego and I went to work as project engineer on LOTOP, a looping nuclear weapons delivery system. From that I took over on ARM, an anti-radiation missile study. We were working on ARM with J. R. (Dick) Iverson and his people at Ryan's Electronics Division, since the company was trying desperately to get into the missile business. ARM didn't make the grade either but out of it we did get a study contract and a 'need-to-know' which helped on later projects.

"In Advanced Systems I had a manpower budget all my own, eight or nine guys, and a charter to get into the missile business. But one morning when I came in, my budget had been cut to one — and it was me — and I had a terrible fight with my superior. I told him what he could do with the job.

"By that time we had our brand new Vice President, a young, very dynamic, outspoken guy by the name of Ed Uhl. He sent for me.

" 'Okay,' Ed said, 'what's the problem?'

"And I said, 'To hell with this damn place!'

" 'All right, Swany, get off of it! I know at least six things around here you're capable of doing, and doing well. What's the one thing you'd like most to do? — And don't hedge with me.'

"I decided I'd better think damn carefully about how I answered that, and while I was pondering his question Ed picked up the conversation again.

"I'll tell you what. We're trying to get into a new product line — reconnaissance drones. I'm not happy with the way it's being run. How would you like to report directly to me on it? Take six or eight people and get going.'

"Well, Ed, that's a hell of a challenge, but I think it's a lousy job. I don't see much future in this reconnaissance drone stuff."

Time proved Schwanhausser wrong, but he proved to be just the guy for the job.

ED UHL to Bob Schwanhausser: *"Take six or eight people and get going."*

Ryan Aeronautical Library

SWANY — LIVING UP to his 'Rapid Robert' nickname — didn't waste a minute in getting under way to provide the Q-2C [later designated BQM-34A] with a recon capability; to prove or disprove what could or couldn't be done.

"From what I heard," Lloyd Ryan was to explain later, "there had been plenty of thought in San Diego about adapting the Firebee for recon missions, but in the labyrinth of bureaucracy they hadn't found us and we in the Air Force hadn't connected right with them."

And, the Ryan company's previous reconnaissance group hadn't proven very creative.

"They had studied the subject," Schwanhausser recalled, "and decided you could not fly one of the Firebee drones farther than 660 miles since the pilotless plane could carry only so much fuel.

"When we first started out," Swany went on, "I knew I could put another gallon of gas in there somewhere, and that it would get us six more miles range. So if we could put another gallon in we could find a way to carry ten more gallons, or 20 or 30. That's about how we started. We refused to accept negative thinking."

WITH BEHIND-THE-SCENES coaching from Colonel Ryan and Ray Ballweg, a background briefing of the Firebee system was laid on early in 1960 for top Air Force brass, comprising the Reconnaissance Panel at the Pentagon.

Swany strode to the front of the conference room to begin his pitch —

Achievements in the field of unmanned aircraft during the past decade are perhaps not generally well understood. A major breakthrough came in 1948 when Ryan adapted the jet engine to a remotely controlled airframe.

Use of the jet vastly increased the performance envelopes in both speed and altitude, providing aerial targets which could match — or even exceed — the capabilities of the fighter aircraft shooting against them.

The refinement of electronic systems within the drone, coupled with more efficient radar tracking systems, extended the range of the targets from a few miles to fifty — from fifty to a hundred — and eventually ranges up to two hundred miles, under remote control.

Today's Firebee is a jet-powered, swept-wing, pilotless aerial target designed to simulate attacking enemy aircraft and missiles. Capable of operating from altitudes as low as 50 feet to as high as 60,000 feet, it is used by the United States Army, Navy, and Air Force for weapons systems training and evaluation.

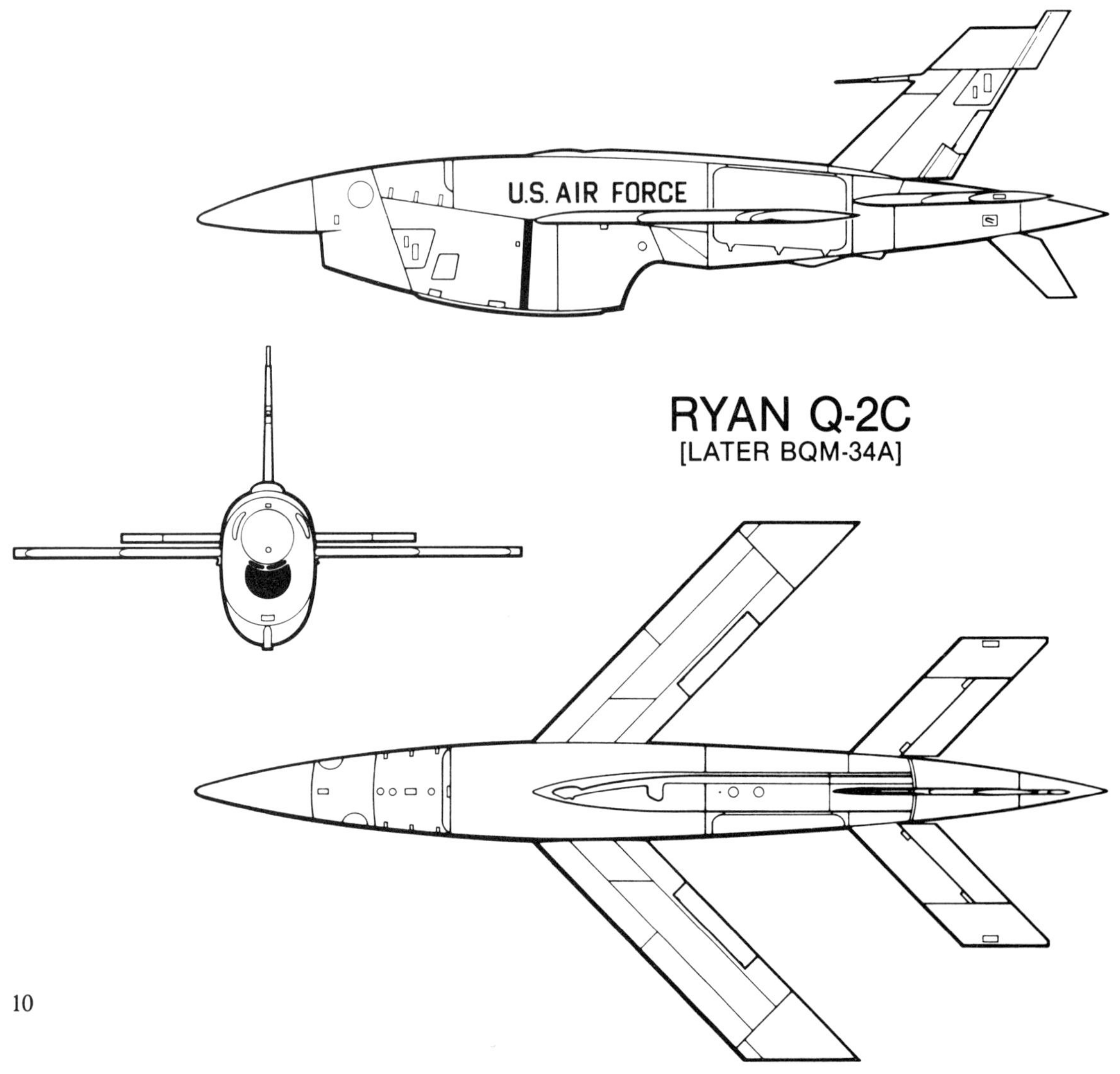

RYAN Q-2C
[LATER BQM-34A]

Firebees are launched from ground installations or from specially equipped aircraft and are remotely controlled by radio through all flight maneuvers. A radar beacon facilitates tracking the drone, while telemetry provides in-flight data such as engine rpm, airspeed and altitude to ground controllers.

Flight path of the target plane and its changing radar altitude are displayed by ink traces on a radar plotting board which enables the controller to fly a planned mission pattern.

Upon mission completion the Firebee is recovered, either automatically or by command, using a two-stage parachute recovery system. This permits the drone to be reused for additional missions.

As I mentioned, Firebee development began in 1948 as a joint program designed to produce a high-performance, sub-sonic, drone aircraft to be used as an aerial target by all three services. From the original vehicle, the XQ-2, evolved the U.S. Air Force Q-2A, the U.S. Navy KDA-1, and the U.S. Army XM-21. Each version incorporated special features dictated by the individual using service.

In 1958, the Air Force backed development of an advanced Firebee, the model Q-2C. Performance and reliability were much improved, and many of the individual service requirements of earlier Firebees were incorporated as standard equipment. Q-2C production was started the first of this year.

Since the Firebee was introduced, operations have been conducted on a wide scale under a variety of environmental conditions.

The basic Firebee is 23 feet long; the wing span is only 13 feet. It is powered by a J69-T-29 turbojet engine, employing two stages of compression, and is rated at 1700 pounds sea-level static thrust.

The Firebee is designed for either air or ground launch. A typical launch aircraft is the Lockheed DP-2E Neptune, which can carry two Firebees.

The flight control system automatically stabilizes the Firebee and executes flight maneuvers upon command. The autopilot uses conventional aileron and elevator control surfaces to provide roll and pitch stabilization and to execute flight maneuvers.

Remote control of the Firebee is normally accomplished through a radio link using a ground transmitter and an airborne receiver. The remote command link permits control of the target either from a manned aircraft or from a surface station.

TRI-SERVICE FIREBEES of early '50s *included from front: U.S. Air Force Q-2A, Navy KDA-1 and Army XM-21. Royal Canadian Air Force Firebee, rear.*

Teledyne Ryan Aeronautical

Teledyne Ryan Aeronautical

RYAN'S TORRANCE, CALIFORNIA, plant, *under direction of G. W. Rutherford, was first to build the Q-2A version of the Firebee training target in quantity.*

U.S. Air Force

REALISTIC TRAINING for Air Force *fighter pilots was provided by unmanned Firebee target drones which simulate action of 'enemy' planes.*

FLOATING DOWN for another flight, *Firebee is recovered by two-stage parachute system.*

When a mission is completed or when fuel is near depletion, the remote control operator maneuvers the target to a suitable recovery point. The two-stage parachute sequence ensures a safe landing impact. The main chute lowers the Firebee in a horizontal attitude to the ground or water at approximately 20 feet per second. Landing impact is absorbed by the keel of the engine nacelle thus protecting equipment in the nose and fuselage compartments.

After landing by parachute, Firebees are retrieved by helicopters capable of lifting a static load of approximately 2,900 pounds. Air-sea rescue type boats fitted with special cranes may be used to retrieve the Firebee from the water.

The limits of the Firebee's speed/altitude envelope vary, depending on the target's weight and the additional drag forces of external stores. The weights shown on the graph, now on the screen, cover the normal changes experienced as a result of fuel burnoff. Firebee speed is varied in flight, by remote command, from approximately 250 knots air speed to the maximum indicated. As you can see, this is approximately Mach 0.95.

Mission requirements frequently dictate specific speeds or altitude, either of which will affect endurance. On this chart, the solid line is the curve for best endurance, and the dotted line shows maximum speed. For instance, for best endurance at 40,000 feet altitude, true airspeed should be about 400 knots. This would give an endurance of approximately 100 minutes. Maximum speed at 40,000 feet would be about 550 knots, but endurance would be reduced to about 50 minutes. This is just an indication of some of the variables which must be considered during mission planning.

''Gentlemen, that's the story of the basic Firebee.

''You'll note we finished this portion of the presentation by referring to specific performance in terms of altitude and endurance.

''Now I'd like to move on to another phase of what we see as within the Firebee's potential. Here, as you know, our discussion is going to border on classified information.

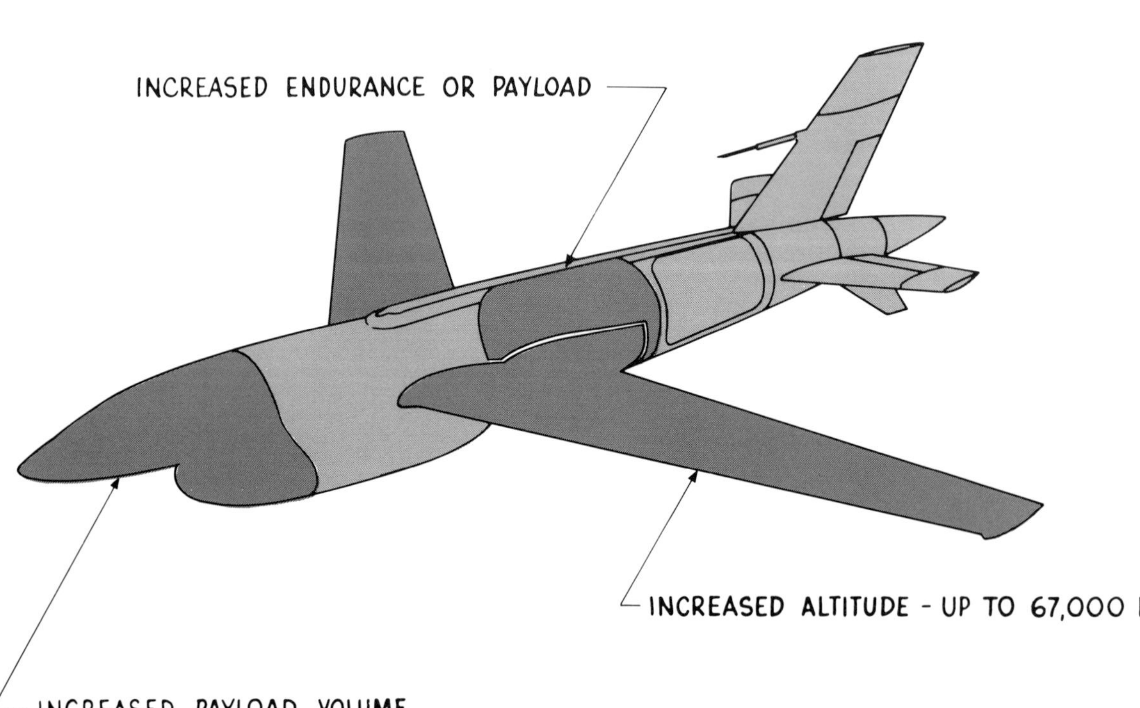

"WE AT RYAN ARE AWARE of the Air Force's requirements for aerial intelligence through use of reconnaissance aircraft. What we want to propose and discuss with you is the means by which the Firebee's altitude and range capabilities can be greatly extended to provide the country with a pilotless reconnaissance vehicle for covert operations.

"The use of U-2 manned vehicles for overflights of the territory of nations unfriendly to the United States creates, we believe, risks which are unnecessary to take. We feel there is a solution to this in the logical evolution of the unmanned Firebee drone system.

"We propose that Ryan customize several Firebees to demonstrate how we can give you increased range and altitude. Nothing more drastic is required initially than to extend the fuselage to provide more fuel capacity for greater endurance. Our preliminary studies indicate the Q-2C can be given a range capability of 1200 to 1400 nautical miles. If the mission requires flying above the known capability of potential enemy anti-aircraft and missiles then we can add additional wing surface and take the bird upstairs to altitudes far in excess of where we are now operating.

"Then, of course, to round out the reconnaissance capability we need to provide the cameras or other sensor packages which have already been proven in your manned reconnaissance vehicles.

"We believe the day need not be far off when, to cite examples readily understood by laymen, it would be possible to launch a pilotless jet aircraft say near Kansas City, and within hours know precisely what ships are unloading in New York harbor, the nationality of those ships, and the type and amount of cargo being unloaded.

"A low-level launch south of San Diego could reveal the condition of rail and road traffic to Los Angeles in minute detail — and cover the industrial area of Los Angeles to determine what manufacturing activity is going on.

"A high-altitude sweep originating over New Orleans could chart strategic sections of the Mississippi River from Baton Rouge to St. Paul, all in a matter of hours — and repeat that survey on a daily basis. Imagine, if you can, these flights being accomplished with precision and accuracy under the guidance of only an electronic brain!

"We would like to get going on the kind of program we have broadly outlined today. We believe that for some missions the cockpit must be taken out of the airplane, put on the ground, and let the pilot fly the vehicle from there.

"With your guidance we are prepared to start on this kind of program."

"WE PROPOSE that Ryan customize *several Firebees [off the San Diego production line] to demonstrate how we can give you increased range and altitude."*

Teledyne Ryan Aeronautical

AFTER THE PRESENTATION Schwanhausser and Colonel Ryan reviewed the possibilities for such a project to be sponsored by the Air Force.

"At that time," Ryan recalls, "the Air Force had no money, no budget items, no line items, but we felt we could sell it internally if we could come up with a reasonable program.

"Schwanhausser took it from there and helped bring the contractor's side of the program along. He was ready with something tangible in two months."

In a full-blown "Technical Proposal for a Reconnaissance Drone," Schwanhausser and his engineering people, aided by Ray Ballweg of Hycon, reached these conclusions and recommendations:

1. There is an urgent requirement for pre-hostility, high-altitude photographic reconnaissance by an unobserved, unmanned, non-warlike drone.
2. While ranges in the order of 1100 n.mi. would allow deep penetrations into the Soviet Bloc, ranges of over 2000 miles are required for overflight from the Barents Sea to Turkey, and from India to Korea or Japan.
3. A Q-2C with minimum modification (60 gallons additional fuel) is capable of flight ranges in excess of 1100 n.mi.
4. A Q-2C with a new and larger wing, carrying all fuel internally, and powered by the projected 2400 lb. thrust version of the J69 engine, is capable of ranges to 2500 n.mi.
5. The Q-2C is in volume production (15 per month presently — accelerating to 20 per month in June) and is readily available.
6. Extremely high mission reliability has been demonstrated in flight test and operational use.
7. All ground support equipment has been developed and is currently in production.
8. Air launch from GC-130 Hercules aircraft has been thoroughly developed and tested. Ground launch development for the Q-2C will be completed in July 1960.
9. All components of the Hycon HR-233A camera have been developed with the exception of the new magazine to accommodate 2500 feet of thin-base film. This camera will provide resolution to two feet from an altitude of 50,000 feet and permit oblique photographs as well as verticals.
10. The Litton P-2000 Inertial Platform is an extremely accurate, off-the-shelf navigation system, and will be even further improved during the next year. This system has been found to be superior to its competitive systems in terms of cost, size and weight.
11. The radar appearance of the modified drone will render the drone virtually undetectable, making it the least detectable existing aircraft.

Analysis of the foregoing points indicates that a reliable high-altitude, long-range drone reconnaissance weapon system can be made readily available through the use of existing components, minimizing system development time and cost.

U.S. Army

GROUND LAUNCH *from New Mexico desert.*

3

RED WAGON

MEANWHILE, LLOYD RYAN undertook the role of recon drone missionary in the Air Force.

"We took the idea and ran it through Dr. Joseph V. Charyk, Under Secretary of the Air Force. We knew a camera would operate in the Q-2C Firebee; that the drone was a stable platform and in tests for the Army had proven that vibration levels were acceptable for photo work. So then the question raised was, could we reduce the drone's radar cross-section sufficiently to give it a reasonable survivability in a hostile environment without having to go back through a basic redesign?"

The first proposal had been for test work and 15 flight vehicles but only enough funds were available for a modest feasibility and systems integration study and test program.

"We briefed it to the Reconnaissance Panel of the Air Staff in mid-April," Schwanhausser recalls. "Then, when Francis Gary Powers was shot down two weeks later, things began to happen very rapidly."

On July 8, 1960, just a week after the RB-47 and its crew had been shot down by the Russians, Ryan Aeronautical Company went under contract to the Air Force [AF33(600)-41898]. It was for only $200,000, but it was a start. Ryan in turn let sub-contracts to other specialists — to Hycon to study the camera system and to Litton Industries for the guidance system.

The initial test phase of 1960's so-called 'summer program' was for Ryan to conduct a flight demonstration program, using two Model 124 Q-2C target drones. [Actually four Q-2Cs were used.] The purpose was two-fold. First, to establish the radar detectability of a drone flying at 50,000 feet; and, second, to demonstrate the degree of reduction in radar reflectivity which could be achieved by radar-absorbing modifications to the airframe — without creating serious aerodynamic penalties.

Preliminary to the flight test demonstration, a series of static reflectivity measurements using one-quarter and one-eight scale models of the Q-2C were made by Radiation, Inc. of Melbourne, Fla.

These tests indicated that radar reflectivity could be reduced by placing a screen of proper mesh over the engine air intake, by painting the nose section with non-conductive paint, and by placing a blanket of radar energy absorbing material on the sides of the drone.

The flight test program with modified Q-2Cs was conducted at Holloman Air Force Base, New Mexico, during 17 free flights averaging 51 minutes each between September 16 and October 12, 1960. Dynamic reflectivity measurements showed significant decreases in detectability of the modified drone. And joint studies with Hycon confirmed the feasibility of installing cameras for the photo mission.

REDUCED RADAR REFLECTIVITY was achieved *by screen over engine air intake, non-conductive paint and radar absorbing blankets.*

U.S. Air Force

The information gained in these initial tests was to be applied in development of the projected Ryan Model 136 reconnaissance vehicle which would emphasize minimum reflectivity in its design criteria. These studies in turn laid valuable groundwork for later development of the Model 147 and for other studies concerning operational drone survivability in a hostile environment.

But at the very beginning even the small study contract came close to being lost, as explained by Lloyd Ryan.

"The Air Force Assistant Secretary for Research and Development, Dr. Courtland Perkins, assuming I was the program manager, called me soon after the contract had been let through regular procurement channels. He said the project was a waste of time, and that I was to stop the program.

"I called the Ryan company to find out how far along they were, and it turned out the Air Force had already committed the money anyhow. So, we just didn't answer Perkins since the directive to stop never arrived in written form. We just went ahead and did the test program, which proved to be quite satisfactory.

"Even before the contract was formally signed, some work had gotten under way, and within a fortnight Francis Gary Powers was in the news. To us it was sort of an 'I-told-you-so' deal because we had started the drone studies in anticipation of just such an event."

Despite the Powers' U-2 incident on May Day, which should have stimulated unmanned concepts, it was not all smooth sailing for drone reconnaissance. An internal struggle developed in the Air Force regarding the expenditure of money for the Firebee at a time when they were spending so much on the huge new SR-71 Mach 3 manned reconnaissance plane.

"It was a problem," Lloyd Ryan recalled, "to explain that a low-to-medium altitude unmanned drone system was not in competition with the big, fast, high-altitude piloted airplane — that it really constituted one of several capabilities the Air Force should have and should continue to develop.

"To obtain additional evaluation of the unmanned system I called on Lt. Col. Fred Yochim, a camera expert, at Wright-Patterson Air Force Base, Dayton. He was head of the advanced techniques branch of the Technical Intelligence Center."

"Soon after that," Yochim recalled, "Bob Schwanhausser and several of his technical people arrived to brief us on their droned jet reconnaissance capability. We evaluated it from an operations standpoint, as Lloyd Ryan had requested, to be certain it would, in fact, meet operational requirements. With minor exceptions we felt the system would do the job."

"Red Wagon" became the code name for the flight demonstration and for the follow-on Model 136 proposed to fully develop the drone reconnaissance potential. The Ryan company, which had won out over Boeing Wichita's proposed "Blue Scooter" program, gave Red Wagon top priority.

Teledyne Ryan Aeronautical

BY PLACING JET ENGINE on top of fuselage, *Model 136 design would reduce not only the radar but also the plane's infrared signature as well.*

"We weren't supposed to know about the competition with Boeing," Swany recalled, "but one way or another you find out about these things. Pretty much throughout, we had the upper hand because we were already in the drone business and had something tangible from which to work. So we were able to watch our proposal go through the system successfully."

THE GOVERNMENT'S TOP SECRET classification kept knowledge of the nature of the new work to an absolute minimum. Even so, when the flight test program got under way in September, Ryan had already moved Red Wagon to a separate leased warehouse on Frontier Street in San Diego to isolate the project from prying eyes and the curiosity of other Ryan employees at the main plant.

Staffing the warehouse activity was carried out with equal secrecy. When Swany needed an administrative assistant he put the arm on Owen S. Olds, head of Ryan Electronics, for the services of J. R. (Bob) Reichardt, then in charge of support functions for that Division. Reichardt had earlier been general operations manager of Philippine Airlines and had set up Ryan's corporate aircraft activity.

"One day," Reichardt relates, "I was asked by Owen Olds to pack up my things and report next morning to Swany at the Frontier Warehouse. I was told not to tell anyone where I was going or that I was taking a new assignment — just move.

"I didn't have the faintest idea why I was being shanghaied. I knew there were some Ryan people in the warehouse but hadn't the slightest idea what they were doing. Swany put me in charge of major subcontracts with Hycon, Litton, Lockheed and

Space Technology Labs (STL) — all of whom would be suppliers on a new program which later became identified as "Lucy Lee."

In the outside chance that some of the test vehicles or modified drones should land outside the secure test area at the White Sands Missile Range or Holloman Air Force Base in New Mexico, Ryan public relations men were ready with a 'cover' story news release describing the 'Q-2D' target drone.

"This ground-controlled target will be flying missions at near-sonic speed," the proposed release said, "and at altitudes in excess of 60,000 feet. It will fly for more than six hours while being fired at by surface-to-air missiles in the Air Force program of training against high-flying enemy aircraft." This information, at least, would disguise the true recon role of any test bird.

T. Claude Ryan, President, and Robert C. Jackson, Executive Vice President, gave personal attention to the Red Wagon project and saw to it that Vice President Ed Uhl was available 24 hours a day to ramrod the recon work.

J. E. (Jack) Lucast became Schwanhausser's right hand man and was named Chief, Reconnaissance Systems and liaison representative with Colonel Ryan's office and other interested Air Force agencies.

With the initial reflectivity reduction tests near completion, Ryan got busy on a larger proposal which envisioned building some 46 flight vehicles. The follow-on recon contract was anticipated by November first.

"We thought we had a going program," said Lloyd Ryan. "Everyone concerned in the established system was brought up to speed and appeared behind the program, although some conflict between headquarters people and procurement people was evident.

"From the Reconnaissance Panel, Weapons Board, Air Staff and General Curtis E. LeMay it went all the way up to Roswell Gilpatrick, Deputy Secretary of Defense, who approved a Red Wagon program in the neighborhood of $50 million for development and the production of 'x' number of birds."

Don Doerr

Jack Lucast
Ryan Navion service man, became liaison representative to Air Force

In the interval, the CIA — for whom Francis Gary Powers flew the U-2 — had been briefed, was in full accord and requested quick reaction. It offered its help with State Department and White House contacts.

It looked like the project was really set to take off. Then Dr. Harold Brown, Director of Defense Research and Engineering, held up the money and effectively killed the program. He had overruled the Deputy Secretary of Defense, which was an interesting situation.

The Red Wagon follow-on was turned down on Election Day in November, 1960. Vice President Richard M. Nixon had lost his bid for the presidency and there would be a new political party in the White House. With the change of administration, which would come the first of the year under President John F. Kennedy, no one was about to embark on new projects.

There were to be no more recon drone contracts for Ryan for 16 months.

SECRET RECONNAISSANCE PROJECT had strong backing *of T. Claude Ryan, left, founder-Chairman of Ryan Aeronautical Company, and Robert C. Jackson, President, of the pioneer aircraft firm.*

Richard Stauss

4

FRUSTRATION

WHO ARE THE REAL DECISION MAKERS when it comes to awarding military contracts, and who has budgeted funds available to finance new programs?

This is the dilemma constantly facing the typical Washington representative and the home-plant requirements engineer.

The procurement system is such that contacts must be developed at every level in the chain of command in the various functional groups in each of the services.

More often than not the industry representative works the new project up through the military organizations, often with a green light at every stage, only to find at the top level that the project really belongs in another agency which is more apt to be able to fund the program. At this point, industry must start all over again to rekindle interest in the hope of finding a viable 'customer.'

So it was when Ryan tried in late 1960 and early 1961 to push for greater emphasis on unmanned reconnaissance — which seemed to make a lot of sense in the light of the U-2 May Day incident over the Soviet Union.

"The night of the election in November 1960," Bob Schwanhausser recalled, "Jack Lucast and I flew east to find out what the hell had happened to our program.

"Of course, what had happened was obvious. All the recon money had been placed on the Lockheed SR-71. But before we were through, Robert C. Jackson, our Executive Vice President, and I wound up in an interview at the White House with the losing candidate, Vice President Nixon.

"Mr. Nixon said that if the problem was either budgetary or political he could help us, but if the problem was operational in nature he would take no part. Then Bob Jackson asked the Vice President what he was going to do to help.

"Our Congressman, Bob Wilson, head of the Republican Congressional Campaign Committee and a member of the House Armed Services Committee, was with us. Mr. Nixon said that Bob Wilson would get us an appointment with the Secretary of Defense, Thomas S. Gates, Jr., who obviously would also be leaving the administration.

"All we could find out from Mr. Gates was that while a million dollars had already been put into drone reconnaissance, he had not authorized anyone to do anything more, and it just wasn't going to happen. As it was, the small program we had was known to only six people in the Pentagon.

"We understood there had been full program approval for the Red Wagon follow-on on the Secretary's desk with the notation, 'Recommend Your Signature,' which would have kicked the entire program off.

"Later we were to learn that the Secretary had added his response: 'I thought we weren't going in this direction'.

"That's the way programs get stopped.

"By this time we were in the Frontier Warehouse. We've got a hundred people on the payroll. We're all geared up to go. But after the turn down we got on Election Day, Ed Uhl decided we couldn't afford the overhead. So we slowly went down to a staff of a couple of guys, one girl and one security guard."

With the Air Force recon drone program in limbo, Schwanhausser and the Ryan company's staff redirected their unmanned drone effort to the 124F model to meet requirements of the U.S. Army for a tactical photographic reconnaissance drone and of the Federal Republic of Germany for tactical reconnaissance. No contracts resulted.

However, analytical and design work on the larger concept was never halted and by April 1961, Ryan was ready to submit a $750,000 proposal to Dr. Charyk for study of "An Unmanned Global Reconnaissance System." It was hoped it would trigger a subsequent research and development program which in turn would lead to an operational reconnaissance system. But this effort, too, failed.

STUDIES CONTINUED within the Department of Defense and, with technical assistance from Ryan Aeronautical, a number of position papers moved up within the Air Force and Department of Defense structures to the Secretary level.

One such report ("Alternative Reconnaissance System," September 25, 1961) from the office of Dr. Harold Brown, later Secretary of the Air Force and subsequently Secretary of Defense, provided this introduction —

The suspension of overflights and peripheral operations by U-2 aircraft is political in nature and has deprived the United States of its most effective aerial intelligence collection capability.

The fact that the Sino-Soviet Bloc capabilities, both offensive and defensive, are dynamic and aggressive, dictate that an almost constant surveillance be maintained to insure maximum U.S. combat effectiveness. This requires high resolution (1-foot) photographic coverage of selected areas and of specific targets within these areas.

Based on the foregoing, the following criteria are proposed for use in the selection of any future vehicle that will be used for overflight.

Unmanned — for political, diplomatic and public acceptability; decreased detectability due to smaller size; decreased design sophistication; increased operational flexibility; increased security and cover.

Operate Independent of Foreign and U.S. Overseas Bases — Desirably, the entire system should be capable of operating from the Continental U.S. and not be dependent on a third country for support and/or policy. The overflight vehicle should be launched and recovered over international waters.

Feasibility and Costs — all of the major aircraft companies have indicated that the technical solution of the reconnaissance overflight requirement raises no problems that appear to be beyond today's state-of-the-art.

Lead Time — it is recommended that the study phase of a drone program be undertaken immediately.

The report continued with more detailed information —

Aerial reconnaissance is the only source of intelligence information in many parts of the world. The information obtained is used to assess current and estimated Sino-Soviet capabilities and in confirming estimates. The lack of this type of intelligence for any sustained period denies the DoD 'order of battle' information and seriously affects the U.S. ability to accurately assess the Sino-Soviet capabilities.

The requirement is immediate and urgent and can only be satisfied by an aggressive sustained peripheral and overflight reconnaissance program. Although the quantity of information collected through other means is substantial, the quality and timeliness is not satisfactory.

Allen W. Dulles, Chairman of the United States Intelligence Board, has stated, "The United States has, and will continue to have for the foreseeable future, a high priority requirement for photographic and electronic reconnaissance of the Soviet Union and other denied areas."

Satellite and aircraft reconnaissance systems are complementary; neither is adequate without the other.

The satellite is able to cover vast areas (weather permitting) by virtue of limitless range. It probably has some advantage over an aircraft with respect to penetrability. In addition, it may be more acceptable politically because of the possibility of concealing its purpose. On the other hand, the coverage that a satellite can obtain has approximately 10-15 feet ground resolution; one-foot ground resolution can be obtained with an aircraft.

An aircraft, in addition to having a great ground resolution advantage, would permit speedier recovery of the film allowing for timely analyses. An aircraft is suitable for coverage on demand, whereas a satellite is not adaptable to a specific timetable.

The Russian threats to use rockets against Pakistan, Norway, and Turkey were and are serious. The existing restrictions that these countries have placed on all U.S. operations are an indication of the seriousness which these countries attach to these threats.

At the present time the Russians have in their possession U.S. photographic balloons and the pilot and wreckage of a U-2 aircraft. They have shot down numerous types of aircraft conducting peripheral missions and have captured and killed some of the crew members. In the case of the balloon program, the high failure rate and the established pattern of operations caused embarrassment and identified the U.S. as the operator.

The capture of the U-2 pilot and recovery of aircraft fragments caused world wide embarrassment to the U.S. The qualitative aspects of the U-2 end product are well known and the urgency of the requirement for continued operation is recognized.

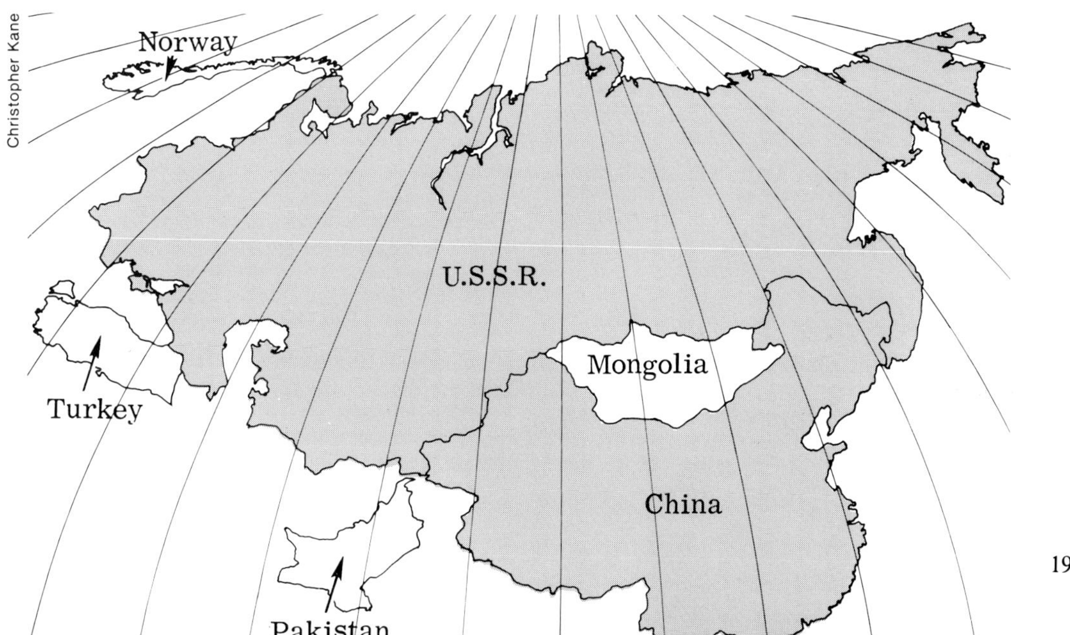

"LUCY LEE," Alias *L^2 or L squared, was spurned.*

Because of problems associated with manned aircraft in overflight operations (selection of pilots, maintenance of secure test and operating sites, the obvious nature of the vehicle to trained observers, involvement of families, travel, physiological and psychological problems, possibility of capture and many other considerations) unmanned vehicles must be considered as a desirable alternative.

An unmanned vehicle could provide the following advantages:

- Would assist in gaining Executive approval since the political risk is minimized due to the absence of a possible prisoner.
- Operational freedom, due to the less stringent requirements for safety and environmental protection than required for a man.
- A smaller and lighter vehicle, thereby decreasing radar cross-section, and increasing range.
- The reliability of an unmanned system can improve with the state-of-the-art and mechanical improvements.
- A computer can handle all programmed turns just as accurately as a man, and activate the sensors.
- Although an extremely distasteful subject, an objective appraisal of the use of a man must also consider the possibility of defection.
- Any system has a limit to its useful life due to improvements in the enemy's defenses. The only way to determine the useful life of the system and to obtain this type of highly important information appears to be to continue until loss does occur. Only a drone could make this possible.
- A man increases technical complexity and at the speeds and altitudes required does not contribute to the operational accuracy or reliability while over enemy territory. The operational parameters of the type of vehicle required are such that they approach enemy missile performance.

In the field of electronic intelligence (Elint) the U.S. has needs which parallel those of photo intelligence. Some examples of Soviet equipment or systems on which we have little or no electronic information upon which to base penetration techniques, include:

- Anti-Ballistic Missile radars
- SA-3 surface-to-air missile system which is estimated to become operational in 1961. Electronic information on this system is required to accurately assess its capability and also to develop countermeasures.
- The U.S.S.R. will probably seek to improve the altitudes and range capabilities and greater resistance to Electronic Counter Measures (ECM) of the SA-2 system for defense against more advanced type aircraft and cruise type missiles.
- The deployment of any new electronic equipment or the improvement of existing electronic equipment along the Arctic periphery will go completely undetected without an active aerial reconnaissance program in this area.

The unmanned reconnaissance drone will be less vulnerable than the manned aircraft but in overflight operations must be designed for minimum exposure to current enemy air defense weapons including Guideline (SA-2) missiles having limited effectiveness to 80,000 feet.

The Soviets are soon expected to have a surface-to-air missile (SAM) capability of approximately 100,000 feet altitude and 60 mile range.

The new delta-wing MiG Flipper fighter with its air-to-air missiles, which increase the intercept altitude up to 10 miles, also poses a threat to U.S. reconnaissance capability.

Highest priority collection areas are dotted with confirmed, probable and possible SAM sites. The necessity for straight and level flight over these target areas dictate that the performance of any peacetime overflight vehicle be far superior to the existing enemy defense capabilities. The nature of peripheral operations is such that the performance should be equal to existing enemy combat capabilities.

The lowest possible vulnerability obtainable is required although no known technique exists today which will provide a vehicle that is invisible to all enemy radars. However, minimum radar, acoustic, infra-red (IR) and visual detectability is a necessity.

Any new system must be capable of operating covertly and eliminate most of the physical and political limitations of existing systems. The operations usefulness and utilization of any covert system is dependent on the ability of the program managers to maintain a plausible cover. There the drone lends itself admirably.

Reliable and satisfactory recovery of the drone's payload is required. Mechanisms for air, ground, water, and aircraft carrier recovery of the entire drone vehicle must be developed but need not delay the initial operational utilization of the system.

Stimulated by the U-2 incident, seven major aircraft companies have submitted various proposals to develop a vehicle. Ten proposals have been received which recommend the use of drones. Due to the lack of experience in this area and the lack of availability to sensitive information, each of the companies used different criteria. Therefore, it is impossible to compare them for evaluation purposes.

All of the proposals had one thing in common; i.e., the feasibility and desirability of drones to perform overflight reconnaissance.

ALTHOUGH THE PENTAGON was beginning to accept the need for developing an unmanned recon capability, funds and contracts were slow in coming.

"When we saw Vice President Nixon, in November," Schwanhausser recalled, "he reminded us about the RB-47 photo recon plane which had been shot down off Scandanavia. He said he felt that a drone operating from the perimeter outside the Iron Curtain made a lot of sense.

"We took this back to the basement of the Pentagon, discussed it with them, and started a new variation of an old theme. It was called "Lucy Lee" (also known as L^2 or L squared), and was to be an around-the-outside-border type of bird for both photo and Elint missions.

"By mid-summer 1961 it looked like we had a new lease on life."

"It was," Lloyd Ryan said, "another program that we pushed in an effort to get the concept up and going in a big way." Meanwhile, the Lucy Lee proposals were realigned in an effort to obtain the necessary sponsorship from the Air Force.

The summary from L^2 stated —

> The drone reconnaissance system will be configured to provide both electronic and photographic intelligence capability. It will have as a primary mission a range of 3440 nautical miles, considering a minimum initial cruise altitude of 65,000 ft. with 72,000 ft. being the terminal altitude. It will be launched at 30,000 ft. from a GC-130 aircraft modified to provide in-flight refueling, allowing all operations to be conducted from the zone of the interior (ZI).
>
> A Litton inertial guidance system and programmer will provide navigational accuracies of 1 n.mi. per hour throughout the flight. The Hycon camera equipment will provide ground resolution of 1.9 feet from an average altitude of 69,000 feet.
>
> Recovery of the drone may be accomplished over land or sea, using a secure command and control system activated at the terminal portion of the flight by the programmer. The radar reflectivity of the drone will be reduced to a minimum using defraction, transmission, and absorption techniques.

Finally, in January 1962, despite support at nearly every level, the Director of Defense Research and Engineering (DDR&E) spurned Lucy Lee.

Somehow the program had again slipped through the crack. Just a week before, Schwanhausser had been called and told the project was 'go'. Presidents of all the supporting companies — supplying the airframe, engine, electronics, cameras, etc. — were called to the Pentagon for a kick-off briefing.

"We were being rehearsed by a Colonel down in the basement, when it became obvious something was wrong," Swany recalled. "Our newly appointed President, Bob Jackson, gave me one of his 'find-out-what's-up, Bob,' glances.

"I ran upstairs and saw a friend who handed me a piece of paper that had gone from the head of DDR&E to Dr. Charyk. It said, in effect, "we don't have the money and we don't approve this program."

"So we all marched into the office to be greeted by a very crestfallen Dr. Charyk. All he said was 'I can't tell you anything except that something has gone wrong. I'm sorry because I really wanted to see this program get going, but my hands are tied."

[Later estimates were that had Lucy Lee made the grade, drone reconnaissance in 1965 in Southeast Asia would have been as sophisticated as that finally achieved three or four years later.]

Again, the operation at Ryan's Frontier Warehouse was on the verge of grinding to a halt. Reflecting back on those days years later, Swany was reminded of a remark by G. W. (Bill) Rutherford, who, as Vice President, Operations was to succeed Ed Uhl as the Ryan executive with management responsibility for the 'black' programs. Rutherford had said, "Swany, you'll have more fun in that warehouse job than you'll ever have in the rest of your business career." And he was right.

© KARSH Ottawa

G. WILLIAMS RUTHERFORD, now a Teledyne Vice-President, *during the first years of reconnaissance was the company's top manager of 'black' programs.*

The Lucy Lee proposal had come out of Schwanhausser's 'skunk works' in the warehouse which was absolutely off-limits to all Ryan personnel including executives unless they had a Top Secret clearance and a government-approved 'need-to-know.' Few had such clearance.

Bill Rutherford, then Vice President of the Electronics Division and himself an experienced navigator, was frequently in Washington peddling Ryan's Doppler radar navigation systems. Competing with Rutherford for military navigation systems business was his friend, Dr. Henry Singleton of Litton Industries.

Early in 1961, Rutherford replaced Ed Uhl as Vice President-Operations, assuming management responsibility for all Ryan product lines, both aerospace and electronics. In his new capacity, Bill for the first time had 'need-to-know' security clearance for Schwanhausser's heretofore secret Red Wagon and Lucy Lee projects.

Imagine Rutherford's surprise, then, when inspecting a mock-up of the Ryan reconnaissance drone to find that it included the competitive Litton inertial platform as the bird's navigational system. It wasn't long after that the Ryan Doppler set replaced the system which had been successfully marketed to the Air Force and Ryan by Dr. Singleton.

[Today — 1981 — Dr. Henry Singleton is founder-Chairman of the Board of Teledyne, Inc., and Rutherford is a Teledyne Vice-President with management responsibility for Teledyne Ryan Aeronautical, Teledyne Continental Motors, and many other Teledyne companies.]

But as 1962 got underway the warehouse again was "down to one light bulb, one engineer, one secretary and a guard." Bill Rutherford told Schwanhausser that at the end of the week "we are going to shut the whole damn program down. You and Jack Lucast will be the only two left to work on drone reconnaissance. We'll close the warehouse and bring you back to the main plant."

Half an hour later, Lloyd Ryan called Swany on the phone and said, "We've got a live one. Let's get going!"

They had played their ace in the hole and it had worked. Along with the $70 million Lucy Lee proposal, Ryan had also submitted a half million dollar study project as sort of a 'green stamps' bonus — an inexpensive way to get something started. With that small amount a standard Q-2C Firebee drone could be modified to reconnaissance configuration.

Lloyd Ryan was ready to embark on "Big Safari" and take Schwanhausser and company along to hunt big game with him.

U.S. Air Force

LT. COL. LLOYD M. RYAN, reconnaissance expert *at the Pentagon, was the Air Force missionary who took the gospel of unmanned aircraft to the unbelievers. He found a 'live one' and got the program up and going.*

5

BIG SAFARI

"NOTHING WE TRIED through usual procurement channels for development of new aircraft seemed to work," Lloyd Ryan recalls.

"So, early in 1962 we went back to the slow, evolutionary type approach in order to justify the expenditure of funds.

"'Big Safari' was a system of procurement that was set up back in the early '50s solely for special reconnaisance. It was an expedited method of avoiding the complexity of going through what is now the Systems Command — the old R&D Command — with all of the approval chains. You could bypass all of this, and once you had a directive from a sufficiently high authority and money allocated, you could go right into contract.

"It was a way to get something done in two months that would normally take two years. It was used solely for modifications to manned aircraft to adapt them to recon use, that is, until this unmanned vehicle system came along.

"We modified existing aircraft to meet special requirements. We customized. We never started from scratch, although sometimes we had only the plane's original canopy and tires when we got through. The rest may have been brand new, but it was modification money. It was in the best interests of the country to do things expeditiously when there was a truly urgent requirement."

Ryan's project "Fire Fly" followed the unlucky Lucy Lee and was the latest proposal up for consideration. Ryan Aeronautical Company had gained a reputation in the industry for its Quick-Reaction Capability (QRC) and said that in 90 days it could produce a drone modified for the reconnaissance mission. This meshed nicely with the Big Safari procurement concept of instantaneous reaction capability (IRC).

Big Safari operated out of the Air Force Logistics Command (AFLC) at Wright Field. The action people were in a group with the code symbol AFSME (Directorate of Maintenance Engineering).

"Once we got something approved," Lloyd Ryan explained, "we gave it to AFLC. They took the money and went through the full procurement procedures.

"We ran the initial drone work straight out of the Pentagon but after the Fire Fly program was accepted, Lt. Col. Walter J. Raynor went out to Wright Field from our Pentagon office to head up the system program office (SPO) and this became the group at AFLC handling all of the manned aircraft modifications under Big Safari, as well as the unmanned — the drone systems."

So with a great deal of push both from within the Air Force and by key Ryan executives at the Washington level, Dr. Charyk, Air Force Under Secretary, early in 1962 gave verbal approval to proceed on Fire Fly using Big Safari funds. This was followed by a formal $1.1 million contract February 2, 1962 to Ryan for four Q-2C Special Purpose Aircraft (SPA) modified to photo recon configuration and incorporating features providing low vulnerability to attack. Later the four birds procured under this contract [AF33(657)-8263] would be designated 147**A**.

Design criteria for the Fire Fly drones were 1200 nautical miles range, cruising altitude above 55,000 feet, and photo resolution of 2 feet at 55,000 feet altitude. The quick-reaction contract was to be completed in three months — by May 15.

In later years, Walt Raynor was to speak glowingly of Big Safari and what could be accomplished with a streamlined organizational approach.

"It was a management concept run with a skeleton force, where procurement and engineering support were supplied by other commands. We were a crisis-oriented group and we often used specialized talent like Jim Regis (about whom, more later) to excite the environment.

"We were recognized as a small but experienced and dedicated group. That was probably why we were given a disproportionate amount of trust, if you compare Big Safari to the routine way of getting things done. This faith, trust and confidence went all the way down the line.

"Exactly how this near-ideal situation happened is hard to realize, and how to recreate it is even harder to imagine.

"Contractors had to be creative, too, and Ryan Aeronautical Company fit that description. They knew how to respond to fast reaction procurement needs, possibly because they had a great deal at stake. They had the hardware, the drone experience and the motive.

"With the passing of time, the drones got larger and more complex, and procurement more controlled and regulated. It is easy to understand why the very size and scope of the project later required a more formalized system to accomplish the task when it got beyond a certain threshold."

"Under Big Safari," explained Lt. Col. Fred Yochim, deputy to Raynor, "most specifications were general in nature and relied 90% on the relationship between the contractor and Air Force personnel handling the project. With Ryan Aeronautical we had a new relationship which had to be developed; it depended on understanding our one ground rule — modify an existing vehicle.

"We were able to take a target drone already being produced and modify it for $1.1 million funding as compared with Lucy Lee which had a $70 million price tag for production of a quantity of entirely new vehicles.

"The whole concept of Big Safari was to obtain special reconnaissance capabilities without going through normal procurement requirements. Usual contracting procedures were abbreviated; much of the routine for monitoring the contractor was waived. What we wanted were airframe contractors that could react in an extremely short time to very sketchy requirements; companies that could hand-build a particular modification and do it right now. Thus we could accomplish something — have hardware in a few weeks — where other programs would take six months just for planning.

"On every program we always had an experienced individual assigned at the contractor's plant. He monitored the project and often made the difference in bringing a loosely written contract to a successful conclusion with a finished project that met a tough, emergency requirement. Any story that doesn't include the contribution of on-the-spot guys like Jim Regis in the early Fire Fly days would be far from complete."

"The 147**A** contract," also recalls Lloyd Ryan, "was a very low price, low burner demonstration phase to prove you could take pictures, could navigate successfully to obtain desired intelligence, and could get through a defense network to obtain the data."

WHILE THE 147**A** was a low pressure effort, it did set the pattern for a whole series of reconnaissance drones customized for special purpose missions by modifying the basic BQM Firebee target vehicle and its components.

Bigger wings of increased area combined with added thrust from the jet engine gave higher altitude performance. Added fuselage length provided extra fuel capacity for flights with greater operational range. Special control and navigation systems, electronic programmers, precision altimeters, camera systems and other sophisticated hardware added to standard equipment made possible a variety of mission profiles, intelligence gathering and counter measure capabilities.

With the 147**A** contract, drone reconnaissance at last would have its day.

IN THE YEARS THAT WERE to follow, Ryan recce drones

- Obtained the first photographic evidence of the SA-2 Guideline missile in North Vietnam (NVN).
- Uncovered arming and fuzing electronics of SA-2 missiles.
- Took first photo closeups of MiG-21D and MiG-21E Soviet aircraft in North Vietnam.
- Provided photographic evidence of Russian helicopters in NVN.
- Provided photographic evidence of the "Cheesebrick" Passive Tracking Station in NVN.
- Photographed launch of an SA-2 missile against a drone flying at an absolute altitude of 600 feet.
- Photographed SA-2 firing at a night photo special purpose aircraft (Model 147**SRE**).
- Established that an unmanned aircraft can be equipped to electronically react to hostile threats and out-maneuver both missiles and hostile aircraft.
- Photographed an SA-2 detonation at close range, 20 to 30 feet, and returned to fly another mission.
- Provided the first remotely controlled real time communications intelligence (COMINT) collection system, manned or unmanned.
- Became the first unmanned aircraft to air launch Maverick and Hobo smart bomb weapons and repeatedly hit the target.
- Provided continuous low-altitude, high-resolution photography of an area denied by political edict to manned aircraft.
- Established the ability of the high-altitude drone to survive defensive reaction of 8 MiG intercepts, 3 air-to-air missile launches, 9 SA-2 ground-to-air launches.
- Flew 68 missions with a single SPA, most of them over North Vietnam, representing the collection of over 100,000 feet of photographic information. ("Tom Cat" was lost on that final mission.)

- Accomplished first surface launch of a photo recon drone.
- Established a response record by flying 5 missions in six days with a single SPA.
- Dispensed leaflets over North Vietnam with a SPA **(NA/NC).**
- Provided the only daily low-level BDA (bomb damage assessment) of B-52 raids during "Line Backer II" in the closing days of the war.

"SOVIET-BUILT MiG-21D Fishbed *Mach 2 interceptor, carrying an air-to-air heat-seeking missile under each wing, begins a flat turn as the pilot attempts to get into position to fire on the U.S. Air Force reconnaissance aircraft that took this picture near Hanoi."*

During the course of the drone reconnaissance program, Ryan probably produced more individually customized special purpose versions of a basic design than any aircraft manufacturer. It was as bad as . . . maybe worse than . . . a jet transport manufacturer having to satisfy the requirements of many airlines for features similar yet distinctly different than those of every other airline.

Since introduction of the 147**A** model, more than 1000 reconnaissance drones have been built in 18 major versions and more minor variations than anyone cares to recall — particularly those whose task it was to schedule and control manufacture of the multitude of airframe, engine and equipment combinations.

In Southeast Asia, 3435 operational drone sorties were flown. But that's getting years ahead of the story.

WITH SIGNING of the Fire Fly program under Big Safari contract, the operations people saw the need to find suitable locations for launch and recovery of operational drones, and to brief the various commands which might be called upon to use the unmanned vehicles.

"There was considerable interest in the Air Force," Lloyd Ryan recalls, "after word got around of the successful demonstration of the low radar reflectivity of the drone. I was given permission by the Strategic Air Command (SAC) to take one of their C-97 transport airplanes and brief the program to potential users in the Far East.

"Accompanied by Ryan's Jack Lucast; Erich Oemcke, a key engineer; and Bill Berry, tech rep; and by Lt. Colonel John Bush of the Air Force Missile Development Center at Holloman, we left SAC Headquarters at Omaha for Elmendorf Air Force Base, Anchorage; from there to Shemya in the Aleutians for our first briefing. Then on to Yokota, Japan; Osan, Korea; Okinawa, Guam, the Philippines and home via Hawaii.

"Primarily we were out there to brief the using commands, but on top of that we were looking for operating locations where the drones could be used advantageously. One such place was Osan, but it was not until nine years later we had an operation going there.

"From Shemya, of course, we were looking at the Kamchatka Peninsula off Russia for possible operation of drones to overfly in that particular area. Out of Guam, we were talking to a SAC Division Commander as to whether or not he would have any use for an unmanned vehicle.

"In the Phillipines, we were looking at an area aimed at Vietnam primarily, but from the standpoint of operating out of there with a DC-130 launch aircraft to cover Vietnam, recovering and bringing everything back, using the Phillipines as a base of operations.

"South Korea, of course, was obvious as an operational base as we were interested in North Korea. Okinawa was also a site to use the legs of the DC-130 Hercules to piggy-back a drone to an area of interest and fly it back with the sensor packages. We were looking across the spectrum at electronic intelligence capabilities and at photographic capabilities, wherever there was an official, validated requirement for reconnaissance coverage."

6

147A

WHILE THE AIR FORCE-contractor group was out in the Pacific surveying operational sites, engineers and production people at the Ryan plant were getting into high gear.

The Fire Fly contract called for four 147**A** birds. One was to be a test bed for the guidance system — a standard Q-2C target drone with a simple navigation system consisting of a timer-programmer and an MA-1 gyro compass.

Since the whole idea was to cut corners and get going fast, the concept of guidance meant the fastest thing the company could get 'off the street'. The system was home-made and used what Bill Rutherford, who had been Ryan's Vice President-Electronics, referred to as the "Alexander Graham Bell" programmer. Ryan technicians used a stepping switch — cost $17 — out of telephone system equipment because it was the most reliable piece of readily available equipment they could buy. The only compass they could lay their hands on was an MA-1, so they had only a Dead Reckoning navigation system which required a lot of preflight programming for wind compensation.

The other three **A** birds would be 'stretched' versions of the regular Firebee target plane. They'd have a 35-inch section spliced into the fuselage to carry 68 additional gallons of fuel for extended range, and nose modifications to accommodate a Hycon camera.

The Big Safari program technique permitted some fancy corner-cutting as explained by Fred Yochim.

"To meet the high altitude requirement we needed more wing area and wanted to try an extended wing. It turned out the Army had bought and paid for some wing tips. By some rather unusual means these tips were diverted to Fire Fly and whether the Army was ever paid back, I'll never know.

"As an example of the informality of Big Safari, one afternoon Ryan's Bob Schwanhausser, Bob Wesselhoff and Jack Lucast came into my office in Dayton. They were reporting some aerodynamic trouble they felt would definitely require wind tunnel time. They had quite a presentation to justify their request. After five minutes I cut Schwanhausser short and asked him if he really needed it, and he said 'yes'. Skipping the rest of the presentation, I made a phone call which got them their wind tunnel time. Wesselhoff wasn't prepared for such fast action. He was on an airplane to the wind tunnel that afternoon and didn't get home for three weeks.

"We had confidence in out contractors and always gave them the benefit of the doubt unless they violated this type of confidence. No matter how detailed your plans and controls, if there isn't complete mutual trust you're not going to get the product you want. Paper work won't guarantee it; too much of it so dilutes the effort you can't operate."

On occasion the Air Force seemed to have more confidence in Ryan personnel than did the management of the company. With a potential build-up of employment, if the drone program got into high gear, the writer in his role as Vice President-Public and Personnel Relations set out to attract the interest of prospective employees in the company by publicizing every new contract which would assure job security.

In that vein a news release was made June 19, 1962 announcing Ryan's receipt of a new contract for Flex Wing vehicles. That afternoon the phone rang and we were soon talking to an irate Robert C. Jackson, President of Ryan. "I'm over at the warehouse . . . get over here quick before we lose this damn contract!"

Not sure just what we'd done wrong we left post-haste for Swany's secret warehouse whose interior we still were not cleared to see. Bob Jackson met us outside with a copy of the afternoon newspaper whose headline proclaimed that Ryan had just received an important new contract. "What will the Air Force officers who just arrived today from Dayton think when they see that. This is a secret program; don't you know that! We'll lose the contract! They'll cancel it because we broke security!"

It took some little time to calm Jackson down and get him to read the detail of the story which concerned not the Fire Fly program but the new Flex Wing contract. The Air Force, we pointed out would appreciate the subtle way in which we were recruiting additional technical talent for the company so we'd have the people needed for the Fire Fly project.

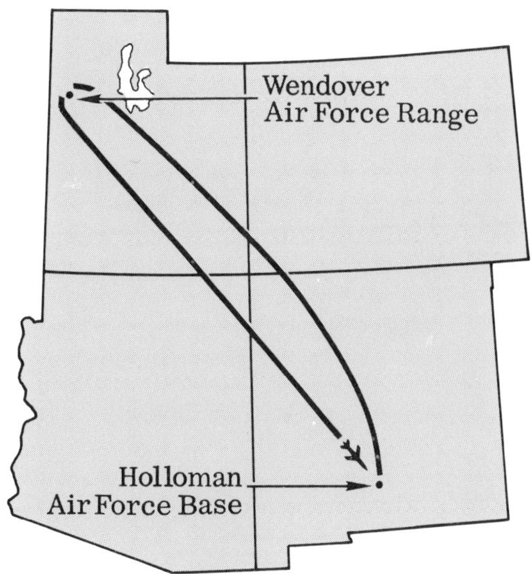

THE STANDARD Q-2C drone with minimum navigation capability, and one with stretched fuselage, would be used in the flight test program. If tests of these birds were satisfactory, the other two 147**A** special purpose aircraft (SPA) would be placed on 72-hour alert for deployment in the event of a crisis where their unique capability might be required.

Two months after award of contract, the first of two test drones was air lifted from San Diego to Holloman Air Development Center. Two Ryan flight test groups, headed by Ed Sly and Al Donaldson, and including Dale Weaver and Robert Todd as launch control operators, were based at Holloman. There, between April 11 and May 16, seven proving flights were conducted. Navigation checks were made in three flights with vehicle 147**A**-1; four flights in the extended-fuselage 147**A**-2 vehicle validated the basic concepts of the Ryan recce drone system.

Using the new navigation system and flight programmer, bird No. 1 on April 20 flew the first off-range test from the Alamogordo, New Mexico, area northwest in the test corridor to Wendover, Utah, where the drone returned to the White Sands Missile Range without commands from the B-57 airborne control plane or from the ground station. The drone had flown 761 n. mi. within predicted accuracy limits in a 98-minute flight and had landed by parachute only 1800 yards from a pre-selected spot.

SHROUDED IN BLACK, the first of two test *147A Fire Fly reconnaissance birds is lifted by Air Force C-123 transport plane to Holloman Base in New Mexico.*

Teledyne Ryan Aeronautical

The navigator/programmer demonstrated it could do the job. Once that worked it was put in the bird having the extended fuselage for added fuel capacity. It also had a new nose section for the camera.

The first flight of a fully-configured Fire Fly drone (147**A**-2) followed a week later, 75 days after contract. The No. 2 test plane returned from a 2-hour 24-minute flight which had covered 1080 n. mi. and during which it had made 17 course reversals. A resolution target had been set out on the ground to check both en-route navigational accuracy and the capability of the camera. The film taken from the camera met all expectations.

But there's more to the story than that as told by Bob Schwanhausser:

"A BIG HULK OF A GUY, J.E. (Jim) Regis, had been sent out to San Diego by the Air Force as a civilian technical specialist to run the military side of the Fire Fly program. He was, said Walt Raynor, 'a one-man panzer division.' An ex-Flying Tiger, he sported a fierce king-size moustache, adding to the impression that he was capable of railroading any job through. And, with his help, we certainly did.

"At Holloman we had borrowed a camera, the optics, from the U-2 program, and built a new frame to hold it because we were in a hurry. We got into a terrible argument with a Lieutenant Colonel on the base about the use of his expensive optics in the test flight of an unmanned, unproved bird. At that time we called the camera a 'scorer', a code name we were using in the drone business.

FIRST 147A FIRE FLY test drone *after arrival at Holloman has its MA-1 magnetic compass checked for accuracy. Posterior view of technician suggests it may be Dale Weaver.*

"Big Jim was over at Holloman and I was in San Diego about to leave for there to be on hand for the first flight with the scorer installed. We kept arguing back and forth on the phone trying to decide whether or not we should make the first flight with the real thing.

"We decided that all the chips being down, we'd go for broke. If we lost the bird, hell, so we lost a bird. But if we lost the bird and still had some good film we would at least prove our point.

"Our Lieutenant Colonel friend, though, worrying about his high priced optics, didn't show up the night before the first flight of the fully-configured Fire Fly. We had the equipment in and out of the bird about three times. Finally I said 'let's go' and Jim agreed.

"In the morning, the Colonel showed up at the 'King One' radar site about five minutes before launch from the mother plane. He had gotten the word that we were flying the real thing. He went straight to Jim Regis, the big guy, and asked, 'Are you flying that camera today?'

"Jim looked at him seriously and said, 'Colonel, that's called a scorer, and that is the code name for the camera, yes sir.'

"All hell broke loose around the plotting board.

"The Colonel said to stop the launch, and that he was going straight to the commandant to get us thrown off the base — permanently.

"In the meantime Regis asked me to try to calm the Colonel down. By then, during the heated argument, we had launched, and at that very moment we were flying — and having a marvelous flight. Everything was going just great.

"I told the Colonel, 'you know when this is all over we will look back at the whole thing and we'll laugh like hell.'

"'This is no laughing matter,' was his unsmiling answer. 'You guys are going to be thrown off this base. This is your last flight and for your sake I hope it is a good one!'

"The only thing that came out of it was that one of our better Ryan guys, test engineer Al Donaldson, got grounded from flying in B-57 chase planes.

A BIG HULK OF A GUY with fierce moustache, *Jim Regis was 'a one man panzer division' and super Air Force expediter.*

"Later we learned from Walt Raynor, Regis' boss, that perhaps Big Jim was losing his touch because it had been 70 days since he had been involved in one of his typical scrapes!"

WHEN 147A-2, the full-configured bird, returned from its long camera mission that memorable April 27, the film was hand-carried from Holloman at Alamogordo, New Mexico, to El Paso, Texas, where Schwanhausser and Regis boarded the first airliner for Hollywood. There Ray Ballweg of Hycon met them and took them to a secret processing laboratory. Regis returned to San Diego while Ballweg and Swany went to the Hycon plant at nearby Monrovia.

"About six o'clock in the morning," Swany recalls, "we found the resolution targets on the film and they were damn good. I remember waking Jim up in the morning to give him the good news.

"As you'd expect, we immediately flew the film to Washington for presentation purposes. We incorporated the pictures from the 'scorer' into a motion picture which went straight into the White House via the Joint Reconnaissance Center of the Joint Chiefs of Staff.

"Meanwhile the test program continued, and by the 91st day after contract we considered ourselves operationally ready to deploy."

There were some tough moments along the way, however. May 3rd was the kind of a day that would be long remembered by the test crew.

After a good launch and an 894 n. mi. flight with 147A-2, up the Wendover Corridor and return, radio control was to be passed to the ground station from the airborne operator in the B-57. A momentary loss of control caused the built-in fail-safe system to be activated.

This initiated automatic parachute recovery while the bird was at 50,000 feet. The drogue chute deployed, followed by the billowing 80-foot main parachute. The drone landed with not too great damage — but at 8,000 feet altitude between two peaks in the Magdalena Mountains 120 miles northwest of Holloman Air Force Base!

But let Schwanhausser describe the outcome:

"BIG JIM REGIS CALLS me in San Diego on the secure phone line from Holloman. All my people are gathered in the office because we know we've got a real problem on our hands with a bird stranded up in the mountains.

"'We've got to get that damn bird the hell out of there, Swany,' Jim says.

"I tell Jim it looks impossible to me, but he explains that they've got a big, twin-piston-engine Sikorsky H-37 military chopper on its way.

"So what happens? With the winds and high altitude the chopper doesn't have enough lift to pick up the drone, and it crashes on the scene.

Teledyne Ryan Aeronautical

NO. 496, THE C-130 launch plane, *with Air Force crew and Ryan technicians who trained military launch control officers. Ryan men are Dale Weaver, fifth from left, standing, and Bob Todd, third from left, kneeling.*

U.S. Air Force

AT 8,000 FEET ALTITUDE in the Magdalena Mountains *the Air Force chopper didn't have enough lift to pick up the drone and so crashed at the scene.*

"Now we've got both an Army helicopter and a classified drone with all its secret gear splashed on the mountain side. Our Colonel friend, who gave us a bad time with the camera we borrowed for the previous flight, provides what to him sounds like a good solution. Just spill some JP-4 jet fuel on the drone and torch it off! It was his idea of the best way to keep drone security from being compromised.

"Bear in mind we have only one flight test bird at this time and it is very important that we keep flying. So Jim, over the telephone, reminds me that he's been in the Flying Tigers and that the Chinese could carry an airplane out of the mountains. So, if the Chinese could do it, why couldn't Ryan employees carry this damn thing out of the mountains?

"Well, that really got under my skin, so I said, 'Alright, damn it, we'll carry it out of the mountains.' Anyway, Sly, Berry and Weaver and the guys had said they'd enjoy a 'picnic' in the back country.

"This was a Friday, so we got a group together, jumped into our battered DC-3 and were on our way out of San Diego post-haste, to join the crew out of Holloman.

"Saturday morning the gang started up the mountains, Al Donaldson and I bringing up the rear. When the Air Force suggested we burn the drone we had refused, so the military pretty well walked out on us and left our people with the problem. Two of our guys had been left there overnight out in the open, armed with guns in their holsters as a security precaution.

"The civilian crew including such Ryan stalwarts as Ted Owens started disassembling the drone piece by piece and bringing it down to an open area; meanwhile Donaldson and I were hauling a case of beer up to them, as we reckoned they needed a little inducement, some encouragement, and a bit of refreshment for their 'picnic'.

"By four o'clock we had completely disassembled the bird. Two Air Force trucks had broken down trying to get to the site. In the meantime we had 'conned' an Army sergeant with a weapons carrier into helping haul some assemblies out. By later afternoon we had the bird sitting in a meadow, some of the assemblies resting on old tires so they wouldn't get banged up.

"The Army sergeant had earned his pay, so we gave him a $20 bill and told him to get a couple of bottles of booze, and 'thank you very much.'

"That's when he discovered we were contractor personnel and not military, and that he had stuck his neck out something fierce. Later we wrote him a personal thank-you letter but decided it was hazardous to send it through official channels as someone along the chain of command might not take kindly to our having liberated the Army truck and driver.

"With the bird secure, we went down to the nearest bar as you'd expect and made a long distance call to Holloman saying to the Air Force that the bird was resting very nicely in the meadow. And, if they would please pick it up with a flatbed truck the next day, which was Sunday, we would be very happy to fly it again on Tuesday, which we did.

"Come Tuesday we flew it over the same area and took stereoptic pictures of the chopper that had crashed in the mountains. We thought that was really quite something and a darn fine demonstration of what Ryan types and their recce bird could do under pressure.

"Jim Regis and Ryan's Bob Jackson were pretty proud of our guys. To compensate for their husbands' weekend absence and hard work the company offered the wives a weekend with their husbands in the motel of their choice, or a $50 gift certificate. I think a lot of egos were badly hurt when most of the wives chose the gift certificate!

"WE'VE GOT OUR CLASSIFIED Fire Fly drone *with all its secret gear splashed on the mountain side." But the Ryan crew had their picnic after all!"*

U.S. Air Force

Wide World Photos

MEDIUM RANGE BALLISTIC MISSILE Field Launch Site — *near San Cristobal, Cuba. This and similar reconnaissance photos provided first evidence of Soviet offensive missile employment in Cuba.*

MACDILL AIR FORCE BASE, Tampa, Florida, August 1962

The August 29th U-2 overflight of Cuba, which had confirmed with photographic evidence the presence of Russian SAM defensive missiles, was not the only recon activity then going on in the area.

Unknown to other intelligence and Air Force units, two C-124 transports and a GC-130A had arrived at MacDill the end of July on a flight out of Holloman Air Force Base. Stowed inside the C-124s, instead of being slung in their usual place under the wings of the GC-130 launch plane, were two recently developed top secret Ryan recon drones bearing the new designation 147**A**. To maintain security, contractor personnel flew in the GC-130 rather than aboard commercial airlines. A third 'standby' bird was carried externally on another GC-130 but it was carefully guarded at the refueling stop.

To further validate recon drone concepts, it had been decided to demonstrate the new 147**A** system, supporting equipment and personnel in a simulated operational environment using the two 'alert' birds. One bird was equipped with a Hycon 233A camera and would test not only the photo equipment itself but also the capability of the camera system to be controlled by a programmer. The Operational Test and Evaluation (OT&E) would be staged out of MacDill and conducted under direction of SAC. Flight data generated would go directly to Headquarters; thus the contractor would have available only partial information of the actual results.

Dale Weaver, who went down to Florida for Ryan as a technician specialized in launch control operations, recalls that the tests were to include two photo flights on the Atlantic Missile Range "where the unique feature was to try to get the range people, usually concerned with tracking outbound spacecraft, oriented to having something flying back up the range against them. We were to launch from downrange in the Bahamas," he continued, "and fly back on a northwesterly course toward Patrick Air Force Base at Cape Canaveral.

"We had run our captive flights trying to get the range stations to report in reverse order which was something they hadn't run into before, so for them it was a different experience.

"August 1 the first free flight was made with the Fire Fly drone (147**A**-3) launched near Grand Turk Island, off the east coast of Cuba to fly a northwest heading. Flying at 50,000 feet on a pre-programmed course, the on-board equipment successfully turned the camera on and off, and activated the radio prior to letdown. After an hour and 47 minute flight, during which a maximum altitude of 54,900 feet was reached, descent was started into the land recovery area.

"Eleven minutes later the Ryan/military team had a crisis on its hands when the engine flamed out at 8,000 feet — while the bird was still 65 miles at sea.

"We were having an excellent flight but had started the descent a little early, forgetting that we had used up quite a bit of fuel in the pre-launch checkout phase. In any case, in those days we didn't have too much data on fuel consumption. This bird had the original short wing of the standard Q-2C and fairly high wing loading so it didn't have much of a gliding range."

All hell broké loose as recalled by Bob Schwanhausser.

"YOU HAVE TO UNDERSTAND that no one at Cape Canaveral was cleared as to what we were really doing. However, one Lieutenant Colonel who had once been an instructor of mine had some background from his own days in recce work.

"Al Donaldson, our flight test engineer, had been down there earlier to explain to the Air Force and Pan American Airways, which ran the range, that we had some very classified gear which could only be handled by classified personnel in case of an accident. Al explained that we had to consider every possible type of accident and, in the course of that discussion, promised that Ryan would provide two experienced skin divers on stand-by.

"I thought that was crazy as hell but there it was in the Statement of Work when I made a preliminary trip through Canaveral. Back in San Diego I got the gang at the Frontier Warehouse together and asked who among the cleared technicians had skin diving experience. It turned out that Howard Allen, one of our principal engineers, was a hell of a skin diver, as was Jack Deegan of Field Service.

HOWARD ALLEN *who had the misfortune to be a salaried engineer*

"So we told the guys to get their gear, that they were going to be on vacation in Florida for a couple of weeks. 'Bring all your gear,' I told them, 'just in case we have a little problem, though we don't expect to have to use you.'

"Among the support equipment for our program was a chopper flown by an old friend from Tyndall. When the bird went down by parachute 65 miles off shore, he picked up our two divers on the beach and headed out over the Atlantic. He knew the gross weight of the drone and what kind of load his helo could lift and realized he had a problem on his hands.

"We also deployed a bunch of guys in a boat so that one way or another we would recover the bird and the pictures we were sure we had gotten, because

Christopher Kane

SIXTY-FIVE MILES OUT into the Atlantic, *chopper pilot Colonel George Skinner, sings out, "We're ten feet off the water, now jump!" Jack Deegan saw to it that he followed Allen.*

it had been such a good flight. However, it would take the boat perhaps two days to make the pickup and get back.

"Meanwhile the C-130 launch plane with an Air Force crew and Dale Weaver aboard was flying cover on the bird floating out there. Dale reported that a good storm was coming up, and that they would orbit the area to keep track of the drone.

"At this point you need to understand the difference between salaried Ryan employees and those paid by the hour. As a key engineer, Howard Allen was a 'blue badge', while Jack Deegan was further down the organizational scale as an hourly-paid technician.

"Anyway the helo gets out there and it's time for the skin divers to get in the water and attach the sling so the chopper can pick up the bird.

"Colonel George Skinner, the pilot, calls out, 'we're ten feet off the water, now jump!' So our guys throw their raft into the water.

"With that Deegan looks down and says, 'That's a lot more than ten feet,' Again the pilot calls, 'Jump!' and that's when protocol-conscious Jack sings out 'Blue Badges first.' So Howard Allen had to dive in first, followed by Jack. Both climbed into the raft.

"With the helo now nearly 400 pounds lighter, Colonel Skinner managed to pick the drone up out of the water. But that's all he could carry.

"That left two civilians in a life raft, 65 miles at sea, with the C-130 orbiting at 6000 feet overhead and the weather closing in. Not a very happy prospect.

"And there's a boat with more Ryan guys and one from Hycon heading into the squall. So we've got people all over the damn place and our bird with its pretty pictures is likely lost. Jim Regis and I see everything falling apart around us, and all we can think to do is have a drink. Then I get a frantic phone call from Lloyd Ryan, who's come down from Washington in charge of the whole operation. By now he's a full Colonel.

"'By God,' says Lloyd, 'the chopper's got the bird in tow and it's going to be on the beach in a few minutes. You and Ray Ballweg (Hycon) get the hell out there and get the scorer. We've got a T-33 waiting for the stuff to be taken to the Air Force processing lab at Del Rio, Texas.'

"By then we recover a bit from our sulk because we know the whole program won't be scrapped since we're going to get our bird and film back. But what about Allen and Deegan floating out there 65 miles from shore?

"This is the first time Lloyd is in complete charge of a flight test operation, and the base commander as you might expect isn't too happy about the visiting Colonel and his secret project, about which he can't even be informed. Lloyd suddenly realizes that he's in charge and responsible for the lives of two contractor personnel sitting on a life raft.

"Later we find out when the guys got in the raft there was nothing left. Everything had been swiped. No water, no food, no anything. And the weather and darkness are closing in.

"Well, Lloyd Ryan is quite an operator when he needs to be. He got Operations on the phone and ordered an SA-16 Albatross rescue plane out there on the double, only to be told that it would be several hours before they could get underway.

"The hell with that,' replied Lloyd, 'you're going to get out there right now, or else!' And with that the SA-16 took off without delay even as the base commander was tracking Lloyd down to remind him he was responsible for the lives of two civilians."

In relatively short order the SA-16 made the pickup and had the guys back on the beach, though they were badly blistered and sunburned. The men in the boat were a long time getting the word to return and didn't tie up until the next morning.

The helo bringing the bird back barely made it to the beach, running out of fuel as the pilot was setting the drone down. At the time, nearly all of the Ryan field crew were either in the boat at sea or in the life raft. That left it up to Schwanhausser, Al Donaldson, Ray Ballweg and Bob Reichardt, the Ryan program manager, to take care of the drone.

The front office types joined by Big Jim Regis suddenly became working troops, disassembling the front end of the bird to remove the scorer. Then, if the drone was to be used again, it would have to be decontaminated. A water truck was standing by to wash the salt water off but within a few minutes the rain storm broke and did the decontamination job for them.

Ballweg, Schwanhausser and Regis took the film magazine out and, lacking security facilities, went to Swany's motel room. "Jim, who was a pretty good film handler," recalls Schwanhausser, "went into the bathroom, locked all the doors and put towels all around to plug light leaks. Then he took the film from the magazine and put it into the film can and ran it down to the T-33 which was waiting to take off.

"Meanwhile Ed Sly took the camera back to his motel room and decontaminated it in his bath tub. It was the best we could do from a security standpoint but a violation nevertheless."

FIVE DAYS LATER the Ryan troops got the same bird up and going again. It was another good photo mission up the Atlantic Missile Range and this time there was a dry recovery with no more escapades at sea.

"On the previous flight," Swany related, "we had dropped the 147**A** to fly a northwest course toward Florida with one leg scheduled over Eleuthera in the Bahamas as a navigation check and camera target. We hit it beautifully, only 150 yards off target. The bird had started to go somewhat off course but the wind blew it right back so we were fantastically lucky in a way. The PAA range officer said, 'You sure must have a tremendous guidance system in there.' I just didn't have the courage to tell him the truth; that we had enjoyed unusual luck on this flight and that all we had was an old-fashioned MA-1 compass.

"During that flight, our first time on the range, the Air Defense Command had been alerted to go find the drone. Though they weren't authorized to shoot it down, they were all so confident that they expected to take pictures of it with hand-held cameras.

"ADC launched so damn many interceptors and flew at so many altitudes, the ground radars didn't track us at all. Instead they were tracking their own aircraft and were chasing each other all over the sky.

"We had radar blankets around the vehicle so it would minimize radar cross section. Nobody got a look at us; nobody even saw us on radar as we came through. We were 200 miles out and so delighted that we decided we could make a beautiful penetration right over the island where there were plenty of photographers to see us; then we'd bring the drone down low and drive it right in to the beach at Canaveral.

"All of us grown men — pilots, aerodynamics engineers, experienced flight personnel, the whole works — forgot that a jet airplane at low altitude uses a hell of a lot more fuel than it does at high altitude. That's how come we fueled out 65 miles at sea. We had an engine rundown, which was the way it was written up, but we flat fueled out. We had screwed it up, but good."

THE OPERATIONAL TEST and Evaluation of the Ryan drone was being staged out of MacDill Air Force Base near Tampa. In addition to flights off the Florida east coast, there were to be three missions flown up the Gulf of Mexico against hot guns — anything that could fire at the drone.

Facilities at MacDill for the Ryan contractor-furnished crew were not the best, the only available area being a sort of nose hangar for bombers.

Because doors had to be kept closed for security reasons the place was unbearably hot and sweaty that mid-summer of 1962.

Jack Lucast was in charge for Ryan. The Air Force had sent Colonel Ellsworth A. Powell of SAC Headquarters, Reconnaissance Division, to Florida to conduct the operation. "Ells" had been one of the key men in drones because as head of requirements of the recce shop at Omaha he had helped push the Fire Fly drone. He was a friend of Colonel Lloyd Ryan's and both men were determined to make a go of the program, having come down to run the job themselves.

With only ten contractor personnel, the hours were as punishing as the heat as the Ryan crew fought to turn the two birds around every two or three days. In the end everyone decided it was just too hot so it was decided to open the doors of the nose hangar even if it meant a lack of complete security.

Ells Powell was the type who ran a really slick operation and a clean shop. At the end of one of those very long working days Dale Weaver, a fine technician, had just returned to the shop when Powell gave orders that the floors were to be swept before anyone left for the motel.

When Weaver was told by Lucast to pick up a broom and start pushing, Dale was so weary he insisted on being given a ticket back to San Diego, then and there. Jack said, "You can't have a ticket until you finish sweeping." Fortunately, by the time the sweeping was done Dale had changed his mind.

WITH TWO FINE PHOTO and navigational flights under their belt (providing one overlooks the unscheduled water landing), action moved to the Eglin Gulf Test Range where operations started August 9.

The flights on the Atlantic Missile Range off the east coast of Florida had been a source of embarrassment to the Air Defense Command. None of the pilots ever saw what they were chasing. The F-102s and F-106s 'painted' the drone with their radars once or twice while the bird was in a turn but nothing more. ADC was pretty upset.

"We weren't trying to pick a fight with ADC," Schwanhausser was to explain later. "We weren't trying to show them up. We were just trying to show we could do our job, but they didn't understand that at all because what we were really doing was classified and not available to them.

"Our second flight on the Atlantic Missile Range off the east coast was a very good one. We landed the drone by parachute right at the point we wanted. By then we had learned all about how to fly drones, and not to fly them out of fuel at low altitude!

"It had been a beautiful recovery and pick-up. Thirty minutes after we were on the ground ADC pilots were still chasing what they thought was us clear across Georgia.

"You have to picture now, a very much upset and defiant Air Defense Command with the top brass at the General level much concerned.

"At the same time the Air Force and Navy,

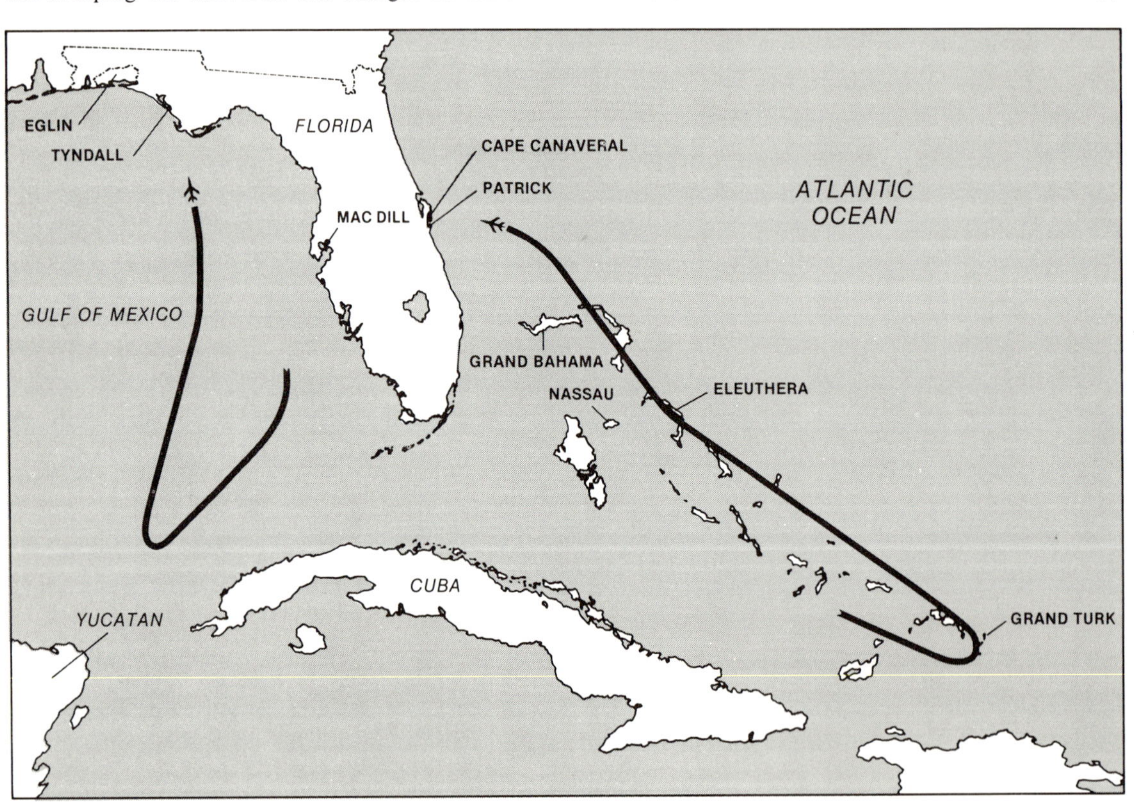

working together at the Under Secretary level, have arranged for three missions with live missiles against the Fire Fly up the Gulf of Mexico. On these missions the birds would serve only as targets against hot guns. Photo equipment would not be carried by the 147A Fire Fly.

"The drones would try to penetrate the air defense of the United States by sneaking in on a simulated mission such as might be flown from unfriendly bases in Cuba.

"The Navy was reluctant to get into this act; they didn't really want to be tested but they had orders to send an F-4 Phantom with some Sidewinders and Sparrows.

"The Navy is to have first crack at the Fire Fly; if they don't get it the Air Force F-104s with guns and F-106s with Falcon missiles will have their turn.

"By this time we're cocky as hell. We decided we'd really show them up. We launched the drone from the C-130 directly over a Navy base on the west coast of Florida. On this first mission on the Eglin range it became apparent that ADC was monitoring our flight pattern, as they had been given our flight plan for reasons of range safety.

"We dropped the bird where the Navy pilot was able to see the condensation trails as we came up to cruise altitude. Ells Powell and I could hear the radio chatter between the pilot and his ground control intercept (GCI). He had better get that bird, or else!

"He fired his first heat-seeking Sidewinder and got a near-miss which was so close the J69 engine flamed out from the warhead explosion directly in its flight path. The bird went into parachute recovery. Now you have to picture the enthusiasm of this Navy pilot and his radar operator. Although the Fire Fly was in the chute, and with its dead engine not generating any heat to attract the missile, the Navy nevertheless made a run on the bird and fired a second Sidewinder out of spite!

"We'd been in the air only 50 minutes. We had a wet recovery, but five hours later the bird was retrieved by boat. We turned it around and flew it again four days later.

"On the next flight — our second on the Eglin range — we decided we'd play some games. We looked at doing things like throwing chaff out of the GC-130, false launches and other dirty work to confuse ADC because everyone was spying on us. You need to understand that safety requires someone at the tracking radar familiar with the planned flight path so that when the operator puts a grease pencil around the wrong target you don't end up with a tragic accident.

"ADC is 'painting' the bird with height-finding radars so many times our on-board beacons are burning out. Everybody is playing an intelligence and con game back and forth. We decided we were going to get the better of them.

"Colonel Powell was working on a strategy that would have us go through ground checks and the countdown but not actually release the drone. We

4080th/100th SRW History

COL. ELLS POWELL and Bob Schwanhausser *decided they'd play some games and try to defeat the Air Defense Command.*

had to abandon throwing chaff to confuse their radars when we discovered you couldn't drop chaff without 'x' hours notice to the civilian Federal Aviation Administration (FAA) and sixteen million other people.

"Once the August 13 operation started we went through a complete check with ground control while cruising in the C-130 at 15,000 feet, then a complete countdown before we called out 'drop.' But we didn't launch. We descended to 10,000 feet and went through another fictitious countdown and again didn't drop.

"At the time we had a six hour 'window' on the Tyndall and Eglin schedules for the operation. It was hot on the ground and we decided to make the pilots sweat it out on the runway waiting for the intercept scramble. We'd hit the 'window' at the last hour and make those poor pilots sit out there in the sun in their high altitude pressure suits, with an umbrella over the boiling cockpit, and really get them pretty growly.

"Next we went down to 5000 feet and another fictitious drop, but still not releasing the bird. Then we flew south down into the Gulf of Mexico until we were out of their radar range so nobody could 'paint' the GC-130. We were in their blind spot out of range and at low altitude. Only then did we launch the drone — toward the Yucatan Peninsula.

"We climbed the bird back out of there and didn't have the beacons turned on until we came up to reasonable cruise altitude and a new heading. We'd also rewired the programmer with some cut and solder type modifications to further confuse the 'enemy.' We really wanted to defeat those guys and were very effective at it. Although we had told our planning guys what the mission profile was to be, Ells Powell and I changed it once more because we felt somebody had swiped our flight plan.

"The Lieutenant Colonel who had come over from White Sands Missile Range found out that we had rewired the programmer without range safety approval and turned Colonel Powell in for a violation. You have to picture the fight that ensued between commands when a Lieutenant Colonel turns in a full Colonel for a violation.

"We had a fine drone flight and good recovery that day. An F-104 got a visual contact from the bird's contrail and got off 15 or 20 rounds before he flamed out. At that altitude the F-104 couldn't support gun fire. On the way down the F-104's trying to relight his jet engine, and the F-106s are starting to come up to get *him.* Everybody is confused about who is going after who, so the F-104 jockey says, 'please leave me alone.'

"When the F-106s tried to jump the Fire Fly they find they can't fire a missile because of time compression. This proved one of the points we were trying to make — that flying a subsonic drone at high altitude is very effective for photo recce work because the airplane trying to shoot you down is supersonic. With time compression he just can't get everything done fast enough. By the time his radar has locked on and the pilot is ready to pickle off the weapon, he's already past the bird.

"Right after this flight, in which Air Defense Command had a terrible time trying to locate and shoot down our special recce bird — and not succeeding — they immediately scheduled a confidence flight at Tyndall. It was against one of Ryan's regular Q-2C target training drones using the same aircraft and weapons in hot pursuit. With no one 'playing games' to confuse them they shot it down with no trouble. That helped relieve a lot of minds that the United States did, after all, have a fine air defense system.

"We weren't trying to prove that our defense system was bad but that we on the reconnaissance side at Ryan could work pretty hard to confuse and defeat any 'enemy' set on stopping our spying capability. But we sure had a hard time trying to keep from looking like bum guys out to make other people look bad.

"As an example, in trying to sell the program we had put together data on all the missile shots that had ever been fired against our jet target drones. It showed the number of 'kills' by various weapons at seven different operating units — the kind of information only a contractor could put together.

"This material was briefed at the deputy level of the Agency (CIA) to an Army General who had run Ft. Bliss, where they were quite proud of their weaponry.

"The briefing was being made by Colonel Lloyd Ryan and right in the middle of it the General stood up and said, 'That's just bullshit, Colonel; you don't

Dave Gossett

CONTROL PANEL at Tyndall Air Force Base *which monitored drone operations including 147**A** tests south into Gulf of Mexico.*

have your goddamn facts. I want to see you back here Monday morning and you have the *right* facts!'

"A very dejected Colonel Ryan called me at the plant and said, 'For God's sake, get me some information here quick; over the weekend.'

"So we had Bill Berry get in touch with our field people and validated all of the information we had. In the meantime the Army general went through his channels, and it was weeks before he got his data back. When he did, it turned out that Lloyd's information was accurate. But that just made our problem with the Army even worse; they weren't happy that we were right. Finally the information was accepted, reluctantly. Then it was classified Top Secret and we were told to burn every piece of paper we had generated.

"On August 16, the last day of our three flight series in August 1962 at Eglin, ADC was getting pretty smart and I guess we were letting up a bit. Although we launched 147**A**-3 out of radar coverage, an F-106 interceptor pilot again acquired the Fire Fly drone visually from contrails. He couldn't get a lock-on with a missile, so drove in close enough to put the infra-red Falcon in it visually after 47 minutes of flight. That was the end of that bird."

"I was in the ready room when they got a hit and shot it down," Big Safari's Walt Raynor recalled. "They had sent some of the best pilots they had up in 106s to challenge the drone. They had both heat-seeking and skin-tracking missiles.

"Lloyd had tried to extract a promise from the pilots that they'd not use the contrails; that they would just operate with the use of instruments — the gunsights available internally in the airplane.

"We were listening to the post-flight debriefing and

it was one of the older, more experienced pilots who shot it down. He said he just barely got it, more by accident than anything else. He just hit it in the very small time threshold they have to get a lock-on before he falls out of the sky. But the fact that they got it took the pressure off this apparent vulnerability of the whole ADC. It had been quite an issue at the time."

One thing was clear. While ground control intercept had difficulty seeing the drone on the radar screen, the contrails often generated by the bird at high altitude did give pilots the visual clue they needed. That raised a new operational problem for unmanned recon vehicles. You could hide it from radar, but not from visual contrail sighting. So a 'no-con' (no contrails) development program would be required.

THE FIVE TEST FLIGHTS in Florida documented the drone reconnaissance system and set the stage for fully operational Model 147 special purpose aircraft (SPA). An ability had been demonstrated to adhere to flight profiles; launch and recovery techniques had been worked out, as had ground control and tracking. Relative vulnerability to interception by manned fighters had been determined. Camera and navigation equipment had been proven adequate. The contrail problem had been identified.

However, despite the Cuban crisis that Fall, it would still be two years before the Fire Fly drones were to go truly operational. But the concept had been accepted that there should be a small, ready, highly mobile drone reconnaissance unit on alert which could be flown in C-130s to world trouble spots. Once they performed their task, they would be ready to move on or return to base and await a new assignment.

The last of the five simulated operational flights in Florida had been conducted August 16. Two weeks later U-2 pilots returned from Cuban overflights with photo evidence of SAM installations.

The next two months brought an unheard of concentration of manned photo reconnaissance. Then just before Khrushchev agreed to pull Russian missiles out of Cuba, Major Anderson was shot down in a U-2 bringing another burst of high-level activity.

"The Ryan people were trying to figure out how their recce drone work might be continued now that testing of the 147**A** had been concluded. Without a doubt they could do a job in Cuba, but who at the highest levels in government would see that they had their chance?

The story has since been told of a contact between Doug Steakley ('Mr. Reconnaissance') and the Joint Chiefs of Staff which served as President Kennedy's eyes and ears during the Cuban crisis.

"As I understand it," Schwanhausser later related, "the Chairman and Colonel Steakley, who was chief of the Joint Reconnaissance Center, were driving across the Potomac River en route to the White House. They were discussing aerial reconnaissance and particularly whether there was some way of doing the recce job without risking the lives of pilots like Major Anderson.

"'Yes there is; we have some pilotless jet drones we've been testing but have only a few of them, and they could hardly be used at this time.'

"'You mean, Colonel, that's all you have in the Air Force right now?'

"'Yes, sir, we just don't have the capability.'

"'Well, tell me what you need?'

"'We ought to have at least ten to get a program started.'"

"It wasn't long after that," Swany resumed, "that my phone rang and the Air Force told us they wanted Ryan to build some more drones."

Dave Gossett

TESTING OF TECHNIQUES to suppress contrails — *which would disclose location of reconnaissance drones — was conducted at Tyndall Air Force Base.*

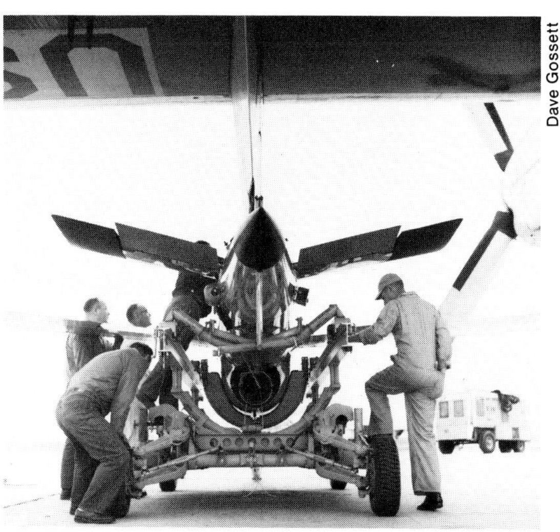

Dave Gossett

DALE WEAVER PICKS UP the Cuban crisis story as it involved Ryan drones.

"Jack Lucast, Bill Sved and I were down at Eglin negotiating to get started on the contrail suppression program when the Cuban panic hit.

"Jack took a phone call from Bob Todd, then in charge of the Ryan group at Holloman. He couldn't be specific over the phone because of security precautions but told Jack that the group from Holloman was to deploy as soon as possible (ASAP) to Tyndall and for Jack to get over there and get things going. Bill Berry, flying west to San Diego, was intercepted at the air terminal in New Orleans to catch the next plane back to Florida.

"We were on a 72-hour alert at that time and Bob was told to get ready to support a two-bird sortie on short notice. They put the two 'alert' birds on the pylons of the C-130 and the 'scorers' inside. Then they put so much support equipment and other cargo aboard that they had to offload some of it when the C-130's nose gear depressed too much.

"At midnight Colonel Powell arrived at Tyndall with a Top Secret message which he waved under the nose of security people at the main gate requesting special security precautions and a prompt meeting with base personnel.

"Tyndall was then under a terrific buildup with C-130s and C-124s arriving with fully loaded complements of combat ready paratroopers. Colonel Powell set up his command post right next to the regular Ryan Q-2C target drone operation. About 2 a.m. our C-130 from Holloman arrived.

"We took the cameras, serviced them, put film in, loaded them into the 147**A**s and went through a quick autopilot check. They had decided they wanted to fly a semi-low-level mission over Cuba so we went through a rapid engineering change in the vehicle and gave it that capability. It was an element of the programmer. Working through the night we programmed the birds by long distance telephone using the computers in the Ryan plant in San Diego. We had it so the bird would round out at about 30,000 feet rather than climbing on up. We modified the cameras slightly.

"The C-130 fired up, all four engines churning. We were parked on the flight line ready to head down the taxiway to the end of the runway for the final word to take off. Just then the mission was aborted by higher headquarters."

Weaver and the others involved in the aborted mission were a long time in finding out the reason for the last minute switch. Colonel Lloyd Ryan later related what had happened at the Pentagon:

"**T**HE 147s HAD BEEN deployed to be available to fly over Cuba should the situation arise. We in the Air Force at the working level and including General Curtis E. LeMay, Chief of Staff, didn't want to use it over Cuba. We had only the two birds. The General wanted to save the capability for bigger things and wanted to go on with further development.

"However, the civilian sides of the Defense Department and Air Force came up with the decision that they wanted to use drones over Cuba in November 1962.

"I was right in the middle because I was in blue suit uniform working for General LeMay. At the same time I was sort of a special project officer for Dr. Charyk, Under Secretary of the Air Force, who wanted to use the Ryan drones down there. They had already been deployed on standby.

"I figured I owed it to the Chief so I went to General LeMay and told him what decision had been made by the civilian side. He took me by the hand, because his office was just down the hall from Dr. Charyk's, and we walked up there to the Under Secretary's office. General Thomas S. Power, Commander of SAC, was in there giving a briefing. General LeMay stuck his head in the door and told Tom Power and his people to get out.

"So that left the three of us in there — the Under Secretary, the Chief of Staff and me. I was in a tough spot.

"To make a long story short, it was not used in November 1962 over Cuba. We got the word to Colonel Powell just in time to call off the mission."

OUT OF THE CUBAN CRISIS a contract was let for Ryan to proceed with the 147**B**, the first true drone reconnaissance vehicle. It came about because of the big argument as to what you do when you have only two recce drones in the inventory. Operations people were faced with a situation where they might want to use an unmanned vehicle so that pilots would not be killed. Major Anderson had just been shot down in the U-2. That tragedy helped generate the November 1962 go-ahead on the 147**B**.

The 147**B** model would be the first high-altitude drone, having a much larger wing so the bird could achieve a 62,500 feet altitude capability compared with 52,500 feet for the earlier model. An improved navigation system using a programmer and Ryan Doppler radar would be included to get rid of the error that existed when having to rely on predicted winds when using the MA-1 compass. The wing would be extended from 13 feet to 27 foot span, with the wing area increasing from 36 sq. ft to 80 sq. ft. Range would be 1680 n/mi. vs 1227 n/mi. for the "**A**" bird.

Nine **B**s were ordered and design work started under the first real production contract, (AF33(657)-10043), which was to reach $13 million in value. There would be two vehicles for test and seven production birds.

One phase of testing which got under way early was evaluation flights with two Q-2Cs of a system designed to eliminate the formation of vapor contrails at high altitude. The Ryan test crew headed by Bill Sved operated out of Tyndall Air Force Base, but as test engineer Al Donaldson reported,

"Tyndall is on an alert status due to the Cuban situation and like Eglin AFB has limited capability to support the No-Con Program. There is no way of knowing when the alert will be lifted and the base capability returned to normal."

The series of no-con tests in which a chemical agent was introduced in the jet exhaust to suppress formation of a vapor trail were inconclusive.

Later other methods and equipment were tried and proved quite successful in operational missions in Southeast Asia but in the long run the best solution proved to be greater altitude capability which permitted flying above the contrail level.

SCHWANHAUSSER RECALLS one personnel problem which also cropped up at this time.

"When we deployed the team of guys for flight test work, we naturally had to have a secretary, but that raised questions. Do you hire one of those 'lovely' male type secretaries or do you risk the problems created by having a potentially troublesome single girl out in the boondocks with a bunch of chargers? We decided to go the girl route, but with poor initial success.

"Finally Jack Lucast wrote up a requisition for a new girl with the requirement that she be old and ugly, not interested in men, but damn good at her job. That was a tough assignment for any Hollywood casting director or industry employment manager.

"Our Personnel people sent Jo Ann Howell to us for an interview. She was one of their department's own employees, and at that time Personnel was known as the 'body shop' because of the classy talent they processed. We couldn't understand how Jo Ann fit our request for an old and ugly type and she obviously wasn't pleased to have been selected as fitting that description.

"But she was single, attractive, had a Secret security clearance, and was willing to travel. Bill Berry, her boss to be, and Jack Lucast recommended her so she went on our payroll.

"Her first assignment was at Tyndall Air Force Base in Florida where we were getting the no-con testing under way. She had flown out of Holloman Air Force Base with 13 Ryan technicians. She was the only girl aboard the C-97 transport. It was trouble-plagued and had a fire in No. 2 engine requiring an emergency stop at Ft. Worth where a tire blew out on landing. The next day, the fourteen civilians grabbed a commercial airline flight to Tyndall at Panama City.

"When I checked up on things there she was having breakfast with the crew at the motel, and I've never seen guys better dressed on a field assignment in my life.

"But Jo Ann was no problem — except with Dale Weaver. She was part of the recce program almost from the start. She ended up being my secretary, one of the most competent in the business, and the devoted wife of Dale Weaver, one of the best technicians we ever put in the field."

"JO ANN HOWELL ended up being my secretary *and the devoted wife of Dale Weaver, one of the best technicians we ever put in the field." — Bob Schwanhausser.*

8

A, B, C, D, E

BEFORE THE 147B could reach final design and production stages, two events, dictated by the necessity of those days, occurred.

First, the Air Force wanted to have the immediate capability envisioned in the concept of a ready, mobile reconnaissance force without waiting even a few months for the new big-wing **B** model. The interim production vehicle delivered to meet this need was a version of the short-wing 147**A** design including provision for contrail suppression. It was designated the 147**C**.

Seven 147**C**'s were ordered in October 1962 and four were eventually used operationally. The remainder served primarily as training vehicles for the Strategic Air Command, and as modifications for later configurations.

Secondly, an Air Force project was undertaken to determine the characteristics of the proximity fuse and beacon transponder used on the Soviet Mark IV and Mark V SA-2 Guideline Missiles. A special electronic-intelligence-configured drone, using CIA furnished equipment, was required as part of this effort. To meet this requirement, Ryan was asked to develop the 147**D** for the Air Force.

Three **D**s, modified from the **C** model in a very short time frame, were delivered to the Air Force and declared operational December 16, 1962, to be available for the electronic intelligence (Elint) effort, then concentrated on Cuba.

Actually the first **D**s went to Holloman, where according to Dale Weaver, they were "received in a basket" and had to be assembled, with new equipment installed in the field. The pressure had really been on the factory at San Diego to get the drones in the hands of operational people.

"We had some new electronic gear we'd never worked with before," explained Weaver, "and tried to put it in a bird that wasn't really designed for that application. We had done our captive flight test work and other preliminary testing at Holloman and Colonel Powell decided March would be a good time to go back down to Eglin and have another shot at Operational Test and Evaluation. We wanted to fully evaluate the 147**D** and all of its supporting elements.

"Also, we had another flight to run on 147**A**-2 and a new air launch scheme we wanted to try. We went down to Eglin with two **A**s and one **D**.

"It was a bad week. In fact it took some doing to live down what later came to be known as 'Bad Week at Black Rock.'

"We had an excellent sortie out of **D**-3 on March 21 but crashed on recovery. Ed Sly was trying to stretch a glide across Choctahachee Bay and it just didn't quite make it.

"The SAC Deputy for Operations out of the 4080th Strategic Reconnaissance Wing, Col T. J. Jackson, was down there and it was the first time he had seen a drone. He was out at the recovery site and the bird mashed in right in front of him. It was too low — it augered in with the chute, which opened just before impact, streaming behind it. Col. Jackson was more than a little disturbed.

"Ells Powell was trying very hard to sell the program to SAC. He had gone on record with SAC that they would take the capability, and he wanted the 4080th to have it.

"Of the other two birds, **A**-4 flew on March 19. The new launch technique didn't work too well! The second, it was 147**A**-2, lost control of its gyro. We found the defect months later. It was an original manufacturing defect in the MA-1 compass.

"The **A**-2 bird went wild. We had modified that one so that the tracking capability was eliminated. It was flying a programmer flight and the only thing that was on was the telemetry signal. The idea was to make an overflight, take some pictures and come in simulating an operational mission as closely as possible.

"When the gyro went, the bird followed its nose around and was flying over Jacksonville control center and none of the GCI sites could find it. They were able to 'dead reckon' it by virtue of the telemetry and when the radio and beacon came on at the very end of the flight, Sly got the recovery command in.

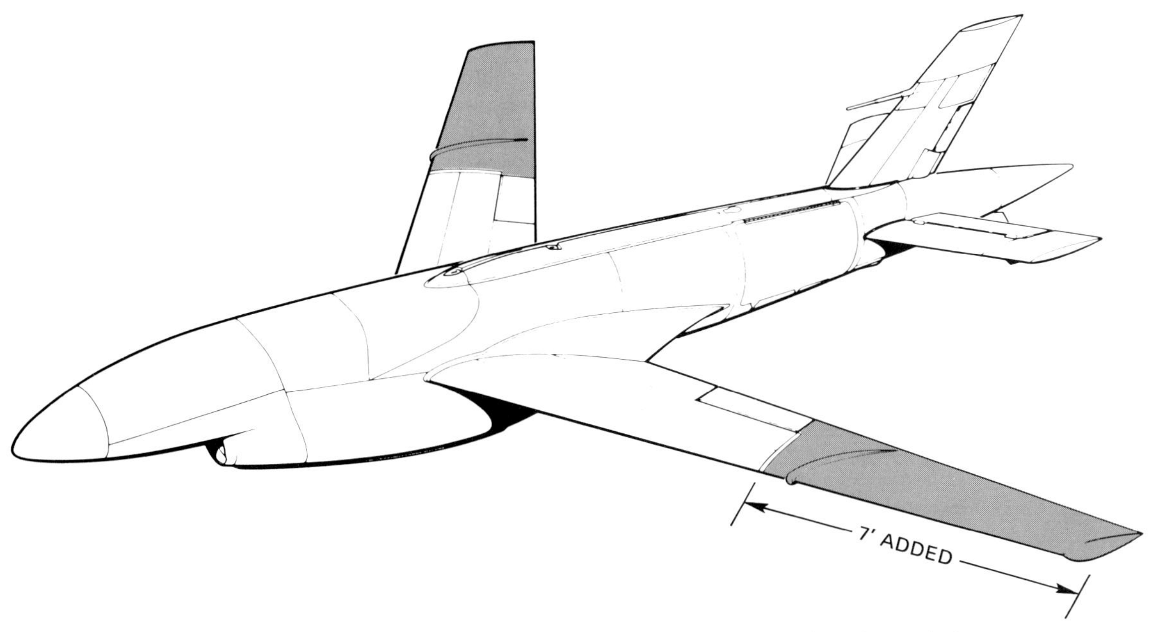

BIG WING B bird. *Span of the wing for the 147**B** Model was extended from the standard BQM's 13 feet to 27 feet, increasing the wing area from 36 square feet to 80 square feet.*

"It was recovered on the Atlantic side after having been launched on the Eglin Gulf side. It drifted and we finally retrieved it at Nassau."

And that's another story as related by Weaver:

"THE RANGE SAFETY officer had predicted that the **A** bird might end up in the Bahamas based on the information of where it went down. A day or two later a fisherman found it. He thought it looked like a bomb so he reported it. A Navy buoy tender picked it up and they said they would deliver it to the nearest port, which was Nassau.

"We took off very early in the morning in the C-130 with Col. Powell and a bunch of people, and a handling trailer to put the bird on. We arrived at Nassau airport at 5:30 a.m. The airport was absolutely deserted and we went wandering around in our bright orange flight suits, through customs and everywhere looking for just anybody.

"Powell and I were supposed to contact the Port Commissioner, go down and look at the docks, etc., and of course we had no transportation, but about seven o'clock a U. S. Customs man arrived for work and loaned us his car. Capt. Robert M. McBratney, the C-130 navigator, Powell and I went into town. We left Bob Todd and Billy Sved with the problem of getting the trailer off the C-130 and finding a truck to haul it and the bird.

"We went to see the U. S. Consul to try to explain what we were doing but by the time we got the PC's office he had gone off somewhere in a very angry state of mind. Since he wasn't there Col. Powell and I just wandered down to the dock area and took a tour. We got on to a huge floating crane which we decided could probably lift the whole C-130.

"When we finally caught up with the Port Commissioner he was in a state of shock and opened the conversation with the comment that he had about decided to close the port and not allow the Navy buoy tender to come in with our wet bird. Col. Powell calmed him down — told him it was hush, hush U. S. government business and all that.

"Shortly thereafter the ship arrived and our guys came roaring up in a truck and some cars. The 147**A** bird had a scorer in it and the nose compartment was full of water, so it presented a rather strange sight during off-loading because of it hanging nose down. It also had radar absorbent blankets on so we had to do quite a lot of manhandling.

"We were just taking the blankets off when the local newsman arrived with his camera. A rather large crowd had also arrived. All this was happening at the docks which were right at a plaza, just down the street from the market place.

"It was his country, so we couldn't really tell the newsman not to take pictures; we could only keep him just a little distance away. So Bob McBratney took his GIs and kept moving them around in front of the guy; every time he'd try to take a shot Bob would run the GIs in so all he got was pictures of the backs of heads.

"We took the wings off and put them on the pickup truck and the rest on the transportation trailer. Nobody had remembered to bring the bolt that goes in to keep the tail down and hold the bird so it wouldn't fall off. So Ted Owens stuck a #2 Phillips screwdriver through the hole and they all took off down the road.

"Powell, McBratney and I delayed our departure for a while. When we finally got on the road, we saw traffic stalled. That #2 Phillips had sheared so they couldn't move for fear the bird might fall off in the middle of main street. They finally got something to hold it and off they went.

"The U.S. Consul meantime had been talking to the authorities trying to explain what we were trying to do. And he finally convinced the Port Commissioner not to throw us off the island. Apparently negotiations had taken place on a high level, but the working level hadn't been informed, so without their cooperation we could have been held up a long time.

"The PC was typically British in appearance and when he finally got into the spirit of the thing, he helped a great deal. The traffic policeman directed the whole entourage down the main street, and it seemed that everybody who had a car followed us out to the airport. We sure had a lot of spectators."

"THE IDEA BEHIND the **D**," Schwanhausser says, "was to equip the drone with a traveling wave tube (TWT) to make it look like a much bigger U. S. aircraft. The drone would then be flown over Cuba at night or just before dawn to draw SAM fire; to bring a SAM up where the CIA electronic gear could effectively get the fusing and beacon information from the Soviet SA-2 missile.

"This was to be done jointly with the Navy which had a ship in the area to track the flashing strobe light we would flash from the drone. The **D** bird would transmit received electronic data and fusing signals to Air Force RB-47 Elint aircraft that would be flying off the Florida coast, and to the Navy destroyer.

"Although we had the Elint birds ready in December as promised, the Cuban situation changed drastically both operationally and politically to the point where they would no longer be able to draw a SAM up for 'inspection.'"

"The first of the **D** birds had augered in [crashed] during the tests at Eglin, but in other flights the program proved the concept because the drone worked better than anyone had expected," Dale Weaver recalled. "It gave us all the data we were after within the limits of the capability we were able to generate in the Eglin test area. We could have brought in the other **D**s and actually run some missions. But basically our birds were just tolerated. The Air Force had their U-2s, and reconnaissance was their baby."

"Though we had a good capability," says Lloyd Ryan, "We never had the chance we had hoped for, late in 1962, to prove it."

Since the Air Force couldn't get SAMs up to expose themselves to electronic intelligence, the **D** drones were 'put in the barn' at Eglin, so to speak. Later two were deployed to Vietnam, in 1965, where they were flown as decoys rather than in their Elint role.

Meanwhile the **C** models were delivered and Ryan's special purpose aircraft activity was moved in January 1963 from the Frontier Warehouse to a new, secure factory building in San Diego's Industrial Park on Kearny Mesa.

Upon completion of the special project for the 147**D**, effort returned to the design and production of the 147**B** which would be the first large wing, high altitude special purpose aircraft.

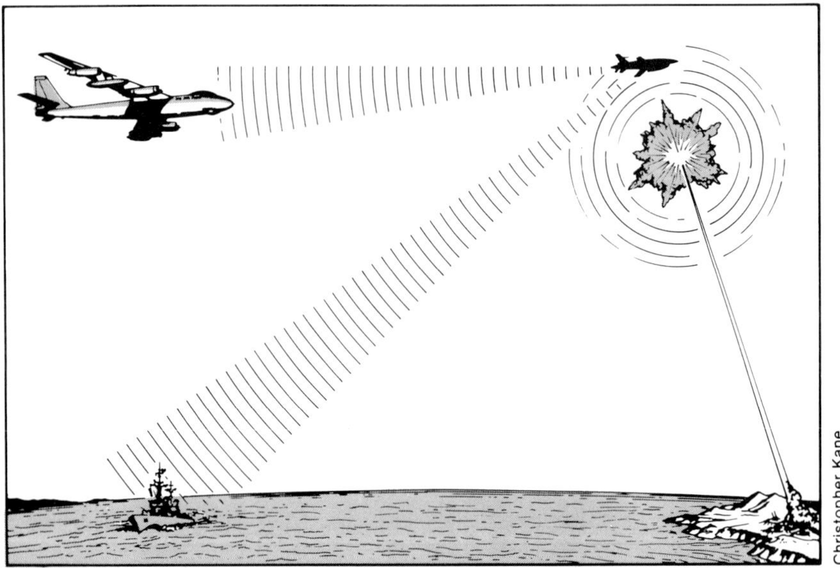

ELECTRONIC INTELLIGENCE configured *147D drone could relay enemy missile guidance information and fusing signals to Elint aircraft or navy ships.*

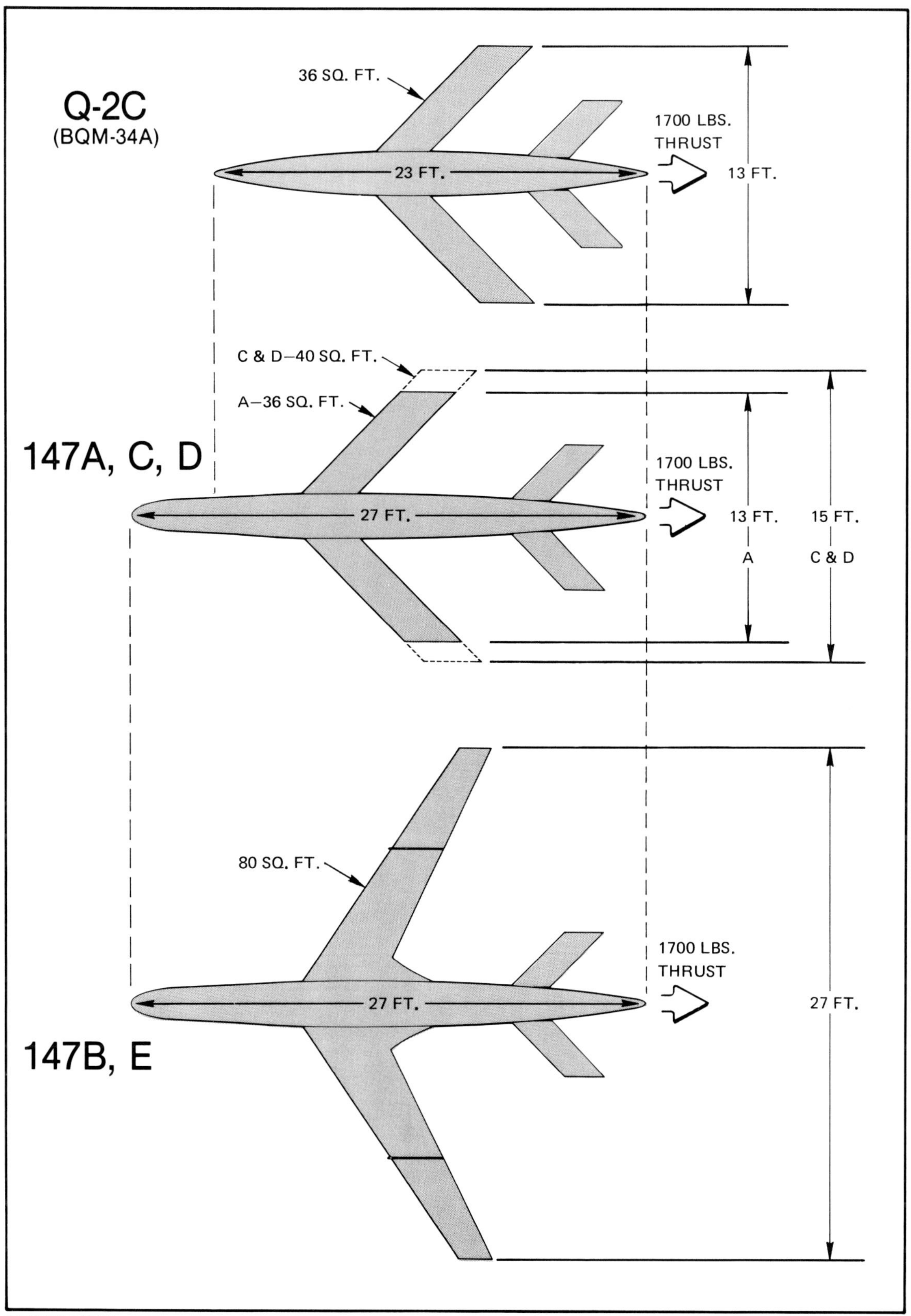

Christopher Kane

HIGH ALTITUDE CAPABILITY for electronic intelligence *missions was provided in the 147E — a customized drone with the large **B** wing and the special equipment of the **D** Elint capability.*

Three vehicles of yet another new model — the **E** — were delivered in January 1964 with training and development flights continuing on other models. The **E** revived the joint CIA/USAF electronic intelligence project begun in 1962 with the 147**D**.

As usual, Ryan production people gave the **E** the old college try. This model had the updated electronic intelligence equipment of the **D** bird installed in a 147**B** airframe. The intention had been to use it in Korea as part of "United Effort" to draw SAM fire, and this required the larger, 27-foot-span **B** wing to provide altitude capability above that of MiG fighters which might otherwise intercept the **E**. Again, everything was set but not deployed. Walt Raynor credited Ryan with "not only overcoming new engineering concepts but the compression of schedules which enabled the company to deliver the third vehicle one day ahead of time."

BY MARCH 1963 when the new flight test program on the big-wing 147**B** version got under way at Holloman, the recce drone code name Fire Fly had been compromised and was succeeded by "Lightning Bug."

Initial testing centered around the 147**XB**-1 which was used for aero-dynamic performance checks, flight loads, stability and control. The 147**XC**-1 model was also used, to support testing of the Ryan Model 523 Doppler navigator — a two-beam continuous wave system developed under direction of Dick Iverson. The flight programmer directed the bird to perform certain functions at specific times or points, while the Doppler velocity sensor provided a cross-track error signal that was pumped into the autopilot to update navigation by making constant corrections to keep the bird on its intended course.

Test results of the navigation system required development of a planar array antenna to provide sufficient isolation of the Doppler signal from the effect of the jet engine compressor blades.

The fully configured 147**XB**-2, the third test vehicle, demonstrated operational mission capability of the total system with Doppler navigation and advanced model Hycon camera equipment installed.

May 3, 1963 the **B** bird made its first free flight. No 'chase' plane accompanied the drone for the simple reason that altitude and range were beyond the 'chase' capability. Ground stations controlled and monitored the **B** as it demonstrated 61,000 foot altitude capability and range of 1555 nautical miles. A new, larger, 100-foot parachute set it down gently.

Each of six flights at Holloman on **XB** drones averaged 2 hours 43 minutes duration.

"On June 4," reports Dale Weaver, "we flew the GC-130 with **XB**-1 and **XC**-1 on the pylons down to Eglin to continue the tests in a more controlled environment where we could actually overfly parts of Florida. The next day another GC-130 carrying **B**-2 on the pylon arrived at Eglin.

"We needed to define the limits of navigational accuracy and to test the Doppler system over calm water to be sure we could get a radar beam return. We wanted to develop a more professional approach to operational problems. Colonels Ellsworth A. Powell and Kenneth R. McCaslin, and Major Andrew J. Corra, from the various Air Force recce offices, came down to Eglin to see how the birds were doing. Actually, we had more problems with the C-130s in those days than we did with the birds.

"While we were running the test program on the **B**s we were also conducting an on-the-job training program for the Air Force — the 4028th Strategic Reconnaissance Squadron (Weather), assigned to the 4080th Strategic Reconnaissance Wing. Many of those people had been on the drone program with us at Holloman and at Eglin. We also gave them some training on the Firebee target system at the Ryan factory in San Diego. The Air Force wanted to have their own internal blue suit operational capability by July 1 with minimum civilian support.''

At Eglin, navigational accuracy was verified by the 147**B** drone's own photo coverage over check points and by radar track and time position correlation. The Doppler radar gave pulse information, which converted into miles traveled, and corrected the drift angle, giving an accurate, updated navigation capability. In 34 flights covering 60 hours in the air, accuracies of 3% in distance traveled and 1.8° in intended heading were demonstrated.

By the end of August the birds had met all requirements. The altitude performance was excellent and the **B** proved to be a very stable camera platform. Several **C** birds had also been flown into Eglin for test flights.

On July 1, 1963 the new pilotless recon drone capability, based at SAC, Davis-Monthan Air Force Base, Tucson, Arizona, had become operational and placed on a 72-hour alert. Ryan assigned Bob Todd to Davis-Monthan as tech rep to help the 4080th out as needed.

Four Lightning Bug drones were assigned — two **C** birds and two **D**s — pending receipt of the new production **B** models.

147B EQUIPPED with radar absorption *blankets hangs beneath DC-130 Hercules launch plane during 1963 tests at Holloman Air Base.*

Dave Gossett

SEPARATED FROM ITS 'mother plane,' *the 147B is launched on a radar reflectivity test flight. No. '496' served as reconnaissance launch plane for many years.*

U.S. Air Force

ON DECEMBER 20, 1963, the Secretary of the Air Force approved a follow-on contract for 14 additional **B** birds to be assigned SAC's Lightning Bug group and placed on ready alert.

However, "There was a great reluctance to deploy the system", Colonel Ryan explained, just before his retirement in December 1963. "It was due to the unknown nature of just how good it would be, and whether we would be giving away a capability that we might want to save for bigger game."

Colonel Yochim, too, recalls the resistance unmanned reconnaissance met at the time.

"Headquarters USAF people had quite a selling job to do to get the Air Force to commit the vehicle operationally because many had serious doubts about the concept. There was real resistance on the part of the manned recon troops.

"After one presentation to the recon requirements office in the Pentagon, an old friend with whom I had worked for a number of years called me aside.

"'Fred, you're not really serious about this program are you?'

"I sure am. Absolutely.

"'Well, it will never replace the manned reconnaissance aircraft.'

"'You're right,' I replied, 'and that's the whole point. It's not going to replace, but supplement, manned reconnaissance. For certain missions it's more economical and efficient to use.'

"The initial, first reaction of people getting flying pay was that they didn't believe the technology was that good, and secondly — perhaps subconsciously — they felt they were being threatened."

Lloyd Ryan had done this job well. From late 1959 to the end of 1963, he, more than anyone else within the Air Force, had kept drone reconnaissance alive. He had done the missionary work.

With modesty he disclaims the credit.

"It wasn't I alone. Hal Wood was Chief of the Division. I was the Deputy Chief. Doug Steakley had been Deputy Chief before he moved up to the Joint Recon Center and I replaced him.

"When I got busy on other projects, Lt. Col. Hayes (Lou) Dickerson took over and then later Lt. Col. Victor W. Rudd monitored the Ryan program. When Vic left, Major Andy Corra came in from SAC reconnaissance operations at Omaha to take over Air Force recon at the Pentagon for the Air Staff. It was not a one-man show by a long shot. But if we hadn't gotten it going then, it wouldn't be in existence today.

"Special reconnaissance — being anything other than tactical — did, indeed, get special attention and handling. It had high level carte blanche which made it possible to move ahead by just taking the bit in our teeth and getting going. A lot of noses were pushed out of joint but that's inevitable when you're dealing with that kind of secret mission. You're involved with foreign countries and American strategic objectives and there has to be a separate channel of communications where you go outside normal procedures, where you can get very high level recognition and support of potential systems to solve highly classified objectives.

"I recall one instance where a high level superior chewed me out because a drone program he 'killed' was still alive. He hadn't heard that it had been approved by one of **his** superiors. That's the type of thing that upsets the military organization structure. But it's the only system that works when things get on dead center. We had our own separate access to the highest levels of government when needed. It was an open secret that when necessary JRC — the Joint Reconnaissance Center — had access to the resident of 1600 Pennsylvania Avenue.

"A lot of generals got very unhappy with the way I had to do business. They breathed a lot easier when I retired the end of 1963."

IN FLORIDA, at Eglin Air Force Base, *a 147B with radar absorption blankets is retrieved after an evaluation flight.*

Dave Gossett

THROUGHOUT THE FIRST HALF of 1964 testing continued on the big-wing **B** birds at Holloman in New Mexico and from March to May with **B**'s, **C**'s and **E**'s at Eglin in Florida.

Early in May, Barnard L. Collier and Laurence Barrett of the New York Herald-Tribune staff reported that top administration officials were giving serious consideration to the use of drones for surveillance flights over Cuba, because loss of a drone to Cuban anti-aircraft rockets would be less likely to provoke a major East-West confrontation than the loss of a manned surveillance aircraft.

The flight proficiency program on the **B** model was completed at Eglin in May and, on the 28th, Colonel Ells Powell of Headquarters SAC declared that "this is one of the finest training programs we have ever had and Davis-Monthan military personnel are ready and operational as of this date." However, Davis-Monthan personnel remained at Eglin on an indefinite stand-by basis, continuing training flights on a one-a-week basis. Ryan personnel returned to San Diego or Holloman, and only Bob Todd remained at Eglin with the SAC contingent.

At Davis-Monthan, one of the young tigers assigned to the 4080th Strategic Wing as Deputy Commander of Maintenance was Colonel William W. Forehand, just out of the Industrial College of the Armed Forces.

"The drone program was so highly classified," Forehand recalled, "that even as a full Colonel I couldn't see it. But I did!

"New on the job, I was out looking at all my facilities and came up to this old World War I hangar. I walked up to the door where this young air policeman was standing. Gun in hand, he said I couldn't go in the building. I told him I owned the damn place and move over, because I was coming in and didn't he see those eagles on my shoulder? It was a little tense for a few minutes, but when I went on in it was the first time I saw the Ryan birds.

Dave Gossett

JUST RELEASED from launch plane, *a 147B begins an extended flight in which effect of radar blankets on reflectivity is studied.*

"I didn't have any idea what they were; they didn't make any sense to me. That's when I went and asked my wing commander what they were. He told me the program was too highly classified for me and that he would have to wait until I got a 'need-to-know' clearance on it before he could tell me. In the meantime I was to stay out of the hangar.

"But I kept nosing around and finally found some Ryan tech reps — Bob Todd and Ted Owens — and started asking them some questions. Their answers were vague and hardly informative but finally I got cleared and found that some 40 of my aircraft maintenance people were qualified and cleared to work on the vehicle."

U.S. STUDIES DRONES FOR USE OVER CUBA

N.Y. Herald Tribune News Service

WASHINGTON—A missile or pilotless plane to replace manned U-2s for surveillance flights over Cuba is being given serious consideration here, it was learned yesterday.

The use of a drone craft, some administration officials believe, would reduce the chances of a brink-of-war confrontation between East and West if the Castro regime decides to shoot down a U.S. reconnaissance vehicle in Cuban air space.

If an unmanned spy craft were brought down by Cuban antiaircraft missiles, it is felt, the incident would not be likely to require the same drastic countermeasures as the capture or death of a U.S. pilot.

May 6, 1964

9

SOUTHEAST ASIA

TONKIN GULF, AUGUST 4, 1964

It was a night of confusion — as is all night combat at sea — as the U. S. Destroyer Maddox (DD-731), recently reinforced by the Turner Joy (DD-951), cruised in a combat ready condition through the South China Sea between North Vietnam and the Communist Chinese island of Hainan.

Two days earlier on a daylight reconnaissance patrol in international waters the Maddox had picked up radar evidence of hot runs against it by North Vietnamese P-4 class torpedo boats. Maddox replied with three warning shots, then destructive gunfire which damaged one or perhaps two of the three 'enemy' boats.

The story two nights later was something else again. It would be hashed and rehashed again and again — just as the 'facts' of Pearl Harbor continued to be debated long after the event.

Was there a contact with the enemy or wasn't there? Certainly everyone at the scene was alert; tension ran high; reports flashed between the destroyers and CINCPAC at Honolulu. There Adm. U. S. Grant Sharp's staff had the task of sorting out fact from guesswork and passing on to Washington as accurate a picture as somewhat sketchy reports made possible. Next morning the United States conducted punitive air strikes against North Vietnamese torpedo boat bases and oil storage facilities.

In retrospect, Washington perhaps gave the North Vietnamese torpedo boats more credit for the naval engagement on the night of August 4 than the facts deserved.

In any case President Lyndon B. Johnson six days later had a mandate — the Tonkin Gulf Resolution — from the U. S. Congress.

From that date there was to be no early turning back from the war in Vietnam.

Things began to move fast at the Pentagon following the engagement with the 'enemy' in the South China Sea.

One move was a flash order to SAC at Davis-Monthan: Get the Lightning Bug drones, the Ryan/military operational team and all support equipment on its way ASAP — as soon as possible. Destination, Kadena Air Force Base, Okinawa.

Four days later a crew of ten Ryan drone experts headed by Jack Lucast was on its way to Operational Location 8 (OL-8).

The deployment plan had been generated long before that; it didn't just happen.

Schwanhausser picks up the story.

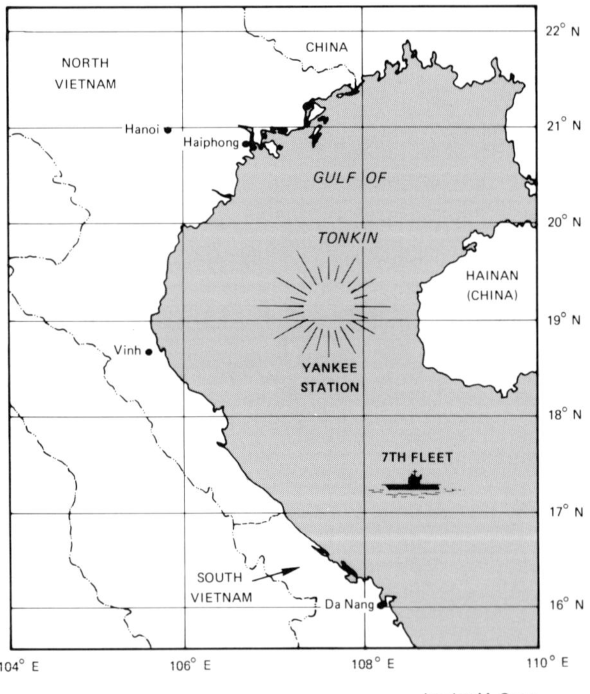

Louise M. Cram

DEPLOYMENT

THE WORD CAME THROUGH about four o'clock on the afternoon of August 4, 1964. It was from Colonel Daniel C. Emrich who had been Ells Powell's deputy at SAC headquarters, Omaha, but was now working for Colonel Doug Steakley in the Joint Reconnaissance Center at the Pentagon. Both had been very instrumental in getting the Lightning Bug program up and going.

We were told to deploy immediately. Get our guys going as fast as possible and be prepared to leave in the small hours of the morning on a series of C-130 transports that would come through Miramar Naval Air Station, San Diego. Others would grab one of the C-130 launch planes or a C-133 out of Eglin.

Our problem was to crank up the team in that short period of time.

Dale Weaver was then running the Navy Q-2C Firebee target drone operation for Ryan at Roosevelt Roads, Puerto Rico, and was on vacation in San Diego.

He was sitting in the lobby of my office talking to Jo Ann Howell for very obvious reasons — still not married, but getting a lot closer to it. I walked out, after I finished a phone call with Jack Lucast in which we were going through the names of the guys we wanted, and I said to Dale "Do you want to go, and he said "Hell yes, let's go." The others felt the same way. Bill Berry was called down off a ladder at home from his housepainting duties.

Then we had to go through the process of going home, getting some dinner, and coming back to work because it was going to be a long night.

We wanted to have each guy go reasonably well equipped. One of the things we needed was at least $500 in cash for everybody, because we didn't know how long we were going to be gone.

By that time the plant was closed, so I had to call Josh Wooldridge, Vice President-Finance, at home and say "Josh, we need $5,000 in cash and we need it tonight." Bob Reichardt got involved in picking up the cash and that's when we found out how honest we were among ourselves as we signed pieces of paper back and forth as to how much money was involved and who was carrying it.

Josh had to come down himself to open the safe because nobody else could get into the damn thing there in the plant. The guy from Finance who was actually carrying the money was taking it out in a briefcase. That's one of the few times the guard on the midnight duty decided to search a briefcase. He found the $5,000 in cash and with that his gun's out and he says "stand up against the wall over there; this is for real."

At any rate, the money is finally given to Reichardt at a bar here in San Diego, in an unnamed location. He signed for it and brought it out to the Kearny Mesa Plant where I was at the time. I signed for it and turned it over to Bill Berry who carried it in his briefcase to Okinawa where he had each individual eventually sign for his share.

U.S. Air Force

JOINT RECONNAISSANCE CENTER chief *Brig. Gen. Doug Steakley, left, shown with assistant, Colonel Dan Emrich, in this 1966 photo.*

The crew never got home to their families that night. We put them up at the Sands Motel nearby but we didn't get the guys off on time. The Air Force had trouble with the airplanes, but the following day they finally got out of here.

Before the group got off I had a terrible argument with another Ryan division head over Dale Weaver. G. B. Doyle said I couldn't borrow Dale for 30 or 60 days, and we got into an awful fight.

I was at home eating dinner before coming back to work. G. B. said "that's fine" I could have him, but Dale would have to be replaced immediately. I said "that's not right; there's no reason a guy can't take a sabbatical for 30 to 60 days." He was insistent and I said "fine, meet me at the office."

I dragged G. B. in here about 9 o'clock that night. I said, "OK, but if it is going to cost Dale his job at Roosevelt Roads, I'm not going to let him go and I'll stop his deployment right now. On the other hand, just so you'll know, I am going to be seeing your boss the first thing in the morning and I am really going to have at you!"

He finally said I could have Dale and he wouldn't lose his regular assignment, which he eventually did, as we discovered while he was overseas.

We got the guys on their way with Jack Lucast in charge supported by the 'first team' consisting of Ed Sly, Dale Weaver, Billy Sved, Gene Motter, Bob Todd, Ed Zelinski, Ted Owens, Bill Berry and Lloyd Morrison. We brought some of them in from their assignments at Eglin, Holloman and Davis-Monthan.

While they were getting out, I was having lunch with Lloyd Ryan and Fred Yochim, by then civilians and staff assistants to me. We decided that as a committee of three taxpayers we should talk to the project office at SAC headquarters and be sure that Big Jim Regis also deployed to Okinawa to give the project the advantage of his unique leadership. That got him the assignment!

You can imagine the hot water that developed at Operational Location 8 (OL-8), Okinawa, when you put that bunch together!

Ed Sly

ONCE ON OKINAWA, Kadena Air Base became the center of operational activity. The idea was to use the long legs of the C-130 to deploy from OL-8, carrying the drone 'piggy back' to a point nearer the 'target' area where it would be launched to fly on its own power. The returning bird would be recovered whenever it could, then if possible be picked up and flown back to a base well removed from the scene of action.

The 147**B**s were to be launched and maintained out of Kadena with parachute recovery being made on Taiwan, some 500 miles to the southwest, only an hour and a half away by T-39.

DaNang in South Vietnam would be an alternate recovery site although it was never actually used for missions originating from Okinawa. With only one MSQ (command, track and control radar) available for the ground-directed recovery sequence it had to be *either* Taiwan *or* DaNang.

The same Lockheed C-130 Hercules used for launch would in most cases proceed to Taiwan to pick up the bird after recovery and return it to Kadena for turn-around.

There were three or four operational people stationed on Taiwan to maintain the radar vans. On the day when a mission was scheduled, flight controllers would be flown in from Kadena for the recovery sequence.

The entire deployment was under the control of the Strategic Air Command out of Davis-Monthan at Tucson. While the military under Colonel Kenneth R. McCaslin were in charge, the Ryan people were there for technical assistance and, after mid-September, Dale Weaver or Bob Todd flew as crew members on the DC-130 launch plane as back-up to the blue suiters.

Jack Lucast, in charge of the Ryan overseas contingent, soon got off a report to Schwanhausser from Kadena —

"Our people and equipment arrived on several different airplanes and it took several days to get things organized. The state of readiness of the squadron for a deployment of this nature was not all one could dream for but they, like we, were certainly rushed into everything. The learning process on this program will continue for some time yet, I'm sure.

"As equipment was not too well identified we had quite a birthday party unwrapping boxes to find out what was in them. Once we got our feet on the ground we decided to put 147**B**-8 and **B**-10 into 'up' condition first. We had the job done in 24 hours, and hung the birds on '496' (one of the C-130 launch planes) and preflighted them so as to be ready when the first operational orders came through. Next we got **B**-9 and **B**-11 into an 'up' condition.

"Then we got word we were in a Typhoon 1 condition which meant winds in excess of 50 mph were expected within 12 hours. Unfortunately the Air Force maintenance officer had downloaded the two 'up' birds so we had to load them back on 496 and load the other two on 497. As soon as both 130s were loaded they took off for Guam to wait out the storm.

"Everyone at Kadena was restricted to base during the typhoon alert; 'C' rations were issued just in case, and worst of all the bars were closed down. Gusts never did get over 40 mph and within three days the C-130s and their four birds were back in business at Kadena.

"Once things were normalized, the day would end with two 'ready' birds on the launch aircraft. Then, starting at 4 a.m., we'd swing into action. The birds would be completely pre-flighted to make certain that everything was in 'go' condition in the event we got an execution order — which should come through between six and eight o'clock. If we didn't get an execution order by 8 a.m. we'd stand down and go back to work on the rest of our equipment and bring it up to condition.

"Finally on the morning of August 20, a little more than a week after our arrival and the day after returning from Guam, came the first operational mission.

"496 and its two birds took off and proceeded to go to work. 497 was scheduled to go to the recovery site on Taiwan to bring the mission bird home so we could rehab it in preparation for the next flight. Col. McCaslin gave me permission to go to the recovery site so I grabbed my gear and climbed aboard.

"When the recovery team on Taiwan picked the bird up on radar on its return leg it was only a few miles to the right of the desired track so indications are that our first mission was a real fine one.

"By the time we got there our bird was resting on the end of the runway. It had been a good flight but the drone sustained major damage on completion of parachute recovery. We worked a couple of hours in the hot sun and high humidity and got **B**-8 loaded back up.

"The scorer material was packed in the film can and shipped off via courier jet to be processed. It will end up at SAC in Omaha.

"The recovery impact area on Taiwan measures a half mile by two miles but as luck would have it on this first operational mission, the bird landed in a rice paddy so the impact switch wasn't triggered, the chute did not disconnect and the bird was dragged until it flipped on its back.

"An Army helicopter came in and picked the bird up in a hurry as we were attracting a lot of strangers who appeared out of the bushes and woodwork."

"When we took off from Kadena on that first operational mission," Ed Sly recalls "we had two birds on the wing pylons, 147**B**-8 and 147**B**-9. The primary bird for this first mission was **B**-9. As the GC-130 launch plane — No. 496 — approached the coast of China we checked **B**-9 out, found everything normal and were ready to launch the bird. As we made our run to the launch point and reached the countdown the bird would not come off the shackle, even with emergency release. We had to come back in

Dave Gossett

PRE-FLIGHT CHECKOUT by launch control officer *(LCO) aboard Air Force DC-130 Hercules.*

for another run as we switched to **B**-8 (Lt. Markle —LCO), the mission backup bird. It launched okay and took off on its programmed photo mission.

"After completing its mission, which we assumed took it over southeast China, the bird came back into control range of our Taiwan radar and the bird descended okay on its 100-foot parachute, but with no disconnect it flipped over and sustained major damage.

"The navigation was not spectacular although it did hit a number of the primary targets. We flew the 'scorer' package back to Kadena and while we didn't see the results at that time we understand the camera brought back significant information.

"The mission was far from a complete success, however. Thirteen minutes after **B**-8 had been launched and the C-130 Hercules was enroute back to Kadena, **B**-9 finally decided to take off on its own. At 24,000 feet it just dropped off the pylon. The engine had been shut down so it just made a graceful descent and headed for the 'deep six'. Something had obviously been wrong when it wouldn't launch on the first attempt, but we didn't expect to see it just plain fall off into space. That SPA (special purpose aircraft) was lost for good in deep, deep water. The bomb shackle did us dirt, but the dye marker worked just fine!"

"ALL THE FLIGHTS OF THE Lightning Bug drones," continued Sly, "were programmed missions. There was no airborne remote control operator (ARCO) aboard the DC-130 nor any ground control except for the recovery sequence.

"We pretty well knew of the routes to be flown in seeking intelligence information because we worked with the military launch control (LCO) and the ground remote control (GRCO) operators to build the programmer inputs.

"The mission plans (routes) were available weeks ahead, and were worked up into the programs which would later be put into the birds. They were of course Top Secret and we had to have access to this information if we were going to help the Air Force plan the mission properly. We worked right with the maintenance people and Air Force LCOs during bird checkout. Pre-flight was backed up five or six hours before scheduled takeoff.

"The necessary electronic inputs were patched into the programmer while the bird was already suspended on the launch rack under the wing. It was patched so events would happen at the proper time you wanted them to, based on the route you were to fly.

"The 147**B** had the Ryan Doppler system so the flight events were programmed at seven mile intervals based on ground distance measurement that came from the pulses generated by the Doppler signals. The backup program, as in the early birds, was based strictly on time so that in the mission planning you had to include wind compensation and everything else which goes into dead-reckoning.

"Early in the program the Air Force had some difficulty with where the birds were flying so we began verifying all the planning that had been done. This led to a two-team military/Ryan concept where each group cross-checked the other. Two groups of people planned the same mission and compared results. This upgraded the whole operation considerably."

NINE DAYS AFTER the first operational flight with **B**-8 the crew got off its second mission, with **B**-11.

"The bird flew its route pattern okay" Sly reported, "and we were looking forward to getting the scorer back into the hands of the customer — the Air Force. But, alas, the ground crew at the Taiwan recovery site had the unfortunate experience of watching the bird fly overhead and disappear beyond the horizon!

"The snafu, it later turned out, was a short in the programmer. Consequently at the end of the mission, when the radio and beacon, telemetry and other systems were scheduled to come back on, they didn't. The birds were built so they could not be recovered except by command. So when the radio command didn't come back up on the program, it was goodby bird!

"A few days later, September 3rd, we got off a good mission with **B**-10, everything going just the way it should except for an engine flame out during the recovery sequence. Only minor damage was sustained, and the 'take' was good. But on the next one, September 9th, our fourth mission, gremlins again got into the system. The engine flamed out at 30,000 feet while we were descending into Taiwan under radio control. Chute was commanded four minutes after engine-off, but the bird was never found. Maybe the bird was jinxed by its serial number, **B**-13.

"A second mission that same day also resulted in disaster. We were flying **B**-6 with some parts salvaged from **B**-8, the drone from our first operational flight which had flipped over in recovery. Shortly after launch from the C-130 the drone was lost during climb-out and crashed in the jungle in Laos. With the engine still running on impact the drone burned in the resulting fire. All parts of the drone were found except the vertical stabilizer leading to the theory that it could have been knocked off in flight due to a possible enemy intercept.

"Clearly we had problems. The system had not yet been de-bugged. Out of five launches, we had only two satisfactory missions. Then on the 15th we had a dual mission schedule but both had to be aborted due to electrical malfunctions. We knew, of course, that unless literally hundreds of events in a complex series occurred at precisely the correct instant, the missions would fail."

KADENA WAS A LOGICAL initial operating base for the unmanned recce birds. It was not in a combat zone, yet offered an ideal opportunity in connection with the Nationalist Chinese on Taiwan to probe Chinese mainland intelligence and defenses, particularly in the provinces bordering on the Indochinese peninsula.

Although the Bamboo Curtain was in some ways more porous than the Iron Curtain, less information seemed to seep through to the outside world than that flowing from Moscow.

The United States and Chiang Kai-shek's regime needed to penetrate the intelligence barrier around mainland China. How near were the Red Chinese to perfecting the A-bomb? What missile sites were being constructed; and what missiles were being installed? Where were the major war-supporting industrial complexes and key military installations?

These were all unanswered questions in the early 1960s and steps were set in motion to find the answers.

For some time there had been a SAC bomber group on Okinawa stationed at Kadena, and U-2s were known to have been based there. Also, the Nationalist Chinese had been operating American-furnished U-2s from Taiwan. Reportedly they had lost some ten of the 'spy' planes, three of them in a matter of weeks before the Lightning Bug group arrived on the scene following the Gulf of Tonkin incident in August 1964. Too, the Red Chinese achieved nuclear capability soon after that when they exploded their first A-bomb on October 16. So, the unmanned recce drones had a logical role to perform if they could 'cut the mustard.'

All of the original Lightning Bug missions out of Okinawa were to be along the coast and interior of southeastern China rather than over Vietnam. One of

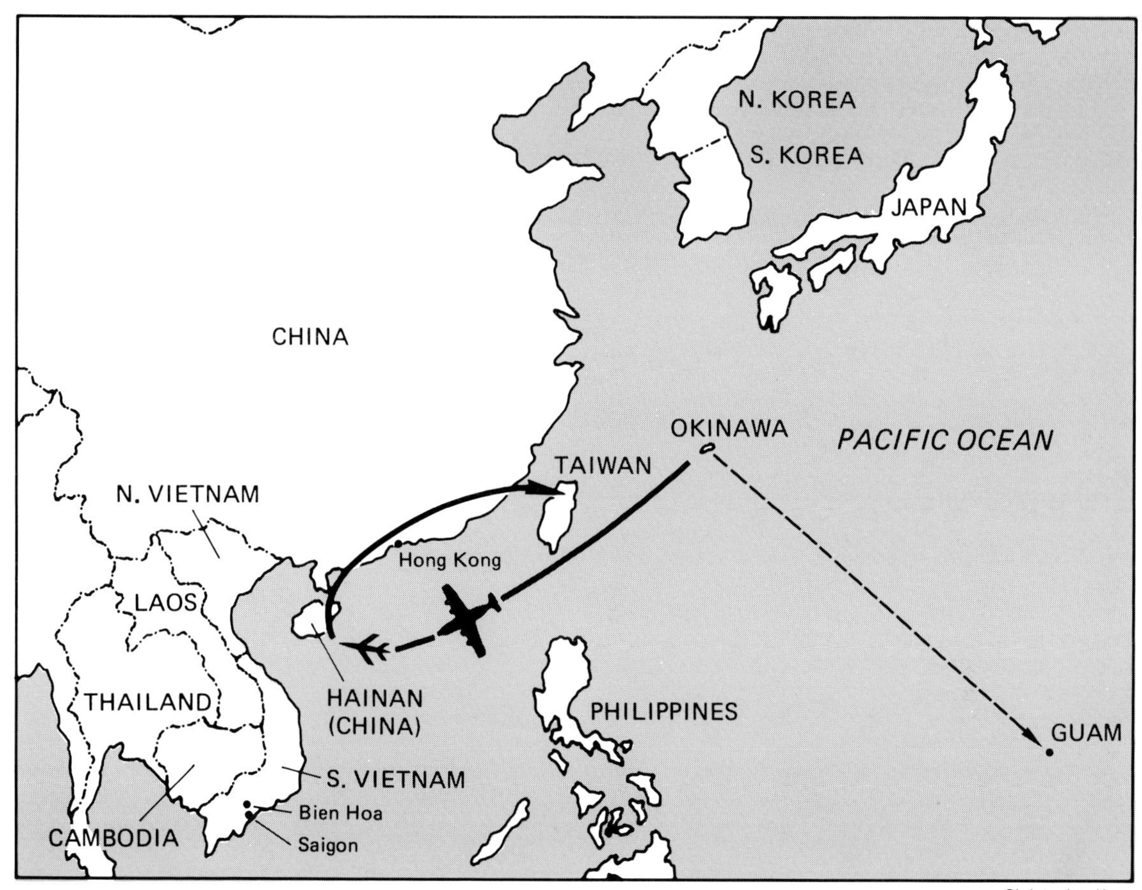

Christopher Kane

the concerns about recovery at Taiwan was its proximity to Hong Kong. The Air Force had to be sure flight patterns did not involve restricted air space. For this reason the drones were usually launched down around the Hong Kong area to fly north over the mainland and then recover back on Taiwan.

Certainly SAM missile sites were one type of target they were looking for. In any case radio "Hanoi Hanna" knew something was up for as Ed Sly reported there were occasional comments about "SAC's hired killers" and references by name to operational personnel almost from the day they arrived.

As a 'cover', Nationalist Chinese insignia was painted on the Ryan drones late the night before a mission out of Kadena. The area around the insignia was then covered over, and the cover removed just prior to the launch plane taxiing out for takeoff. When the returning 'spy' drones were recovered on Taiwan, the insignia was apparently removed because when the birds were returned to Kadena it was possible to see the outline of the star under a freshly painted-over portion of the wing.

There were plans for removing all identification marks from the drones and their on-board equipment but this idea was abandoned as explained by Colonel Lloyd Ryan:

"We had talked about a destruct system, just as the U-2 people had, but the problem of eliminating all identification was not as simple as you would think. If we took name plates of American manufacturers off the airplane (Ryan) and engine (Continental), for instance, they would still be on electronic components, cameras and every kind of equipment. But suppose we took them off that gear, too, there would still be other identification marks. And imagine the problem of assembling and servicing an airplane without identified parts!

"How in the world could you ever eliminate knowledge of the fact that the thing was built in the United States? Any reputable engineer here or abroad can take a piece of equipment and tell you its origin. So if you can't do the job completely, why bother at all to try and disguise it.

"So we said, forget the destruct system. You can't destroy everything. If they shoot one down and announce it publicly, don't deny it; but don't acknowledge it. Just reply, 'no comment' and sweat it out. The one thing you don't say is 'It's a secret project,' because that only confirms that such a project exists."

HABU-BOOS AT KADENA

WHEN THE RYAN TYPES first arrived at Okinawa they lived on the base in the air-conditioned Bachelor Officers Quarters and were soon indoctrinated in local customs.

Their base was only 20 miles from Naha, the capital, where the Navy's VU-5 drone squadron operated Firebee target drones for training. Ryan had one tech rep there and the Lightning Bug group used those facilities for decontamination whenever they had a wet bird — one which had landed by parachute in the ocean or a rice paddy, and been retrieved. They were also able to exchange equipment which was common to the 147 and the Q-2C target drone. The Naha group, however, had no operational knowledge of the 147 missions.

The Kadena Air Base information bulletin called particular attention to the Habu, the local poisonous snake with a bad reputation for an unusually aggressive nature when disturbed. One form of local entertainment for tourists was a fight to the finish between the Habu and the mongoose.

With all the problems which arose in the early Lightning Bug days, it was to be expected that major glitches, gremlins, snafus, mistakes and assorted booboos came to be known as Habu-boos.

Operational problems there were aplenty. The Taiwan recovery site was very small and the winds unpredictable, resulting in many birds being damaged after good parachute recoveries.

Too, the weather was a problem. In the first month there were two typhoon alerts. Everything which could be loaded aboard the C-130s was flown to Guam; what was left behind was locked up and battened down.

Personnel, both military and civilian, were affected by the Habu-boos.

Jim Regis had been pulled in on the program as expeditor of logistics and general coordinator. He wore hats from two different commands and used to kid about writing himself messages and then answering them.

Bob Todd was in the Army hospital in Naha with blood poisoning. Seems he was paying off a native taxi driver when a kid came up and grabbed some money out of his hands. Bob gave chase, fell and barked his shin, which became infected.

All military and contractor personnel were deployed initially for a 30-45 day period — which was extended regularly. With the first flight a good one, everyone felt that they would be on the way home before too long. Instead, departure was postponed again and again. Everyone felt that what was needed was three or four consecutive good missions. Then they could go home, regroup and come back again.

"The schedule for work here doesn't seem to have any end," Jack Lucast reported. "We are now working two shifts but the first week everyone was on a 24-hour shift, with very little sleep.

U.S. Navy

FIREBEE TRAINING TARGET is ground launched *at Naha, Okinawa, by members of Navy's VU-5 utility squadron.*

"The sooner we get out of the operational end of the business and leave it up to the blue suiters, providing the Air Force capability is adequate, the better off we will be. As time goes on and the work load levels off we should be able to get down to four or five Ryan people here. If the program succeeds this can turn into a pretty long-term operation. But we'll stick right in there as long as it appears we can be helpful.

"Maybe we're so used to putting so much of our own hearts into the program that it makes it difficult for us to understand why other people don't feel the same degree of responsibility that we do.

"And, we would never tolerate such loose security as exists here. I've twice found the hangar unguarded. There's little effort to cover the bird to disguise it when outside the hangar. An unnecessary amount of curiosity is generated by the way the program is handled."

Bill Berry, accompanied by three others, returned to the States to prepare and select personnel for rotation necessary to keep the off-site facility going. The Air Force also came to the conclusion that they would need a proper staging area. This was to be done at Davis-Monthan in Tucson which would be responsible for getting the equipment in proper operating order before shipment, and personnel trained and ready for deployment.

In retrospect, the Lightning Bug program would never have succeeded without the Ryan troops. They not only gave technical advice and actual mechanical help with the equipment when needed; they flew as direct control operators (DCOs) while training military personnel to take over the in-flight checkout responsibilities and launch of the drones.

And the physical assets — the birds included — were pretty well depleted.

"When you have only a couple of birds left you find yourself pretty short," Sly recalled. "For example, after we'd moved to a new operating location, we had a good flight on **B**-15 on October 13, with moderate damage on recovery; then turned it around for another good flight on October 18, which ended in a salt water recovery. But we turned the bird around yet again and got off another good mission four days later with **B**-15."

It was typical of the pressure under which unmanned recce drone operation came to maturity.

AFTER LESS THAN A MONTH at Kadena the Lightning Bug group got orders to pack up everything and move to South Vietnam to stage their intelligence gathering missions out of Bien Hoa Air Base, 20 miles north of Saigon. It lasted only eight days.

The Ryan crew wrote company officials in San Diego about the aborted relocation of the operation. "The trip south," they told Schwanhausser, "was pretty gruesome with the usual frantic last minute packing and getting ready to go." Conditions they had to live and work in at Bien Hoa were pretty dismal.

"The misnamed bachelor officers quarters (BOQ) consisted of open-air type shelters with cover overhead and sides screened for mosquitos and flies. But there were a lot of rats running around and that was the reason for plague shots for everyone. Of course the GI's had it worse, but for tech reps the facilities were about as bad as we've ever seen.

"Then there was the symphony of music at night too. A lot of heavy guns going off in the area and machine gun fire constantly. On one flight, '497' — one of our C-130s — was being fired on with small arms. The area was terribly hot, muddy and muggy and just an overall bad place in which to work."

When the crew got back to Okinawa after those eight days in South Vietnam, Kadena looked like heaven. But that wasn't the reason they came back from Bien Hoa.

"Frankly," Schwanhausser reported later, "we were premature in basing in South Vietnam. They didn't welcome our guys very well. The Air Force wasn't ready either facility-wise or psychologically to introduce an unmanned recce bird into their operations. Lines of authority within the Air Force were not clearly drawn, nor was the role of the contractor. Too, the South Vietnamese government hadn't been fully briefed.

"We withdrew to Okinawa until the wheels could be properly greased; then, when we later returned, it was as a permanent operation at OL-20 at Bien Hoa."

ALMOST FROM THE BEGINNING Bob Schwanhausser got directly and personally involved, for the word had reached SAC headquarters in Omaha that all was not going well with the OL-8

RYAN'S 'FIRST TEAM' plus Big Jim Regis

AT KADENA AIR BASE Officers Club, *Ryan's 'first team' poses for formal picture after arrival in Okinawa. Rear, left to right, Ed Zelinski, Gene Motter, Bob Todd, Jack Lucast, Ted Owens and 'Big Jim' Regis. In front row, Lloyd Morrison, Billy Sved, Ed Sly, Bill Berry, Dale Weaver.*

Bill Berry

operation at Kadena.

"They sure had their problems," Swany recalls. "I had been very optimistic as were Ells Powell and Major Andy Corra, then working for him at SAC Headquarters. I found myself in Omaha at the time they were scheduling a dual mission.

"It's daytime in Okinawa, so that means everything happens at night in Omaha. We went out to dinner because we really expected to celebrate the first dual mission. Instead we had a real calamity that night.

"Right in the middle of dinner the phone started to ring and the officers — Powell and Corra — got called out. I went back to the motel and just stood around trying to decide what to do next. Ells called me early in the morning and said, 'You've got to come directly over here. General A. J. Beck wants to see you.' He was the Deputy for Maintenance at that time. He was hard pressed. He had had this failure on the dual mission and said 'I'm going to take a team of experts; we're going to go over there immediately to see what the problems are.'

"The general questioned me as to who should go from Ryan. Of course I said, 'Well, I'll go,' and he said 'I don't want to talk to you. I want to talk to your president and I'll let him decide who is the right guy to go.'

"I said that was pretty fine but I was sure I was going to get tagged for it anyhow. 'Be my guest,

Dave Gossett

'NAKED' BIG-WING B bird *without the same radar absorption blankets seen in a similar picture on Page 49.*

here's his home phone number.' Then I ran out the door as fast as I could and called Bob Jackson and explained he was going to get this phone call, and here's how to answer; and these are the guys that are going to go.

"The general called me back in and said 'we're going' and would I please run down to the hospital and get my shots and be ready as they would pick me up someplace out in California the next day. A C-135 flew into March Air Force Base in Southern California and off we went August 30 — Chet Bergman, Erich Oemcke, my right hand guy, the general and I.

"After we arrived in Okinawa there was a big investigation and there was much in-house fighting. SAC people were dedicated enough but really not fully proficient at that time though they had worked together most of a year. It was not that they were unconcerned but they had not planned on going and they went in a heck of a hurry. Our people went in a hurry, too, but they pressed harder and were far more dedicated and committed to the unmanned drone concept, for their whole future — and the company's — was at stake.

"Our real problem — the human problem — was trying to get our customers, the blue suiters, to accept some help where we felt they needed it. At the same time they had pride, and had attested they were completely trained and ready to go. I stayed overseas as long as I did on this and later trips because we were trying to warm up the atmosphere. We wanted the bird to look good and we wanted the Air Force to look good, and we needed to have a lot of cooperation.

"The personnel problems were pretty obvious. Poor Jim Regis got terribly flapped up in the thing and got sent home by the general. We decided one of the things we had was too many contractor personnel out there so Jack Lucast, Dale Weaver and Lloyd Morrison from the original group were put on the airplane for San Diego. That was supposed to have fixed everything up.

ERICH OEMCKE, Chet Bergman and Schwanhausser, who returned from Okinawa with the 'excess' Ryan tech reps, had been home less than two weeks when the phone rang at Swany's house about 5:30 in the morning.

"You always knew" Schwanhausser said, "that when the phone rang at that time you really had a problem because it was 8:30 in Washington and all hell had probably broken loose.

"It's our Washington guy, Jim Wells, on the phone. He had been working with Colonel Steakley to make an offer to send some Ryan guys over there to help out, without any cost. I said this is a hell of a change from ten days ago when we just got back.

"He said, 'yeah I know, but they've caught on now.' When Bob Jackson got in the office at 8:30 I

ON-SITE COMMANDER of recce operation *was Col. Kenneth R. McCaslin, left, shown with Col. John A. Des Portes, right, 4080th Wing Commander.*

4080th SRW History

saw him and he called the general and offered free Ryan help which again included Chet Bergman, Dale Weaver and myself. At 11:30 that morning we left in a C-130 from Miramar Naval Air Station, San Diego, with some extra drones. That was a pretty fast departure.

"We were accompanied by Colonel John A. DesPortes, the 4080th Wing Commander, who was being sent over to sit on the job and sleep with the project until it got straightened out. The assignment was a real sacrifice for him because he was about to make general and be put in charge of the new SR-71 manned reconnaissance operation at Beale Air Force Base, California.

"To use DesPortes own words shortly after his arrival at Kadena, 'Most of our personnel out here have about as much knowledge of the Lightning Bug as when they caught them when they were kids on the farm and put them into bottles!'"

Less than a week after Schwanhausser's arrival on his second trip to OL-8, a message came in from SAC at Omaha requesting a joint report from the top Air Force and Ryan people at Kadena for recommended improvements to the birds and to the recce operation.

In a three-hour Saturday afternoon brain-storming session, the Ryan group came up with nearly one hundred suggestions for improvement. That evening at the Command Post the Ryan technicians presented their findings for nearly four hours. When the Air Force's turn came, there wasn't one of their suggestions that Ryan people hadn't already covered. The Air Force also frankly reviewed their personnel problems, acknowledging they were not completely prepared due to rotational problems and that they needed up-dating in their training, and refresher courses for the crew chiefs.

The leadership qualities of Colonel Jack DesPortes and Bob Schwanhausser brought the military-contractor team into a more harmonious, open relationship which was soon reflected in improved operational capability.

What was needed most was to get three or four consecutive good flights; then move the entire squadron back to the States for retraining, refitting the drones, getting supply lines in shape, and then deploying back to the Far East.

The evening previous to the Air Force/Ryan meeting things had not gone so good for new arrival Schwanhausser. Swany, Chet Bergman and several others had visited Bob Todd at the hospital in Naha then gone to the Ryukyu Tokyu Hotel for dinner with Len Sinfield, the Ryan Firebee target drone representative on Okinawa, and his wife.

"Chet and I," read Swany's weekly report to the home office, "innocently ordered a half dozen oysters on the half shell to accompany the nine-course Polynesian dinner.

"Thinking they would be just like good old Chesapeake Bay oysters or some Blue Points, we chomped down on those things, and I have to tell you that it was a real taste sensation. Weaver and Sly, by that time old Okinawa hands, sat there like Cheshire cats, and watched the agony Chet and I were going through.

"Those things must have been grown in all the slops coming out of the Mekong Delta and South China Sea put together. Boy, what an aftertaste!

"But back to business, and to summarize:

"We don't want to dig in so hard as to bother anyone here, but if there is any way we can help, we would sure like to do so. Again, per the SAC directive, we are not evaluating the military people; we are just trying to help them."

10

OL-8 TO OL-20

October 2, 1964

To: Robert C. Jackson, President

From: R. R. Schwanhausser
Transient Officers Quarters
Kadena Air Base, Okinawa

Dear Bob:

I AM WRITING from our room where it is more secure and quieter than the hangar or Command Post, so you will have to bear with my typing.

Chet Bergman, Dale Weaver, and I departed San Diego 14 September and spent the evening in Honolulu, departing early on the next morning for Wake Island and Okinawa. After crossing the date line and losing the 15th (my birthday) we arrived late the evening of the 16th.

That night there was a standdown so all got a good night's rest. Following this there have been three flights, but before describing them let me discuss a typical day here.

We rise between 1:00 a.m. and 1:30 a.m. on a mission day and split into two groups. The operations people and our RCOs (remote control operators) and DCOs (direct control operators) go to the Command Post to plan the mission and calculate the flight plan and drone program. The other group goes to the launch aircraft and begins the preflight on the bird.

Both birds have been hung prior to the cessation of work the previous day. By approximately 3:30 a.m. the operations crew arrives from the Command Post and commences programming the birds. This is done with USAF people on one bird and Ryan on the other. One man reads the program while another patches it. Then the two fellows change places and the patcher reads while the other checks. Then the Ryan and USAF crews exchange birds and check each other. In addition each crew has done their own planning and program calculations independently and then cross-checked each other.

During this period I tend to stay at the launch aircraft. If everything goes according to schedule, and it has since I've been here, the birds are buttoned up by 6:00 a.m. and the C-130 takes off at 7:00 a.m.

The worst difficulty we have had in this operation was on the first scheduled flight after I arrived. At about 4:00 a.m. one programmer went up in smoke while it was being stepped through and checked. A malfunction caused the programmer to stop operation at pulse 70 or 80. We now feel sure that this is what occurred on flight #2 when the bird overflew the MSQ and continued on to fuel out and destruction.

One of our DCOs, either Dale Weaver or Bob Todd, leaves with the launch aircraft and regular crew. They ride as instructors behind the USAF DCOs. Incidentally, these fellows have been well received by the customer and this has worked out real well. It has certainly steadied down the two lieutenants and provides reassurance when they were in doubt or encounter new experiences. I feel both Air Force operators are qualified; they just could use a little more experience with the occasional abnormal circumstances to round them out.

At 8:00 a.m. the second C-130 takes off for the recovery site. Col. Des Portes leaves on this aircraft with one of our RCOs either Bill Sved or Ed Sly. Lately our Ted Owens has been joining this party to help on dismantling the bird to bring it home. The balance of us try to rest and grab a nap and sweat out the mission.

The launch aircraft flies past the MSQ at the recovery location for beacon and radio checks and then heads for the launch point.

The drone, which has been riding along as a leech, is usually dropped about 12:00 noon and recovered between 2:00 and 3:00 p.m. After pickup the bird should be back between 7:00 and 11:00 p.m. The launch aircraft returns and is loaded with one or two more drones as required.

On days when we stand down we are not awakened and sleep through until the morning and a normal hangar maintenance day. On days after a mission all officers, Sly, our DCO, and I attend a 10:00 a.m. debriefing. This schedule is good for seven days a week, rain or shine. Each night when we go to bed we have to be prepared to awake at 1:00 a.m. This certainly provides a much different set of working conditions than most of us are used to and I'm sure you can understand why these guys are tired after two solid months of this.

MSQ COMMAND, TRACK and control radar *van. At recovery location, the launch aircraft flies past for beacon and radio checks with Sgt. Ed Wahl, then heads for the launch point.*

Dave Gossett

The three flights that have been flown since my recent arrival are as follows:

Flight #6 Route 5021 21 September 1964

This bird (**B**-12) was dropped in a good location on time but a little to the right of the intended point. The course was about 2 degrees to the left of the intended course and crossed over it passing to the left. After the first leg it rolled out onto its new heading about 8 n.m. short but on a perfect heading. Approximately 120 n.m. out the bird turned 40 degrees to the right on a new unexplained heading. Fortunately this was well within the MSQ limitations and control of the drone was taken.

On the initial pass over the recovery area no command of recovery, either normal or emergency was effective. Beacon track was also erratic and telemetry (TLM) failed after one minute of operation.

Bill Sved convinced them to attempt a second pass at the recovery site before heading out to sea. On the second pass he had all recovery commands sent and the two transmitters cycled. This time recovery was accepted by the bird and impact was on the recovery range on a knoll in winds blowing about 20 knots, gusting to 40 knots. Winds at impact probably were 25 knots. The chute did not disconnect and the bird was dragged upside down into a ravine. The nacelle broke loose and the wing and empennage were badly damaged.

This was the first flight for bird #12. Post flight inspection showed a faulty power supply and improperly installed parachute release wiring. No malfunction occurred or could be found in the autopilot or programmer or radio. As a matter of fact, the bird was immediately placed on external power the next morning without any repairs despite the rough handling received the previous day. Unfortunately the entire route had 8/8 cloud coverage and we refer to this flight as Nimbus #2.

Flight #7 Route 5020 25 September 1964

This bird was dropped in a very poor launch area due to navigation difficulties in the launch aircraft. Practically no Loran exists in this area and the C-130's Doppler was inoperative. Present information shows a good launch followed by a first leg that was 2 degrees to the left and ran about 8 n.m. long. The second heading was 1 degree to the left and 10 or 12 n.m. short. The third heading appeared good but was soon overtaken by command control for let down.

Recovery was normal but **B**-14 hit the ground moving sideways and the nacelle sheared off. This was reported by the USAF as major damage, but by cannabilizing some fittings off **B**-12 we had the bird back up in three normal working days. This included going into the fuel tank and resealing it. I consider this a fine job by all concerned. This was **B**-14's first flight.

U.S. Air Force

'LIGHTNING BUG' 147B reconnaissance drone *is carried by DC-130 to program initiation point (PIP) where pilotless photo plane is released to begin its scheduled route over enemy territory.*

Flight #8 Route 5021 29 September 1964

This drone appeared well launched but 1 to 2 degrees left of intended heading as an average. Actually the first 60% of the leg appears to be 2 degrees left and then changes to an almost convergent heading. The drone was 34 n.m. long on this leg and our information shows a very slow, wide turn. The second leg commenced with about 5 degree left heading error and halfway down reduced to a 2 degree error. Control was taken at that point with the drone 19 n.m. to the right of the intended track and recovery was very smooth and normal requiring 25 minutes. The impact was satisfactory and damage minor, although the location prevented helicopter removal that night. This was the second flight for **B**-10, the first being on 3 September.

At this point let me interject several thoughts. First, the source of our plot information must remain unknown except, of course, from the camera 'take'. We have established a good manner for receiving this and the additional information is gathered from friends who really are not supposed to do this, but it is essential that we have this info.

Second, we know we have been consistently off to the left on the last three missions and need similar info on our previous missions to determine if we could calibrate this error and factor it out in our flight planning.

Third, we have been jumped by enemy aircraft on all our recent sorties. On the second last flight (25 September) we were trailed by at least four aircraft in pairs. These appeared about 10,000 ft. below us and we photographed them and their contrails. At least one fighter was seen 5,000 feet below us on our last flight, and many more have been seen on previous flights.

You'll recall our 'William Tell' missile firing exercises against the Firebee targets at Tyndall Air Force Base, Florida. Well, we're apparently experiencing here what our guys refer to as a 'Chinese' William Tell.

The photo equipment is not working too well. We do not know if this is equipment trouble or maintenance difficulty. Their tech rep is enroute. Also understand the processing on the last picture batch at Guam was terrible. Light struck and blotchy. This we know is causing quite a stir and is not too good for our morale. You might give Hycon a call to be sure that they are doing everything they can to help. Their reputation appears to be sagging in the eyes of the customer.

Colonel Des Portes, the Wing Commander, has been doing a fine job and I feel we are getting along fine. Hope it continues! He has been with the 4080th for four and a half years. He is apparently a good friend of Kelly Johnson [of Lockheed U-2 fame], and a great believer in him. He is still a manned aircraft guy, but is dedicated enough to his job to have an honest desire to get this project up and going. Underneath, however, I sense a strong manned vs. unmanned feeling and Col. Des Portes certainly isn't looking real kindly at this unmanned stuff right now.

The trip to OL-20 (Bien Hoa) sounds and must have been hideous. Lots of mud, heat, humidity, no hangars, rain, etc. At this point, I have the dubious distinction to report to you that as soon as we get the next successful mission off here, we are returning to OL-20 where the night musical serenade consists of bombs, grenades, mortars, machine gun, and of course light arms fire. I shall report to you further from there.

We operate from two maintenance locations, here and OL-20, which I described on the previous page. We recover in two locations, Tua Yuan on Taiwan, just east of Taipei, and Da Nang up north on the coast of Vietnam.

I have decided to have Chet return home and hand carry this to you. In this manner you will receive this on 6 October and will allow us to add to this for two more days. Chet has also fulfilled his mission in fine shape and now can do us more good supporting us at home. He can also carry many impressions of what must be done that cannot be reduced to writing.

The fellows here have all done a splendid job, but they have just about had the course. They are tired and want to go home to their families, but it is next to impossible to do this until the next three sorties are flown. Des Portes himself cannot leave. He tells me they must have one RCO at the MSQ (Sly/Sved) and one DCO (Todd/Weaver). I concur and the problem is we have no replacements.

Maybe this is where you could help us in Washington by trying to have someone make up his mind as to what the future of our operation looks like. We have heard nothing from Lucast or anyone in this respect and anxiously need it. In my own case, I am afraid I must recommend that I stay here with the guys. They will feel deserted and abandoned if I walk out now. I probably should stay too, as long as Des Portes does. He seems overanxious and joyous about exposing Weaver and me to OL-20. They have apparently been operating U-2s there for some time.

Claude Ryan's letters to the fellows arrived yesterday and were very well received. I was surprised myself (pleasantly) to see how much affect they had.

All of our recoveries on Taiwan have been watched by very high level personnel. The Nationalist Chinese Chief of Staff has been to each one and he is reported to me to be very enthusiastic. He has lost three U-2 pilots recently and likes the unmanned concept. On one flight I was told the manned aircraft was shot down immediately upon penetrating the mainland.

I think you know, but if not, we are flying with ChiNat markings. This should be held very closely by you. We are not even allowed to see this. It is painted on at the very last moment by two GIs and painted out at recovery. Unfortunately, they don't sandpaper the markings so you can see the shape of it pretty well.

Des Portes wonders why our birds haven't been hit yet, but I feel their small radar cross-section is effective against some of the SAM site radars and I doubt if they have the capability to fuse such a weapon against us. Our altitude capability has thus far been sufficient. We are watching to see if newer aircraft may appear. At any rate it is the SAM sites which apparently are getting the U-2s.

THE COMMUNIST CHINESE were indeed 'getting' some U-2s. As early as October 1959 new weapons provided by the Russians were aiding Red China in slowing up manned reconnaissance flights which had been going on over the mainland ever since the Korean War.

With late model MiG-19s available, the People's Liberation Army Air Force was able to do a better defensive job. In October 1959 an RB-57, one of many furnished by the United States but flown by National Chinese pilots, was downed over northern China by a MiG-19. A year later, several months after the ill-fated U-2 mission of Francis Gary Powers over Russia, an RF-101 was brought down while taking photographs over Fukien Province.

Then, on September 9, 1961, a U-2 piloted by Colonel Chen Wai-sheng was shot down over Nanchang. The U-2s had been deployed to improve intelligence gathering on the nuclear development center at Lop Nor. In the next several years three more U-2s were brought down. But, due to the U-2 missions, the U. S. was not unprepared when Red China exploded its first A-bomb on October 16, 1964.

BY LATE SEPTEMBER, five weeks after the first operational mission and ten days after Schwanhausser's second inspection trip, things at Kadena were looking up.

Swany had been able to report "the situation is tremendously improved from what we saw a month ago.

"The last two times out we had both birds on the

launch racks and checked out for the mission in not more than 2½ hours. That includes the entire flight course programming as well as mechanical checks. We found no discrepancies at all, so it is getting to be a real smooth, clean operation.

"Morale has improved in the military group in large part because of Colonel Des Portes appearance on the scene and the personal interest he has shown. And all our people have been taken into Colonel Des Portes' full confidence.

"One of the things most needed is for us to have more access to information on actual tracks flown vs. the intended routes which were programmed. If SAC at Omaha will let us come in, with some security requirements relaxed, and plot actuals vs. the intended, we can do the necessary calibrating to improve the 'take' of intelligence information.

"Ed Sly has been doing all of the data reduction work here and is very familiar with the planning of the routes and the method of laying out the navigational problem. Again, we think that very careful post-flight analysis here will help us run better tracks in the future."

With the improved operational capability, quite good flights had been conducted September 25 and again September 29. The photo take on the first flight was good; on the 29th the film was overexposed but acceptable. But again there was damage to the birds on recovery for, as Swany reported, "as long as we are operating with the present recovery site on Taiwan, we're going to have to expect damage of this nature. At the time of day we make the recovery, winds are generally 20 knots or more with gusts running from 25 to 40 knots.

"Dale Weaver," continued Swany "flew two recent missions and is much more satisfied with the capability of the blue suit operators. Today's mission is being flown by recently hospitalized Bob Todd, who will continue from now on.

"The operation really appears to be a heck of a lot better — looks like a very steady operating thing now with good records, good work, good time schedule and pretty good attitude on the part of the people who know that they can't get on home until this thing gets working."

But within the week the Habu-boo hex took over again. Two missions in a row were aborted on October 4, one for a ground condition at the recovery site; the other for navigational equipment difficulties in the launch aircraft. Other troubles were also being encountered with the launch aircraft, one of which was sent off to Japan for repairs.

In preparation for operations expected to be conducted out of Bien Hoa, Gene Motter and Bill Sved boarded a special flight out of Okinawa for Da Nang, the alternate recovery site. Sved was to be assigned there permanently. Two flights were being scheduled which would take the unmanned drones over hostile territory, and the launch aircraft, too, would be operating in an area considered hazardous. Dale Weaver volunteered to ride the launch C-130s as DCO (direct control operator), back-up to the Air Force lieutenant on both the flights.

In a message back to the home office in San Diego, Schwanhausser urged that personnel being assigned to overseas locations be protected with adequate visas.

"For their own personal protection," he wrote, "people traveling out here should not only have a valid passport but also adequate visas. Because we travel on military orders on military aircraft we get into some places where from a personal security standpoint it's bad business not to have proper documents. Sometimes you can get them on the spot and sometimes they are very difficult to come by.

"On their recent trip to OL-20 (Bien Hoa) our people never did get visas. It's really dangerous for them to be wandering around the streets with no visas. So let's get them covered for Vietnam, Taiwan, Japan, perhaps the Philippines and maybe even Korea."

In truth, the Ryan technical crew members were in for some interesting times!

"We were having as much trouble with recovery as with anything else. The birds were flying pretty well and coming home, but then we'd have problems. We were having trouble with chute disconnects, for instance. They were programmed for salt water, so we had a salt water switch, but if we landed in a rice paddy — with fresh water — the chute would not disconnect and the bird would be damaged from being dragged.

"Then there were the mechanical problems like the programmer door. This was the door which pinched and tore the wires on the bird that overflew Taiwan on return from a mission, and kept right on going out to sea. We were fighting all the problems — the debugging — you never find until you actually get into an operational environment.

"One night at the Officer's Club, while at Kadena on my second visit, we were notified about eleven o'clock that we were departing for Bien Hoa in the morning, and to be packed and ready to go.

"When we moved into Bien Hoa permanently it was done with great haste. Weaver, Sly and Todd went out in 496, the first plane. Ed Zelinski and I were on the second aircraft carrying some equipment. The remainder of the equipment and crew came on the next two planes. Colonel Des Portes was in the last one out of Okinawa. Within 20 hours after the word came through, everything and everyone was out of Kadena.

"Being a wise guy — I thought — I had bought some speakers for my stereo at home in San Diego at the PX in Naha and had them in my room at the BOQ expecting to take them with me on my return to San Diego. Instead came the word to depart for Bien Hoa, but now! So I had to ship the speakers by express; they didn't get to San Diego until after my return, and including shipping charges, cost me far more than if I had bought them in San Diego in the first place!"

REPORT FROM OL-20

Operational Location 20
Bien Hoa, South Vietnam

SCHWANHAUSSER TO SAN DIEGO:

We arrived here Thursday afternoon, October 8, about 3:30 p.m. By seven o'clock we were in a position to declare both birds and the launch plane in an 'up' condition and ready to go in the morning.

Friday we expected to go; however, the word did not come through. I am not sure whether it was weather or some reason dictated by decisions made in Omaha or Washington.

Saturday was a down day and as we got the word Saturday night that our first mission out of OL-20 was doubtful at that time, we thought a little party was in order with out military counterparts. We all got to bed late expecting to get a good night's sleep. Then in the middle of the night the word came that the mission was on, so we rousted everyone out.

This was the first of three consecutive good missions during our first operational week at OL-20.

Dale flew that first mission as LCO in the C-130. This flight of **B**-14 on October 11 was an interesting mission as far as we were concerned — the bird a hundred percenter until recovery.

During recovery the main chute blew off leaving only the risers. The bird went in and dug a big hole. It was returning about 20 miles off to one side. We know nothing yet of its track along the flight path, only that it returned about 20 miles off.

The chute was commanded at 30,000 feet and the bird descended through a very heavy rain storm. Then the main chute blew off on deployment. Now there is a big muddy hole in the middle of a rice paddy; little or nothing has been carried out at the present time. The bird went through a very heavy rain squall and we're curious as to how much water we collected in traveling at 200 knots for 4 plus seconds in a main chute reef condition. We feel that was the cause of the chute blowing and breaking off. At any rate, upon drone impact a helicopter and three 4080th airmen were dispatched to the scene. The helo ran into heavy fire from the Viet Cong. The three men were let out and dropped into the hole. Then another chopper came out carrying the Marine Colonel who runs the Special Forces there. It also was shot up pretty heavily — punctures in both fuel tanks, slashed canopy and the crew chief got cut up a bit with the broken canopy.

The fellows then felt they had a fight on their hands for possession of the bird and they were just in

"WE ARRIVED HERE AT BIEN HOA on Thursday *afternoon. By seven o'clock both birds and the launch plane were ready for a morning take-off."*

the process of checking Gene, Bill and Dale out with the AR-15 automatic rifle when it was decided to leave the bird alone, pull everybody out and go back the next day.

The following afternoon armed helicopters went in, straffed and shot up the area very badly, killed a few V. C. and we still had no bird. After sanitizing the area, they were still digging and trying to get the water out of the hole so we could find whether or not the scorer material would be returnable. We are still looking for the material; however, at this time we have no report on it. The airplane RON'd (remained overnight) at Da Nang that night and came back the next day with very beat and tired stragglers.

We heard that Sunday would be a down night so most of us went into Saigon — the first evening actually in town. We stayed overnight, picked up our passport visas on Monday and returned here in the afternoon anxiously looking forward to the next flight which we felt would come that evening.

Sure enough at 1:30 Tuesday morning, the 13th, the next flight was commenced. This was one of our best. The checkout went extremely smooth. Actually on both the last two missions the checkouts were right on. The aircraft took off on schedule, encountered a little difficulty at drop time — fortunately, on this flight, Dale was along and could help the LCOs. They had two minor difficulties which caused one orbit and the bird was dropped ten minutes later. The flight apparently was excellent.

We turned on schedule about 7 miles to the left but on course. This is a very difficult U-shaped course. After completing its scheduled route, telemetry told us the chute had been commanded. At 49 minutes

'TOURISTS' IN SAIGON

Bruce Engman

TYPICAL TOURIST Bruce Engman *takes a break from his tech rep duties. Right — two wheels rather than four are standard transportation in Saigon.*

Bruce Engman

Ed Sly

RYAN TECHNICIANS Ed Sly, *left, and Dale Weaver make friends with Vietnamese children.*

JINRIKISHA PASSENGERS Ted Owens, *left, and 'Rapid Robert' Schwanhausser see the sights of Saigon the easy way in 'pedicabs.' Right — the slit-skirted beauties on the boulevard are eyed by Bruce Engman's camera.*

Ed Sly

Bruce Engman

after the hour we knew it was down. Sharp at the hour we had a message that it had been picked up by the chopper and was en route back home with a condition 1 bird. Only damage we found was a broken keel and it is being repaired, so we don't consider this major damage. We are even trying to fly a keel in from Naha to replace it.

It was very satisfactory to all of us. We were quite rewarded, frankly, to see that hundred percent mission as we had been wanting and hoping for this one badly. The mission was flown by **B**-15. Five days later, October 18, we sent **B**-15 out again. The bird returned after a fine flight to a good salt water recovery.

With these good flights under our belt I am going to suggest to the people here that three of us return this weekend. That would be Dale and Ed Kraus and me. Then we would return the entire crew around the first of the month when the contract runs out and we are recommending that from then on perhaps two representatives from our place stay out here. One being an all-around fellow who can also act as LCO or RCO; the other a Doppler man.

I should point out that the last missions were running very smoothly. These guys are in real fine shape to take over and fly this bird now. It is beginning to look more like getting up in the morning and starting the car on the way to work. At this time, too, we feel we now have too many people here. Really there is little more that we can do and we felt that perhaps by returning a little early we could get extra work done back there to support these people here.

The GIs now have a lot better morale since getting off a couple of good flights. It had done wonders for them. The officers certainly are all getting with the program and we're extremely happy with it right now.

I'm convinced the combat bonuses we scrapped for are more than justified. As a matter of fact we have armed Todd and Dale. Both are now happily, or reluctantly, carrying .38s.

When you see Dale in his flight suit with this big holster hanging down by his side, he looks like a pretty sad example of an American cowboy. At any rate they have all done a good job. They've had some very interesting missions and Dale has cranked off four that could be considered combat missions. At this time Todd is on duty for the next one to go.

They have, as you probably know, a DL (Dragon Lady: U-2 manned recce) operation out here.It's been very interesting for us to be able to sit and talk in private conversation with some of the pilots who fly that machine. Most of them are a little nervous about flying these days. They had two up today, one aborted with a mechanical problem en route which worries everybody here considerably.

The other pilot with whom I spent the time landed 15 minutes ago and he's being debriefed right now. He believes he'd like to get out of this business and sees quite a future for the type of operation that we have been proposing and trying to sell.

So as each day has gone along here, and as the operation has gotten better, we not only have created better relationships with these people but a real understanding as to what the equipment can be made to do, especially with some additional modifications. We have been gathering some converts to the cause!

As to expense money, checks will do us no good at all here at OL-20. A maximum of $100 per month can be cashed and that requires going downtown through a special embassy agreement.

They just don't want American cash over here, so if any of us linger here you will have to send us money — cash — by registered mail. It is a little dangerous but it is the only way we can get it, and you can't live without it.

BEFORE things got rough: *Ryan crew at Bien Hoa, November 1964. From left, Bob Reichardt, Tom Wood, Todd, Owens, Sly, Norb Cormier, Bob Price, Zelinski.*

Ed Sly

AFTER things got rough: *Viet Cong raids found the crew busy sandbagging their quarters. It was Halloween — time of "The Great Pumpkin."*

Bruce Engman

SWANY WAS NOT THE ONLY one reporting back to home base.

Correspondence from the Operational Location overseas and from the Air Force at Omaha, Washington and Dayton didn't go through the company's usual business channels. Early in the program, to protect the highly classified work, two post office boxes at suburban San Diego substations were rented in the name of key employees who acted as trusted couriers for the sensitive documents.

Thus Dale Weaver was conducting a correspondence half way around the world, in as veiled language as possible, with Swany's secretary, Jo Ann Howell:

Bien Hoa, 9 October 1964

You should see me now. I am truly the front line combat troop. Flight suit, go-to-hell hat, .38 cal. pistol and all. Kidding aside, the game they are playing here is not too nice although I must say, as far as this base is concerned so far, it's a spectator's war.

I was standing outside the hut last night with a drink in my hand watching flares go off and listening to bombs, rockets and small arms fire. To tell the turth I feel a little bit like joining the local Special Forces on a night raid just for a little action, but I guess I'll content myself with flying combat missions in '496'.

Bruce Engman

"YOU SHOULD SEE ME NOW! *I am truly the front line combat troop, go-to-hell hat and all." That's Dale Weaver at left with Capt. Charles West, DC-130 navigator.*

Bien Hoa, 12 October 1964

Just got back from a trip to Da Nang. Yesterday's mission was perfect except for the recovery. We have Billy Sved and Gene Motter at Da Nang, where I stayed last night and they have it pretty plush compared with this 'garden spot' at Bien Hoa.

You should have seen us yesterday after **B**-14 dug the hole after its chute failed. Bill, Gene and I were set to go to the impact site and help fight for the pieces, especially the scorer. We had been given our AR-15s and instructions on how to use them and were just getting ready to climb into the chopper when the word came back that the VC had shot up the H-37 pretty badly and that both HU-1s had engaged in a hot fire fight. The base commander decided to send in an Army group instead of some crazy civilians.

At the time — and later — a lot of activity involved China just as it had on missions out of Okinawa. Dale recalls, "We were launching quite a lot over Laos; often we'd make it almost to the Chinese border to launch."

TWO MORE SUCCESSFUL Lightning Bug photo missions were flown out of Bien Hoa over North Vietnam on October 22 and 27. Bob Reichardt had flown out from San Diego a week earlier in a C-130 Hercules to OL-20 with a load of new drones to replace Schwanhausser as Ryan's on-site program manager to provide the interface between SAC's OL commander and the plant to be sure problems in the field got prompt action.

Swany and Dale Weaver flew westbound out of Saigon for Washington, D. C. and Omaha to report in with the first-hand information on operational successes and difficulties and on the continuing personnel problem. There was still no firm plan for rotation of either military or contractor personnel and it was further aggravated by inadequate communication. As Reichardt wrote:

"For the long haul a better method of communication must be worked out. Letter exchange takes too long; telephone is extremely unreliable because of transmission difficulties. It remains to be seen how cable will work. While you in San Diego were working on one approach to rotation, I was working on another here. Coordination is virtually impossible."

Reichardt didn't have long to wait for action — but of a different sort. "The Great Pumpkin" — Ed Sly's description — arrived at Bien Hoa with a flourish on Halloween!

That night the Viet Cong, out to play trick-or-treat, threw everything they could at military installations on Bien Hoa airfield. They had a tempting target. For months, row after row of U. S. aircraft stood wing to wing on the field. The VC crept to within 2500 yards of the flight line, then blasted the airstrip and barracks with 81-mm

'WARRIORS' IN BIEN HOA

Ed Sly

IN CONTRAST TO SAIGON, Bien Hoa *is 'combat' territory for Ryan tech reps. From left, Bob Todd (his infected ankle still in bandages), Ed Sly, Ted Owens and Gene Motter.*

Bruce Engman

NEW ARRIVAL, tech rep *Coy Himebaugh, pictured in a 'bad area' near the compass rose at Bien Hoa.*

Ed Sly

MILITARY AIR CREWS who manned *launch planes have a more soldierly bearing than Ryan's motley civilian group.*

HEDGING THEIR BETS lest things *get too rough, Ed Zelinski, Bruce Engman and newly arrived Chet Bergman and Bert Winslow find a visit to the Chaplain's Office good insurance. Below, Zelinski hedges his bet even further.*

Bruce Engman

Bruce Engman

mortars. A lot of airplanes were wrecked on the flight line but fortunately neither the C-130 launch planes, the Lightning Bug drones nor Ryan personnel were hit. It was the Ryan civilian crew's first exposure to honest-to-gosh combat, and they weren't exactly enthusiastic.

"It was the first time in twenty years," Reichardt reported, "that I found myself crawling on my belly in the mud in the middle of the night."

There had been a lull in photo reconnaissance missions, but the Lightning Bug group continued to maintain a ready-alert status. Finally on November 7 they got off another good mission. As Reichardt reported:

"This gives us a string of six good missions now.

"It was quite a relief to have work to do after eleven days of inactivity. Eleven build-ups and eleven let downs! Nothing to do but eat, drink and sweat. Believe it or not I was hoping for another Great Pumpkin barrage to relieve the monotony; assuming of course we could again come out of it with none of our people injured.

"The general level of this type of activity has increased considerably during the past week. The sound effects are in the background every night now; sometimes carrying on into the next morning. It's getting so we don't even get up to watch any more — just roll over and go back to sleep. But I do have a loaded AR-15 within reach. All our people are carrying side arms just in case. They need them especially when flying for if you have to land somewhere, you have no way of knowing what the conditions will be.

"Night before last there were 3000 'bad guys' just twelve miles from here. This makes me kind of wonder whether the top people in Washington are aware of how exposed our recce birds are — needlessly, I think, because the job could be done equally well from less exposed locations.

"I don't care to go downtown (Saigon) too often these days. Not to sound melodramatic, but our people are in ever-present danger for their very lives, and I kid you not. Bombings of American personnel in the big town nearby are routine occurrences and the probability of another Halloween Great Pumpkin affair is real.

"To illustrate — whenever I go to the john, about half a block from our sleeping quarters, all the way there and back I look for the nearest ditch into which to dive on short notice, if necessary. Yesterday a bomb was tossed into Saigon's Tan Son Nhut commercial air terminal restaurant, killing or injuring 18 people eating their lunch. Bombs are regularly thrown into night clubs patronized by GIs and officers, and hand grenades are being tossed into passing vehicles. And, the local bad guys have passed the word around that they expect to have their Thanksgiving dinner in the Officer's Club here at OL-20 with American officers serving them!

"To us here on the spot it's very real. The AR-15s by our bunks are very real, too. So it's a little difficult for us to understand why the bean counters [accountants] in San Diego can't accommodate our requests for vacation time in Hawaii for the men enroute home after three months under war conditions.

"We should keep Ryan personnel to a minimum and avoid needlessly risking our people's lives. I'd like to get our LCOs (launch control operators) off the planes. They simply are not paid to take the same risks as military personnel; they are not in uniform but are subject to the same hazards.

"Of course we do appear in uniform — unintentionally — now and then. The other day returning to Da Nang in a C-130 from a combat mission I was wearing a flight suit borrowed from the co-pilot. When we went into the Officer's Club for lunch I discovered I was 'impersonating' an officer in uniform. At 41 years of age I was probably taken to be the oldest First Lieutenant in the Air Force!

Teledyne Ryan Aeronautical

SHRAPNEL from 'honest-to-gosh combat' *was sent off to San Diego as a reminder that the Ryan overseas crew might qualify for hazardous duty pay.*

Ed Sly

"YESTERDAY A BOMB WAS TOSSED into Saigon's *Tan Son Nhut commercial air terminal restaurant, killing or injuring 18 people eating their lunch."*

"When one of the guys got out here expecting to fly as back-up LCO and found out that aircraft get hit by ground fire on takeoff and landing, and that pilots downed within a few miles of Bien Hoa sometimes cannot be reached in time, he lost his enthusiasm for the assignment, and I don't blame him.

"There are still skeptics about our drones in the top Air Force levels here. They feel we sold the Air Force a 'bill of goods' on a piece of equipment that isn't ready, and that they're being expected to meet operational standards the hardware isn't capable of achieving.

"As you can see we still have a long, hard road ahead to gain acceptance of unmanned photo reconnaissance."

IN FAIRLY SHORT ORDER drone operations fell into a planned routine which, of course, had to be flexible enough to meet the unknowns which continued to crop up.

One of the San Diego-based program managers, the late Dave Williams, a 23-year veteran with Ryan, explained the operational concept as applied to later low-altitude operations:

"After each mission, the bird which returns home goes into the hangar for a complete recycling. Following any structural repairs, the drone goes to the electronic console which 'exercises' all of the systems just as though the bird was flying. Then comes an engine run, and if that checks out okay, the drone is up-loaded on the launch aircraft.

"Now it's ready for a flight line check with the bird on the launch pylon. This check is to verify that all of the connections to the DC-130 are working properly and to confirm that the bird is still performing as it did when it came off the checkout console. Everything is ready for a 'go' on the mission.

"The flight crew is composed of pilot, co-pilot and flight engineer, plus a launch control operator (LCO). If they have two vehicles, then there are two LCOs, each of whom can see his own bird. Only major functions are checked during the pre-launch sequence. When the bird lets go of the pylon on launch the LCOs job is completed.

"Up front in the DC-130 are one or more airborne remote control operators (ARCOs). They have a display panel which tells them where the bird is and instruments which show what the bird is doing. They can fly the drone through the microwave command guidance system (MCGS) exactly the same as does a ground remote control operator (GRCO) through the ground station.

"The reconnaissance mission is usually an automatic one, pre-programmed to fly a precise intelligence gathering route. But anytime either the ARCO or GRCO feels it is not doing what the program called for he can cut in and correct it or take over and fly the drone manually.

"At launch time it is important that the DC-130 be at an exact predetermined point so that the programmer can then pick up what has been put into the program. The compass heading being flown also has to be precise so that when the drone is launched the programmer will pick up the necessary initial heading.

"Navigation aids on the DC-130 get the launch plane and drone to the drop point and on the correct heading. Lateral location must be precise; vertical position in terms of altitude is not as critical to mission success. Even on low-altitude missions altitude is not critical because right after launch a dive is commanded to take the bird to a specific altitude, so whether you launch at 10,000 feet or 20,000 feet you end up at the same altitude for the low-level mission.

"In a typical SEA (Southeast Asia) mission, we take off from Bien Hoa and fly far north of Da Nang, sometimes being airborne up to five hours before launch off the coast of North Vietnam. Up to 20 minutes before launch the drone is just hanging there as a parasite on the pylon. Then the LCOs start checking out the systems.

"On the way north we will have flown over the ground station at Da Nang so he can make his checks to be sure he can 'talk' to the bird. Da Nang will not see the bird again until it is on its return mission leg.

"After launch the ARCO will be tracking the bird through the entire mission. When the drone starts its return trip to the recovery area the ARCO picks it up as a blip on his radar scope and gets it almost home to Da Nang then turns it over the GRCO who performs the final inbound leg and recovery.

"Occasionally ground control can't acquire the bird so the ARCO takes it all the way to the recovery area. Sometimes ARCO and GRCO pass it back and forth because of problems in one or the other of the control stations."

DANANG WAS FINAL check point for missions *flown north, and recovery location when drones returned. Ryan's Ed Sly, left, with Lt. Ed Beverly, Air Force RCO (remote control officer) at DaNang.*

Ed Sly

11

COMPROMISE II

HONG KONG, NOVEMBER 16, 1964 — Peking announced tonight that the Chinese Communist air force had shot down a pilotless United States reconnaissance plane.

The incident, described by Marshal Lin Piao as a 'major victory', took place over central south China, according to Hsinhua, the Chinese press agency. The announcement said:

> **''A pilotless high-altitude reconnaissance military plane of U. S. imperialism, intruding into China's territorial airspace over the area of south central China on Nov. 15, was shot down by the air force of the Chinese People's Liberation Army.''**

This was the first report from Peking or elsewhere abroad that pilotless aircraft were being used for reconnaissance. Flights are made across Chinese territory by pilots of the Chinese Nationalist air force and some coastline patrols are known to be made by planes of the United States Seventh Fleet.

These reconnaissance flights are so extensive that the United States was able to forecast China's recent nuclear explosion, having spotted the site from the air. Observers said that if pilotless planes were being used for flights over China, one might have produced the pictures of the nuclear test site.

Peking has reported the shooting down of 10 ''U. S. -Chiang Kai-shek spy planes'' in the last few years. They included three U-2 aircraft.

The last of these was downed in July. Chinese Nationalist authorities announced that a plane on a spy mission had failed to return to Taiwan after Peking had reported shooting down a U-2.

The United States is believed to have relied mainly on the Chinese Nationalists for aerial reconnaissance over China to avoid giving Peking a chance to make propaganda capital out of captured American pilots. The use of pilotless planes would enable the United States to make its own flights without concern over this possibility.

RYAN 147B MISSION LOG

Date	**15 November 1964**
Location	**OL-20**
Vehicle	**B-19**
Launch	**Okay**
Results	**Lost enroute during penetration phase** **SPA DNR (Special Purpose Aircraft. Did Not Return)**

Bob Reichardt to Bob Schwanhausser, by tape recording, 19 November:

''About the occurrence of the past week-end, this was more or less expected here. Possibly the goal was a deliberate attempt to find out exactly what they could or could not do.''

What Reichardt was reporting, in thinly veiled language, was that the mission was run as a planned effort to get the Red Chinese to fire on the recce drone. Undoubtedly there were U. S. Elint aircraft in the area to record and analyze electronic fusing data which would be useful in planning a better system of defense against Communist ground-to-air missiles.

Schwanhausser recalls other reports — unofficial — that something like 16 to 20 MiG fighters went after the bird that day and made perhaps 30 to 50 passes at it before they got it.

''We had their attention,'' Swany recalls. ''They were mad and they were really flying virtually a 'William Tell' Weapons Meet against us.

''One of the main targets we had down there was the island of Hainan as well as North Vietnam on the mainland side in the Gulf of Tonkin.''

Red China Says U.S. Spy Plane Shot Down

LOS ANGELES TIMES Nov. 17, 1964

IN A MINOR, "WHO ME?" repetition of the Francis Gary Powers U-2 incident, official Washington was caught somewhat off base in commenting, or not commenting, on the reports out of Peking.

As United Press reported, "If there was a mystery, officials were willing to let it deepen." No official spokesman in Washington denied the Chinese claim, but collectively they asserted ignorance of the matter.

White House Press Secretary George E. Reedy: "I know nothing about it. This is the first I've heard of it."

The State Department: It had no information to support the Chinese claim.

The Defense Department: After deliberating all day on what to say, Pentagon spokesman finally came out with a statement: "No comment."

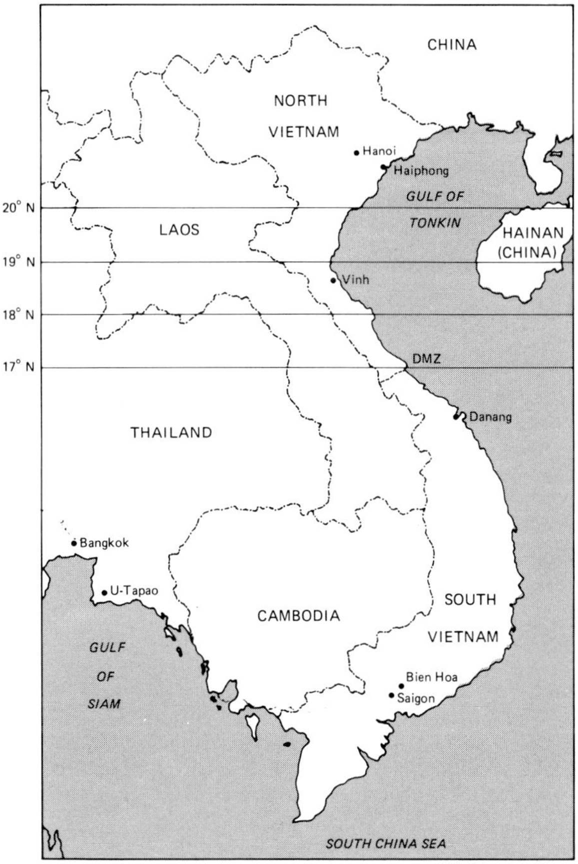

CHINA
NORTH VIETNAM
Hanoi
Haiphong
GULF OF TONKIN
HAINAN (CHINA)
20° N
19° N
18° N
17° N
LAOS
Vinh
DMZ
Danang
THAILAND
Bangkok
U-Tapao
CAMBODIA
SOUTH VIETNAM
GULF OF SIAM
Bien Hoa
Saigon
SOUTH CHINA SEA

Christopher Kane

WASHINGTON, Nov. 17 — Administration spokesmen declined comment unanimously yesterday on Red China's claim to have shot down an unmanned American "high-altitude reconnaissance military plane" Sunday over south central China.

Some American officials suggested last May the United States was considering the development or use of unmanned planes for reconnaissance flights over Cuba.

Informants here said they did not know if this country was using unmanned aircraft for reconnaissance flights. There were comparable disclaimers, however, at the time Francis Gary Powers was shot down in a U-2 over the Soviet Union.

SAIGON, Nov. 18 — The U. S. Air Force is launching pilotless reconnaissance aircraft from "mother" planes based in South Vietnam, American military sources reported today.

The small photo-taking drones, said to be jet-propelled, have been sent on missions over North Vietnam, by remote control, these sources told UPI.

The disclosure was made two days after Communist China claimed to have shot down a U. S. reconnaissance plane with no pilot. The Chinese report said the craft was downed Sunday by fighter planes.

U. S. military sources said only that the drones have been sent to North Vietnam.

(The Chinese claim was met with silence by U. S. officials in Washington.)

(Washington officials said there would be no technical obstacles to sending a pilotless craft on a reconnaissance mission but added there were no known robot-controlled craft specifically designed for such work.)

The U. S. Air Force here has refused to comment officially on the drones.

UPI obtained a photo of one drone earlier this month. It showed the craft slung beneath the wings of a turbo-prop C-130 Hercules "mother" plane.

The picture was made at an air base in South Vietnam. [Perhaps due to high level security considerations, UPI did not distribute the picture at that time. Later, Associated Press distributed a photo on April 17, 1965 of a drone at Bien Hoa after Peking had released a picture of the first recce bird shot down. — Ed.]

Questioned about the drone at that time, an Air Force spokesman said the black, unmarked craft was "a secret project". [Thereby inadvertently confirming that the reconnaissance drone project did indeed exist. — Ed.]

Wide World Photos

AFTER PEKING RELEASED a picture *of the first recce drone shot down, this photo taken a month earlier at Bien Hoa appeared in American newspapers on April 19, 1965. In addition to 147**B** at right, two more birds are in the hangar.*

The C-130s involved are devoid of the usual Air Force markings and carry only a small white star with red and white strips on dull gray fuselage.

Military sources said it was conceivable that the Hercules could launch the drones for flights to Red China from a position over international waters in the South China Sea.

Nationalist China has openly admitted sending U-2 planes over Communist China but it denied any of its planes were shot down over Chinese territory Sunday.

(In Hong Kong, the China Mail, an English language newspaper, reported today that the downed craft was "a U-2, piloted by Nationalist Chinese." It attributed the report to "impeccable sources.")

—————

"Now, get this straight, because we're tired of being misquoted in the press. We authorize only accidental flights over Communist China."

DEPENDABLE DALE WEAVER left San Diego November 21 for his third war-zone tour in a matter of just four months, flying over in a C-135 'flying submarine'. "It was," he said "just so many hours in an aluminum tube."

Also arriving fresh on the Bien Hoa scene was Colonel Bill Forehand from Davis-Monthan AFB. He had been working hard back in Tucson to train more people because the 40 men at the operating location were long overdue for rotation.

"The only place I could get the people," Forehand recalled, "was out of the U-2 outfit. So we robbed them and with a minimum amount of training put together a new team of 48 people and headed for Southeast Asia. We had only two tech reps teaching maintenance on the bird and it was mostly verbal. We were short of test equipment, printed tech data and test vehicles.

"We assigned this group man for man to those already on station. The man due for rotation home could go, I told them, as soon as he had trained his replacement to do the job as well, but until then he couldn't go home. Then I'd sign the new guy off as being certified. That really moved the replacement program along in a hurry."

When Weaver arrived at OL-20 he found operations running at a pretty slow pace. "The primary effort now," he wrote, "is in training and qualification of the people who came over from Davis-Monthan at Tucson. We had a mission cranking but it was cancelled about 4 a.m. because the tail end of a typhoon was very close to the recovery area.

"Tuesday night we all had a chance to relax and let our hair down. I joined in a little recreational drinking with Col. McCaslin and Col. Forehand. The prime topic was ways to improve the program. Col. William E. Bethea, Bien Hoa base commander, joined us for a while and mentioned he had been called in by top brass and asked about the 'news release' made by someone here, after the Red

Commies knocked down a bird, which confirmed our operations out of the Saigon area. He knew nothing about it but noted it probably happened because so many newsmen came in after the Great Pumpkin Halloween fiasco to report on the extent of Viet Cong attacks on the base.

"Just as we finished the Scotch we heard a frantic knock on the door. Col. Forehand opened it to complete darkness outside and a loudly whispered request to turn out the lights because we were under attack. We turned out the lights and charged around in the Scotch-filled darkness looking for weapons. I ended up with an AR-15 and Col. Mac with a .38. After about 15 minutes lying in the wet grass to the accompaniment of small arms fire in the distance we decided that since the Scotch was gone we might as well go to bed. The typical uniform here after dark seems to be shower shoes, shorts and an AR-15.

"Wednesday I took a gooney bird (C-47) trip up to Da Nang to see Big Daddy Sly. Ed feels we should get out of the LCO business and I feel we should get out of the RCO business. Hopefully we can phase out of the operations end of this job, but it just won't happen until the new military people are trained and qualified.

"Yesterday was fairly quiet and the Thanksgiving turkey pretty good but somehow you lose that holiday feeling when you can hear 500-pounders going off in the distance."

Despite the international publicity disclosing the Lightning Bug reconnaissance flights and the reduced activity during a training build-up period, half a dozen more operational missions were flown before the end of December. The mission of December 15, after a 30-day lull was, according to Weaver, "the best to date."

Ed Sly

A GOONEY BIRD TRIP by some of the Ryan crew *got them up to DaNang to see Big Daddy Sly, shown here at left with Bob Todd at the Monkey Mountain Heliport near which was located the MSQ van for drone tracking and recovery.*

Ed Sly

THE NEW YEAR, 1965, started off with another blaze of publicity when, on the night of January 2, Communist China announced that its air force shot down a second pilotless U. S. high altitude reconnaissance plane.

Hailing another "major victory", Defense Minister Marshal Lin Piao issued a commendation order to the defense unit which shot down the drone.

Press reports said that the U. S. was keeping central south China under surveillance because that is where a build up of Communist Chinese forces would take place prior to any major intervention in Vietnam.

The Ryan flight log for January 2, 1965 from Bien Hoa, for vehicle 147**B** serial number 21, merely noted: DNR — did not return.

On March 31, **B**-20 was also reported as DNR and the following day Radio Peking announced that a third pilotless U. S. plane had been shot down by Red Communist liberation forces.

A day later, April 2, wreckage of a plane which Red China claimed was a U. S. pilotless spy drone made by Ryan Aeronautical Company went on exhibition in Peking. Thirty thousand red Chinese filed by the wreckage displayed in a military museum. Hsinhua, the Chinese Communist press agency, released a photograph and said it was the plane which was shot down "by the air force" January 2.

Other newspapers published pictures of camera equipment said to have been caried by the plane and of a plaque bearing the name of the San Diego, California, manufacturing company.

No sooner had the American 'spy plane' been put on display than Peking announced, within 24 hours, that yet another pilotless reconnaissance plane — the fourth — had been shot down. The fifth was bagged two weeks later, the same day that U. S. newspapers for the first time carried photos of a Ryan Lightning Bug drone waiting to be hung beneath the wing of a Lockheed DC-130 Hercules launch plane. Someone, somehow had gotten a copy of the picture taken months earlier at Bien Hoa not long after operations started there.

Three days later the story of the 'secret' drone operations really hit page one when Peking released a photo showing three downed Ryan drones on display at the Chinese People's Revolutionary Museum in Peking. They were identified as the unmanned planes shot down January 2, March 31 and April 3.

Wire services, news magazines and trade journal editors burned up the phone lines from New York and Washington to San Diego. The author fended off all calls neither confirming nor denying the accuracy of the description which accompanied the photos.

"You say they look like BQM-34A Firebees with extra long wings? Well, if you describe them that way, that's your responsibility. We have no comment!

"What our customers — the Army, Navy and Air Force — do with our Firebee drones operationally is up to them. We just don't speculate. Better check with the Department of Defense," we told the press.

The press was of course correct.

The Chinese could claim whatever they wanted but they didn't have a captured 'spy pilot' as evidence. Though they did have aircraft and identification name plates, no one volunteered to confirm the 'facts' and a name plate doesn't receive the same public attention as an American pilot in prison.

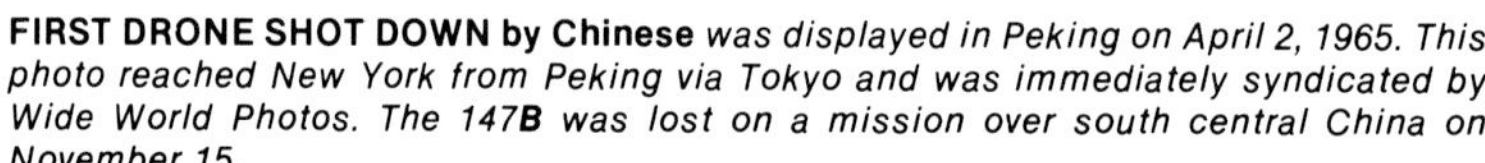

FIRST DRONE SHOT DOWN by Chinese *was displayed in Peking on April 2, 1965. This photo reached New York from Peking via Tokyo and was immediately syndicated by Wide World Photos. The 147**B** was lost on a mission over south central China on November 15.*

Wide World Photos

e World Photos

TOK/SF 35 LCP184 TOKYO 224SQCM 20 2359 PPD Re Radio

ssociated San Francisco (TOK-4) Peking, April 20 (AP) People of Peking iewing the wreckage of three U.S. pilotless high altitude reconnaissanc ircraft shot down by the Red Chinese Army at the Chinese People's Revo-ution Museum in Peking. The aircraft in the background was shot down anuary 2. The one in the middle on March 31 and the one in the fore-round on April 3.

12

WILD BILL'S BIRDS

Buck Lee

COL. BILL FOREHAND, OL-20 commander: *"On my first day of command I dropped one vehicle on the ramp and crashed the other!"*

RETURNING TO BIEN HOA in late January 1965, Col. 'Wild Bill' Forehand, who had recently resupplied uniformed manpower for the drone operation, took over as commander of OL-20, relieving Colonel Ken McCaslin.

His first day in command was not an auspicious beginning.

"I took over at midnight," Forehand related, "and the next day they had a mission on for me. The only two vehicles we had were already uploaded and on the launch racks.

"We were short of equipment and had a camera in only one of the birds. While we were trying to get the thing in commission, we had all the power off in the DC-130 — we thought — and all circuit breakers pulled — we thought. Dale Weaver was at the launch control panel. When he turned an electrical connector plug around, a piece of solder hit the jettison pin causing a short circuit. The bird came off the launch rack and dropped on Bruce Engman, one of the recently arrived Ryan technicians. I thought we had killed him — we certainly could have — but **B**-18 dropped between his legs and he was not hurt.

"I went in to report the accident to the Vice Wing Commander and he asked, 'Bill, are you gonna report you dropped that bird on the ramp?' I said it was my first day of command so there's no sense in me starting off lying. I got Col. Ells Powell at SAC headquarters in Omaha on the single sideband radio and told him I had dropped the only available operational drone on the ground.

"Just then Major Linus L. (Buck) Lee, my chief of maintenance, interrupted to ask me 'what are we going to do?'

"Take that damn camera out of the drone lying on the ground," I ordered, "and put it in **B**-10, and let's go!

"If we didn't get off by eleven o'clock the mission would be scrubbed, but the DC-130 came off the runway at 10:55 and we were on our way.

"The bird flew a good mission and came on home. Unfortunately my recovery control officer reduced

MAJOR LINUS L. (Buck) LEE *was Air Force's chief of maintenance for the drone squadron.*

the throttle too far as the bird came into the recovery area, causing the engine to flame out.

"**B**-10 crashed in a river just south of Da Nang, setting off one of the largest searches anyone ever heard of, trying to locate the bird and its scorer package. We had U. S. Navy skin divers, Vietnamese rangers, an Australian platoon, an Army squad and I don't know who else looking for that airplane.

"Next day we learned a Vietnamese gunboat disguised as a sampan had seen something black coming out of the sky. That gave us a definite spot to look. Sure enough we found it in the bottom of the river. I told the skin divers to bring me the biggest piece of anything they could find. When they came up they presented me with ten pieces about as big as my hand! That finished that bird and its pictures.

"On my first day of command I dropped one vehicle on the ramp and crashed the other!"

Forehand stayed on for a three months tour and had the operation running smoothly by the time he left, though there were still problems aplenty. Not only were personnel constantly rotating, but conditions in the field left much to be desired. Test equipment had been designed to operate "in some nice dry, cool shop like the factory, but we were out there trying to maintain drones and equipment in the dust, mud, rain and everything else. In fact, if you would reach over and turn on the test equipment master control switch while it was raining, it would knock you flat!

"WE OF COURSE LAUNCHED north of Da Nang, then came back in and landed our C-130 there, awaiting return of the bird. I'd go to the GRCO (ground remote control operator) van and direct the recovery actions from there.

"About 100 miles north of Da Nang, radio on the drone was programmed to come back on so we could take command and bring the vehicle back for recovery in the designated area. Then a helicopter would go out and pick it up. We'd bring it back to the launch rails under the '130' wing, attach it, and fly home to Bien Hoa to prepare the bird for another mission."

Later, Major Jay Merz was to describe the trials and tribulations of the uniformed drone recovery officer:

He is an Air Force pilot who never flies a flight plan. He's not allowed to pre-flight his airplane. He never gets to strap in. They won't allow him to start the engine. He never sees a cheerful thumbs up from his crew chief. He never gets to taxi.

Nobody will fly with him. He's never permitted to make a takeoff or landing. He never gets to hear the reassuring roar of his engine. He can't even raise and lower the gear. He's not allowed to look out the windows.

He only gets to fly when there's a problem or he's running out of gas. But . . . you let one little thing go wrong and we confiscate his tapes, drag out the manuals, and hang the guilty bastard!

TRAPPED INSIDE the MSQ van *in the ground control complex at DaNang, the remote control officer is "an Air Force pilot who's never permitted to make a takeoff or landing . . . and is not even allowed to look out the windows."*

Ed Sly

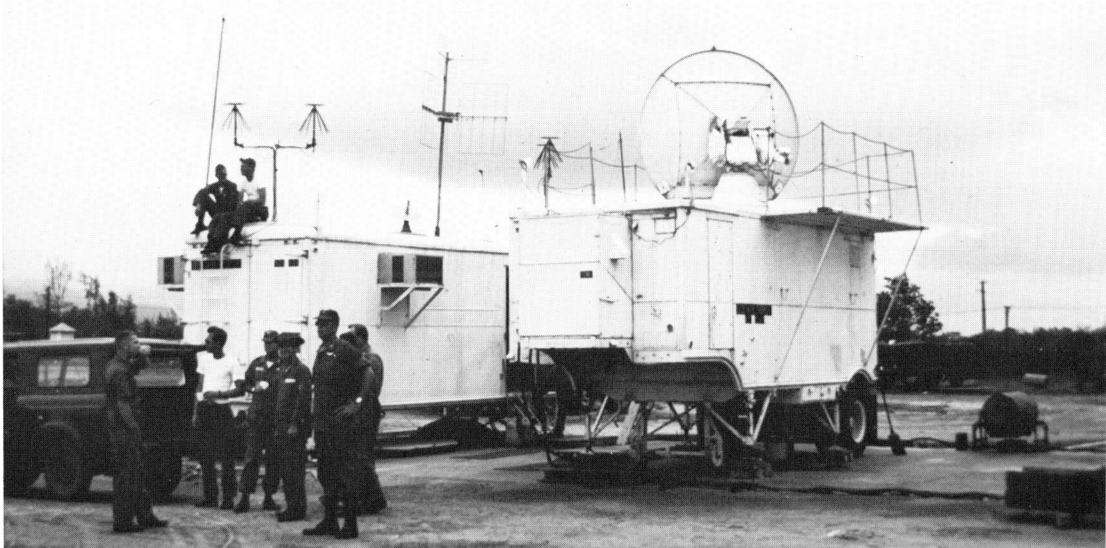

"Things didn't always go perfectly," Forehand agreed. "I particularly remember the flight of B-15 some six weeks after arriving on my first tour.

"We were flying north up over China and were supposed to come back around over the island of Hainan in the Gulf of Tonkin. Here we were programmed to turn west. But the plot on the radar screen in the van showed it had turned east instead and for the next few minutes it looked like our vehicle was somehow being steered. By Chinese radar? Was someone trying to steal the bird?

Passing over the technicalities, the facts are that on the spot I worked out pilot procedures, just as if flying a manned aircraft, on how to make timed turns with the bird when we were getting intermittent tracking. I had to act like I was flying on instruments and try to think for the bird up there over 100 miles north.

"It was a hell of a thrill to bring that bird home 'flying blind' from a remote control station. It was truly an RPV (remotely piloted vehicle). And we recovered it okay.

"When I got off my message about the mission to SAC headquarters, I sent them a real cocky wire about getting our bird back from that far out even though it appeared the enemy was trying to steal it away from us with overriding commands. They didn't appreciate that nor the fact that my message signed off 'the hell with it, I'm going down to happy hour'. That caught everyone's attention.

"The next morning I sent them another wire apologizing, 'sorry about that'. There'd been a hang up in the MA-1 compass that had never been experienced before.

"But, by that time, messages were flying back and forth and everybody was getting mad. I was sending some pretty terse wires myself.

"The Reconnaissance Branch of SAC Headquarters caught the Vice Wing Commander in mid-air and diverted him to San Francisco to catch a flight for Bien Hoa. I was being relieved — but immediately! In the meantime the Recon Branch had to go in and see General John D. Ryan, SAC Commander, to inform him they were going to fire me.

"He read the exchange of messages, and said, 'so what else is new! It doesn't bother me a damn bit. Just sounds like two of my Colonels are fighting, and that doesn't worry me. Forehand's flying the airplanes better than anyone else ever has. Leave him alone.'"

"YOU HAVE TO UNDERSTAND how carefully everything about reconnaissance operations is monitored. Route packages — the actual flight tracks we were to fly — came out of SAC headquarters through the Department of Defense and the Joint Chiefs of Staff in Washington with obvious high-level decision as to where we would operate. In the field we had to program their mission plan into the airplane. We flew only where we were told to fly.

"At every step of the mission OL-20 reported back to SAC headquarters by single sideband radio, in code. You reported when you broke ground, you reported when you were in the launch area, you reported when the bird was 100 miles out and coming back, you reported it when the bird had been recovered. After that you confirmed it all back to headquarters over secret communication lines. You were busy as hell reporting!

"In the early days, the U-2s were covering North Vietnam as there was no shooting war going on in the air to oppose them at that time. We were covering China with the reconnaissance drones because it was politically acceptable since it had no pilot aboard. In this way we could still see what the Chinese were doing; see if there was a build-up which could indicate they were moving south.

"When Russian SAM missiles put in an appearance in North Vietnam and began knocking down American aircraft, I recommended to SAC headquarters that we pull the U-2s off and start flying the drones over North Vietnam. We didn't want to lose U-2s and their pilots, so they were assigned to stand-off reconnaissance."

"We flew only where we were told to fly."

After a three months tour, Forehand went home.

"By then I had built up a pretty good file of things I didn't like and that included everything from SAC Headquarters to the 15th Air Force to my Wing and my Air Division. I put it all down in cold turkey and was told in no uncertain terms that the report was pretty rough. Before it was over I was so damn mad I put in my retirement papers. It didn't seem anyone was paying much attention; that anyone was as concerned as I was about the OL operation.

"Not long after that, I got a call from SAC asking would I please volunteer to return, even though I'd put in my retirement papers. They wanted me back as OL Commander, they said, because the program was in serious trouble. They said I could have every asset in the inventory — everything — and take it out there with me. I could take anybody out of the Wing I wanted, too.

"Fifteen minutes later Bob Schwanhausser called and volunteered anyone in the Ryan company I felt was needed. So I picked several of the finest tech reps I had ever met — men who really knew what they were doing — and we went back out there in August, 1965.

"It was during that period we had the finest 45 days the program had ever seen. We had our first double sorties — two birds launched and a double recovery off the same '130'. It was a high point not matched for two years. At that time we had only the one launch plane and one air crew out there but we flew 28 days in a row without being down.

"I'd been warned on this tour that I'd better damn well go through channels or get courtmartialed. Two days after I arrived I sent a wire direct to General Ryan at SAC, requesting permission to violate the tech data which was designed for contractor personnel rather than for Air Force field use. Nobody could check out a vehicle with the tech data we had! That wire caused some furor including a written reprimand and word from General 'Brick' Holstrom that he was going to come out there personally and courtmartial me if I did anything like that again. Later he looked into the tech data thing, saw that I was right and said 'I hope you tore that message up.' I had.

"WHEN THE MiGs out of North Vietnam first started jumping our birds they would go after us with what seemed to be almost their entire air force. They just plain clobbered the drones. But we did get some pictures of MiGs that didn't know we were up there above them.

"Sometimes we had pure luck with us on photo missions. We'd been after this one air field in South China with manned recces for I don't know how long. The day we were after this photo target with a drone we had nothing but clouds — except for shots made in a few minutes right over the air field. Thunderstorms were all around but the clouds opened up briefly just as the bird flew overhead to give us a perfect picture. Five minutes sooner or later; or slightly off course and we'd have come back empty handed. It was the only picture we got that day.

"THE LIGHTNING BUG DRONE was a rare bird *so I hollered, pulled my gun out and waved the chopper down." Was it A LIFE photographer?*

"ONE OF THE THINGS that kept me hot under the collar was that we had no official, and little unofficial, access to the results of the camera 'scoring' on our missions.

"Usually the Air Force had a B-57 waiting at Da Nang to take me and the scorer material back to Saigon as quickly as possible. I would hand it over the side of the airplane, and they would take it over to the photo lab, but I never saw any of the results — officially.

"Every time I turned around someone would be raising hell about the film being overexposed or underexposed, or some other complaint. How could I defend the job we were doing if I never saw what we were getting?

"After about six weeks of this I went down to Saigon and into the processing lab. I've always been a bomber guy; not a reconnaissance type who's supposed to know something about cameras and film processing. But I found out the film was a hell of a lot better than people were reporting. They were processing it wrong! I created a big stink over that because I don't like people raising hell with me when I haven't got the facts to defend my operation.

"The bad thing was that in the drone squadron we had a bunch of kids working 16 or 18 hours a day, seven days a week, with no time off, and never getting an opportunity to see the results of what they're doing. Morale just goes to pot. So finally I went down to Saigon again and this time selected some real good shots, had prints made and brought them back to show the guys. At last they saw what they were accomplishing.

"But I got reprimanded for a violation of security even though everyone out there was cleared for the 'Blue Springs' operation, our code name, and knew what we were doing. So what?

"The photo might show an air base, but who knows what air base; or a road that no one can identify. No one could tell whether the pictures were taken over China or North Vietnam or what. They didn't have big signs down there telling you where it was. Anyway no one at that level was privileged to know the route so no positive identification was possible. So there wasn't any violation of security and they finally decided there wasn't.

"After that morale got pretty good.

"Of course we were pretty sensitive about the security of **our** program. No pictures were allowed of the drone or of our operation at any stage; nor were any cameras permitted in the area.

"One day we were sitting in my car up at the north end of the field at Da Nang when along comes a helicopter with a civilian in the door holding a camera with a long-snouted telephoto lens like you never saw before. I hollered, pulled my gun out, pointed it in his general direction and waved the chopper down. I sped to the scene followed by the base commander. Here was this LIFE photographer taking pictures like crazy.

"We had brought a bird we'd just recovered back to the base and had it on the positioning trailer ready to put it back on the launch rail of the '130' so we could fly it back to Bien Hoa. Because the drone was a rare bird to him he was taking pictures of it like mad, figuring that some strange vehicle like this must be news.

"It appeared someone had given LIFE permission, but I told the base commander no one was going to take pictures of our mission and that I was going to have someone's head if those pictures of the Lightning Bug drone ever saw print. I had to get on down to Bien Hoa but anyway the pictures of the drone must have been confiscated properly, because I have never seen any of those shots of our bird.

"Our instructions were if we saw anybody taking pictures of the drones to take the camera, jerk it open and rip out the film. I tried that on a General once, but it didn't work. He didn't have any written paperwork that said he was cleared to take pictures of the program but he said that General LeMay or Secretary McNamara or somebody important wanted pictures of the operation. I warned him about three times and he finally got a bit angry with me and mentioned that he was a General and that he would take any goddam pictures he wanted and do anything with them that he wanted and that he also understood his responsibility for security.

"He got his pictures!"

It took a bull-in-the-china-shop, to-hell-with-channels type like Bill Forehand to wrestle the drone operation into shape. As one general said, "As a combat commander I couldn't ask for a better guy than Bill, but as for a diplomat I'd sure have to look elsewhere."

Forehand remained at the OL until November 1965 checking out his replacement, then finally let his retirement papers go through. His was the kind of talent Ryan could use and civilian Forehand joined the Ryan company in January 1966 as Operations Research Engineer.

DEFENSE SECRETARY MCNAMARA, second from left, *apparently wanted pictures of the Lightning Bug drone operation at OL-20 where he is pictured with General William Westmoreland, far left. Unknown photographer wrote that he was 'hobnobbing with the big shots.'*

13

FIREBEES AND RPVs

AS THIS WAS BEING WRITTEN in mid-1972, the magic new acronym — alphabetical code name — in military aviation was RPV. It was being used as if someone had just made a fabulous new discovery! Not so. Remotely piloted vehicles in their less sophisticated form had been around a long time.

Twenty-five years earlier Ryan took the cockpit out of the airplane and put it on the ground!

The company had won a tri-service competition in 1947 against 13 other designs for a contract to build the first Army-Navy-Air Force pilotless jet plane — in other words, a remotely piloted vehicle. At the time, the vehicle was classified as a missile; still later as a training target; then as a drone. But all basically meant the same thing — a pilotless jet plane capable of being operated as a remotely piloted vehicle.

Starting out as a rather simple jet airplane flown by an operator on the ground, the Q-2 model Firebee went through a series of engineering modifications which converted it over the years into a highly sophisticated, electronically controlled, electronically navigated weapons system. Its capability was expanded far beyond its initial role as a target for training and evaluation of weapons systems fired against the sub-sonic Firebee.

As described in the preceding chapters, the Firebee was readily adapted to its new role as a reconnaissance aircraft of unique capability. And, with minor modifications, it could carry a variety of munitions to assume the role of a weapons delivery system; it could fly through and sample A- and H-bomb clouds; it could carry TV cameras for real-time transmission of combat information; it could engage an enemy fighter aircraft in aerial combat. It could be — actually long has been — a highly successful RPV.

If one were to select a date when the remotely piloted target drone gained recognition for its combat potential it would have to be May 19, 1970. On that date a classified symposium on RPVs was convened by the Air Force Systems Command and RAND Corporation, the military think tank, to study the future role of pilotless aircraft.

David Koser

DOC SLOAN — pilot, writer, character. *More about him on* *pages 149-150.*

How did the RPV evolve?

Lt. Col. William P. (Doc) Sloan, a veteran Ryan pilot and drone program manager, describes the background in the following report:

THE STORY OF RPVs

IN THE FOURTH CENTURY B. C., a small boy stood on a lonely windswept hill in China and flew recorded history's first remotely controlled vehicle. True, the aerodynamics of the kite left something to be desired, and his down-link was a piece of string, but history was in the making. And today, 24 centuries later, men sit in dimly lighted rooms on lonely hills and silently guide unmanned aircraft to a pinpoint on a map hundreds of miles away.

KETTERING AERIAL TORPEDO bi-plane drone *of World War II had pre-set flight controls.*

Air Force Museum

Little progress was made from the flight of string-held kites to a free-flight robot until shortly after the dawn of the 20th century. True, tethered balloons were used as photo platforms during the Civil War, but it wasn't until a still larger war in 1915 that the first attempts were made to design and launch an unmanned powered aircraft.

After three years of research by Charles F. Kettering (later of General Motors fame), the first reciprocating-engine biplane drone, mounted on a jury-rigged cart on rails, roared into the air. The Kettering Aerial Torpedo, often referred to as the "Bug," was built for the U. S. Army Signal Corps by the Dayton-Wright Company. Carrying 180 pounds of explosive, flying at 55 mph and with a range of 40 miles, the Bug was to have been guided to the target area by pre-set flight controls. At the target, the wings would be released, and the fuselage would plunge earthward as a bomb.

Recommendations springing from the Kettering plane led to the first successful droning of a commercial Curtiss Robin monoplane in 1928. This radio-controlled, bomb-carrying airplane floundered through the skies on and off for four years before expiring from lack of funds in 1932.

It wasn't until 1938 that serious interest was shown by the armed forces in developing remotely controlled offensive weapons. Again Kettering came into the picture, teaming with General H. H. (Hap) Arnold to spearhead a new breed of "special weapons". Among the several projects started were the development of radio-controlled target planes of the PQ series, a glide bomb (GB-1), a controllable high angle bomb known as AZON, a surface-to-surface "buzz" bomb, later called the General Motors "Bug", a glide bomb known as the "Bat" and several other projects which were subsequently discontinued.

Of all of these wartime experiments, perhaps the GB-1 proved to be the most effective. Utilizing a 2000 lb. demolition bomb as a fuselage, the airframe consisted of twelve-foot plywood wings and twin plywood rudders. Actually, the GB-1 was the first of our modern "stand-off" weapons. Radio-controlled, they could be dropped by B-17 bombers well out of reach of highly protected areas, and visually guided to the target. In 1943, a group of 54 bombers from the 8th Air Force performed a mission against the city of Cologne, carrying 108 GB-1s.

In 1944, a "war weary" program for droning tired B-17 and B-24 bombers was initiated, but abandoned because, to be flyable, the war-wearies had to be overhauled and updated almost to a new configuration. Several of these were flown out of England against German targets, but the cost was prohibitive.

The Air Force also duplicated the German V-1 "Buzz-Bomb" and released it for production in the winter of 1944-45. Original plans were to employ it in the Asiatic theater, since the war in Europe was drawing to a close, but the A-bomb negated its use.

With the conclusion of World War II, the missile program was greatly accelerated, and the Guided Missiles Section of the Air Force was formed in September 1946.

From this Section came the first Pilotless Aircraft Branch, the grandaddy Project Office for later target and reconnaissance drone configurations.

In late 1946, the Pilotless Aircraft Branch was assigned the task of coming up with the requirements and performance characteristics for three separate unmanned aircraft to be utilized by the Army and the Air Force as targets for various applications.

As a result of these studies, a small, reciprocating-engined target capable of speeds up to 210 knots and an altitude of 25,000 feet was specified for the low-performance regime. For the intermediate requirements, a pulse-jet powered aircraft with performance set at 300 knots at 15,000 feet was released for bidding. For the high performance target, a specification was released for a jet-powered aircraft capable of 521 knots at 15,000 feet, but with a service ceiling of 40,000 feet.

Industry attention was centered on the high-performance jet target designated as the Q-2. Sensing the potential magnitude of this project, thirty-one companies responded to the first request for quotation, but after analysis by the Air Force, none was accepted and the project was opened for rebid with a due-date of January 1948. Eighteen of the nations top aircraft manufacturers responded, and 14 actual designs were submitted.

In August 1948 the Ryan Aeronautical Company was awarded the first contract for a subsonic, jet-propelled unmanned aircraft. Thus began a segment of aeronautical history that is today still in the formative stages, foreshadowing eventual offensive and defensive tactics of air combat by remote control.

The U. S. Navy, cognizant of the preliminary design studies conducted by the Air Force, took more than a passing interest in the development of the Q-2, and prior to procurement, agreed to pick up the tab for half of the initial research costs. In effect, the program became a tri-service effort with the Air Force as the contracting agency for themselves, the Army Ground Forces and the Navy.

Pioneering a new aeronautical concept can be an inspiring and rewarding achievement. It can also be frustrating, disappointing and sometimes hopeless. The problems facing the services and the contractor in the development of the first designed-from-scratch pilotless jet airplane took months of designing, testing, discarding and redesigning. The major areas of experimental development were propulsion, track and control, launch and recovery.

In keeping with the procurement policy of negotiating separately for airframe and engines, the Air Force selected the Flader XJ-55 turbo jet engine

UNCLASSIFIED

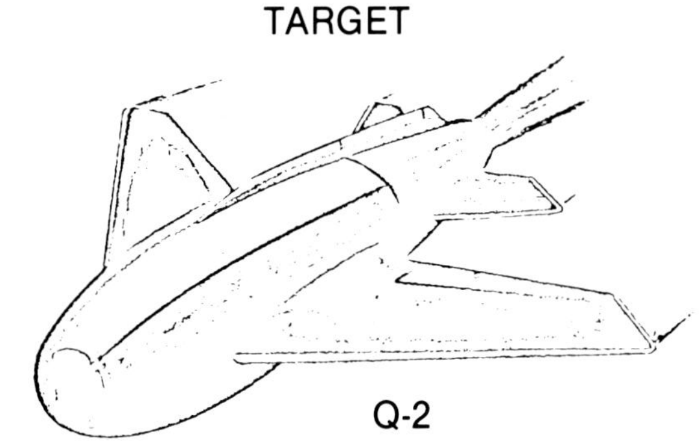

Air Materiel Command

HIGH PERFORMANCE JET TARGET designated Q-2 *was put out for bid in 1946. Configuration shown here was an early concept. In 1948 competition, Ryan Aeronautical Company won contract over 13 other designs for the tri-service sub-sonic unmanned jet aircraft training target.*

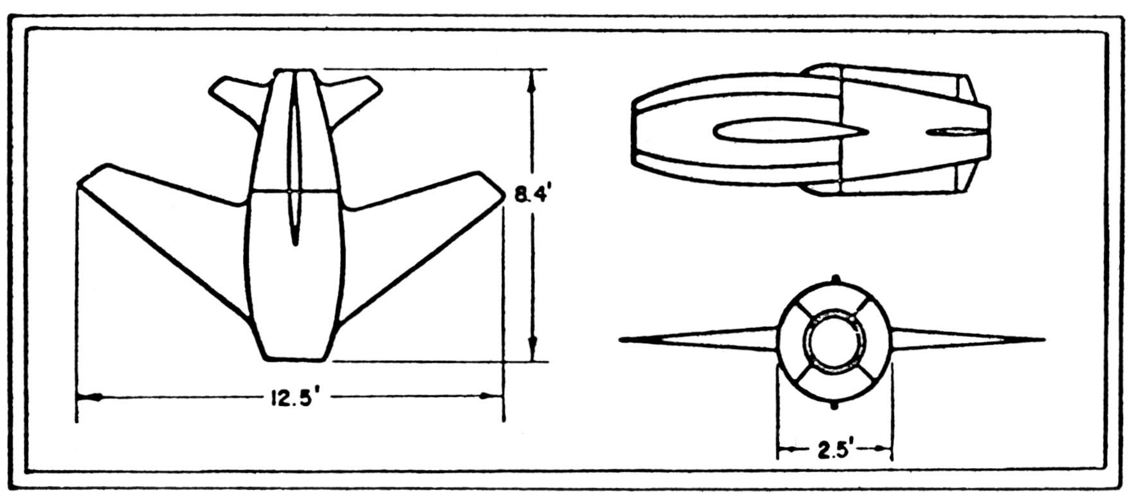

U N C L A S S I F I E D

proposed by the Frederic Flader Company of North Tonawanda, N. Y. A radical departure from the standard four-stage compressor turbo jet, the XJ-55 was single stage, weighed 300 pounds and was theoretically capable of developing 700 lbs. thrust.

Whether Flader was ahead of his time in design or incapable of making his stated performance during the four years from 1947 to 1951 is problematical, but after numerous tests and ground runs in the XQ-2, the contract was terminated and the Fairchild J44 designated as the replacement engine. Fortunately, the Ryan design of the engine nacelle for the new bird was a modular unit, and the changeover was made without a time-consuming major redesign.

As the developmental program progressed, more and more stress was placed on altitude capability, and eventually the Continental Aviation and Engineering J69 version of the French Turbomeca Marbore II engine with a static thrust of 880 pounds was introduced into the system. The early production version of the Air Force Q-2, and the Navy configuration, utilized both the Fairchild and Continental engines.

In the early stages of design, the limited endurance capability of the Flader engine led to a unique method of flight control to minimize the time necessary to complete the standard 180 degree turns in the oval patterns to be flown. Instead of making standard race-track type turns, a method was proposed to program the bird into an Immelman turn (half loop and half snap roll on top of the loop), dive back to pattern altitude and make the target presentation. The design headaches associated with this maneuver were finally dissipated when the Flader faded and the Fairchild J44 was installed.

Finally, after many innovations, a control system known as the Ryan automatic pilot system (RAPS-4) was integrated into the design and the XQ-2s were retrofitted with it.

The original specification for the Q-2 called for both an air and ground launch capability. Early launching aircraft for the Q-2, as well as the launching vehicle for the parachute recovery tests, were many and varied. The first launching (unpowered) of the Q-2 took place from the wing of a B-17 bomber, and a B-29 was also used for a short period for chute tests. Eventually, the B-26C light bomber was adopted as the standard launch vehicle. Actually, the Navy was the pioneer in this phase, using their JD-1 version with a single target on one wing with water ballast on the other. The final configuration with a target under each wing was tested at Holloman AFB with the Air Force.

IT WAS IN THE SPRING of 1951 when the first successful powered free flight of the XQ-2 was accomplished, following launch from a B-17 at Holloman. In 1952, the Research and Development Board Panel for Target Drones, including

Don Doerr

FIRST XQ-2 FIREBEE drone was powered *by 700-lb. thrust XJ-55 Flader jet engine around which Q-2 had originally been designed.*

U.S. Navy

U.S. NAVY USED JD-1 twin-engine *launch plane with water ballast on left wing to counterbalance KDA-1 Firebee on right wing.*

U.S. Air Force

FAIRCHILD J-44 JET ENGINE succeeded *the original Flader installation in early Firebees like shark-nosed bird on B-26 wing launch rack.*

LAUNCHED FROM BELLY of Air Force light bomber, *Firebee streaks over New Mexico desert. Same B-26C bombers later launched birds from wing racks.*

KDA-4 FIREBEE suspended beneath *maple leaf of Royal Canadian Air Force 'Lancaster' bomber was used in cold weather testing.*

GROUND LAUNCH OF Q-2 FIREBEE was accomplished *with 11,000 lb. JATO (jet assisted take-off) booster and rail launcher.*

representatives for the U. S. Air Force, Navy and Department of the Army convened at Holloman Air Development Center in New Mexico to witness the formal demonstrations of Radioplane's XQ-1 and Ryan's XQ-2. Some 32 Ryan drones were built for test and evaluation.

After sweating out a flight a day for two weeks, both contractors were overjoyed with the results. In December of that year Ryan received a letter contract for the production of 35 XM-21 targets (Army designation), and the lengthy, exhausting period of initial development became a thing of the past.

Ground launch experiments started with a 4000-foot set of rails to determine the effect of acceleration on the target during and after launching. All of these tests were captive, with the trolley-held bird screaming down the rails under jet assisted take off (JATO) and engine power. Decelerations were accomplished with a scoop attached to the trolley which was dragged through a series of reservoirs containing water.

From the 4000 feet rails, the tests proceeded to the KC-9 catapult launcher with 99-foot rails. The catapulting force was obtained from a powder charge fired from the breech mechanism of a standard 6-inch naval gun. Fortunately, powder with the desired burning characteristics was not available, and use of a standard A-1 guided takeoff launcher with an 11,000 lb. JATO bottle for initial boost was adopted.

One of the first attempts to zero-length launch the bird from a standard road vehicle produced a truly spectacular flight. Shortly after takeoff, the target commenced a slow roll. The JATO continued to burn until the Q-2 was in an inverted position, at which time the JATO separated, the bird completed its slow roll and reassumed level flight. Had not complete confusion reigned at the control station, the flight might have been a success, but the target impacted almost immediately.

Unperturbed, Ryan's Mickey McDaniel walked over to the Army officers watching the tests and asked, "General, can you top that?"

It was the Army which was responsible for tests from an 80-foot rail and later conducted the successful tests from the standard 8-foot rails now in use all over the world.

Parallel with their interest in the XQ-2, the Navy also sponsored a program for a target powered by a ram jet. However, after witnessing demonstrations at Holloman, this project was cancelled in favor of the Ryan drone. Officially designated by the Navy as the KDA-1, forty of the targets were ordered by the Navy with deliveries beginning in September of 1954. The Air Force followed suit with an order for 89 Q-2As, and jet powered targets were in all three service inventories to stay.

Canada joined in 1957 with an order for thirty KDA-4s in 1957 for cold weather testing at Fort Churchill, Canada. By 1958 nearly 1300 Q-2 birds had been ordered by the three services, and pilots,

Teledyne Ryan Aeronautical

Q-2C FIREBEE (later designated BQM-34A) *can be equipped to simulate a wide variety of conditions necessary to provide realistic targets for training and for evaluation of weapon systems.*

gunners and missilemen were finding the small jet plane-without-a-man-in-it to be a realistic threat simulation.

To remain static in the aircraft industry is to stagnate and perish. Heedful of this axiom, developmental studies on a bigger, faster and higher version were begun. In 1957, the Air Force assumed procurement responsibility for all jet drones, and funded the improvement program for what was to become known as the Q-2C (since redesignated BQM-34A).

Longer, sleeker and powered with Continental's J69-T29 engine developing 1700 lbs. thrust, the C target drone exceeded the design specifications in nearly every category. It has attained a speed of Mach 0.97 in level flight, has climbed higher than 60,000 feet and flown as low as 50 feet. With a variable speed range from 200 to more than 600 knots, it has remained aloft for more than 115 minutes. It has flown more than 200 nautical miles from its remote control site and has the capability of an hour and seventeen minutes about 50,000 feet. So advanced was the Q-2C in its early flights that chase pilots of the 1959 era had difficulty staying with it.

And with the new bird came other developments and improvements. Scoring systems were developed to give the missilemen an accurate appraisal of their firing accuracy. Augmentation devices were invented which gave a radar return to simulate a small fighter or large bomber. Flight control systems improved to the point where the Firebee could make as good climbing and diving turns as the manned fighter pursuing it.

Electronic counter measure (ECM) devices were flown to further simulate the combat environment. Various infrared augmentation sources were tested and adapted to meet the specific demands of those weapons, both air-to-air and surface-to-air.

JATO power was increased to allow a one thousand pound payload to be ground launched with the target. The development of towed targets (Towbee) produced a major cost-saving device wherein the missiles sought and killed the tow, leaving the Firebee untouched for flight after flight. Reliability of the system and skill of the ground crews grew to a point where less than three out of every hundred flights had problems, and the flights-per-target number has grown to more than fifty in automatic weapons firings.

The far shores of the Pacific are no stranger to the Firebee, where it has been flown by the Air Force in the Philippines and the Army at Okinawa, Korea and Taiwan. It has become the standard workhorse for the Navy in Hawaii and Okinawa as well as the Atlantic Fleet Weapons Range in the Caribbean. It has performed for the Army's Hawk missiles in the subzero weather of Alaska, and been flown from the

U.S. ARMY FIREBEE is ground launched *from Pena Beach, Canal Zone, during annual Hawk missile training exercises in March, 1968.*

Dave Gossett

deck of a Japanese target ship. It has participated in every anti-aircraft weapons development in the United States from the Missile Center at Point Mugu to the Florida waters off Eglin AFB. It has been the elusive enemy of the Air Force at every Tyndall 'William Tell' weapons meet since their inception back in '57. Over 6,500 of these versatile jets have been ordered by the services, and they have racked up an impressive 30,000 flights in every conceivable climatic and combat environment.

But despite this impressive record, the potential use of unmanned aircraft is in its infancy. A third major step in the development and advancement of the state-of-the-art was undertaken with the supersonic version of the Firebee.

Funded by the Navy in 1966, the newest member of the Firebee family completed an unusually successful flight test program at the Pt. Mugu Naval Missile Center in 1970. Capable of Mach 1.8 speeds at 45,000 feet, the BQM-34E Firebee II has flown at Mach 1.5 above sixty thousand feet. With a combined sub-supersonic endurance of 74 minutes, this sleek threat simulator can be controlled out to 200 miles from home base. Continued interservice cooperation was evidenced with the placement of quantity production orders for Firebee II by the Air Force in 1970.

And where to from here? The applications of a plane that thinks and responds as though it were a pilot are unlimited. Already the Firebee has proven it has the eyes of a man through television. It can be remotely controlled by a 'pilot' from a presentation of television pictures secured by a camera in the vehicle and relayed in real time. Digital programmers give it a capability of thinking and responding at precise intervals to complicated commands. With a photographic memory, it is capable of returning intelligence in an environment too hostile for man to survive.

This is what RPV is all about.

ELUSIVE ENEMY of Air Force pilots *at famed William Tell weapons meets in Florida, the Firebee has been a challenging target for fighter aircraft crews since 1957.*

Ed Hayes

U.S. Air Force

AIR FORCE DC-130 LAUNCH PLANE IS CAPABLE OF CARRYING AND CONTROLLING FOUR FIREBEES

Dave Gossett

AFTER COMPLETION of its mission *as a target, Firebee is returned by helicopter to Roosevelt Roads, Puerto Rico, base.*

Gossett/Stauss

ARMY FIREBEE roars off zero-length *ground launcher at White Sands Missile Range in desert area of New Mexico.*

BQM-34E SUPERSONIC FIREBEE II

14

FLYING HIGH; FLYING LOW

WITH ONLY FIVE MONTHS of drone reconnaissance operational experience, much of it spent de-bugging the system, Washington in January 1965 was nonetheless sitting up and paying attention.

As so often happened in the past, and would in the future, confidence between the Ryan Aeronautical Company and the Air Force was such that programs got started even before contracts were let. Soon after New Year's 1965, Ryan started cutting metal on the 147**G** model, an updated version of the **B** which was then seeing 'combat' in Vietnam.

The principal change was in a new T-41A version of the J69 engine. This produced 1920 pounds of thrust, 220 more than the power plant of the **B** model and gave the **G** higher altitude performance over mission areas. The already stretched fuselage was extended two feet more to 29 feet. A new system to suppress high-altitude condensation trails which formerly gave the enemy a visual sighting, would be included.

The first formal **G** contract, for 28 birds plus spares, was received in March. By July the first of the 56 **G**s eventually built was delivered. They became operational the last day of October 1965 replacing the **B**s which had flown the first 70 'combat' missions.

In all, **B** birds flew 78 missions; 48 of the **B**s returned okay for a 61.5% successful operational average. One bird flew 8 missions while the **B** type averaged 2.6 missions per vehicle. It was a satisfactory but not spectacular performance for an entirely new type of reconnaissance. Greater success would come with future birds and missions.

While the first of the **G**s were coming off the production line, the **H** model, also using the 1920 pound T-41 engine, was placed under contract. To give this version still greater altitude capability the wing was extended from 27 feet to 32 feet. Area of the wing increased from 80 to 114 square feet and the fuselage was stretched yet another foot. The **H** would have a range of 2415 nautical miles compared with 1455 nautical miles for the **G**.

By this time need for a low-altitude photo capability had been identified and the 147**J** model, developed from the **G**, went under contract in October 1965. In quick-reaction time the first **J** was delivered the next month and went operational the last of March 1966, nearly a year ahead of the **H**. The **J**, too, used the 1920-pounds-thrust engine.

C BIRDS

THE COMING OF THE MONSOON season in Southeast Asia each year aided the enemy in several ways. The low-hanging overcast made the high-flying **G** photo missions quite unproductive. The bad weather also greatly increased the risks to pilot and aircraft in low-flying U. S. manned reconnaissance flights. In order to gather more definitive photo intelligence by operating under the overcast, a new unmanned capability would be necessary.

Overcast skies weren't the only problem. The high-altitude birds had to face the twin hazards of frequent attacks by SA-2 missiles, then being more widely installed in North Vietnam, and by the Russian-built MiG fighters. "We needed to get under the weather," Bob Reichardt recalled, "where we could get meaningful photo intelligence and hopefully be able to escape at least the SA-2 missiles which we believed could not be fired in a flat trajectory to catch the birds if they were flying at 1500 feet altitude or less."

"We were sending out our high-altitude birds," Dale Weaver related, "but smoke and ground haze and monsoon rains were so severe we weren't getting back good photo intelligence — we just weren't adequately covering the areas the Air Force needed.

"SAC Headquarters, particularly in the person of Colonel Ells Powell, was wanting to develop this low-altitude capability. He had heard that Ryan had developed a barometric low altitude control system, (BLACS), for its Firebee target drones. He had some old 147**C** birds available at Davis-Monthan in which he wanted to put BLACS and a low altitude

Teledyne Ryan Aeronautical

LOW-ALTITUDE 147C BIRD with barometric *low altitude control system. Bill Forehand made a special 'duck head' to hold the larger camera.*

camera.'' Colonel Bill Forehand claimed the camera was too big for the bird but made a special 'duck head' for it and got it installed.

Ryan sent Bernard D. Paul, a control systems engineer, over to Tucson in August 1965 to help install BLACS. Later Bernie went with the modified **C** birds to Eglin Air Force Base, Florida, where they were flight tested; then cleared Davis-Monthan in a C-130 with the low-level drones aboard for the flight to OL-20.

''While Ells got his low altitude **C** machines up and going,'' Weaver continued, ''the company got interested in adapting its newest high altitude birds — the **G** — to the low level role. With the **G** in flight test, we started development of the new **J** from it and had the first one flying in November at the Navy's Missile Test Center at Pt. Mugu, California. We knew that the **C**s were marginal at best and that we needed a better bird to carry the BLACS system and develop a good 1500-foot low-altitude capability over the target.

''We needed better reliability too. Over Luang Prabang, the capital of Laos, we'd had a hairy experience. On release from the DC-130 pylon, the bird pulled straight up in front of the launch plane, stalling out about 500 feet directly overhead. It augured in about seven miles back of the point where it had been air launched. The crew discovered that the 130 is capable of some very fine evasive action when the pilots are properly motivated! We found out from that incident that maintenance on the **B** bird had to be pretty good to survive a three-hour mission enroute before you get to the launch point. That really started a new, hard look at reliability.

''Two Air Force-modified **C** versions were deployed October first and second, 1965. Both were lost to enemy action or simply went astray. I happened to go along for the ride as back-up LCO October 12 on the last flight of the remaining **C** model. I was probably one of the few U. S. civilians to see the coast of North Vietnam for over a year — maybe longer.

''We were to launch in the Gulf about 15 miles off Haiphong, which took us within 22 miles of a new SAM site. The Air Force wanted to get some information on these low-altitude birds for use in our development of the **J**. They scheduled four F-4s to fly combat air patrol (CAP) on us. One was assigned to follow the bird in and take pictures.

UPDATED VERSION OF THE BIG-WING B WAS THE 147G *with larger engine.* ***G*** *model is shown here with its support equipment. New Continental J69 engine had 1920 lbs. thrust vs. 1700 lbs. for engine used in 147****B*** *model.*

Dave Gossett

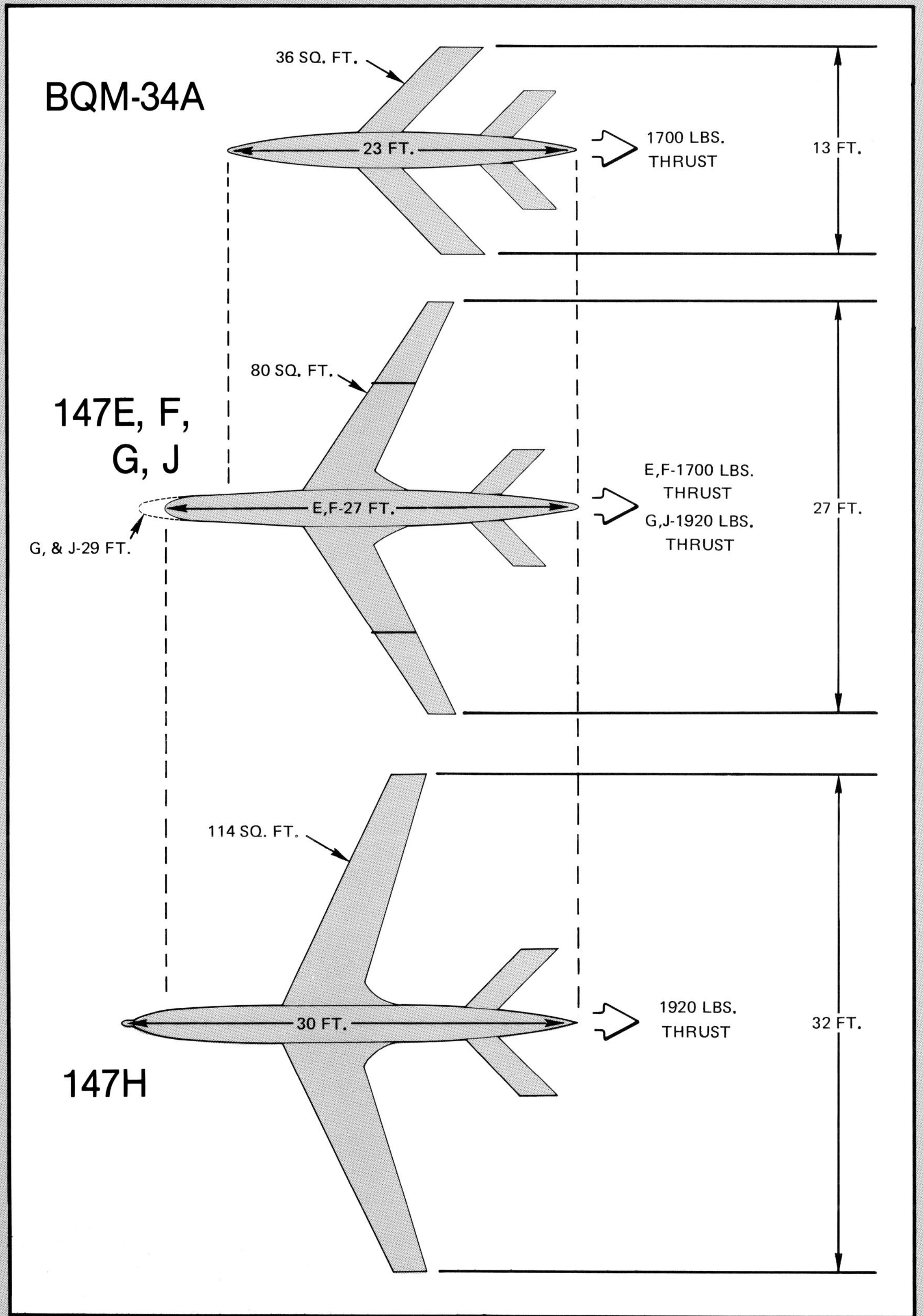

Christi De Lacey

"We went charging up into the Gulf and could hear the fighter CAP overhead but they couldn't find either us or their aerial tanker; they locked onto somebody else. Finally they got the F-4 refuelings started but the last plane — the photo man — bounced the KC-135, broke his refueling probe and had to return to Da Nang.

"As we started in, the bird had a minor autopilot malfunction in the roll system. We continued to work with it. Then we had an indication from U. S. 'spook' planes that we were being 'painted' by radar from an SA-2 missile site. Our 'spooks' provided general alert information over guarded channels. The grid coordinates showed we'd been tracked all the way up the coast by the NVN [North Vietnamese] tracking chain. As we turned in to launch we looked to them as if we were pretty hostile and I imagine if we'd gone much closer they would have fired.

"The 130 started in at about 3K (3000 feet), and the launch plane flight profile required we come down to around 500 feet until we got about 20 miles from the coast. Then we were to go up to 3K to locate our position, and then to 5K for launch.

"Well, we had gone through an aborted launch because of a problem with the roll system. The crew knew a SAM had locked on them and was in the fire mode. Torching it off at the 130 might be the next step. All this time our fighters were looking for us. The water was loaded with North Vietnamese fishing boats. It wasn't exactly the safest area in which to fly a holding pattern. Things were getting a little sticky and at a very critical stage."

COL. STANLEY W. BEERLI, Director of Reconnaissance, *SAC Headquarters, on inspection trip at DaNang while 147***G** *began operations in December 1965.*

R. R. Schwanhausser

Dale went on laconically to describe the subsequent launch of the **C** bird after 23 minutes spent straightening out what he later called "a simple logic problem in the roll channel of the flight control system."

Later testimony of the crew is that Dale remained pretty cool through the crisis except for a "damn it, make another orbit and I'll get the son-of-a-bitch off!" Which he did.

Right over the North Vietnamese fishing fleet.

"You could see the people down there shaking their fists," Dale reported. "I don't know if it was because we were ruining their fishing or if they were just angry with us because we perhaps seemed unfriendly.

"After the bird was pickled off it looked fine until the barometric altitude command came in. The drone went right up to about 8K and then dove to about 3K until it rounded out on the BLACS pre-set barometric altitude and correct heading. It probably pulled too many G's in the up-and-down maneuver to complete the flight. Still, it looked good going into the target area. The bird flew into the clouds and we never saw it again or found out what happened to it.

"Our fighters finally found us on the way home and one joined up with us for a while."

HAZARDS ALOFT-HAZARDS AGROUND

"WE OFTEN HAD INDICATIONS of ground fire while landing and taking off both at Bien Hoa and Da Nang," recalls Weaver. "I remember in 1964 we were flying up through Laos and we had two birds on the racks. We had launched one successfully and were coming back. We decided to try to match up the camera image motion compensation (IMC) with our altitude and our airspeed and just run the photo materials out on the bird which was swinging under the C-130. We wanted to see what sort of terrain we were flying over. The photo interpreters would take a look at it later since naturally it was put on low priority and it didn't get processed for quite a while.

"Later we heard we had flown over some of the better gun emplacement positions along our flight path in Laos. Shortly thereafter they changed our flight path on the C-130 to minimize its incursion into Laos and go up through Thailand. But there were no actual interceptions of the 130s by enemy aircraft and no ground-to-air missiles fired at the launch planes."

Col. Bill Forehand recalls that the hazards were from friend and foe alike.

"On two occasions, right after takeoff in the 130 from Da Nang, we found ourselves right in the middle of a flight of U. S. fighters. They were going after ground targets, diving all around us too close for comfort or safety. Concentrating on their targets, they just didn't see us. We came pretty close to mid-air collisions several times.

"Other times it was the enemy, and then generally in the landing pattern at Bien Hoa, or Da Nang. Almost every landing you could see the tracers coming at you.

"Final approach at Bien Hoa had to be pretty steep — almost straight down it seemed. If you were under 1500 or 2000 feet more than two miles off the end of the runway you could be sure you were going to be shot at.

"I had a young troop take us into Bien Hoa one day in one of those huge C-141 transports. He was doing practice ground controlled approaches (GCA). He was making those long, low, flat approaches and I began to see those little wiggle worms coming at us. I finally looked at him and said, 'Lieutenant, do you know what those things are that you just saw going by?' He said, 'No, Colonel, what's that?'

"I told him he was being fired on from the ground and that he'd better get up and out of there. He really hauled it back in a steep climb. But quick!"

It wasn't only over enemy territory that flying in the DC-130 launch planes was hazardous. In a short letter to Swany's secretary, Jo Ann Howell, in September 1965, Dale wrote:

"The DC-130 returned cancelled from what was to have been a double launch. We had a fuel leak in number three tank, a fire warning light on number two engine on takeoff and a fire light on number three engine 15 minutes after takeoff. With smoke coming from number two engine, we chopped power, feathered the prop and hit the fire extinguisher bottles. Then we observed fluid — thought to be fuel — in the area of number four engine. That did it! The pilot declared an emergency and went in for a very rapid landing at Da Nang escorted by fire trucks, a rescue chopper and lots of other attention."

Often, some of the equipment took an unnecessary beating according to Weaver —

"We launched three **B**s and two came home. The third one was presumably zapped. Both of the recovered birds came down in the water. After an hour and a half floatation **B**-35 still had a dry scorer (camera) compartment, but the recovery crew opened the compartment in the surf and doused the scorer. Still the 'take' was dry.

"The other bird, **B**-37 didn't fare so well. The recovery boat ran into the floating drone, turned it over and then towed it, submerged, to shore. Needless to say, it is in pretty bad shape."

Weaver was not the only one to report an occasional un-scheduled 'incident'. Ed Sly cites these two —

"We had **B**-28 returning from a mission up north. It landed by parachute in Da Nang Bay and an Army Huey chopper was sent out to pick it up. Unfortunately the chopper developed trouble and had to be ditched. In no time the chopper began to sink so the crew and the drone recovery team abandoned 'ship' and took refuge on the floating drone. Meanwhile the Navy sent out a landing craft, tank (LCT) to pick up the survivors. By the time the LCT arrived, the chopper had sunk and the rescue boat had a terrible time trying to figure out how the unmanned jet drone could possibly have flown with such a large flight crew aboard!

"Some of the returning birds of course parachuted into rice paddies in an area which was friendly by day but swarming with Viet Cong after dark. Natually we tried to retrieve the drones and get them back to base before dusk. On one retrieval mission the chopper hovered over the downed bird to drop a GI whose job it was to attach the drone sling to the chopper winch. Water in the rice paddy looked about two feet deep so the GI jumped in with small tool box, rifle and ammo and disappeared from sight in the water and quagmire. Incidentally, Ryan people did not participate in these recoveries. That was left to the military."

Bob Reichardt reported a similar incident which had taken place late in 1964.

"An Air Force sergeant had to get into the water from a helicopter to help pick up a bird that was down in a rice paddy. While he was in the water getting the riser attached to the helicopter's sling, the Viet Cong moved in on the scene with bullets banging the water all around him. Meanwhile the downwash from the chopper above him was about to drown the sergeant.

"Finally he got the bird hooked on, and they hauled the drone and the sergeant out of there plenty fast. Later I visited the base hospital where they were giving him first aid for shock. Colonel McCaslin, the OL commander, came in to congratulate the sergeant on his performance under fire.

"This little, skinny, scrawny sergeant looked up at this great big, bull Colonel and said, 'Colonel, I want you to know something. I ain't gonna do that anymore. I ain't ever gonna do that again."

When the birds were on their way home, the recovery area, which was just a few miles from final approach to the air base at Da Nang, would be pretty thoroughly sanitized.

"A company of South Vietnamese and a company of our own military would come in ahead of us and secure the area so we didn't have to worry too much as long as the drones parachuted there, either over land or water," recalls Bill Forehand.

"The recovery area was really pretty small. The air base was to the south, mountains to the north and west and water on the east. That meant we had to land those fool pilotless airplanes by parachute right smack down through the traffic pattern.

"Nobody even knew they were coming because of the security on the program. Even the base commander didn't know what the hell we were doing, but in time he caught on.

"In any but wartime conditions what we were doing would have been impossible if not illegal. They would have F-4s and other fighters, and larger craft coming in there, and here would come a parachute with a drone hanging on it, down through the whole traffic pattern.

"As far as firefights are concerned, during my command I never had a drone I had to fight for. We got shot at some, but it was of pretty short duration because we were in there and out too fast. The helo would already by airborne and if things were going properly we would get the hooks into it and out of there as soon as it touched down."

WEAVER TO HOWELL reports continued to flow into Schwanhauser's San Diego office:

Bien Hoa, 1 March 1965

Our particular cross last week was a Class II alert created by the air strikes up North. As a primary crew member I spent a good portion of one night with tin hat, AR-15 carbine and 357 magnum hand cannon guarding Old Dum Dum (one of Lockheed C-130 launch planes). We were preparing for an evacuation — even if we have only three engines operative.

Bien Hoa, 20 August 1965

If you consider that this is a new maintenance crew, a new flight crew undergoing check flights and two new LCO teams; that we have three models of vehicles; that we have flown three successful flights, been cancelled on two missions and that we've turned around seven drones — all in eleven days — then you will understand that most of my time is taken up on the job. My so-called free time is spent conferring with the Colonel on future plans and on potential problems.

The mission today should have been a lulu except for the weather which caused a cancellation of the mission ten minutes before scheduled launch. I was disappointed because today was the first anniversary of operational use of the 147**B**.

Bien Hoa, 26 August 1965

The Viet Cong attack here two nights ago was pretty spectacular. There were about 30 rounds fired — mixed 60 mm, 80 mm mortar and 75 mm cannon. The closest hit was ten huts down and it pretty well rattled stuff all over our hut. There were several hits on the flight line, trailers, hangar and such. Our new DC-130 got a crease and ole 'Stupid Water Bug'(147**B**-28,

VIET CONG ATTACKS at Bien Hoa *could be pretty spectacular, particularly to non-combat civilian technical personnel on the base.*

Ed Christian

4080th SRW History

"IT WAS THE SAME PEOPLE moving back and forth *across the two 4080th SRW operations: Blue Springs and Trojan Horse."*

which had landed in the water on five of its six flights) got a hole or two in its nacelle. The casualties were relatively light — eight uniformed people hit by flying metal, 46 by running into barbed wire, plus miscellaneous stubbed toes, bumped heads, and so on. Somehow, it's easier to sleep when we are pounding them.

The results of the last three missions have been excellent; actually much better than our competition (manned recce birds).

Bien Hoa, 19 October 1965

The 15th started the official VC 'hate Americans' month. Minor acts of terrorism are expected to increase; however, rumor has it that Charlie might try something big.

Yesterday morning we watched our planes striking with napalm less than three miles from the runway. Some were also using high explosives and machine guns. It seems that about two battalions of VC were caught in that area. Word is 200 were killed.

It's interesting to have a show like that going on while you are outdoors patching in the programmer for a mission with the bird already on the launch plane waiting to go.

MANNED VS. UNMANNED

ACCEPTANCE OF THE UNMANNED aircraft was slow in coming, but little by little the manned reconaissance aircraft people were getting the message. No small part of this was because reconnaissance with drones and with piloted U-2s was under the same commander.

"It was," said Schwanhausser, "the same people moving back and forth across the two operations: Blue Springs, the drone activity, and Trojan Horse, the manned U-2 flights.

"As the SAMs started to be deployed around Hanoi, the Air Force scheduled a dual mission one day. One of our drones was to fly over the SAM site while a U-2 flew off to the side to witness what happened. His mission was to observe the 'yes or no' of an SA-2 Guideline missile.

"From his offset position, the U-2 pilot saw the Lightning Bug drone shot down. Back at the Officers Club later at Bien Hoa, he told me how he watched the 'telephone pole' consume the drone. The rivalry stopped when he said, 'From now on, you guys can have that mission.'

"Our biggest 'sales' problem has always been that just about every customer wears a pair of wings on his chest, so the fight for the unmanned aircraft has always been uphill all the way. It's being extremely well received now. We call them remotely piloted vehicles (RPVs) and leave the word 'pilot' in there! Still there are ingrained jealousies between the manned and the unmanned mission.

"The manned mission is very obvious; so obvious it's subject to the spotlight of unwanted publicity — even when it involves just one pilot like Francis Gary Powers. But contrast this with minimum exposure and low readership when a reconnaissance drone is shot down and reported by Peking or Hanoi."

WHEN THE SA-2 'telephone pole' *missile shot down the 147 Lightning Bug, the U-2 pilot decided "you guys can have that mission."*

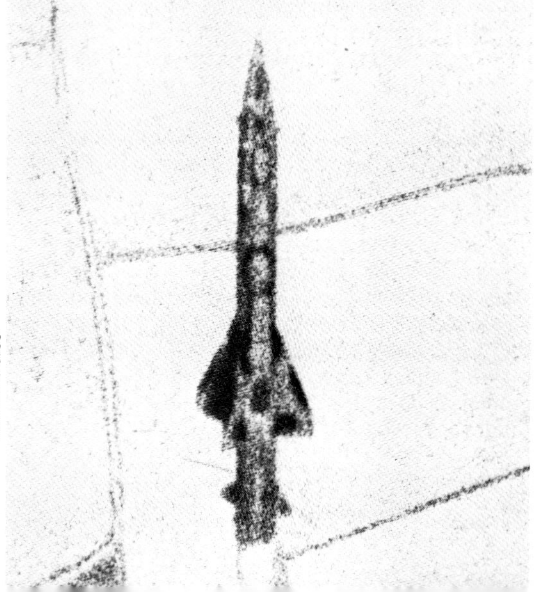

U.S. Air Force

FOUR MANNED U-2 reconnaissance planes *shot down by Red Chinese were displayed in August 1965 at Peking's Chinese Peoples' Revolution Military Museum.*

"When a U-2 was shot at over North Vietnam," Dale Weaver recalled, "they were, essentially, run out by the SA-2 missiles, and it became our task to provide the high altitude recon.

"Other recon elements, RF-101s, were also operating but at lower altitudes and, until the bombing started up North, all the drone recon was high altitude.

"At that time I heard a comment which has often been repeated, but the first time I heard it, it really made the whole operation seem worthwhile. A couple of captains at the bar at Tan Son Nhut were discussing the fact that they didn't have to fly the next day because the Lightning Bug had already made the mission!"

IN A MORALE-BUILDING message to the security-cleared production people at San Diego who had been working round-the-clock for several years to make drone reconnaissance possible, Dale Weaver wrote that "the birds are flying well and the data has been excellent. The results speak for themselves.

"Quality workmanship is producing a quality product. The manufacturing and quality control people should know that their efforts are appreciated out here where our vehicles are playing a vital role in U. S. policy in this area. Since the Department of Defense issued its directive concerning SAMs, we have the only acceptable device, in certain areas, of getting the information necessary for evaluating the strategy of the air power we have committed. Certainly the lives of many men depend on the success or failure of each flight.

"A responsibility like that is more than most of us bargained for at the start but it should not be more than we are willing to accept."

FOUR A4 SKYHAWK Navy fighters, led by an A6A Intruder, left the deck of the aircraft carrier Independence on Sunday morning October 17, 1965. Their target was a missile site 52 miles northeast of Hanoi which had been located two days earlier by a Lightning Bug drone — 147**B**-37 — which returned unscathed to its base from an "excellent mission" over Route 5109.

Again, the drone had done its job without exposing a pilot to the hazards of a target identification flight. It was typical of scores of similar drone missions.

As reported in "Stars and Stripes," the pilots of Carrier Air Wing 7 that Sunday morning counted five or six missiles, presumed ready for firing, when they streaked in with 8½ tons of bombs to reduce the site to rubble.

Commander Harry B. Southworth described how one of the destroyed missiles was seen "snaking" around on the ground like a toy balloon propelled by the air as it is released to "squirt" around a room.

All five Navy planes returned safely to the Independence.

E FOR ELINT

WHILE THE NEED for both high- and low-altitude photo missions continued, there still remained the requirement for electronic intelligence (Elint) flights from which data on enemy intentions and capabilities could be obtained.

Ryan's star commuter, Dale Weaver, made his umpteenth trip to Saigon in late 1965 with a dual assignment. The drone operation had slipped somewhat in maintenance reliability and Dale was sent out as the eyes and ears of Ryan management to find out what was wrong. Secondly, the Air Force and Ryan were in the process of fielding the 147**E** model. This was an up-dated, higher altitude version of the 147**D** Elint bird, and had been built in January, 1964, using the 147**B** airframe. Along with the three **E**s, two **D** models were shipped to Vietnam.

"By October 1965, better black boxes had been built," Weaver recalled, "and we were certain with the testing we had done that we could get the intercept intelligence we were after."

The concept of the **E** had been developed from the earlier 147**D**. All electronic signals received by the drone were converted to video or continuous wave (CW) level signals and transmitted to monitoring RB-47 aircraft and strategically located surface stations.

"We were preparing the **E**s for launch against the SA-2s in North Vietnam. We were reasonably sure we could jump them up, for by that time they were firing quite frequently. With the addition of a traveling wave tube (TWT) to augment radar return, the **E**s could be made to look like U-2s.

"Then too, some of our missions, including the high altitude, were being scheduled to locate SAM sites. Whether or not photography came back out of it, it was worthwhile to send a bird in just to locate a missile site. If we came back with photographs fine and if we jumped one up and got a reaction that was fine too. Other observers in the area would see the action.

"When we actually started flying the **E**s they had a fair task force built around us under the code name 'United Effort.' It was originally aimed at Korea where there were SAM sites. The **E**s were never deployed there, however, for reasons which were perhaps political rather than operational. United Effort did involve a large number of people and the airplanes receiving the electronic data. In addition there were Navy and Air Force observer airplanes preparing to strike if they could in fact identify a particular SAM site they thought they could hit.

"The first three launches of the **E** in late Fall 1965 were not 100% successful. In the first, the mission Elint payload package quit operating 20 seconds after launch. But the bird came back and was recovered, primarily because it wasn't augmented and so didn't look like anything the North Vietnamese wanted to waste a missile on.

"The second and third were both fired at; the Elint receiving airplane on the second mission actually saw the missile burst and got a 35 mm picture of it from 40 miles away when it came up to meet the bird contrail. The electronic data was great until 3 or 4 minutes before intercept so we missed some of the prime information we were after.

"Incidentally, I'm now identified as a SAC hired killer. That's what 'Peking Polly' says we are. The other night we were listening to shortwave and they made reference to the civilian SAC hired killers at Bien Hoa. Somehow the word has gotten out about

OMINOUS-LOOKING 147E Elint drone *obtained key data needed to build electronic counter measures (ECM) equipment which improved survivability of American pilots and airplanes.*

Dave Gossett

the gun-carrying civilian types. Next they will probably have our names, if they don't already."

While the **E**s did succeed in jumping the SA-2 up, the highly desired electronic information had not been obtained because some onboard government furnished equipment (GFE) was not functioning properly. Ryan felt there was an environmental problem — excessive heat in the compartment where the black boxes were stowed.

"Schwanhausser went to the Air Force," Weaver continued, "and made a pitch that as system integrators Ryan wanted to bring the material back from overseas and not risk it again until adequate testing had been completed in San Diego.

"His suspicions were confirmed in the environmental chamber so we fixed it and shipped it back overseas early in 1966. Despite the electronic complexities involved, the bird worked perfectly and drew the shot we were after.

"I was on the launch February 13, 1966 and its checkout was fantastic. It flew its mission very well and was shot at within 50 miles of where they figured. The intercept was perfect. All of the data received on SAMs was capable of being analyzed. We got the proximity fusing information, plus some radar guidance data we were after when the fusing came on; also the over-pressure that killed the bird. We needed to know all these things to go farther in designing and building electronic counter measures (ECM) equipment to improve the survivability of our pilots and airplanes in the bombing phase. That led to some significant changes in the ECM business for protecting our airplanes.

"We were told that Dr. Eugene Fubini, Assistant Secretary of the Air Force, agreed with Doug Steakley that it was the most significant contribution to electronic reconnaissance in the last 20 years; that that particular mission had paid for the entire drone program up to that date.

"The information obtained on that one flight was to save scores of lives and aircraft in the months and years to come. The U. S. had been trying every way in the world to get the SA-2 information; they had used every kind of manned reconnaissance airplane, every kind of sensing and listening device. But they couldn't find out what the fusing was. It's fantastic that the drone got it all."

Six years later on a visit to the CIA, Bob Reichardt was pleased to have confirmation that the data obtained February 13, 1966 was still valid.

"My host at lunch" he said, "was a guy I felt pretty sure was aware of what we had done with the **E** model. I asked him if the name 'United Effort' meant anything and he said it certainly did; that the results obtained were even then being demonstrated daily in flights of manned aircraft over North Vietnam. He told me that the ECM equipment carried to this day is designed directly from the technical information obtained from the 147**E**'s flight."

THE F BIRD

THE 147**F** (CONVERTED FROM **B**-7) was a one-of-a-kind bird designed and flown in a multiple role on a couple of sorties in July 1966. It had the first of the ECM defensive systems in a photo recon bird.

"The **F**," Schwanhausser recalls, "was to fly the ALQ-51 package, an ECM box called 'Shoehorn,' for the Navy in a high-threat area. They wanted to try Shoehorn in a drone to see what it would do to confuse incoming SAM missiles. This is a good example of one of our better successes.

"Some of the customers had looked at the size of the box — it was a big unit that went into a manned aircraft — and said you couldn't put it in one of the Ryan drones. That got our attention. If somebody said we couldn't do it, we said 'the hell we can't.' Our guy who integrated that design was Howard Allen of 'Blue Badges first' fame. We literally shoehorned it into the drone and flew it overseas.

"I was in Washington at the time. We were having dinner on a Sunday with the Steakleys and he took me over to the side and said he'd just been in the Secretary of Defense's office. He was extremely delighted because we flew this particular **F** bird and drew 10 or 11 missiles before it was hit. Our flight log for July 22, 1966 shows 'Good flight. Did not return.'

"The trade off in the number of missiles you could make the enemy expend to get one drone was extremely worthwhile. So we had a bird that had the capability to go and test equipment in the real live environment without risking a man's life."

15

IMPROVISATION

"THE RECCE DRONE business thrives on crises — plural."

It's Bob Schwanhausser speaking and he should know. For ten years — except for a heart attack in 1968 — he'd thrived in the quick-reaction atmosphere which is the natural climate of the intelligence business. The **J**-bird was a good example.

In the Fall of 1965, T. Claude Ryan, founder four decades earlier of the Ryan Aeronautical Company, accompanied Schwanhausser to SAC Headquarters at Omaha. Swany saw some merit in bringing the two Ryans together — Claude, and General John Ryan, SAC commander.

"Our early birds overseas were all high-altitude," Swany recalls. "General Ryan's Deputy for Operations asked me about low-altitude birds. I pointed out I didn't think it was a very good idea — another case where I was obviously pretty stupid because it's been one of our biggest flying birds. We had lots of problems then, and continued to have, with low-altitude navigation because you don't look very far ahead.

"Anyway, several days later a phone call came at 4 p.m. from Doug Steakley. He said they wanted a low-altitude bird and would like it in four weeks. They wanted the Cost Proposal and Statement of Work by 0700 Washington time next morning!

"By that time we had the **G** model and we modified it to make it fly low. It became the **J**.

"During testing, one of the first **J**s flew into the 130 launch plane — nobody was hurt and that was the only near fatality we have ever had in the drone program. It knocked a propeller off the 130, badly damaged that engine and the other propeller on that side. Although the drone exploded and broke in half, fortunately there was no fire on the 130."

But let's review the official reports of Ryan technicians — Bob Todd and Bernie Paul — who were aboard the launch plane at the Pacific Missile Range out of Pt. Mugu, California, on January 3, 1966:

The DC-130A launch aircraft proceeded outbound shortly after noon to the launch point and scheduled 4,500 foot altitude. Direct control checks of the systems on 147XJ-2, including the BLACS barometric low-altitude control system, were reported by LCO as "completed satisfactorily; standing by for remote checks." The remote commands were completed normally using the remote control transmitter from San Nicholas Island.

With the drone engine operating normally, the mission countdown was placed at the "minus five minute mark and holding" while the F-8U chase and F-4H photo planes joined the launch aircraft.

All systems were operating properly and the drone was reported as ready for launch at the minus two minute mark. The countdown continued normally with launch occuring at the "zero" count from the remote control site.

"Bird clear" was called out as the drone dropped away normally, but after bottoming out 10 to 15 feet below the right pylon it began moving forward, then suddenly pitched up at about a 20 degree angle impacting with the number 4 starboard engine.

That called for an immediate "May Day" alert.

It appeared that the front of the drone was ahead of the number 4 propeller before impact and that the prop hit the drone fuel tank.

There was an immediate explosion and ball of fire with the major portion of the drone vehicle continuing up and over the C-130 wing. The propeller and gear box separated when the drone hit. The number 3 propeller and engine nacelle was also damaged.

Flying back, the debris punched a hole in the fuselage above the aft door near Todd's position. Six feet of the starboard horizontal stabilizer was torn off.

There had been the usual buffeting of the aircraft when a drone is launched but this was followed by a big jar a second or two later when the drone hit the C-130 engine, then another when the wreckage hit the horizontal stabilizer.

Thirty minutes after calling "May Day" the pilot made a perfect landing at San Nicholas Island. AMEN!

U.S. Navy

"THE DRONE (147J) PITCHED up in a violent maneuver *and took out No. 4 engine . . . then became one big ball of fire which went right over the top of the C-130 wing. Flying pieces knocked holes in the fuselage and tore into the tail feathers."*

Bernie Paul describes the incident in more personal terms:

"I was sitting in the flight engineer's seat between the pilot and co-pilot positions. In this case Captain Marvin Bixby, the plane commander, was in the right-hand seat because we were to launch from that side of the C-130.

"I wanted to be where I could study the **J**'s tendency to porpoise — see what the bird was actually doing immediately after launch.

"Everyone on board was required to wear a parachute as a safety measure, but they're cumbersome so we would strap them on, get them properly fitted and then stow them nearby in case they were needed in an emergency. D. H. (Blackie) Blackmer, our Doppler expert, who's about my size, was another of the Ryan technicians aboard.

"Anyway, the second the bird was launched I felt a huge rocking motion, the drone pitched up in a violent maneuver and took out No. 4 engine, leaving its hardware guts just hanging there. The prop on No. 3 was also damaged and Bixby feathered it immediately. There was nothing left to feather on No. 4, but he pulled its extinguisher and shut off all fuel lines.

"Then we heard 'May Day'

"The drone became one big ball of fire which went right over the top of the wing. Flying pieces knocked holes in the fuselage and tore into the tail feathers.

"Our launch altitude had been 5,000 feet and as we rocked back and forth Bixby quickly got control,

Bruce Engman

CAPT. MARV BIXBY came back from OL-20 *to test the J bird but ran into a 'May Day' problem which he deftly handled.*

pulled back and before you could say 'uncle' we were at 10,000 feet, a better spot from which to bail out.

"I went back to get my chute and there was Blackie with it strapped on.

" 'Blackie, you've got my chute on,' I said, 'It was right here under my jacket.'

" 'I've got it on,' Blackie said, 'and I'm not taking it off.'

"I grabbed another chute and probably fit it faster than I'd ever done before, pulling straps here and there like a madman.

"It wasn't funny at the time, but the chute incident has been a standing joke between Blackie and me ever since.

"Bixby did a fine job of getting us in to the 10,000 foot strip at San Nicholas Island, 75 miles off the California coast. There a helicopter picked us up and flew back to Pt. Mugu.

"As I look back on the incident now, I really didn't have time to be frightened.

"As soon as the film from the chase plane could be developed we had a debriefing and only then did I realize the imminent danger that was involved because it was terrifying to see that huge fireball rip right into the launch plane.

"There had probably been some failure in the circuitry which had caused an up-elevator position on launch. After that we made some circuitry changes.

"That January 3rd was the absolute low ebb of the **J** program. From that point on we really picked up our feet — worked day and night — and I can't recall any group of people turning to in such a tremendous way. Two months later we were in Vietnam with the **J** birds."

Losses during flight testing are always a matter of concern, but after all that's what testing is all about — to assure reliability when the vehicle goes into routine operation.

The **J** had it's share of test problems.

"One of the biggest headaches we had with that big-wing bird," recalls Bernie, "was to keep it from porpoising. It had a tremendous fugoid aerodynamically right after launch and this had to be worked out.

"We started off with a black mark against us even before X**J**-2 flew into the C-130 wing. On our initial test flight — with X**J**-1 — we were experiencing porpoising and, thinking it might be due to the BLACS system, turned it off and commanded parachute recovery. But the chute didn't pop and the bird just augered into the ocean off Pt. Mugu."

A third bird was also a casualty, but by the end of flight test the **J** had undergone the most comprehensive and productive evaluation of any of the 147 series. **J**-4 for instance, flew seven times successfully in flight test, was then moved to the OL and in its first three months flew five good missions. On four of these operational missions there was a good MARS (mid-air retrieval system recovery by helicopter). On the fifth, there was no attempt to use MARS, but the bird parachuted properly to a recovery in salt water.

"When we got to OL-20 and started operating," Bernie continued, "our initial flights were just tremendous. We ended up getting stuff back that was just unbelievable. I got into the photo recon center in Saigon and saw some of the material that was coming back. It was really amazing looking at the detail of the ships up there in Haiphong harbor."

Bernie Paul

IF HE HAD TO BAIL OUT, Blackie Blackmer, *right, had a head start on Bernie Paul. Others in photo at Bien Hoa are Gene Motter, left, and Bruce Engman.*

THE J PITCHED UP and impacted *with the No. 4 engine leaving its hardware guts hanging there.*

U.S. Navy

Dave Gossett

Dave Gossett

ALONG WITH Gs and Js, THE 147H with the biggest wing yet, *was tested at Point Mugu with Navy cooperation. At left, an* ***H*** *bird is returned by helicopter after a successful flight. Test bird XH-11, right, is ready for launch from its rack on DC-130.*

THE **G, H** AND **J** MODELS of the 147 were getting a lot of attention from Ryan engineers and production people early in 1966, and flight test programs for the three models were under way at Pt. Mugu, some 120 miles up the coast from the San Diego factory.

As in the past, orders for additional quantities of the drones were being released by Ryan management to the factory even before the contractual paper work was processed through government channels.

Just as the military used Big Safari procurement procedures to expedite drone reconnaissance so was it necessary within the contractor structure to by-pass normal procedures. Thus, for many years, Schwanhausser ran what was virtually a company within a company, having great latitude and independence in developing his own technical sciences, engineering, program management, production and field service capabilities.

To wrap all Ryan drone activity — both security classified reconnaissance birds and the unclassified target systems — into a single grouping, Schwanhausser had been named Chief Engineer of Drones and Special Projects in May 1964.

Recognizing that new generations of high performance drones would be required as follow-on vehicles to the subsonic Firebee training targets and 147 series of reconnaissance vehicles, the Schwanhausser group obtained new contracts in 1965 for the development of the supersonic Firebee II target and for the classified Model 154 reconnaissance drone in 1966.

MODEL 154 FIREFLY, new 48-foot span *high-altitude surveillance RPV was developed by Ryan for a potential follow-on drone program while the 147 series of reconnaissance 'spy planes' were operating in Vietnam.*

U.S. Air Force

VICE PRESIDENT BOB SCHWANHAUSSER *In 1966, he became the company officer responsible for all Aerospace Systems*

Bob Wilson

At that period Ryan management was having to devote ever increasing attention to running and staffing its new Continental Motors subsidiary, making necessary the selection of other executives for key posts in top management of the Ryan Aeronautical unit.

While executive management then had some understandable reservations about the effervescent Schwanhausser's maturity, there was no denying his capability as leader of a team which was then generating well over half of all company business volume. As the company's then Vice President-Public and Personnel Relations, the writer strongly supported Schwanhausser's selection because of a natural disposition not to argue with the kind of successful performance he had demonstrated.

In July 1966, the Ryan board of directors named Schwanhausser Vice President-Aerospace Systems.

BY APRIL 1966, 'combat' operations with the **J** had begun in South Vietnam. In June the first of the extended-wing, longer range **H**s had also been delivered to the Air Force. They were deployed overseas in December, 1966 and had their first operational use in March, 1967.

"I kept an eye on development of the **H**," Dale Weaver recalls, "because I knew I'd eventually become involved in its operation overseas. It had the larger 1920-pounds-thrust J69 engine. While the bird had the same general family appearance of the **B** and **G** series, it was a new airplane designed almost from the ground up to achieve a needed weight reduction but retaining the same thrust as in the **G**. It wasn't just a 'mod' based on original BQM-34A pieces as were the **B** and **G** birds. It also had new features like a detachable nose for camera installations.

"We also fielded the microwave command guidance system (MCGS) which had the capability of launching and monitoring the **H** around the flight path within a 200-mile tracking range.

"This did away with the former beacon/radio control which had caused us some difficulty late in 1965. We had found out the hard way that assignment of radio frequencies in the corner of South Vietnam in which we were operating was poorly coordinated. We had three birds spin out of control because some Vietnamese outposts were operating on our control frequency."

EXTENDED WING, LONGER RANGE H model with larger *1920-pounds-thrust jet engine also had new microwave command guidance system (MCGS).*

U.S. Air Force

Ken Martin

MARS Mid-Air Retrieval System *is depicted in artist's sketch, left, as helicopter snatches drone's parachute and winches in the reconnaissance plane. In photo below, drone is ready for mid-air recovery.*

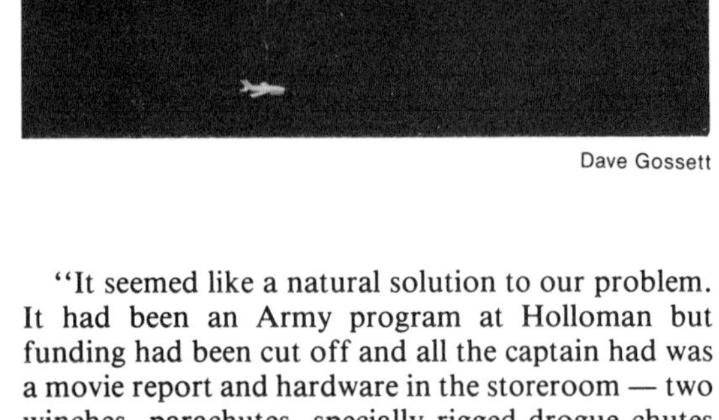

Dave Gossett

"THE **H**" relates Weaver, "was geared to use the new MARS (mid-air retrieval system) in which a helicopter snatched it during its descent by parachute. The MARS system had been fielded earlier that year and was first used operationally for the low-altitude **J**."

A lot of returning drones were getting badly clobbered as they parachute-landed into rice paddies, jungles and the ocean off Da Nang. Many others landed with relatively little damage in the designated recovery area.

Ryan experts felt there must be a way to eliminate the hard contact with mother earth; some method to retrieve the drone in mid-air and return it gently and directly to the air base. One who thought so was Fred Yochim, former deputy SPO at Dayton, who had joined Ryan in March 1964 following his medical discharge from the Air Force after a heart attack the previous Fall.

"There was always some damage on ground impact," Yochim had said, "and I felt there ought to be some way to lick the problem. I'd heard of a young captain at Holloman who had been making mid-air retrievals of weights up to two thousand pounds with a helicopter.

"I went over to see him and he gladly opened up his records and showed me the equipment built by All-American Engineering Company to snatch payloads in mid-air.

"The idea of mid-air retrieval had first been developed six years earlier with C-119 and C-130 aircraft especially equipped to snag the camera capsule ejected by SAMOS and other reconnaissance satellites as they parachuted to earth in the mid-Pacific.

"It seemed like a natural solution to our problem. It had been an Army program at Holloman but funding had been cut off and all the captain had was a movie report and hardware in the storeroom — two winches, parachutes, specially rigged drogue chutes and allied gear. He said he'd turn it over to us.

"The movie was pretty exciting so I brought it back to San Diego and showed it to our people. Their enthusiasm rubbed off on the Air Force and we got the program up and going.

"In the combat environment, you might have a fire-fight on your hands to get your bird and its sensors back. If it came down hard in the chute or winds were heavy it could get pretty well beaten up on ground contact. If it went in the water — particularly in the ocean — you had a serious decontamination problem.

"So the obvious answer was to snatch it in mid-air, but to achieve some success, we went through a long, strenuous development cycle, and we aren't over it yet.

"The basic principle is to deploy the chutes at medium altitude — somewhere around 15,000 feet. The retrieval helicopter is some 3,000 feet lower. As the bird descends through that altitude, the helicopter flies past with a grappling hook and engages a part of the parachute system.

"Once hooked up, a release mechanism frees the drone's main parachute to float clear. Then the chopper's winch pays out line just like a fisherman who has hooked a marlin. When they get the drone velocity matched to that of the chopper they begin reeling the bird in until it is stowed about 15 feet below. Then they bring it home, set it gently on the ground and separate the line.

"Since then MARS, incorporating customized engineering changes, has become the primary recovery system for recce birds overseas. It went into service out of Da Nang with the **J** birds in April 1966."

In extended operation in Southeast Asia, 2655 MARS 'catches' were made in 2745 attempts for a pace-setting 96.7% success record.

Mrs. Fred Yochim

FRED YOCHIM felt there ought to be *some way to lick the problem of recovering returning drones. He found the answer in MARS.*

SCHWANHAUSSER WAS NOT exactly popular with his secretary, Jo Ann Howell, during the early Southeast Asia operational days. "Each time we would bring Dale back home, and they were about to get married, we'd send him back in a hurry because we needed help over there.

"On one occasion when Dale was returning from OL-20, Jo Ann flew up to San Francisco to meet him and get married, but Dale made the mistake of calling the plant in San Diego and ended up going right back to Saigon.

"So I promised them the next time he came back the marriage would go through. When he returned in November 1965 I told Jo Ann to take the next two days off and get married. I even threw a party for them, but we all had such a good time celebrating their coming marriage that it had to be delayed two days!

"Again there was a call for Dale to get back to the scene of drone operations, but this time we kept the bridegroom home for a week or so.

"Dale or Bob Todd flew practically all the early missions. We always had a Ryan guy who was a LCO along with the Air Force guy. However, Air Force personnel would always 'pickle' the bird off.

"During the first 18 months of overseas operation, Dale flew most of the missions and ended up flying more combat time than any Air Force guy because the blue suiters were rotating and we were sending Dale back again and again for extended periods.

"When Colonel Bill Forehand, OL commander in 1965, returned to the States he called me and said he wanted to do something for Dale . . . put him in for the highest award that could be given a civilian. I told Bill I thought he was out of his mind, that it would never go through, but he insisted on going ahead. So we got his bride, Jo Ann, to put together the information about how many combat missions Dale had flown; then Forehand wrote up the justification on the basis he had spent more time overseas than any GI on the program and had flown more combat time and missions, than any military LCO.

"As one could expect, it was not approved by the Air Force because they could hardly go on record with the information that a contractor guy had put in more combat time than a blue suiter.

"An interesting sidelight of the period is that all of the information flowing into my office on the drone program was treated as Top Secret. The only secretary we had with Top Secret clearance who could read and distribute the dispatches from the OL was Jo Ann. She read all of the incoming mail from the field including Dale's reports and those about the very hazardous flights on which he was a crew member. It was kind of a sticky situation."

While willing to admit the risks, Dale was inclined to shrug them off. "When the Air Force was trying to develop its operational capability and had very few qualified people I was doing a lot of flying and soon had more operational missions than any of their people. I long ago quit counting but the number of sorties is in the hundreds.

"That one off Haiphong when we had to orbit 23 minutes at low altitude got pretty hairy. And the one I mentioned over Laos when the bird got away and flew straight up only to disintegrate over the top of the DC-130 was more than a little scarey. The other sorties were pretty much routine."

THE N DECOYS

THE BOMBING PAUSE over North Vietnam starting December 24, 1965 brought some new problems for the recce drone squadron. Without the confusion of an accompanying air strike, the unmanned Ryan birds became very vulnerable north of the demilitarized zone (DMZ) and so the attrition rate went up sharply.

That situation led to still another family of drones as related by Dale Weaver:

"On one of my trips back to the States early in 1966, Bob Schwanhausser and I went to Washington to meet with General Steakley and the Joint Reconnaissance Committee. They wanted to know if we could build a decoy; something that would provide some confusion and cover for the high-altitude birds. They wanted it quickly and in this business quick means cheap because you don't have time to get fancy and design anything.

"I told Swany we could do it; that it wouldn't be very difficult to modify some of the standard BQM target drones for that role, and that if they thought it necessary we could augment them with TWTs to look like larger aircraft. We started on the job that afternoon.

"There wasn't enough time to do the work through normal procurement channels — even the Big Safari route — so the company sent me over to the 4080th at Davis-Monthan Air Force Base in Arizona as a tech rep with instructions to go ahead and build them if I thought I could. The Air Force waived the company of all responsibility, feeling that if the idea worked that would be fine because the task was urgent, and if it didn't, it would be no great loss."

To get the job done in the limited time available, Col. Ells Powell arranged to team Dale Weaver with one of his key maintenance engineering officers, Major Harold F. (Red) Smith, who served as special projects manager.

MAJOR HAROLD F. (RED) SMITH was not only project manager *on the* ***N*** *decoy program but was regularly called on by the Air Force on tough assignments.*

"Dale brought the technical expertise," Smith related, "while my contribution was to locate and collect the necessary assets. Using the prestige and priority of SAC Headquarters I was able to accumulate hardware from existing assets in Air Force depots all over the country and had what we needed within a couple of weeks.

"The physical task was overwhelming. Normally the planning of such a task takes months for the acquisition and transportation procedures in the military supply system. That is, if you expect to have all the material for a special project funnel into one place at a given time. But we did it in two weeks because we had the priority to bypass all the red tape."

Weaver took Gene Motter and a technician named Charles (Mac) MacFarland over to Tucson, recalling that "we designed and, with GI labor, did the modification of 10 standard BQM-34A target drones in about 10 days. I don't recall where we got the birds but we attached a 147**N** designation to them to keep the nomenclature straight.

"I don't believe I've put in as tough a period as those 10 days at D-M working on the **N**, at least not since the early days of the recce program. And, at the time, I told Swany that if another group of **N**s was to be built, I hoped it could be done in the factory."

"The theory," explained Bob Reichardt, "was to launch one of the high-altitude **G** or other operational birds almost simultaneously with an **N** decoy. They would be programmed to fly parallel for a while and then diverge as they approached the target area. The split pattern would confuse the enemy's ground radars by giving them a choice of two birds at which to fire — sort of a 'which twin has the Toni' challenge."

Without the decoys, the Commies could readily locate the **G**s and go after them. The drone squadron had lost 16 birds, ten of them **G**s, in 24 missions. With the **N**s in there to confuse things, enemy radars would often pick up the decoys and ignore the **G**s, greatly increasing the survivability of the high-altitude birds which were important to the intelligence program as they were equipped with very effective high-resolution cameras.

SINCE THE **N**s were flown into the target area at a vulnerable altitude, the possibility of their survival was so marginal that the decoy missions were considered to be one-way flights. As a result, the parachute recovery system was replaced by sand ballast.

During March and April 1966, eight **N** missions were flown and all the birds were lost. But, reports Reichardt, "several of them did come back and of course were flying around in circles over Da Nang virtually pleading, 'recover me, recover me', until they fueled out and crashed with their load of sand bags. We couldn't do anything about it because they had no parachutes."

LETHAL-LOOKING 147G was probably accompanied *on this mission by a 147***N** *decoy to confuse enemy ground radars.*

R. R. Schwanhausser

Bob Schwanhausser felt the lost birds ought to receive recognition as 'aces' for five MiG kills. "Not many people," he told us, "knew that the **N** birds did not have chutes and consequently could not be recovered.

"Typically, one decoy flew over NVN then exited over the Tonkin Gulf where it ran out of fuel. The MiG chased it so long that it too ran out of fuel; the pilot ejected while his MiG plunged into the sea. Four other MiG 'kills' by drones followed in short order.

"One MiG was shot down by a North Vietnamese surface-to-air missile chasing a drone. Another was shot down by a MiG which mistook an accompanying MiG for the drone he was trying to shoot down."

Dale Weaver wasn't flying in the launch plane as LCO back-up at that time so had to get some of his information second hand. "The flight crew on the first **N** mission on March 3, 1966," he said, "reported lots of ultra-high frequency (UHF) activity right after launch. That would indicate maximum effort and lots of confusion on the part of our friends up North.

"Reports were that the **N** bird made it through to the target area and the **G** came home, but I guess we will never know why the **N** didn't make it back to the Da Nang area.

"The next day we flew again and the **N** bird did the exact job for which it had been built. Again the flight crew reported lots of UHF warning right after launch. And, at the time when it should have been providing maximum cover for the **G**, there was a UHF-reported SAM firing at the **N**. I can't say positively what happened, but there was just the hint of a smile on Colonel Charles D. Rafferty's face when the mission was completed and the **G** recovered. The **N** was not expected to return on that mission since it was limited by fuel to 90 minutes flight.

"The third mission was the next day and this time the **G** didn't come home. I have a feeling that the **N** made it through, but was too limited on fuel to make it home.

"We'd done what we said we could at that meeting in Doug Steakley's office; that is, provide a decoy capability in a very limited time frame. The decoys did the job, but later the Commies were able to figure out the radar signatures of the birds and identify which was the real one.

"Some of the **N** birds also flew cover for the **J**s which had begun operating the end of March."

In August another order for 10 decoys was placed by the Air Force reportedly for use in connection with B-52 bombing raids against North Vietnam. They were designated **NX** and like the first of the **N**s were converted from basic BQM-34A target drone hardware. They were equipped with traveling wave tubes (TWTs) to make them appear like large aircraft to enemy radars. Although their primary mission was as decoys, they also carried a camera.

The first **N**s had so consistently defied the laws of probability by coming home that the parachute recovery system was reinstalled and an inexpensive low-resolution camera put in the nose compartment. Missions with the **NX** version began to be flown in November 1966.

They would fly in a general area as a confusion factor, rather than a well defined photo mission against a specific camera target. If photography came back it would be useful in a gross sense. Targets and objects maybe six feet large; trucks and things like that could be identified. One couldn't make an accurate determination as with 1-foot resolution photos, but the extra data from these decoy missions was useful even though the **N** when compared with other machines had a limited photo capability.

MAJOR JOHN DALE . . . .

. . . who proposed "a cross-eyed potted monkey as pilot of the NX," and wondered how the enemy would react to his arrival in Hanoi.

LIFE WITH THE AIR FORCE drone Squadron at OL-20 was not without its lighter moments as related by Major John Dale. Years later he recalled that "we had a cross-eyed monkey at the 'O' Club at Bien Hoa who always sat on the sand bags out front looking for a free drink. He was potted most of the time.

"My plan was to put this monkey in a flying suit (made by mama-san), place an oxygen bottle and cheap camera in the forward bay of the **NX**; launch it on a mission to Hanoi as a decoy for a **G** and command chutes over the city.

"I wonder what the Commie Intel world would have put over the wires when they found a frantic monkey with a camera peering through the glass at them!

"My boss wouldn't allow it, but we had lots of laughs over the idea."

Despite some reports that morale among Air Force troops was poor, John Dale did not agree. "We were too busy," he said, "making a 'go' of something new, and happy to be in on the beginning of a new weapon system. It was damn hard work and required you to put every bit of yourself into it. I saw no slacking off, and it was tremendously rewarding when things went as planned. From a crew-member's viewpoint, it was one of the best jobs I've ever had!"

'65 — '66

IN THE FIRST TWO YEARS of reconnaissance drone operations in Southeast Asia, more than 160 sorties had been flown against targets about which better intelligence was needed by U.S. forces. About one of six drones launched was lost to 'hostile' action or for operational reasons.

The first 70 missions, during the initial 14 months of operation, had been flown with the 147**B** models. A total of 37 **B**s were produced, of which 32 reached the OL operational location. They flew 78 missions in their life span. One bird, **B**-32, flew eight missions. Sixty-six of the **B** flights were exposed to hostile fire, and 12 were lost to enemy action. Two out of three birds launched returned to the recovery area, and most of these could be flown again.

As a follow-on to the **B**, the first of the **G**s became operational the last day of October 1965, the same time that the Air Force-modified **C**s were used on low-level sorties.

Three **E** models flew their electronic intelligence gathering missions in late '65 and early '66. The **N** decoys started their razzle dazzle flights during the Spring of 1966, and the low-altitude **J** also entered the flight inventory during the same time period. The approximate 100 missions flown during calendar year 1966 were primarily by **G**s, often accompanied by **N**s, and by the new low-level **J** model. Forty-two of the **G**s flew 83 combat sorties through mid-1967. The other 12 **G**s were modified to **J** configuration.

Dave Gossett

Teledyne Ryan Aeronautical

TO MEET REQUIREMENTS for low altitude *missions, this* ***J*** *model was developed from the big-wing* ***G*** *bird.*

Although operational use of drones was being stepped up, the "Lightning Bug" still played second fiddle to the more glamorous manned U-2s. It wasn't just a matter of prestige to the Ryan people; the Air Force personnel working on the 147 "Blue Springs" program also found themselves at a disadvantage for they were merely the 'bug' section of the U-2 wing out of Davis-Monthan.

One Air Force officer who recognized the problem and was instrumental in correcting it was Major Red Smith. After completing his 147**N** assignment and returning to SAC Headquarters at Omaha, Red was determined to do something for the military personnel assigned to the drone section, so they would receive proper professional status and pay. He drafted an appropriate staff paper to establish the Airborne Missile Maintenance Squadron (AMMS), walked it through Headquarters and got equal status with the U-2s, on a squadron basis, for the reconnaissance drones.

Smith also found that the Air Force was not adequately staffed with engineering talent — too much reliance had to be placed on contractor personnel. Other major SAC missile wings had technical engineering assistance teams attached to their organization.

Again Red 'cut the paper' which set up a Technical Engineering Assistance Division (TEAD) within the drone squadron. It authorized the Commander to have three or four professional engineers on his staff so there would be a continuing evaluation of technical problems and recommendations for their solution: Established in 1966, the TEAD capability proved invaluable in improving operational efficiency in Southeast Asia.

Although contractor personnel were becoming less involved in actual flight operations, Bob Reichardt and Dale Weaver still managed to participate in some missions as reported by Reichardt:

"Dale and I went along on the operational flight of **G**-55 on June 30, 1967. It was extremely interesting and I got some good color movies of the up-loading, the launch and of recovery of the bird. They show a tremendous capability, for the same C-130 that launched our bird also participated in its recovery.

"As we were approaching Da Nang on our return after the launch, we could see the main chute of our **G** bird floating down by itself. The MARS (mid-air retrieval system) helicopter had already snatched the bird and would have it in Da Nang by the time we landed to take it back to Bien Hoa."

One of the **G** birds was launched over Laos on a mission 'up north' despite a severe storm through which it had to fly. When contact with the bird was lost no one was greatly surprised and the drone was written off. Obviously it had crashed, would probably never be found, and was soon forgotten.

Some time later a Laotian native walked into a base where there were U. S. forces and reported he had found a crashed airplane near a jungle trail. He reported it was in pretty fair shape. An examination of all available records failed to reveal any aircraft which had not been accounted for. The native must have been confused about what he had found.

Not to be put off so easily he returned a week or so later with a part he was able to get off the plane. After much checking and rechecking someone finally established the fact it was from a 147 reconnaissance drone.

A call went out to the OL-20 drone squadron at Bien Hoa which sent Major John Dale and a maintenance sergeant, both wearing civilian clothes. They were picked up by an Air America helicopter out of Vientiane.

"A stop was made at Pak Sane," Major Dale related, "to pick up fuel and five Lao soldiers, several of whom became sick and tried to puke out of the side door as the flight progressed. Air flow deposited the used rice on me as I held one of them from falling out of the chopper.

"Several stops were made near villages before a young Lao who knew where the drone was located was found. He directed the chopper to a clearing and after landing the team walked through forest for about a mile and found the drone on top of a lightly forested knoll and the ground covered with vines.

"While I was standing on the wing, one of the Lao soldiers caught his foot on a trip wire among the vines. It broke off a nipple on a mortar shell that had been placed in the wreckage causing a loud hiss and smoke. Someone yelled 'BOMB!' and everyone ran.

"After 30 minutes, we approached the drone to retrieve a tool box and camera but the fuzed mortar shell began smoking again. The camera and tool box remained in the wreckage, which was subsequently destroyed.

"During the team's return trek to the chopper, drums were heard and the Lao soldiers broke into a run, departed the trail, and plunged through the forest with the sergeant and me close behind. The helicopter was waiting with rotor turning when we reached the clearing, as the pilots had also heard the drums.

"It seems the bad guys were waiting to ambush the team along the return trail when they did not hear their booby trap detonate."

In Major Dale's trip report he recommended that Green Berets do the job next time as that wasn't his bag. What was left of the bird wasn't worth hauling out of the jungle, so the wounded recce drone was blown up and destroyed.

LAOTIAN NATIVES finally convinced *authorities at a U.S. base that they had found an airplane when they brought in parts of a drone.*

16

BEHIND THE BAMBOO CURTAIN

CHINA AND NORTH VIETNAM understandably continued to be irritated by the overflights of the non-combat pilotless jets. Whenever possible they shot the drones down, often at the expense of giving up electronic intelligence information which enabled U. S. aircraft to operate with reduced exposure to SAM missiles.

Reports of downed Ryan drones continued to be given the world press by Peking and Hanoi. Articles and pictures describing the San Diego-built drones and their operational capability continued to appear. By the Spring of 1966, Hanoi claimed to have downed 14 drones while Peking said it had chalked up seven 'kills'. Through it all, official Washington — and the writer as spokesman for the prime contractor — kept a steady "no comment" posture which neither confirmed nor denied press reports.

Occasionally a writer got behind the Bamboo Curtain for a first-hand report.

In the spring of 1965, Lisa Hobbs, a San Francisco newspaperwoman, managed a visit to Communist China. An Australian by birth, Mrs. Hobbs arranged to join a tour group organized by the Orbit Travel Agency in her native country. On her return she wrote "I Saw Red China" in which she reported:

At my request, we stopped at the Military Museum of the Chinese People's Revolution. I wanted to see for myself the three American robot spy planes which had either crashed or been brought down over Chinese territory.

They were assembled in a central courtyard and all around the roped-off area the youth of China passed in thousands. Trucks of soldiers arrived while we were there and when we left they were still lined up waiting to see the 'proof' of American's 'aggressive intent.'

I found this a profoundly upsetting experience: in fact, when I moved in close, ducking under the roped-off area, to get a closeup of the manufacturer's nameplate engraved on a steel plaque (Ryan of San Diego), I found that my hand was shaking. The Chinese had set up white cardboard plaques with black arrows pointing to the cameras nestling in the front of the plane. Lying now, glittering sightlessly in the weak sun, they looked alien and ugly. Despite my continuing irritation at the anti-American propaganda, I left the museum thinking over what Yu [a Communist Party official — Ed.] had said the previous day, and wondering how it would feel if several Russian or Chinese-built planes crashed in the Midwest.

Back in the bus — a couple of the Australians had refused to come in because they said it was all 'propaganda' — a lively discussion on the use of spy planes followed.

Ironically enough, Mrs. Chia [interpreter — Ed.] expressed my thoughts when she said with no little disgust:

"How would the rest of the world like it if we sent spy planes up over their countries?"

Paul Morawetz, the Australian economist, said it was foolish to adopt a moral attitude about it, that the spy planes were simply an improvement on the old trench-coat method of spying.

"All countries have spies," he said.

"We don't have one spy plane up," said Mrs. Chia.

"Because you don't own one," said Morawetz.

"Oh!" said Mrs. Chia, her breath expulsed in a flash of anger. I felt that if she had been French she would have hit Morawetz on the head with her umbrella. Instead, she just stomped it on the floor."

————

In April, 1966, Frank Touhy, a British newspaperman visiting China, filed a story datelined Hangchow for Associated Press. It read, in part:

Large groups were being harangued in the museum of the Chinese Revolution in Peking. In the courtyard of the military museum, children lined up on a freezing day to inspect the reassembled wreckage of a U-2 and several pilotless spy planes.

A plump girl soldier with braids pointed to the trade

name: Ryan Aeronautical Co., San Diego, California, Model BQM-34A. Ser. 64-14875, produced 11 August 1964.

"This is proof of American aggression against China," she said.

The bringing down of yet another U. S. pilotless spy plane, two days after my arrival, was treated as part of a regular series of booster-shots for public morale.

How genuine is all this propaganda? Is it for war or just for increased productivity?

Harrison E. Salisbury, an assistant managing editor of the New York Times was one of two American newspapermen permitted by Hanoi to visit North Vietnam during Christmas week, 1966. His report, in part:

The alert yesterday (at 2:25 p.m.) was only six or seven minutes long. It was caused, the authorities said, by the appearance of a pilotless American reconnaissance craft near the city.

The three tremendous blasts [after which an air raid siren caused Salisbury and other guests in the hotel to seek shelter — Ed.] presumably were SAM surface-to-air missiles. The same kind of robot plane, it was disclosed, caused Hanoi's Christmas alert at almost the same hour.

Today the foreign press corps was taken to see where the drone that appeared on Christmas was shot down.

The drone downed on Christmas Day fell 12 or 13 miles northeast of the city in the Tienson district of Habac Province. It proved to be a Ryan model with a wingspread of about 18 feet that the Americans call the Firebee.

The wing and fuselage, somewhat crumpled, lay in a pile. Eight or nine girls dug in about seven feet deep for the engine, which was gradually being recovered.

The robot plane, which was shot down adjacent to the main rail line linking Hanoi to China, presumably had been dispatched to transmit photographic intelligence on rail conditions and traffic movement. According to the girls digging out the engine, the drone was at an altitude of only about a mile when downed.

HONG KONG HAS LONG held a unique position in Southeast Asia. Although dependent upon mainland China for its water supply and much of its food, the Communists have found it convenient to not disturb the status quo of Hong Kong which provides an important commercial meeting place for East and West.

Because of its unusual economic/political role, Hong Kong also became a center of intelligence activities, more prosaically called spying, agents often working as a exchange place for both sides.

Edward Neilan, writing for Copley News Service in May 1966, filed a dispatch which included these comments:

Wide World Photos

"CRAZY LEGS," 147B-23, shot down April 3, 1965 *got plenty of attention and this news photo when displayed at Peking Museum the following year.*

How can the United States, which is barred entry to Red China, know what is about to take place inside the mainland's supersecret facilities?

These questions stir the public imagination as it waits for the third Chinese (A-bomb) detonation. Peking's first blast was on Oct. 16, 1964; its second in May, 1965.

Overflights by pilotless drone aircraft equipped with cameras have proved one of the most effective ways of gathering this type of information.

The Communist Chinese usually refrain from mentioning these drone flights except when one of them is shot down. Some half-dozen have been shot down over the mainland, according to Peking. From time to time photographs of the wreckage appear in the Peking Review and other Communist publications available here.

The drones — the most common type used is the Firebee, manufactured by Ryan Aeronautical of San Diego, Calif. — are launched from under the wings of C-123 transport planes [actually C-130 — Ed]. These planes take off from airfields in South Vietnam, Thailand, South Korea, Okinawa and Formosa. The drones are electronically guided.

One of their best qualities is that by being remote-controlled the United States is saved the embarrassment of a pilot being captured if the craft is shot down.

Another advanced intelligence tool is the network of supersensitive listening devices around the rim of Red China.

Some of these are land-based in the Philippines, Laos, Thailand, Vietnam, Okinawa, Formosa (and the Quemoy-Matsu offshore islands), and South Korea.

Similar equipment is aboard aircraft and Navy ships on patrol off the coast.

These sensitive snooping devices record such seemingly innocuous details as how many telephone calls are made into a certain command headquarters or city, fluctuations in electric power generated at a specific point and similar facts. These figures can be projected and analyzed giving an indication of increased activity in certain areas.

In some cases actual telephone and radio conversations on the mainland of Communist China are monitored from hundreds of miles away.

Information gained from these electronic devices is pooled with word-of-mouth reports from old-fashioned spies, agents, travelers, diplomats and published items. Sometimes even the Communist Chinese press itself gives valuable clues that can be pieced together.

Smaller provincial newspapers especially are of use when they report items that give hints as to movements of personnel, storing of food for troops and other details.

For this reason, there is a regular traffic here in Hong Kong of certain newspapers and publications smuggled from the Chinese mainland.

The buyers are both the obvious research institutions and also the undercover intelligence agencies of many nationalities that abound here.

〔左〕撃墜されたアメリカの無人偵察機。完全な姿ではないが、どうやら、ターボジェット推進のBQM-34Aファイアビーの特殊偵察型のようである。1965年5月に中国領土内で撃墜されて問題になったのも、南ベトナムを基地としているC-130から発進したこの特殊偵察型であった。この無人機は超低空をものすごいスピードで進攻するという。

THIS 147J LOW-ALTITUDE bird never made it home. *Instead of returning with pictures, it had its own photo taken, upside down, for appearance in Japanese Koku Fan magazine.*

WE ONCE ASKED Colonel Bill Forehand how it was that he seemed to have so much information about what took place on individual drone flights in North Vietnam and over South China.

"The information filters back one way or the other," Forehand explained. "Our intelligence people get it sorted out somehow. The Chinese watchers and listeners in Hong Kong listen to the scuttlebutt that comes across the border. They made a profession out of seeing just what the tone is in China; and they feed the information in the opposite direction, too."

New York-based newspapermen and newsmagazine writers continued (unsuccessfully) to try and pry details out of Ryan Aeronautical Company which pretty well had all inquiries channeled through a single spokesman to reduce the possibility of an inadvertant admission of its role. It took a bit of fancy footwork but the company avoided the pitfall of admission which goes with the "that's a secret project and we can't talk about it" type of answer.

TRUTH MAY BE STRANGER than fiction. Yet, occasionally, fiction is used as a medium through which one hints at a truth still cloaked in official secrecy.

In 1966 an English novel, "Tree Frog", began circulating in the United States. Its author was Martin Woodhouse, an R.A.F. pilot and medical researcher who had designed pure logic computers and done research on high-altitude physiology.

The spy thriller centered around an experimental pilotless reconnaissance drone aircraft, the T. F. Mark 2 (Tree Frog) whose design was based in part on the Jindivik target training drone, the Australian competitor of the Ryan Firebee. The fictional Tree Frog was powered by a French Turbomeca Marbore jet engine, a development of which was also used in the Firebee.

17

PROLIFERATION

IN 1967, THINGS REALLY began 'flying' with more sorties over North Vietnam and Communist China than in the previous two-and-a-half years. The low-altitude **J**s accounted for more flights than any other single model but high-altitude missions with the **G** and **H**, often accompanied by the **NX** series decoys, made up the bulk of operations.

Another new vehicle, the mass-produced low-level 147**S** model, came into the inventory in midyear with 13 missions flown in December 1967, its first month of operation. New versions of the basic **N** were also being developed and flown — **NP, NRE** and **NQ.**

This proliferation of models, each for a special purpose, each with special equipment and operating techniques unique to that version, raised anew some personnel problems. It was clear to see that reliability was dependent more upon maintenance than upon in-flight factors once the bird was launched on its mission.

Eventually 39 of the 147**J**s were built for the Air Force including the 12 which had been reconfigured from the production **G** models. Between March 1966 and November 1967, the **J**s flew 94 operational sorties and proved to be one of the most remarkable SPA of the 147 series. As a low-altitude bird, the big wing taken from the **G** model did not make the **J** too efficient but it did field a capability the fastest way it could be done.

Using the BLACS for low-level altitude control and two cameras, one scanning fore and aft and the other side to side, remarkable intelligence results were achieved. One photo sequence taken by the bird itself showed a SAM missile firing at — and missing — **J**-14. The primary **J** mission was to fly below the overcast, during the rainy season, over North Vietnam.

Reliability at launch, over the target, and on recovery set new standards. Surprisingly, too, even the drones' photo magazines were intact in almost every case where the bird had been severely damaged on impact at recovery.

The low-altitude day photo **J**s had 61 good returns to base in the 94 missions flown, for a 65% success rate. One **J** completed nine missions.

THE H BIRDS

IN MANY WAYS the new, more sophisticated, **H** bird was the 'white hope' of the drone program. Operational results of the **B**, and later the **G**, had demonstrated that higher altitude greatly improved survivability, and that mission effectiveness improved with increased range.

With the **H**, the Air Force was thinking in terms of a mid-route altitude above 65,000 feet and a fuel-out altitude of nearly 70,000 feet. This required new aerodynamic approaches as well as modification of the T-41A version of the J69 jet engine to maintain effective thrust at altitude.

Reduction in airframe weight was a necessary design requirement, and to achieve the longer operational range the **H** would be the first SPA (special purpose aircraft) with a wet wing — one that carried fuel internally in the wing, as well as in the fuselage. This would bring the range to in excess of 2400 miles. The C-130 launch plane would, of course, fly the captive drone north from Bien Hoa, extending the total mission range by several hundred miles.

Since neither speed, altitude nor range by themselves guaranteed survivability over enemy territory, several other innovations would be tried. These included:

Rivet Bounder — A sophisticated electronic countermeasure device to jam the SA-2 missile guidance system.

HIDE — High Absorbency Integrated Defense against electronic warfare, installed in the air inlet duct to reduce radar reflectivity while in a hostile environment.

HEMP — H Evasive Maneuver Program designed to give the drone the ability to evade high altitude interception and destruction by manned aircraft. When triggered by airborne radar as carried on MiG aircraft, HEMP would make programmed turns to elude the attacking aircraft.

Dave Gossett

FOUR BIRDS OF A FEATHER — all 147 recce drones, on the ramp at Bien Hoa, *with their DC-130 launch plane in the background. Clockwise from the left: 147**J**, the first low-altitude day mission bird;* ***H** model high-altitude drone with extended range; 147**G**, a basic **B** model but with larger engine; and the **NX** decoy and medium-altitude day photo plane. (February 1967)*

Dave Gossett

'WHITE HOPE' of the drone program *was the new, more sophisticated H model with improved high-altitude performance.*

HAT-RAC — High Altitude Threat, Recognition and Counter-measures. An evolutionary outgrowth of HEMP enabling the H to dodge and turn when the system is alarmed by either airborne intercept radar or ground controlled missile track-while-scan radars.

CRL (Cambridge Research Labs) — A contrail suppression system to lessen visual detection at specific altitudes.

The **H** also carried a new Hycon camera designed to scan an area some 780 nautical miles long and 22 miles wide, and give better resolution at mission altitude.

DALE WEAVER WAS BACK at the OL to help field the 147**S** and to observe the **H** model, the introduction of which had been complicated by the fact that "we've got 16 vehicles over here now with nine different configurations.

"The **H** was giving us some problems particularly with the modified T-41A engine because of the maximum altitude performance we were asking of the bird. The RPM just did not come up to the required speed, remaining in the launch RPM mode setting. Attempts were made by MCGS (microwave command guidance system) to command an RPM increase, so it appeared we were having a throttle actuator problem.

"Too, we've had problems with engine oil, airspeed calibration, temperatures as low as -80°C at 65,000 feet, engine starting, and contaminated fuels."

The **H** program in the end probably had more hardware problems than any of the 147 birds.

OPERATIONAL PROBLEMS weren't the only source of uneasiness at Bien Hoa. Things with the ground war weren't going too well and the Bien Hoa-Saigon area was in the midst of the heat of battle.

It was bad enough in 1968 that the United States was humiliated January 22nd by the capture of Comdr. Lloyd Bucher's USS *"Pueblo"* which was on Elint patrol off North Korea as an electronic scavenger, scooping up every electronic signal for miles around. Adding insult to injury, the Viet Cong and North Vietnamese broke the New Year's holiday "Tet" truce and launched the most vigorous attacks yet against Saigon.

A major attempt was made to cut the vital ground link between Saigon and Bien Hoa as part of the widespread Tet offensive which was combined with heavy mortar and rocket attacks on Tan Son Nhut, the terminal for Saigon commercial air traffic.

The Pueblo incident, of course, caught the U. S. off balance. How to respond, and how to learn more about the fate of the eavesdropper and its crew?

Manned aircraft could be used for reconnaissance, but the added risks of additional prisoners were all too obvious if one of the planes was shot down. Why not use the 147 capability?

The drone squadron at OL-20 was tasked to deploy to Osan, South Korea, standing by there for the word to undertake the mission. Ryan tech reps were left behind; this was to be strictly a military operation with additional support coming from Davis-Monthan in the States. While primed and ready at Osan, the 'go' order never came and after a month the unit and its **S** birds returned to Bien Hoa.

"Like many other proposed solutions to the Pueblo incident," recalls tech rep Jeff Grady, "the flights were never flown so far as I know. For one thing it would have been a pretty involved operation requiring a good CAP (combat air patrol) cover as the North Koreans were expected to counter if we overflew their boundaries. No civilian technicians went along with the detachment so we don't have positive knowledge as the whole assignment was kept pretty quiet."

Major Red Smith found himself caught up in one phase of the Pueblo incident. The **S** bird was having technical flight problems and Red was on his way to OL-20 to meet Dale Weaver for a personal review. He had insisted that the company make Weaver available because he had worked with him on the 147**N** and was familiar with Dale's expertise.

Just before departure from Travis Air Force Base in California, Smith was called on the p.a. system. "Word had just come in that the Pueblo had been seized. I was told I was the senior officer on the flight holding a top secret clearance and that I was to be the official courier.

"I assumed I'd be responsible for a small package of data but soon found that half the plane load was cryptographic data being sent in a panic to Southeast Asia to replace crypto tapes throughout the Pacific theater because the Pueblo seizure had undoubtedly compromised those which had been in use."

War always brings its off-beat events and one such incident caught up with a subcontractor's tech rep responsible for the Rivet Bounder missile jamming device. Due to a family emergency at home, his company granted him emergency leave to fly back to the States.

The first commercial jet available to Europe and thence home was an Air France schedule and the rep booked passage hardly bothering to check the route. France, despite the disaster of Dien Bien Phu fourteen years earlier, was on good terms with North Vietnam and Air France held landing rights in that country.

JUST BACK FROM A LOW-ALTITUDE MISSION, a J bird *is picked up at DaNang to be placed on the rails of its DC-130 and flown back to Bien Hoa.*

Ed Christian

Imagine, then, how Mr. Tech Rep must have felt to find himself, a bonafide U. S. passport-carrying technician supporting the secret reconnaissance program, landing at Hanoi! Fortunately he was not required to enter the in-transit area where his passport might have been checked. He was able to remain aboard until takeoff.

The writer well recalls his own vacation visit to Southeast Asia in May 1969, flying along the coast of South Vietnam with Da Nang Air Base just off our right wing tip, then over CamRanh Bay and the Mekong Delta en route to Hong Kong on Malaysia Singapore Airlines. Later, aboard a French Caravelle transport of Thai International Airlines out of Bangkok we flew the commercial air corridor high above the ground war going on below as we crossed Cambodia, Laos and South Vietnam on the way back to Hong Kong. Everyone recognized the need for continued commercial air service and there was never any interference with such flights.

FIRST HAND REPORTS of fighting during the Tet offensive of 1968 reached San Diego from Dale Weaver via the secure, suburban post office box number -

"The VC decided to celebrate the 'Year of the Monkey' by hitting us with rockets and mortars. Enclosed are three solid state pieces [shrapnel — Ed.] from a 122-mm. rocket which should be sufficient justification for the 50% bonus.

"The attack started a little after 3 a.m. on the morning of January 31st. Our unit had received word the previous afternoon that the four birds launched that day — two **H** high-altitude drones and two low-level **SA** birds — had been successfully retrieved in midair by MARS choppers at Da Nang at the end of the missions before the base there was put on Red Alert.

"The base here at Bien Hoa has been on Red Alert since the evening of the 30th, and there is still a lively firefight going on at the east end of the field inside the perimeter. This is still a spectator's war and it is easy to watch from the hangar since it's only about a mile to the fighting. I guess they have a small group of infiltrators trapped down there.

"I was up until 2 a.m. talking with crews that had successfully launched the first double-double mission. Despite the precautionary alert, because Saigon and Da Nang had been attacked earlier, I went to bed completely confident. I even had my flight suit in my locker, and no socks on.

"When the first round hit, I made it from hut 241 to the bunker between huts 239 and 240 without getting my feet dirty! The next 122-mm. rocket hit just across the road in a Vietnamese Air Force training compound about 25 yards away. Those rockets are something else!

"One of the men in 239 was wounded by fragments. The concussion in the bunker was enough to make your teeth rattle. The barrage didn't last long and I had a chance to get into my flight suit. It looked like the SAC compound might be on fire so I took off for there. Although there was some damage I found the whole gang still huddled in their bunker and all in good shape.

"I managed to borrow a .38 special from McBratney and went back to check on the rest of our Ryan group. Lloyd Palmer and Jeff Grady called in from the flight line to report that when a plane blew up one of its 500-lb. bombs also exploded and fragments hit our DC-130, putting some pretty big holes in it.

"Total count for the night was 23 rounds of 122-mm. rocket fire and 54 rounds of 81-mm. mortar. Infiltrators were spotted immediately after the barrage and one hell of a fight broke out down by the main gate and the east end of the field."

Four days later Weaver reported that "Things are starting to return to normal after the grand and glorious New Year celebration. There is still quite a bit of fighting in Saigon but most of the cleanup around here is over; at least for the time being.

"The casualties as a result of the rockets, mortars and infiltration were four killed in action, one heart attack, 19 wounded by enemy action and 79 'panic' wounds. The VC lost 60 KIA [killed in action] and 24 captured. But the word is that the VC are going to hit the base again soon.

"Shortly after that one of the bunkers took a direct hit from a 122-mm. rocket, killing one of the Air Force drone maintenance people and injuring another. Fortunately none of the Ryan people were hit. However, Gene Raymond, one of the Ryan types was responsible for digging one of our friends out of the debris. Gene knew the Air Force men in there and went in right after the blast to get him out."

Red Smith who had flown out to meet Dale Weaver and help on the problems with the **S** bird, only to run into the Tet offensive, was loud in his praise of the drone personnel, both uniformed and civilian.

"Night after night," he recalled, "throughout this barrage which lasted for 18 days, Air Force and company people were subjected to what I would call intense bombardment. Not once did anyone connected with the drone program show any sign of stress or failure to perform his duty in carrying out our reconnaissance missions. As soon as the field at Bien Hoa was declared operational we were ready and able to launch the drones on schedule.

"Everyone withstood the pressures of that very intense wartime experience very well. I am proud of the way our people responded. Dale and Gene Raymond, and other Ryan people, were diligent in carrying out their responsibilities, working endless hours without sleep through the bombardment and ground attacks.

"They carried on and succeeded in getting the turn problems with the 147S corrected and the bird flying well again within a matter of weeks."

Ed Christian

RESPITE FROM VIET CONG attacks during Tet offensive, *including destruction of F-100 fighter aircraft, above, could be found at Rosie's Bar.*

Ed Christian

MINIMUM MOD; LOW COST

"EARLY IN 1967," Bob Reichardt recalled, "it became obvious that low-level reconnaissance missions were proving very productive. The Air Force was concerned that this capability might be lost between the time the last **J** would be expended and the first recently ordered **S** models come off the line and get into action. So they gave us another QRC (quick reaction capability) contract to produce a dozen birds to do the job.

"With their high-resolution photo capability, they became another version of the **N**, designated **NP**. It meant going back, essentially, to the original 147**A** adaptation — a BQM wing mounted on a stretched out BQM fuselage. All our **N**s were based on one design philosophy: minimum modification and low cost."

Before the **NP** birds were completed, yet another requirement came up.

The very effective U. S. tactical air strikes of the previous Fall had forced the North Vietnamese to a much higher level of nighttime troop and support activity.

Could this activity be photographed with an unmanned vehicle?

To find the answer, four of the **NP** low-altitude day photo drones were diverted from the production line to be modified into **NRE** night birds.

The **NRE** (night reconnaissance-electronic) camera system consisted of two cameras sequenced with an alternately flashing light mounted in the belly of the bird. No effort was to be made to conduct covert flights.

Ed Christian was a camera 'scorer' expert and photo interpreter from a Marine Corps Photo Squadron who had joined Ryan early in 1966. When it came time to develop the night photography capability, Ed's experience in camera systems was called upon:

"We had two of our four **NRE**s in flight test up at Pt. Mugu. Most of the work had to be done with the drone captive on the launch rack because we were worried about letting the bird go out at night by itself since we didn't really have a night recovery system.

"There were two Russian 'fishing' boats' — probably electronic picket ship eavesdroppers — in the area at that time. They kept most of their gear covered up by day so their equipment couldn't be seen and analyzed. On one of our night test flights we flew over with a captive **NRE** and decided to exercise the bird's night photo system. The Navy kept the 'take' but I heard they got some useful information out of our unscheduled mission.

"Finally we decided to launch one of the **NRE**s about 4:30 in the morning to fly over San Nicholas Island in the Santa Barbara Channel to see what photo results we could get. We recovered the drone by the dawn's early light and the results were quite good considering it was a very compact electronic flash system that had never been tried before. It was strictly state-of-the-art with a white light system which meant that it was going to be very visible to the 'enemy'.

"The tests were sufficiently encouraging for the Air Force to decide to take all four birds and go overseas with the capability immediately. So in May of '67 I found myself at Davis-Monthan packing the birds and support gear. Three days later we were in Bien Hoa.

"I went as a civilian courier with the C-141, two birds and the only box of suitable film in existence at the time. The film was very sensitive to heat and that almost became our undoing. Its loss or damage would spoil all our chances for the **NRE** so we really hovered over that box of film to keep it out of the sun at the expense of almost everything else.

"From Davis-Monthan we made a refueling stop at Midway Island, then on to Clark Field in the Philippines. There we developed engine trouble and I soon found I was in charge of a C-141 and everything on it. I asked the pilot to call the tower to tell them we had a classified load on board and would require 24-hour guard service. So now I've also got this idiot box of film that we can't let sit there in the 120 degree heat. We had to hike half a mile across the flight line with it; and then no one has a refrigerator where we can store the stuff. Finally the security guards tell me they have a refrigerator that's half full of beer.

"Well, I need all the space in that refrigerator for my film so I have to buy all the beer. With the film safely on ice there was nothing to do but help the guards consume the beer.

"About nine o'clock that night, after 14 hours at Clark Field, the C-141 is packed up and we're ready to go. Now, with my precious film tucked under my

Teledyne Ryan Aeronautical

QUICK REACTION CAPABILITY of Ryan factory *workers, like this crew which built the **NP** birds, made it possible to meet changing requirements in the field.*

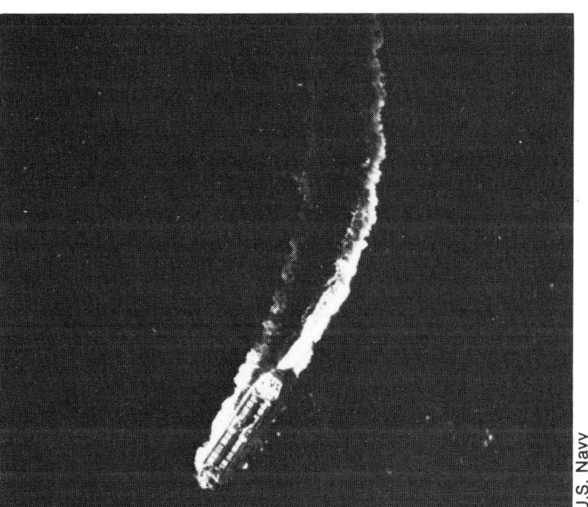

U.S. Navy

RUSSIAN 'TRAWLER' is photographed off the coast *of Southern California by the night photo system of the **NRE** (night reconnaissance-electronic).*

Dave Gossett

DEBRIEFING OF FLIGHT CREWS and maintenance people *followed every mission at OL-20. Photo taken in February 1967 when Col. Harvey B. Logan was CO.*

arm, I discover for the first time I don't have a piece of paper to identify myself so I can get back on *my* airplane.

"There'd been a crew change and they didn't know me from Adam. This led to a 15 minute argument by which time the aircraft commander announced he was taking off. Just then the guard turned to move away and I boarded the plane.

"We got into Bien Hoa about three o'clock in the morning. It was one of the most miserable days in my life. I had no idea where I was or what I was getting into. Nat Summers, the Ryan Rep. met me at the flight line and we signed the load of drones and equipment over to the Air Force.

"Nat got us into one of those little hutches for the rest of the night and we ended up sleeping in the same clothes we had been in for three days.

"We had a real rush to get one of the **NRE** missions off. Apparently they had something they wanted to look at real bad. We took both night photo birds down to the flight line and started putting them together. Meantime there's the little old problem of getting passport and visa squared away in Saigon because, technically, civilians can't come in on an Air Force plane and land at a military base.

"In a couple of days we had the first **NRE** put together but then got into all kinds of trouble because the high voltage lines in the bird weren't sealed, so they got moisture in them from that terribly humid climate. As soon as we would hit the 'operate' switch one of the cables would explode just like a shot.

"It looked like we would have to postpone all our effort until we could get new cables from the States, and that would be a matter of weeks. So we hunted around in other units' hangars and found some co-ax cable in F-100 Maintenance which was sealed, and good for high voltage, so we borrowed 50 feet and began making our own for the four birds.

"We were putting new cables in **NRE**-1 at 2 a.m. on May 17th when all hell broke loose with a big bang. It wasn't the cables exploding this time; it was Viet Cong mortars. Bien Hoa really got a terrible raking over that night. However, all our hangar got was a good shower of shrapnel and rocks.

"When the next mortar came in I was out from underneath the bird I was working on right now and decided that the 'head' offered the most protection. In no time I was on the floor wedged between the toilet bowl and the cement wall; then everyone else arrived with the same thought in mind. It sure got crowded behind that toilet bowl!

"During a lull in the attack we decided a better place for all of us was in the nearest bunker — a quarter of a mile away. The only trouble was there was a 12-foot wide ditch, full of barbed wire, between the hangar and the bunker. We were so inspired to get to the bunker that not one of us hit it going through! Then we found that Nat Summers was missing, so it was back through the barbed wire and ditch for me.

"I found Nat in the hangar underneath a heavy work bench. So back across the barbed wire we went and this time I got hooked good. We watched the counter-attack the remainder of the night from the bunker. It was a pretty good show. In all some 115 mortar rounds came in during a 15-minute period.

"At five o'clock we went on back to the flight line and en route there looked over the ditch through which we'd been running a couple of hours earlier. We found a huge hole with a 122 mm. rocket that hadn't gone off embedded right where we'd been going back and forth across this damn thing during the night.

"Finally on May 25, 1967 we got off our first flight with **NRE**-1 but it proved a rather sad occasion because it never came back. We never found out what happened.

"We'd plan a mission for the terrain clearance and ground speed we assumed we'd be flying; then set the strobe lights accordingly. Flying at 1200 feet terrain, for example, we'd program the electronic flash at the rate of one every second. No one on the ground could see the bird but the flashes were a great attention getter. And if you were flying in a cloud you really illuminated the whole cloud."

Dave Gossett

WITH G AND H BIRDS on the launch racks, *the DC-130 heads out from Bien Hoa on a mission to be flown 'up north' by the reconnaissance drones.*

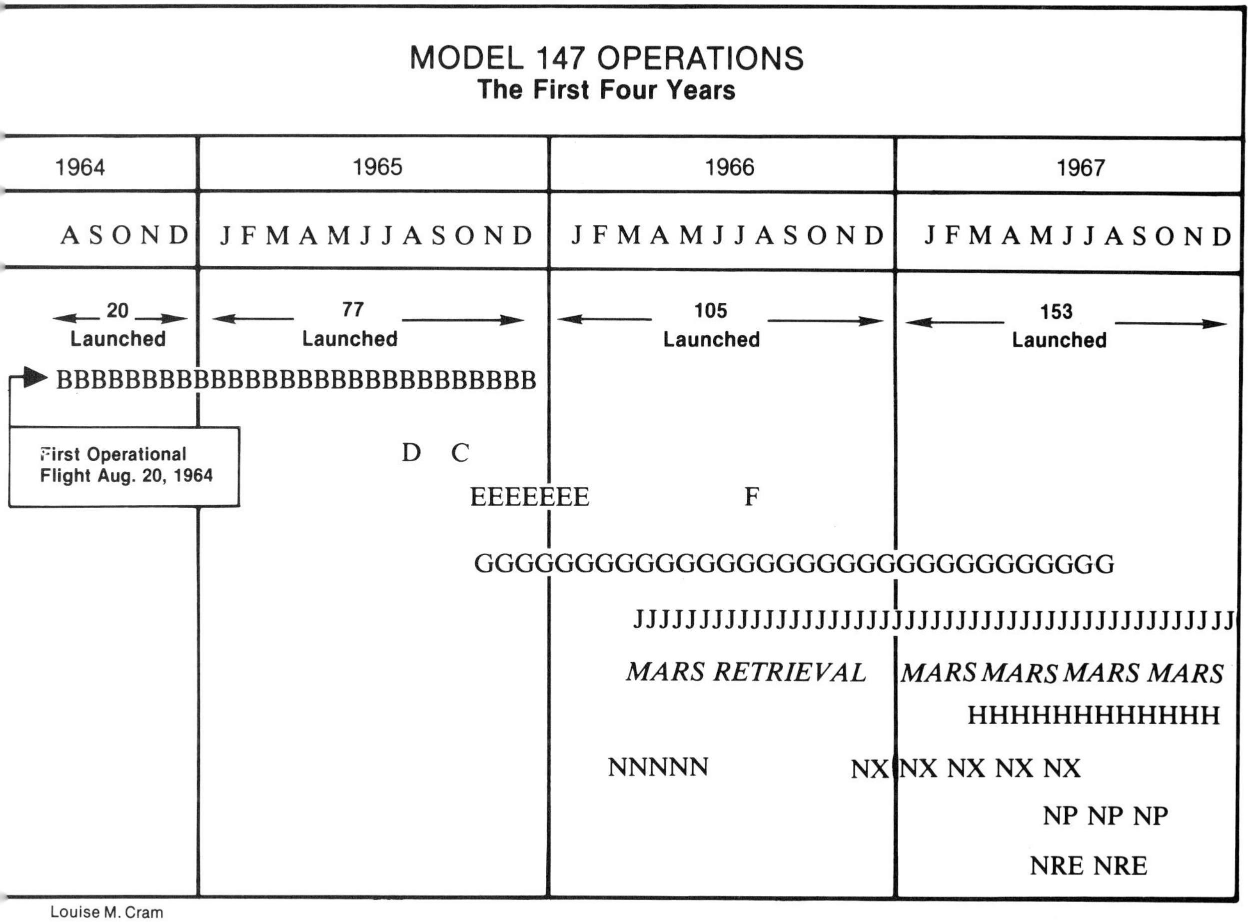

MODEL 147 OPERATIONS
The First Four Years

1964	1965	1966	1967
A S O N D	J F M A M J J A S O N D	J F M A M J J A S O N D	J F M A M J J A S O N D
← 20 → Launched	← 77 → Launched	← 105 → Launched	← 153 → Launched
BBBBBBBB	BBBBBBBBBBBBBBBBBBBBBB		
First Operational Flight Aug. 20, 1964	D C		
	EEEEE	EE F	
	GGG	GGGGGGGGGGGGGGGGGGGGG	GGGGGGGGGGG
		JJJJJJJJJJJJJJJJJJJJJ	JJJJJJJJJJJJJJJJJJJJJJJJJJJJ
		MARS RETRIEVAL	*MARS MARS MARS MARS*
			HHHHHHHHHHHH
		NNNNN NX	NX NX NX NX
			NP NP NP
			NRE NRE

Louise M. Cram

18

A CHRISTIAN IN THE JUNGLE

"ON JUNE 5, (1967) we got off a good one with **NRE**-2 which was launched right up by Haiphong," Ed Christian related.

"On this mission I flew into Da Nang in the launch plane but got off to watch the whole flight on radar plot, and to be there for the recovery.

"The chopper for the early morning mid-air retrieval of the drone, after the flight over the target area, never got a chance at the bird. Apparently the main chute separated on deployment so the drone came down in a remote area on a load line, drag chute and the chopper engagement chute.

"The first we knew about potential loss of the bird was when the radio came on with 'I just saw a bird with a drag chute going by, and the main chute is floating down on the other side'.

"The engagement chute caught the top of the trees. It stretched out and let the bird down quite gently in the trees. They marked the spot as best they could; then with the additional light after dawn the choppers came back and found the engagement chute which marked the location of the bird in the mountains way up north of Da Nang. There in the jungle was the **NRE**, all intact.

"Now that we knew where the bird had impacted, I told the OL commander that I wanted that drone — real bad. He said, 'I want it, too, but I don't know how to get it,' and I replied that 'I'll get the damn thing if you'll let me.'

"He hemmed and hawed about it for ten minutes, and having thought the thing through, went out and asked for volunteers, but none were forthcoming. He came back and asked, 'Hey, are you still serious about it?' I told him yes, that I wanted the bird more than anything else. His reply was that 'if you're volunteering, off we go!'

"We refueled one of the CH-3 choppers and got an explosive ordnance disposal (EOD) team from the Air Force on board. They would take care of blowing up the bird if necessary, so it wouldn't fall into enemy hands. I borrowed the Colonel's sidearm and an M-16 rifle and went off to play hero.

ED CHRISTIAN, Ryan camera systems and photo *interpretation expert told the OL commander "I'll get the damn drone if you'll let me."*

"It was a good 40 minutes north of Da Nang, way up in the mountains, where we spotted the engagement chute hung out and the **NRE** buried way down in the jungle. We were to have had Marine gunship coverage but they were nowhere around; however, moving up the side of the mountain was a whole group of soldiers — apparently Viet Cong — there to get the bird before we could get to it.

"While the chopper hovered, I was let down a line from the winch into the jungle to salvage the scorer and what else we could. An axe in one hand, the M-16 on one shoulder, and trying to hang on to the 'horse collar' the best I could with the other hand I was probably a sad looking sight as I finally disappeared into the jungle growth.

"I found myself 15 feet from the bird in elephant saw grass higher than a person and the usual undergrowth and vines. Right off, I found I couldn't move. On the steep hill, I couldn't go up and I couldn't go down. I'd have to work my way across to the **NRE** by pushing the axe and M-16 in front of me, then pick my feet up as high as possible and push forward and down over the trampled jungle growth.

"When that elephant grass touches you, it's just like a razor blade. The sleeves of my flight suit had pushed half-way up my arms and were cut to shreds. I tried to wipe the blood from my hands, arms and face but made a bloody mess of everything. Finally I got to the bird.

"It wasn't in too bad shape. There were dents in the wing leading edge where it hit tree branches and the wing tips were broken off. My real interest was of course the film in the scorer, so with axe in hand I proceeded to chop into the fiberglass cover. Both rolls of film were recovered out of each camera and sent up the winch line to the chopper.

"By now I'm getting interested in those Viet Cong uniforms I know must be coming up the mountain to visit me, so I try and motion the chopper away since I can't hear a damn thing with them right overhead. Also, I have a hearing problem which adds to the rather uncomfortable situation. The chopper doesn't get the message; they just decide to sit there; but they don't send the winch line down either.

"Because they have the EOD team aboard I assume they are going to send them down to destroy the **NRE**. Later I found out they think they can recover the bird but not knowing this I'm busy seeing how I can punch a hole in the fuel tanks to set the bird on fire. Then I destroy the cameras by shooting through them with the M-16 rifle.

"Just then the chopper leaves and we have nothing but dead silence. Here's Ed Christian all alone in the jungle — and what I can hear now that the whirlybird is gone is not very comforting. Then two Marine gunships show up and start circling around trying to locate my 'friends.' I tried to motion them away; I didn't like the idea of them pinpointing my location, but they thought my waving was a cheery hello so they just buzzed around a bit closer.

"Now the second support chopper — the regular recovery chopper — comes cruising in with its load line down and then it dawns on me the first one had to leave because it was about out of fuel.

"I get the message that they want to recover the bird so I grab the line and hook it to the chute bridle and give them the signal to hoist away. I wasn't so smart.

"Dumb me, I'm on the downhill side instead of uphill. When they lifted the bird, all the fuel comes pouring out of it — a good 40 gallons. The downdraft of the chopper blades gave me a fuel bath the like of which you've never seen. Then the chopper romps off with the **NRE** dangling beneath it and again I'm alone in the jungle.

"Within five minutes the first chopper reappears after refueling and sends the horse collar down for me.

"We left in a hurry just as other people were arriving on the scene to the accompaniment of bullets coming from the Marine gunships just down the hill from me. In fact we exited so fast we had a hundred feet of jungle to go through with me still dangling from the winch line before we were free of the tops of the trees. When we landed at Da Nang both fuel warning lights were on, so we just barely had enough to get back.

Christi De Lacey

Ed Christian

SAFE-CONDUCT PASS which Ed Christian carried *would not have been of much help as the Viet Cong were coming up the mountain to visit him.*

"The rest of the morning was spent getting the **NRE** apart and stuffed into the C-130 for the flight back to base, but we were going into Tan Son Nhut at Saigon this time instead of Bien Hoa. We fired up for takeoff but one engine wouldn't start so the plane commander decided not to tell the tower it wasn't running. He just let it windmill and off we went into the wild blue yonder. Only trouble was we lost another engine in flight but we didn't tell Tan Son Nhut either, so we landed with two engines running and two windmilling.

"One of my reasons for being at Tan Son Nhut was that ours was a special new photographic system. It required different handling and there were few people who knew anything about it, so I had delegated myself some days earlier to get involved with the 12th RITS (reconnaissance intelligence technical section) showing them how to process and interpret the film.

"I deplaned with the film and what was left of the cameras and went on into the 12th RITS which would process the film for us. I can't tell you now what it was we were after but the photo interpretation confirmed that we covered it!

"June 5th was a long, long day."

NOT LONG AFTER his venture into the jungle, Ed Christian had an even more electrifying experience.

"I had gone up to the main ramp at Bien Hoa on a bicycle to await arrival of a C-141 coming in with new birds from the States. We had been up there perhaps 20 minutes and were watching a tropical thunderstorm coming up from the other end of the runway. Bolts of lightning were stitching their way across the field like a giant sewing machine moving toward us.

"Suddenly, without any further warning, my whole body stiffened from some giant electrical shock and I literally lit up like a Christmas tree. The sensation was like getting hold of a 440-volt line. Sparks jumped between my stiffened, outstretched fingers. A blue halo of electrical energy glowed about an inch away all along my arms. A blue glow and sparks came off my shoes into the ground.

"A dozen yards away the shouldered rifle of a guard acted as a lightning rod and drew a larger bolt. One big spark and he keeled over. Incinerated by the giant electrical charge, he died instantly.

"The guard and I were the two tallest objects protruding into the sky and acted as natural lightning rods. Except for the momentary electric shock and subsequent shock reaction, I was unhurt, largely because the rubber tires of the bicycle on which I was resting provided some insulation as the electrical energy grounded.

"That was enough of high-voltage electricity for me. I don't go out into storms anymore for anybody!"

But there was more to come.

"Charlie — the VC — was playing games around Bien Hoa all the time and we never knew what to expect next. One evening about 7:30 I was lying on my bunk when a terrible explosion went off. The whole hut lifted up a foot or so off the ground and then settled back. We ran outside to see the bomb dump at the south end of the field, about two miles away, going up. Just then the second huge blast went off. That's the one that converted the Officers Club into a shambles.

"More bombs continued to go off — until four o'clock in the morning. One of them was all tear gas. A huge cloud of the stuff floated up above the base and just hung there. The irritating part of it — pardon the pun — was that they issued gas masks to all the guards and military police, and everybody else had to shift for themselves.

"Operations on the flight line, of course, had to be called off because of all the grenades, ammunition rounds and unexploded shells scattered all over the runway".

MAY THE 25TH the first **NRE** had been launched on a night photo mission; a week later the **NP** day low-level photo bird left Bien Hoa on its first operational flight. Unlike most other operational drones, which were black, the low-level **NP** model flew with a camouflaged paint scheme.

"The navigation system on the **NRE**" Reichardt recalled "was not adequate for the pinpoint type of target identification required for accurate night photo intelligence because the field of illumination is so small that electronic flashes have to be almost

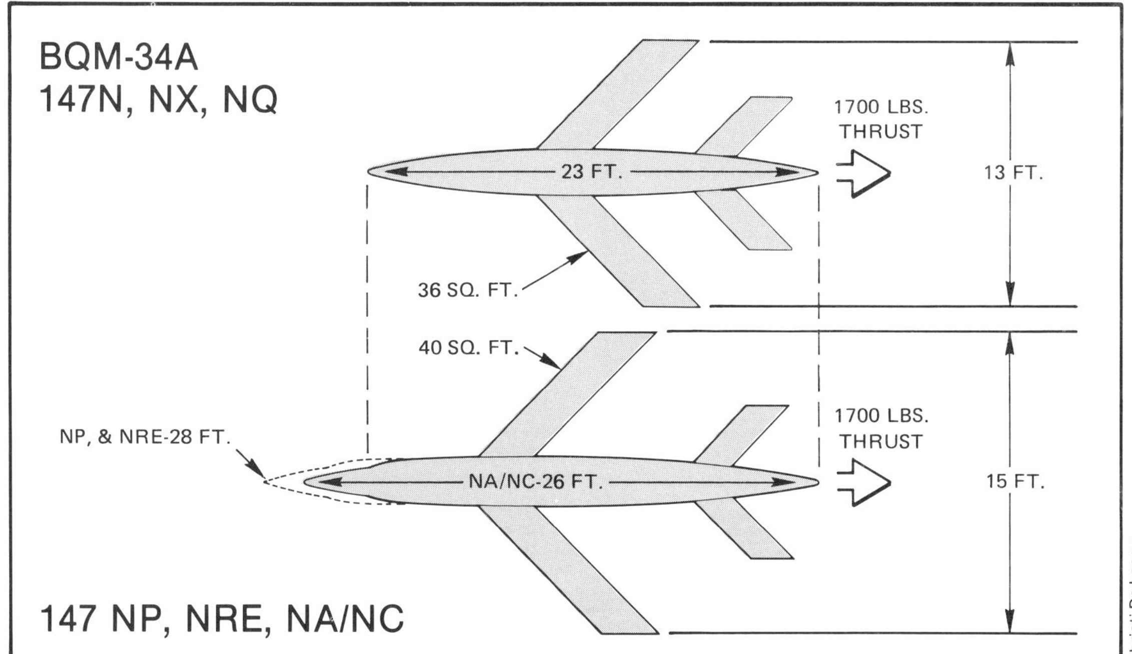

directly over the target.

"However, a lot of very interesting bonus intelligence was obtained by shooting the **NRE**s in almost at random. I remember General Steakley saying, 'I really don't care whether the camera was even working as long as the bird flew over North Vietnam with that strobe light flashing. It would bother them so much that it would accomplish a great deal just by being there.'

"In operation, the **NRE** proved the validity of the night photography concept. Its successor would be introduced later in the 147**S** model line, but with major improvements to enhance both its photographic ability and survivability. When we received a contract for the advanced 147**S**, we were asked also to develop a night reconnaissance capability with the **SRE** version."

Also entering the inventory in January 1968 for another special mission were ten **NQ** birds, a low-level version of the **NX** equipped with a higher resolution camera than the less sophisticated photo equipment provided in its predecessor. The **NQ** was not equipped with a flight programmer; instead it was controlled directly by the ARCO at his plotting board on the C-130 launch plane.

"Its mission in May 1968", Reichardt said, "was to photograph Haiphong every day to get an idea of the shipping activity in the harbor. It was a very successful program with extremely high survivability. At one time it had the record for the greatest number of operational flights per loss.

"Sixty-six **NQ** missions were flown but all ten drones were expended by December of that year. However, in 57 of the 66 missions, the **NQ** birds returned okay, setting a new mission-success record of 86½ percent."

LT. COL. ANDREW J. CORRA of the Reconnaissance Division, Headquarters USAF, in the basement of the Pentagon, was worrried. Reports coming in to SAC from the 100th Strategic Reconnaissance Wing (formerly the 4080th) at Bien Hoa were a cause of great concern. Operation of the Ryan drones was slipping in reliability. What could be done to get at the root of the problem?

During one of Dale Weaver's liaison trips to the Pentagon, Andy Corra asked the veteran Ryan tech rep to give him an objective assessment, in writing, "for my eyes only."

As Bob Schwanhausser later recalled, "Dale wrote the letter and Lloyd Ryan [by then Swany's civilian assistant] and I decided we'd better look it over pretty darn carefully. We knew these things have a way of falling out of the pattern, and we knew we were playing with dynamite. We edited it just a little and let it go."

Somewhat condensed, Dale's letter went like this:

17 June 1967

Dear Andy:

The greatest single problem we have at the OL is lack of experience. For all intents and purposes, it's brand new as far as the people are concerned. There is no lack of basic skill or capacity, but there is a lack of specialized experience developed through training. I'm speaking mainly of the maintenance aspects of the program.

The operational crews are overtrained, overstaffed and underworked. The current ratio is 24 working operational people to 54 working maintenance people. My point here is that there is very little the operational crew can do to promote a good flight if the SPA has not been properly maintained.

Teledyne Ryan Aeronautical

LT. COL. ANDREW J. CORRA, one of the key officers in Air Force reconnaissance, *requested a written 'for my eyes only' report which stirred up a real hornet's nest.*

"THE REAL SUCCESS OF A MISSION rests in the hands of the airman *in the maintenance organization." — Dale Weaver to Andy Corra.*

Dave Gossett

The LCO contributes to the success of a mission by applying the simple draftsman techniques of basic navigation, simple manual dexterity and the ability to recognize a bad bird. The RCO has only the job of making the pen on his plotting board go where he wants it. These two facets of a mission are important; however, they are also the more enjoyable features of the mission.

The launch and recovery phases are the glory end of the business; the real success of a mission rests in the hands of the airman in the maintenance organization. If one half of the time, money and effort that goes into training, retraining and certification of the operational crew were devoted to the maintenance aspects, the program would be much better off.

An unmanned vehicle program by its very nature must depend approximately 95% on maintenance for the success of its mission. I wish the idea that the 147 program is 95% maintenance could be disseminated at the proper levels, as well as the fact that the 147 is not a mature, stable weapon system and it cannot be managed or evaluated in the same light as systems that have gone through the normal development cycle. At best the 147 is just one jump ahead of R&D because of the requirement for quick reaction.

At present, there are nine different configurations of the drone at the OL. Under these circumstances maintenance proficiency cannot be measured by a run through of the check list. Experience, training, proficiency and understanding are so interwoven as to be inseparable. Nothing can explain the current rate of reported hardware difficulties except for statistical failure coupled with inexperienced maintenance. I don't mean to imply that the people aren't trying very hard to do a good job, because they are trying, even though they are confused by the number of configurations and bewildered by the conflicts in direction (''do it by the book or we'll hang your ass'' or ''let's get the job done at all cost'').

The maintenance people are also discouraged by the lack of appreciation as to their role in the mission, and they receive very little information concerning the results of their efforts. From the nature of the problems, you would think that the first operational deployment had taken place in May of 1967 rather than August, 1964.

I hope my opinions concerning long range improvement of the program are not so blunt or tactless as to create hostility by the commands involved. I am trying to act as an interested and objective individual and not necessarily as a spokesman for the Ryan Aeronautical Company. If there are criticisms they should be directed at me and not toward the Company, the OL Commander, the troops involved, or any other member of the evaluation team. Pure augmentation of the OL by Tech Reps is not the answer. Any solution suggested should have complete concurrence from your office, Hq. SAC, 15th AF, 100th SRW Wing Commander and the OL Commander to be effective.

Yours truly,

D D Weaver

Dave Gossett

THE RECONNAISSANCE DRONE COMPOUND at Bien Hoa, *with one of the DC-130 Hercules launch and control planes in the foreground. Arrows point to four 147 birds being readied for flights 'up north.' In background are fighter aircraft which were operated from the same base.*

As Dale later explained, "The number of different machines we built was one of the biggest problems the Air Force had in developing their blue suit capability. Every time they learned how to make a particular model work, we would make a model change, not because we wanted to but because there was a change in requirements.

"When we changed the hardware, it would knock the blue suit training capability into a cocked hat and they would be lost again."

Not aware then of how far the matter was eventually to go, Colonel Corra decided that the information in Dale Weaver's letter should come to the attention of Dr. Alexander H. Flax, Assistant Secretary of the Air Force, and General Steakley, head of the Joint Chief's Reconnaissance Panel.

Swany continued with his recollection of the touchy situation:

"Doug Steakley agreed 100 percent with the letter and decided, unbeknownst to us, to shake it in SAC's face; that it would do everybody some good.

"We weren't aware of what was going on until I got a phone call from General William Martin, head of the 15th Air Force. He said he wanted to come down from March Field and see us. I said fine, and he showed up in San Diego several days later.

"We gathered the top Ryan troops, a passel of Vice Presidents — that sort of crowd — and sat around in my little office making small talk about football and baseball and what a nice place San Diego was to live. With Bill Martin were his Deputy for Maintenance and Colonel Marion C. Mixson, commander of the 100th Strategic Reconnaissance Wing from Davis-Monthan, the officer to whom the OL operation reported.

"The small talk didn't last long.

"The General became very serious and looked me straight in the eye and says, 'Now, about that Weaver letter!'

"My first reaction was 'what letter?' and he says, 'You know what letter.'

"You mean the 'eyes-only' letter? and he says, 'That's the one.'

"With that we shut the door so Jo Ann Weaver, Dale's wife, who's my secretary, couldn't hear.

"Well, immediately Dale was banned from every SAC base in the world, and Ryan was a bunch of bums, and we were told very point blank that if we had difficulties with the 15th AF, would we please come to them and stop these letters.

"We apologized and out of that came a very fine understanding, thanks to General Martin who was a great help in getting things properly squared away.

"In another few weeks I went overseas again with three of our best people because of a problem we were having with some J69-T-41 engines in the high-altitude **Hs**. When we came back our report went in direct to the Commander of the 15th AF. So while Dale's letter gave us one very difficult day it broke the ice and from then on we did very well with those contacts.

"We had some management in-fighting about the T-41 engine (by then Continental Aviation and Engineering which built the J69 series of engines for the drone, was a Ryan subsidiary). Top management was saying 'we have no engine problem' but I'm still insisting we do have a problem and it isn't going to go away. That night our Continental engineering friends called and say, 'Hey, we've got an engine problem!' That cleared the air. It was quite a stew at the time but we got the technical problems cleared up in short order.

"It was about sixty days after Bill Martin's visit before Dale got reinstated. Since then we've called him the 'water walker' — he can do no wrong — and he's known that way by the customer, too!"

A month after Dale's letter 'hit the fan', Colonel Mixson received an offer of training assistance from Ryan 'at no expense to the government' transmitted through William W. Forehand, former OL commander, then in a civilian capacity as the company's Location Support Manager.

The company proposed to send a staff of instructors to Davis-Monthan to conduct formal classroom training in all maintenance areas. Additionally, Forehand suggested that four technician/instructors proceed to OL-20 to assist the Commander in the performance of his mission.

Heading the list was D. D. Weaver, "who has the most comprehensive operational/technical knowledge of the 147 of anyone in the Company and who during 1965 performed outstandingly as the OL Commander's [Forehand's] personal advisor on maintenance and operational matters." Also in the suggested group were Gene Motter, Blackie Blackmer and Ted Owens.

INTELLIGENCE-GATHERING mission of 147 drones *required continuous surveillance of area to maintain military security of the program.*

Dave Gossett

LOW-ALTITUDE 147 day photo J bird *on launch rack of mother plane at Bien Hoa, April 1966.*

Bernie Paul

BY THE END OF AUGUST, 1967 Weaver was back at his old stand doing business at Bien Hoa.

Weaver to Weaver —

Bien Hoa, 1 September 1967

The last of the **G**s (-43) was launched the day after we got here and it didn't come back. **H**-16 went the same way three days later and no word on it either.

Bien Hoa, 3 September 1967

Big day today. It was a double go with **H**-21 and **J**-37 and another one of those 99.9% successes. The MARS recovery chopper dropped the **J** because it was oscillating violently. The Marines are trying to dig the package [camera and film] out now.

Bien Hoa, 14 September 1967

My biggest problem is what to do with the 60-year-old lush, one of the subcontractor reps sent out here. Yesterday morning he came in and told me he would pull himself together. When I came back today he was drunk in the Club again and according to Motter had only been on the line for an hour-and-a-half the whole day. I'm too soft-hearted to have to fire a man old enough to be my father, but for his own good and that of the program, I'm going to be forced to send him home.

Da Nang, 19 September 1967

I came up here on the 17th and rode along on the launch of **H**-21. It was a good bird but as we were watching it via MCGS the bad guys got it.

Launched **H**-14 and **J**-4 yesterday. Neither returned. The **H** bird quit about 100 miles up track; it just went dead. I feel there was probably an electrical failure due to some severe thunderstorms in that area.

J-4 was something else. The ARCO (airborne remote control operator) had taken control over the target area and the bird either got shot down or ran into a mountain. The last few days haven't been too good. Things are bound to improve. We'll give'em hell if the weather will just clear for a while.

FOR NAVIGATIONAL ACCURACY, compass of a recce drone *is checked at Bien Hoa as Continental Airlines transport takes off for 'home.'*

Dave Gossett

FROM THE SPRING of 1966, when Chinese Communists claimed their seventh downing of a recce drone, until early in 1968 both Peking and Hanoi were strangely silent, making few press announcements of 'spy plane' activities.

Then in repetitious, almost sing-song style — and perhaps in recognition of the Tet offensive — the Peking Review began reporting how

> The Air Force of the heroic Chinese People's Liberation Army, which is boundlessly loyal to Chairman Mao Tse-tung's thought and Chairman Mao's proletarian revolutionary line, shot down a U. S. imperialist pilotless high-altitude military reconnaissance plane when it intruded into China's air space over southwest China for reconnaissance and provocation.

In almost identical phrasing, Peking Review in three successive weekly issues, reported the downing

Ryan Aeronautical Library

WIPE OUT THE U.S. AIR BANDITS! read the headline *in a Red Chinese propaganda magazine showing militiamen celebrating shooting down of 147H-18.*

on March 7, 15 and 22, 1968 of the 16th, 17th and 18th drones.

On the evening of April 8, leading Chinese officials including Chou En-lai received airmen of the P.L.A. who had distinguished themselves in shooting down or damaging "intruding U. S. imperialist military planes."

Peking Review had reported that

> Han Young-wu, deputy group leader of a P.L.A. Air Force unit, and airman Chou Young-cheng, were both awarded an order of merit, first class, for shooting down an intruding U. S. imperialist pilotless high-altitude military reconnaissance aircraft on January 20 [1968].
>
> The Chinese officials "shook hands heartily with the airmen and warmly congratulated them on the splendid victories they had won at a time when the great proletarian cultural revolution was winning all-round victory. The leaders urged them to hold the great red banner of Mao Tse-tung's thought still higher, guard against arrogance and rashness, continue to make determined efforts to wipe out any enemy who dares to intrude, and strive for still greater victories.
>
> Waving the revolutionary treasured red book 'Quotations From Chairman Mao Tse-tung,' the heroic airmen who had performed meritorious service repeatedly shouted [Mao slogans — Ed.] with great enthusiasm."

It was a series of high-altitude, broad-winged **H** drones which were the victims of Chinese gunners. The birds were **H**-25, **H**-5, **H**-34 and **H**-39.

Soon Hanoi, through a Reuters news agency dispatch, was reporting its successes, too. On April 21, **S**-17, a low-altitude bird, was shot down over Haiphong.

Agence France-Presse on April 30 had a dispatch from Hanoi that "air raid sirens sounded this afternoon for the first time in a month" and that "anti-aircraft crews sent barrages against United States reconnaissance planes flying low over the capital." "The planes," they said, "appeared to be pilotless." S-39 was on a mission that day.

Similar reports came from Hanoi during the next few months including one on July 7 that "a pilotless reconnaissance aircraft flew over Hanoi for 10 minutes today." It was **SB**-14.

Understandably people in Hanoi didn't feel too comfortable with U. S. camera planes — even though unarmed — flying low overhead.

Laurent Schwartz, a professor of mathematics at the Sorbonne, and a vice president of the so-called War Crimes Tribunal, visited North Vietnam in September, 1968.

"The prolonged absence of air raids around Hanoi," he said, "has allowed the people to relax somewhat, but pilotless American reconnaissance planes still pass over or near the capital fairly frequently. They caused several air alerts when I was there. The people were careful but they did not go to the air shelters."

PEKING AND HANOI were not the only ones shooting down 147 series drones. A strange story was filed out of Saigon May 5, 1968 by Associated Press.

U.S. Drone Mistaken For MiG, Shot Down

> U. S. Navy pilots who believed they shot down a Communist MiG-21 interceptor last Thursday actually shot down a pilotless American plane, informed sources said yesterday.
>
> The plane was shot down over the Gulf of Tonkin. It was not clear why a drone was over the gulf, but apparently it strayed off course, the sources said.
>
> The U. S. Command has not commented on the downing of a drone. Their use in the Vietnam War has been an issue of complete official secrecy, with the U. S. Command declining all comment on them.

[A dozen years later, a Navy officer visiting a Teledyne Ryan Aeronautical executive admitted mistakenly shooting down the unmanned reconnaissance plane. He was then awarded the same 'Kill Plaque' presented to combat pilots who shoot down Ryan Firebee drones in realistic aerial target training practice!]

19

QUANTITY PRODUCTION

PRODUCTION OF ANY aircraft, manned or unmanned, in relatively small quantities inevitably results in a relatively high unit cost. Somehow, if the Air Force and Ryan could agree on a bird which might satisfy the low-altitude requirement over a considerable operational time period, an order for more of the birds could be justified as cost per vehicle would be materially reduced.

The **J** was doing a fairly good job of low-altitude photography. "Enough," Bob Reichardt recalled, "to encourage the Air Force to ask us to produce a new bird that was directed more toward that specific requirement than the **J** which was a hurry-up adaptation of the high-altitude, big-wing **G**.

"The guy who gave me a clue to the real potential of the low-level recce bird was Big Safari's Walt Raynor. At a dinner in Washington one night he said, 'If you guys could come in here with a plan for a low-altitude photo reconnaissance bird to replace the **J** at a very low price, just as low as you can get it — I can assure you hundreds will be required.'

"At that time, two hundred was an enormous number. We hadn't yet built more than 30 or 40 of any one model.

"We got to working on the problem and instead of starting with a **G** model and working backwards to cut out cost, we started with a bare BQM target. We kept more of the BQM than we had in the **B** or the **G**. In fact we used the regular BQM wing which, in itself, saved a lot of money compared with the larger, more expensive **G/J** series wing.

"In general, the name of the game was to get the price down. We had been given a target price of $150,000 a copy for this version by Walt Raynor. We didn't quite reach this — it was closer to $160,000 — but in any case unit price came down approximately 40 percent from earlier models. That's one reason the resulting **S** series ended up with the longest production run of any of the Ryan reconnaissance drones."

Bob Watts

BIG SAFARI'S WALT RAYNOR *had the clue to the real potential for quantity production of a low-level recce bird.*

"SURVIVABILITY in a hostile atmosphere at low altitude," continued Reichardt, "was a key consideration in the Air Force studies leading to the quantity-produced **S** series of Model 147 special purpose aircraft.

"As an interim measure, five of the last 147**J**s were changed to enable the vehicle to fly at other than a single, fixed low altitude. The 'poly-profile' modification permitted varying the launch altitude as well as providing three pre-set cruising altitudes below 5000 feet to confuse the enemy.

"Operational and production analyses resulted in the new model 147**S** being placed under contract in December 1966.

"The two cameras we were using in the **J** gave good results but were limited in film capacity. With improved 'scorer' equipment available, one new camera in the **S** replaced two of the earlier model, provided an 80 percent increase in footage and better quality."

While engineering design and operational problems with any of the birds were the attention getters, program managers had more than their share of work in keeping things coordinated.

William P. (Doc) Sloan, a Ryanite whose employment dated back to 1936 and who had done a World War II stint as a Lieutenant Colonel in the Air Force, was senior program engineer on the **S** birds. His boss was Dave Williams who, in turn, worked for Bob Reichardt.

"With its big flexible wing," Sloan recalled, "the **J** bird was somewhat unstable at very low altitude and so not ideal for this type of work, nor could it turn in the sharp radius we needed when flying down on the deck.

"We flew **J-26** at Point Mugu on our first test flight with the new 'poly mission' equipment designed to improve survivability by giving us a multiple choice of operating altitudes. We were going to level out at around 2500 feet on this first flight. The chase aircraft provided a running commentary:

> 'Nice launch . . . you've got a good bird . . . flying nicely . . . descending through 5000 feet . . . at 3000 and descending . . . at 2500 . . . passing through 2000 . . . at a thousand . . . sorry we have to break off . . . too low for us . . . there it goes into the water!'

"It had tried, but there was a lag in the system. As usual that required a 'fix' or kit to make the thing get well, so this came to be known as the Polly Get Well Kit.

"Six weeks after that the bird was flying alright, but we still needed a completely new configuration since the more expensive big wing bird was not ideal. That brought us back to the short wing of the standard BQM training target series.

"Requirements were then changing so rapidly and the state-of-the-art was growing so dynamically that we had no sooner decided on the **S** configuration, after going through flight test, than everyone wanted to add new capabilities to improve it.

"Running through production quantities of 200 vehicles with no changes would have been ideal, but it wasn't like that. There were calls for anti-flutter kits, different yaw rate gyros, multiple altitude control, radar altimeters, a digital programmer, and so on. How to keep all the changes straight?

"If we scheduled a change at #17 bird and another at #26 and kept going this way we'd never know what equipment was in which bird, nor would our engineering drawings properly reflect the different configurations so we ended up grouping the changes so that all **SA** models would be alike; the same with the **SB**, **SC** and **SD**."

"After the first of 40 **SA**s went operational," related Reichardt, "another 40 vehicles, designated **SB**, went into production in March 1968. Within a

U.S. Air Force

Although large photo (at left) has been widely reproduced, only the full horizon-to-horizon print on page 136, opposite, reveals the full sweep of the reconnaissance drone's photographic capability.

Photo opposite was taken as drone flew from left to right beneath the high tension lines. Flight was made 6 October 1968 by 147 SB-12.

few months after arrival at the OL overseas, 35 of the **SA**s had flown operational missions.

"On one mission in October 1968 when the low-altitude control system wasn't working properly, **SB**-12 came back with a truly spectacular picture. Instead of flying about 1500 feet over North Vietnam it came in at about 150 feet above the terrain, flying under a major power transmission line and taking a remarkable series of photos in which natives in coolie hats can be seen on the road staring up at the drone overhead.

"One of our tech reps, Jeff Grady, told us that someone used to see to it that the ground crews got to see some of the better photo 'takes.' In the case of the power line shot, the squadron commander reportedly posted this particular picture on the bulletin board with the congratulatory reminder that 'the FAA frowns on this bullshit!'

"The first pictures I recall seeing of a Russian SA-2 surface-to-air-missile were taken by an **S** bird. They show the SA-2 flying 'in formation' just off the drone wing-tip, followed seconds later by a picture of the burst of the SA-2 out in front of and below the bird. Obviously, the drone, though slightly damaged, made it back home with the pictures.

"In the **SB**, the barometric low altitude control system (BLACS) was replaced by MACS, a multiple altitude control system, which provided a new versatility. Survivability was improved by giving the **SB** three pre-selected altitudes from 1,000 to 20,000 feet to be programmed into the mission profile with the ability to repeat these altitude changes as required during the mission. Moreover, the **SB** could be launched from the DC-130 at any altitude between 2,000 and 25,000 feet.

"Other improvements in the **SB** included new yaw rate gyros to provide an increased bank angle capability which made possible more precise, steeper turns and a smaller turning radius.

"The largest production of the 147 birds was the **SC** model, several hundred of which were built, with deliveries starting in mid-1968. They have flown over sixteen hundred operational sorties providing photo coverage horizon to horizon 155 miles along the low-level flight path. Navigation accuracy is improved through use of a cross-correlation Doppler radar and missions are pre-programmed through the digital programmer. At mission-end, the **SC** climbs to high altitude for egress and for parachute recovery by the MARS helicopter."

"We had some truly spectacular missions," recalls technician Jeff Grady who was at OL-20 when the first of the **S** birds were being introduced.

"I don't recall whether they were **SA**s or **SB**s but the mission that thrilled me most was the day we flew four birds and got all of them back — retrieving all four in mid-air with MARS helicopters.

"The MARS retrieval on the first one broke the helo's winch, but they didn't drop it. They brought it back okay, but couldn't use that chopper the rest of the day. So the second helicopter had to MARS the other three.

"As I recall this was the day we flew two of the drones in very close proximity across Haiphong harbor. The Russians had claimed that the U.S. had torpedoed one of their ships coming into the harbor so the drone squadron was asked to fly over, take a good look with their cameras and see if the ship was damaged.

"The **S** birds flew right over the Russian ship in the harbor nearly criss-crossing. They got pictures right down the cargo hold. The photo interpreters could see there was no damage whatsoever. But when the North Vietnamese anti-aircraft went after the low-flying drones there was undoubtedly considerable damage for they were shooting at near zero elevation angles from both sides of the harbor. If there was any 'bombing' of populated areas, they were doing it to themselves with their own AAA fire."

INSTEAD OF BEING KNOCKED out of the sky, *the recce drone used its camera to photograph the SA-2 'telephone pole' missile and its subsequent destruction by its own proximity fuse. The drone survived.*

U.S. Air Force

Dave Williams, one of the senior program managers, commented on some of the accomplishments of photo intelligence —

"A number of different cameras are available for the various drones and missions, whether high-altitude or low level, and they provide different results in terms of ground resolution.

"When we speak of 1-foot resolution, or 3-foot resolution, we mean that on the photo print a skilled interpreter can identify objects as small as one foot, or three feet, as the case may be.

"For low-altitude runs with the **S** birds we average about 1-foot resolution of a 60-mile long strip. On some missions 6-inch objects can be identified. I've seen a picture taken during an actual combat run showing truck tires stacked up against a fence in a storage yard where the trademark of the tire can be read.

"One day we 'drove' right down the main street of Hanoi. Pictures showed boys on bicycles and some of the local citizenry diving for potholes for protection — though the drones, of course, carried no armament.

"Our equipment has taken many pictures of one of the main bridges outside Hanoi which was constantly being hit and rebuilt, so it was necessary to monitor it frequently.

"Many times the drones would go on missions where they missed the prime target but photographed targets of opportunity on low-level runs from which they picked up more intelligence than they were expecting in the first place. It was just an unexpected plus.

"Usually the mission is to look at a supply line or SAM site. Is it still there? Are they getting ready to move? Or is it fixed in place? These are the assigned targets, but we may get off track a little from the programmed mission because of winds or navigation problems. That's when they find something they didn't even know existed.

"On high altitude missions resolutions run from 2-1/2 to 5 feet depending on what you are looking through. Looking down through haze cuts resolution sharply; with solid cloud cover you get nothing. But on a clear day 3-1/2 feet is a good average. Photos of a strip over 700 miles long are possible.

"If the vehicle doesn't come back to the recovery point or if we lose it for any reason, we've lost all the data which had been 'scored' on the camera film. That's why a lot of attention must be given to real-time transmission of pictures. Meantime, real-time transmission of electronic data direct or by relay aircraft is being done; the photo problem is much more complex."

Some of the missions brought air-to-air encounters with Russian MiGs flown out of North Vietnamese air fields as well as with SAM missiles and AAA fire.

A series of photos taken by a reconnaissance drone show a SAM missile which had been launched against the bird passing through the full sweep of the camera, then blowing up in front of its flight path.

Although the drone is constantly being tracked, the on-board telemetry equipment does not report whether or not the bird has been hit. But when other telemetry information transmitted to the remote control station is unusual, such as the engine suddenly stopping, or the bird suddenly rolling over from its normal level flight attitude, it must be assumed the event is the result of enemy action.

Other 'scorer' pictures show MiGs taking off from their bases but no pictures of them attacking the drones because the airborne camera is looking down whereas the MiG approaches from behind. An exception was the oxygen-starved MiG-21D Fishbed fighter which had its picture taken from directly overhead as it tried to climb to the altitude where the high-altitude drone was carrying out its intelligence assignment. [See photo page 25 — Ed.]

THE FIRST NIGHT photo missions had been flown with one of the **N** models — the **NRE** — but when the large production, low-altitude **S** series went under contract, twenty **S** vehicles — designated **SRE** — were ordered for the night mission.

The **SRE** was equipped with an improved night illumination system using electronic flash in the near infra-red spectrum so as to make visual detection difficult. In addition the lens filter greatly enhanced haze penetration.

Recovery of birds returning from night photo missions was also improved by development of a night mid-air retrieval system (MARS) capability. A light source on the drone illuminated the engagement chute so that the chopper pilot could successfully snatch the drone as it was descending on its parachute.

Dale Weaver related that "we turned up some interesting things in the way of intelligence with the **S.** We found that there was a lot more activity at night than the Air Force thought possible."

Some of the **SRE**s and other low-altitude birds came home with bullet holes on the underside of the drones indicating they had been hit but not knocked out by AAA batteries. Generally Russian-built 37mm and 57mm AAA weapons, which were effective up to 10,000 feet, were used against the low-flying drones, rather than SAM missiles which went against the high-flying pilotless blackbirds and manned aircraft. [Post-war analysis indicated that some 5000 AA guns, half of them radar-controlled, ringed Hanoi. Highest proportion of U.S. losses was to AA guns as the effectiveness of the SA-2 Guideline missile continued to be degraded by electronic countermeasures. — Ed.]

JUST AS HE HAD DONE with the first night photo recce bird, the **NRE**, Ed Christian flew out to OL-20 at Bien Hoa in October 1968 to help introduce the specialized equipment. His knowledge of cameras was valuable, but even more helpful in evaluating the night system was his background as a photo interpreter with experience in near-infrared photo imagery.

(text continued on page 142)

Ed Wojciechowski

ROUND-THE-CLOCK MAINTENANCE of drones *at Bien Hoa kept the low-level 147**SC** birds in an 'up' condition for mission assignment.*

U.S. Air Force

U.S. Air Force

Small photo at left shows details greatly enlarged for study by experienced photo interpreters and other intelligence experts.

Horizon-to-horizon photo capability of 147S series of low-altitude reconnaissance drones is shown in vertical panel at left. Path of flight is from left to right, the lens taking a 180° view of terrain beneath the drone.

Panel directly below is an enlargement of about one-third of the negative.

Photo on opposite page is a still greater enlargement showing detail of operational AAA battery with seven gun emplacements disguised to look like a SAM (surface-to-air missile) site.

Notation on negative indicates photo was taken 6 October 1968.

U.S. Air Force

U.S. Air Force

"We had a modified, updated photo system which we put into the **SRE**," Ed recalled. "This bird had a Doppler navigation system which the **NRE** didn't. It had a semi-covert night system on board; in other words the **NRE** was a white light system while the **SRE** was a near-infrared system.

"You didn't attract anyone's attention unless they were looking directly at it and then the only thing you would actually see was just a red light — similar to the red beacon on an airplane. All the camera equipment, film and lens filters were geared to the infrared end of the spectrum.

"When I arrived, two **SRE**s were already on station; the balance were shipped overseas to us each week, a couple at a time. While I was there, eleven missions were flown and I was aboard the DC-130 on each of them for the launch sequence and until recovery. I worked on the birds at Bien Hoa and helped check them out but once the drone was hung on the pylon for launch my role was strictly that of observer.

"Well, that's not quite right. I probably overstepped my bounds considerably but I was the only civilian technician aboard the C-130 on actual missions and found myself acting as back-up LCO. I would go through checks with the Air Force LCO and if he got into trouble advise him and help evaluate the seriousness of the problem.

"Generally we uploaded the birds around six o'clock in the evening. The flight control, Doppler navigation and command guidance systems checks would be completed by ten o'clock. I would come down then to install and check out the camera system.

"After we buttoned up the scorer we'd take a roll of scotch-lite reflective tape and put sections of it on elevators, ailerons, umbilical plug, chute cans and engine inlet covers. We'd cut the tape through a center line so we could have a reference to gauge against to tell how much the elevators or ailerons had moved, and in which direction.

"This visual night reference was necessary as no detail whatever of an absolutely black bird can be seen against an absolutely black sky. But with a flashlight to illuminate the scotch-lite tape we could see what the bird was doing as it went through the final pre-launch checks.

"We got off our first flight November 7; and four more the balance of the month. In December we flew six **SRE** missions. That of course isn't all that was going on. We were flying a lot of **SB**, **H** and **NQ** flights during the same period.

"The second **SRE** mission — perhaps because it was on the 13th — ran into problems coming home. It flew a perfect track to the target area with timing impulses to the flight programmer right on the money and turns on schedule. Climbing through 45,000 feet on the way back to DaNang the bird experienced an engine rundown. The SPA went into glide mode and was directed to the nearest Navy on-station ship. Chutes deployed okay and the bird went into the water normally. The impact point was approximated from plot-board and an air search was begun.

"Forty minutes later we spotted the **SRE** floating level, with just the vertical fin above water. Ships were notified and were on the scene in half an hour. The '130' directed a chopper from one of the ships in marking the drone with a smoke bomb. As we left the area — the 130 was getting low on fuel — one ship came alongside, got a line on the bridle and had the bird hard against the stern. A chopper went out from DaNang to bring the bird home. The scorer material was received dry and in short order was in the hands of the RITS photo intelligence people at Tan Son Nhut.

"We all had to be educated to some of the facts of life about low-level missions as related to altitude settings based on barometric pressure vs. terrain clearance. We almost forgot that all terrain is not at sea level. With terrain profiles that vary from sea level to over a thousand feet above sea level, we often had a narrow window — maybe 250 feet — through which to operate if we're scheduled for a 1250-foot altitude mission controlled by barometric pressure settings.

"When I looked at the 'take' of our first mission, November 7, 1968, I found some railroad tracks and scaled them, giving a bird altitude above terrain of 670 feet. On our second **SRE** mission we flew as low as 540 feet over the terrain. The exposure was great, but it should be at that altitude!".

As an aside to the folks back home in San Diego, Christian reported on December 9 that "**NQ**-4 went to the happy hunting grounds today on its 19th mission." It was a new record for a single combat bird. **SRE**-3 didn't do badly, either, getting in nine missions in less than three months.

DECEMBER 19TH was quite an operational day for **SRE**-2 on its second mission in three days according to Christian. "This time it took a picture of a SAM missile — which had fired at the drone and missed. Actually you couldn't see the missile — just the tail burn of the SAM overtaking the bird, then the impact of the SAM as it hit the ground beneath the **SRE** and exploded.

"The night photo was taken from about 1200 feet and the first of those frames shows a North Vietnamese AAA battery being set up; the next the hot blast of the missile which came in from behind; and the third the impact three seconds later.

"Soon after this another SAM was fired against this mission — a side shot which came in from the left. The SAM passed close enough to the camera window that it completely burned out that frame of imagery. In the next frame from the right hand camera you can see the tail come off the SAM going down to impact.

U.S. Air Force/Ed Christian

"HOT BLAST OF THE SAM MISSILE." *Infrared night photo taken by 147* ***SRE****-2 on December 19, 1968.*

"We had launched this mission over the Gulf just off of Haiphong to cover the dock front and seaplane base; then we were supposed to turn almost due west toward Hanoi to overfly the seaplane base there, then exit back out.

"The Doppler was pulsing wrong and our turns were coming in too late, consequently we flew right up into an area northwest of Haiphong where contour maps showed razor backs along a 1500-foot elevation ridge were coming down into the delta region. So the bird made its turn but it made it too late. Flying at about 1000 feet it just barely skimmed over the tree tops. It missed the ridge seven times, coming as close as an estimated 10 to 20 feet; maybe even closer.

"When that bird came home we had some extremely interesting infrared pictures of North Vietnamese trees as the drone made its turn snuggled up close to the slope of the ridge."

"Most of the missions were pre-dawn launches just off Haiphong. We wanted to take a look at Haiphong and Hanoi and the air fields in that area. Several birds were also launched to cover the air fields at Vinh just above the 18th parallel.

"You may wonder why we didn't launch in the middle of the night but from the best intelligence we had, there was nothing going on in those areas from midnight until early in the morning. We wanted to take a reading on the situation at their going-to-work hour so that a photo mission later in the day would indicate what if anything had changed; what the North Vietnamese were up to. This gave the intelligence people something tangible which could be measured about the enemy's preparations.

"In the darkness at 2500 feet over Haiphong harbor I could look down and see the ocean and the islands leading into Haiphong. The sky was just beginning to lighten but the programmed altitude for the birds was from 1200 feet on down and, with the difference in light level at that time of morning, things on the ground were still plenty dark. It was so dark in fact that if the strobe light on the bird misfired or didn't fire we would come back with an absolute blank on the film."

DURING THIS TIME frame the Navy had no official access to the Air Force reconnaissance drone program but clearly had some general knowledge of the operation. In fact, the Navy was considering a program of its own and as a part of the process of getting up to speed and learning more about the photo birds began tracking them with radar and feeding useful information back to the Air Force DC-130 launch planes.

BARELY SKIMMING THE TREE TOPS, the SRE came home *with extremely interesting pictures as the drone snuggled up close to the slope of the ridge.*

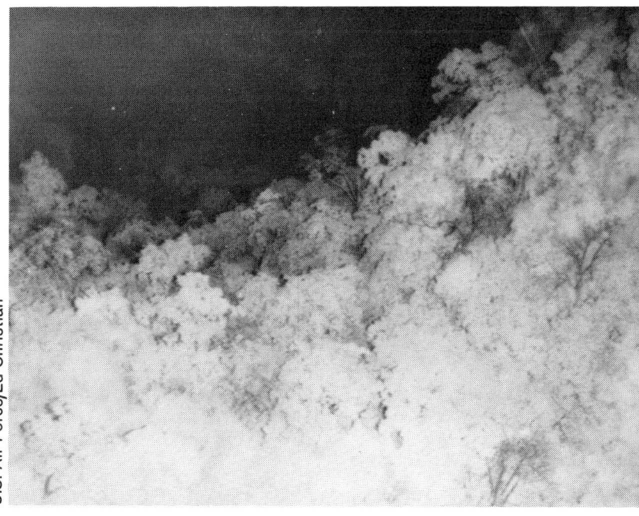

U.S. Air Force/Ed Christian

Ed Christian was on the December 31, 1968 mission with an **SRE** and recalls this incident:

"We had been in over Hanoi again with the bird and on the way out the Navy contacted the DC-130 on a radio voice link. We were orbiting the area waiting to head south as soon as we were certain the bird was over the coastline on its way home. The Navy informed us that their skin tracking of the drone had picked up some information they thought would interest us.

"They said Charlie had launched some MiG-21s which were tracking the drone and closing in on it as it was coming on out. The Navy gave us closing rate and closing distance information. We hung in there until the MiG's were about eight miles from the bird. Then we put it into the climb mode and it disappeared. Its high rate of climb saved it from the pursuing enemy planes. Had we left it on the programmer it would probably have been shot down.

"While our missions were programmed, we had guidance and control override from the DC-130. We had gotten confident enough to fly what we called 'noisy birds' where the MCGS (microwave command guidance system) was on all the time for tracking and control functions. While we could track the bird we had no way of tracking threats to it, but the Navy did and would feed us this information. Of course we would leave the bird on its programmed mission unless, as in this case, something got way out of order. Then we'd take over to see that the drone got safely home, if possible."

The blue suit military personnel, according to Christian's reports to San Diego, were having some problems adjusting to the infrared aspects of the new night photo drone.

"They hate the **SRE**," he wrote, "and are trying to kill it! It's too much work to put together, to check out, and to read the material; it makes a person think and read.

"After a mission I would go to the 12th RITS and review all of the film out of the **SRE**s for content and for any system problems that had come up. Prior to fielding the **SRE** I had spent several weeks educating them on how to process the film. They had never processed anything like this before and were not set up then to process near-infrared film.

"They did not have interpreters trained in viewing near-IR optical material. This is one of the reasons the **SRE** system wasn't used more extensively because data coming out of it was too foreign to the people trying to use it.

U.S. Air Force/Ed Christian

SHIPPING TRAFFIC IN HAIPHONG HARBOR is revealed *in nighttime infrared photo taken May 5, 1969 by an* ***SRE*** *recce bird. Photo intelligence picks out details of armed patrol boats and lighters. Middle shot is of North Vietnamese Coast Guard air station.*

"I personally knew of a target of interest on a recent mission and pointed it out to the photo interpreter. His comment was he didn't see it, and anyway he didn't want to fill out the necessary paper work.

"The same was true of the prior mission. After they had finished with the material and had noted no targets, I found a new section of railroad being constructed using pre-fab rail and tie sections. Again the comment was that it's too much trouble to file the paperwork. However, on the **147SB** follow-up mission they went over the same area and low and behold — new railroad!

"One of their problems is no one is accustomed to looking at flat-lighted targets. I could go on with some other examples, but it won't change any attitudes. Having someone unassociated with the operation doing your processing leaves a large gap in the information loop."

"ON THIS TOUR I didn't make like a hero as I had done the year before in trying to recover the **NRE** from the jungle; yet there was always an element of danger present.

"Games were being played by both sides and I have to assume that there were real bandits chasing us on some night sorties.

"Air cover for the launch plane was supplied on night missions by a Marine Corps group out of DaNang. One night they told us over the radio they were low on fuel and had to get on back to base. About three minutes later we got a call from the Navy guardship that we were being tracked. Just then the 'christmas tree' on the '130' lights up confirming that we're being tracked and that an enemy missile is armed and ready to fire. Whatever and how many it was, they got within four miles and then broke off.

"We were locked in on a launch heading which would make us pretty much of a sitting duck if we held on long enough to launch our **SRE** on its proper course. It's times like that when everyone gets pretty much up tight.

"On several occasions going in deep to launch we nearly got inside the apex of the SAM missile ring and have seen the 'arm' signals come up and their prelaunch signals come on. That's a good time to break off and get out of there.

"When the North Vietnamese radars associated with the Russian SAM missile system began tracking American aircraft they would put out a low pulse rate signal which meant they were beginning to track. When ready to launch the missile they would switch to a high repetition pulse rate which provided the signal for the final guidance data, location and tracking data going into the missile. Generally, launch of the missile would follow in about 30 seconds.

"On the C-130 and other aircraft we had an electronic sensor which could tell the difference between a potential missile launch and an actual firing.

"We referred to it as a 'christmas tree' because different colored lights would come on higher and brighter as things got worse.

"When the 'tree' began lighting up you knew you were in the SAM apex. The only way out was to launch the bird and turn just as steeply as you could and get the hell out of there the same way you came in. This happened on at least three occasions. It's just part of the game, but nonetheless a bad situation in which to be caught."

Major John Dale monitored every one of the **SRE** missions and had a healthy respect for the enemy SA-2 missiles. "The drone launch points," he said, "were planned to remain well outside the lethal range of the SAM installations.

"Indications from enemy electronic gear made your heart rate go up and crew chatter reflected that fact. Once in range of SA-2s in their territory you might just as well 'drive' over the enemy targets with the DC-130 and flip on the drone's scorer! The crews were pretty cautious about getting too close. Hell, they're like me — chicken!"

"One night," Christian resumed, "we had a mission to be launched just south of the demilitarized zone, going up across the DMZ at the 17th parallel then coming out at Vinh and returning back to DaNang. There was almost continuous south-to-north artillery bombardment going on over the DMZ with the apex of the trajectory from 10,000 to 15,000 feet.

"Our flight plan called for us to cross the DMZ at 13,000 feet then let down to 3,000 feet to launch the bird. The artillery was to shut down during the 20 minutes we'd be operating in the area. Obviously they never got the message because we could look out of the '130' and see the artillery bursts from the guns in back of us and the impact explosions ahead of us.

"DaNang control finally found out and told us that no one had gotten the message through to the artillery people to shut down and that our best chance was to get out of there. We were already committed — something like 30 seconds from launch — so we just hung in there until the bird was launched, then we high-tailed it out. We had a dual mission so had to orbit outside artillery range until eight a.m. when we launched the day photo bird from the other wing on the same mission route in order to get good comparison pictures.

"On that launch they had the artillery shut down as the word had gotten to them."

A creative streak runs through Ed Christian as it does through other ingenious technicians. Insects were a constant pest in Vietnam but the military PX offered no aerosol spray cans for a counter attack. But hair spray for women they had in abundance. So why not use it to attack the insects? The idea worked. Their wings laden with sticky lacquer 'holding' spray, the insects stalled out and lost flying speed, then plunged to earth!

20

THE MANAGERS

DRONE RECONNAISSANCE had finally gotten off the ground in 1962 because the Big Safari quick-reaction concept made possible procurement and management outside normal channels. This also was conducive to military security for the drones became a 'black' program so deeply buried that few knew of their existence.

This was well and good until the Red Chinese and North Vietnamese began publicizing the covert flights of the 147 drones. This not only brought competitive aircraft companies out of the woodwork, seeking a bit of the drone action, but also stimulated procurement agencies in their effort to get reconnaissance drone purchasing back into normal channels.

Thus the procurement responsibility began to move from the Air Force Logistics Command (AFLC), whose charter it is to maintain and modify assets already in the aircraft inventory, to the Air Force Systems Command (AFSC) whose responsibility is the development of new aircraft systems.

For too long, many felt, the ASPRs (Armed Services Procurement Regulations) had been disregarded. Now with some public disclosure of reconnaissance drones — albeit by the enemy — a more formalized system was needed to open up procurement and competition and to minimize the 'inside track' long held by Ryan. The change was gradual and took several years — until September 1969 — to consummate.

Recalls Schwanhausser: ''When Col. Ells Powell left the Air Force and retired from the AFLC side, the action moved over to the Aeronautical Systems Division on the AFSC side of the house at Wright-Patterson. Later, the SPO (System Program Office) became an RPV SPO responsible for all remotely piloted vehicles, both for reconnaissance drones and for target drones, the latter used to sharpen the skills of air defense crews.

FAR EASTERN ECONOMIC REVIEW of Hong Kong *offered this photo December 26, 1968 of a throng of militiamen inspecting wreckage of a Ryan drone that didn't make it home to Bien Hoa.*

QRC — QUICK REACTION CAPABILITY — was the commodity the Air Force treasured most in its relations with contractors like Ryan Aeronautical Company. Technical sophistication, production and operational know-how and on-time-delivery were the keys to success in the unmanned recce business.

If Ryan could continue to do the job it was virtually assured of retaining its dominant position in the field. But, how, during a decade-long period of unending crises, did the team Schwanhausser put together manage to keep at the peak of performance?

"We had an unbeatable combination of factors going for us," Swany recalls.

"First of all it was done under a cloak of great secrecy in a 'skunk works' type operation. And, it was done by the best mavericks and rebels we could find in the company — men who were tired of the system; tired of doing things the standard way when they thought there was a better way to do it.

"There was a national need, too, which was recognized by everyone working on the 'black' birds. It gave them a purpose they hadn't had before. There was pride; they'd been chosen for the 'elite' service like a bunch of submariners. And the security regulations helped develop an unbeatable espirit de corps. It molded the group together because there was no one they could talk to about their work, outside that group.

"We had our own shop in the warehouse away from the plant and the rest of the company's activities. What they were doing was new; they were part of a larger national effort. It was stimulating and brought out the best in everyone. And the customer was responding so rapidly to changing requirements in the field that every day was a new challenge. If we grabbed hold of a 90-day delivery contract everyone knew it meant working 70 or 80 hours a week, seven days a week. Then things might get back to normal, but it was never long before we had to face the next crisis.

"We chose the 'can-do' type of people for the drone program. As I said, many were rebels who didn't fit well into routine channels. For them the chips were down. They'd stepped on too many toes and knew they couldn't go back to their former jobs. We told them they'd have just one crack at working on the black drones and if they felt they couldn't take it, they'd better stay where they were.

"Our operations people at overseas locations got a large share of the credit; that's where the action was, but for every Dale Weaver, Bob Todd or Ed Christian there were scores of engineers and dozens of production workers who did fantastic behind-the-scenes work that is too seldom recognized.

"When material came in from the field — fine aerial photos which were the end result of what all of us were striving to achieve — it was a tremendous boost. There was great satisfaction, too, for the technician coming back from the boondocks overseas, making suggestions to the military for new hardware and then taking it back overseas and making it work.

"The manufacturing people back in the main plant gave us tremendous support. They knew something important was going on although they didn't know any of the specifics. But that didn't stop them. Our operation at first was very small compared with what was taking place on the main production floor so it was easy to 'red tag' important parts and assemblies through the line.

"We chose the 'can-do' type of people . . ."

"When we started on the first 147 in the warehouse we took Bob Guyer along to handle final assembly. He was a veteran from the manufacturing organization and knew how to dog a part through the plant. We took guys of long standing who knew how to work something through the production system; how to hand do it if necessary. In turn these workers would 'nominate' friends they knew and had worked with to join our elite corps.

"We had engineers, too, who liked to work right on the assembly floor. It was necessary in this kind of custom tailored aircraft production. They'd be on the floor redesigning a part at 11 o'clock at night or 3 a.m. if someone was having trouble. Some were even available for three shifts in 24 hours when necessary.

"We found you could go just so far in short cuts, and no farther. On the **H** we decided to take the drawings as they came off the board and start manufacturing right then. We were building tools on drawings that had not been checked, and we ended up having to change tools later on. We found it hurt us timewise, rather than helped.

"Fact of the matter is that in our own way we were a Big Safari type operation working outside the normal routines within the company. That didn't endear us to a lot of people, even those who recog-

BOB GUYER
knew how to dog a part through the plant

Teledyne Ryan Aeronautical

nized the need for short-cutting many procedures in order to respond on a timely basis to a national need.

"If we saw we weren't getting what we needed and some guy got in our way who didn't understand how things really were, then we'd have to go right smack over his head and he would be told to go do it. You just had to push this kind of program through in an unorthodox way to get it done.

"The impression the rest of the organization had was 'how come Schwanhausser can get anything he wants by invoking the secrecry of what his people are up to when the rest of us can't have anything?' Most people on the management side understood it, especially top management, but not everybody liked it.

"You can see that over the years we ruffled a lot of feathers, but we did get the job done.

"Both in the military structure and the contractor organization, you had to go right to the top because there they knew why it was necessary to operate as we did. In the Air Force, the Logistics Command (AFLC) had the quick reaction capability to get the job done rapidly and at less cost.

"In the early days, the Systems Command (AFSC), bound by routine, couldn't respond as timely, and out of that grew up a rivalry between these two commands to develop the SPA — special purpose aircraft. Today we have the new acronym RPV — for remotely piloted vehicles — and now AFSC has the ball."

". . . we ruffled a lot of feathers but we got the job done."

MANNED VS. UNMANNED reconnaissance in the military had its parallel in aircraft design philosophy within the Ryan organization.

Bill Rutherford as Vice-President for operations and programs from 1961 to the Summer of 1964, was Ryan's top manager of the reconnaissance drone activity and well aware of its importance as a profitable product line.

Just before leaving for Detroit to assume direction of Ryan's acquisition of Continental Motors, Rutherford found himself in direct conflict with aircraft designer Frank W. Fink, Ryan's Vice-President of research and engineering.

"We had a lot of 'black' drone business then and more coming up," Rutherford recalls, "but Frank told top management that we shouldn't spend one more dollar on development of drone reconnaissance but spend everything available exclusively on manned aircraft — and electronics. He was absolutely committed to manned aircraft and, under the circumstances, the rest of us could hardly believe our ears."

Some incidents in the early recce days which were not very funny — verging on the near tragic — took on a much lighter aspect when retold many years later.

Take the case of the mislaid *highly classified* technical proposal which Rutherford, Schwanhausser and support aides hand carried to Washington.

"In those days," Rutherford related, "everything was a life and death situation. If we got another contract we were still in business; if not we had to shut the place down.

"This particular proposal was tremendously important to the Air Force and to Ryan. It was highly classified and we had been warned that one major security leak and that would be the end of our relationship. So we guarded the briefcase very carefully.

"When we got to our Washington hotel we thought we should leave one man to guard the briefcase while the rest of us went out to dinner but finally Swany and I agreed we'd take responsibility for it.

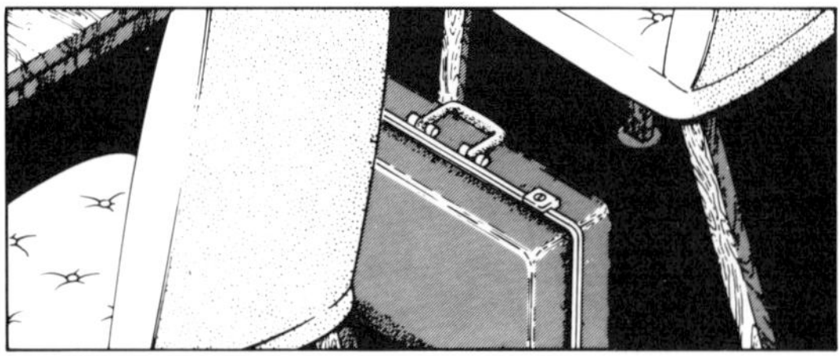

Christi De Lacey

"At dinner the briefcase was on the floor between Swany and me. We had a fine dinner and drinks and left the restaurant in good cheer, climbed into a couple of cabs and went back to the hotel. As we were going in the door, someone said, 'Where's the briefcase,' and we all looked around. No briefcase. We'd left the damn thing at the restaurant!

"You never saw guys pile into a cab faster in your life! When we got back there, the place was locked, but we hammered on the door long enough for the maitre d' to come out of the kitchen and assure us our briefcase was in the cloakroom.

"That was a close call! I think that was one of the contracts we *did* get."

"Lucy Lee" was one of the early proposals the company was almost certain to get. Top Ryan executives, and officials of sub-contractor companies, had been called to Washington for the contract signing.

Ryan would have to quickly expand its factory facilities. Rutherford called in H. L. Fontaine, then Vice-President of manufacturing. Rutherford told him, "Hugh, we've got to put a second story on the assembly building; get started on it *right now.* And I don't want to talk about it any longer. Get going."

Fontaine got going. He had crews in immediately; the cement floor was jack-hammered into bits and pieces for new piers for structural steel.

The multi-million-dollar Lucy Lee proposal was one of the contracts Ryan *didn't* get. Fontaine had to replace the cement floor in the factory.

When Jim Regis was sent out to San Diego during the early recce program as the Air Force's resident civilian manager he was accompanied by several uniformed officers. That called for proper hospitality on Ryan's part, in this instance an over-the-border visit for dinner and refreshments in Tijuana.

Everyone had a fine time. It was a pleasant interlude before the following day's conference which was predicted to be a bit grim. It was.

One of the officers (who shall remain unnamed) showed up with a badly cut face and head. The others looked equally grim; some having difficulty in getting their eyes focused.

Subsequent inquiry disclosed that the one officer had mistaken a picture window for the front door of the house they had rented at the beach.

While some individuals from time to time had lapses, the critically important reconnaissance program was kept on track by an unusually dedicated group of military and industry personnel.

IT COULDN'T BE SAID that managing four or five different recce birds through the contract, engineering and manufacturing process was 'no big thing.' Matter of fact it was close to being a man killer.

In such a highly-energized, top-priority, electrically-charged atmosphere, blood pressures had a way of going right on past allowable tolerances.

Doc Sloan, the program head responsible for the S birds, was able to capture the dynamics of the situation.

"You couldn't help but feel that the work you were doing was vital to the national interest," he remarked. "We figured if our birds were going in and coming back with the pictures that were saving lives of American pilots and others who might be in jeopardy, then doing our jobs right was truly a matter of life and death.

"So when those of us in the program offices ran into anyone in the plant or the military who was grumbling about having to work overtime, or dragging his feet, or saying 'it can wait until tomorrow,' your blood pressure got higher and higher. Pretty soon you were fighting with everyone in the plant; you ceased to be a nice guy. And because you were deeply involved emotionally, you always operated under a full head of steam.

"The program manager had to pull everything together. He was the liaison between the company and the customer — and the Air Force had its own staff right in the plant looking over our shoulder all the time.

"First there had to be a requirement; then you had to define that requirement. Next came a work statement. These proposals and counter-proposals might take two or three months to work out before we had a contract.

"In the meantime you're working with engineering on aerodynamics, weights and balance, electronics, structures — the whole package. With that in hand the estimators go to work and try and determine from past experience just what the job is going to cost.

"In those days everything was a life and death situation."

"It's a constant struggle keeping everyone going in the same direction; and everyone meeting his always-too-tight deadlines. With the contract finally in hand there are more inputs to come — from engineering, tooling, procurement, outside production, fabrication, sub-assembly, final assembly, support equipment, ad infinitum. Now comes flight test, AGE (aerospace ground equipment), engineering changes, technical data and finally production and delivery. It's a task which ends only when the last bird is clobbered at some overseas operational location!

"Monitoring production of the bird once it got onto the factory floor was part of the job, but often the project engineer felt like little more than a parts chaser seeing that everything needed on the assembly line arrived there when required."

The 7 a.m. factory stand-up meeting was where the kinks got ironed out.

L. M. (Larry) Limbach, Ryan's hard-hitting, super-efficient Executive Vice President in charge of plant operations, was the father of the stand-up meeting. It was an innovative technique which produced results. Engineering, tooling, procurement, fabrication, assembly, quality control were all represented at the early morning meetings held every Friday.

"At these Limbach meetings," recalls Sloan "you didn't spend a lot of time sitting around discussing your problems. You stood up, literally, to the display of charts and technical information, and got going on the problems. Generally it was pretty chilly that time of morning out in the factory and you kept things moving at a fast pace if for no other reason than keeping warm.

"We were ironing out our own internal laundry in those stand-up meetings attended only by invitation. It was the project office's job to keep the Air Force apprised of what was going on.

"Our relationship with the customer was pretty much dependent on the attitude of the current commanding officer of the detachment at the plant. Fortunately we had real continuity with some of the Air Force troops like warrant officer R. D. Scruggs and Capt. Dick Wright. They were the backbone of the operation; they understood the problems thoroughly. But we did lock horns quite often.

"Because of the security involved, the national importance of the reconnaissance drone program, the time-compressed scheduling and the huge amount of money involved, tempers often got pretty short.

"One day in August 1968 I was rewriting the 147**SD** Statement of Work for the fifth time. We were on dead center with the Air Force about an engineering 'fix' for the elevator control. We'd come up with five different fixes to satisfy five different Air Force people. On five occasions, one at a time, they'd approve it and the other four would disapprove it. I told them 'you're all a bunch of damn juvenile delinquents;' then slammed the door and went back to my office.

"I ran into Colonel Randa M. Brewis, the detachment commander, coming down the hall. I guess I looked a little wild-eyed. He asked what was the matter.

" 'Colonel,' I said, 'you've got nothing but a bunch of idiots working for you down there.' I went into the office, slammed the door and resumed work on the umpeenth draft of that damn Statement of Work.

"Within 30 minutes there were apologies all up and down the line and it was apparent how ridiculous the situation had gotten.

U.S. Air Force

COL. ELLSWORTH POWELL

". . . .a remarkable man totally committed to reconnaissance drones . . . knew more of their details than any man who ever wore a uniform."

"They hauled me off in the meat-wagon . . ."

"That afternoon it caught up with me. I had a hell of a belly-ache which got worse and worse. Then I began to get shooting pains in my arms. Finally when the elephant climbed up on my chest I suddenly realized I was having a heart attack.

"I went down the hall four doors to Art Sullivan's office. His back was turned. I said, 'Art, I think I'm in trouble.' He said, 'Doc, don't bother me; you're always in trouble, and anyway I have my own problems.'

"When Art turned around and took one look at me things began to happen. In minutes the company paramedic was there with oxygen. They hauled me off in the meat-wagon to the accompaniment of appropriate sirens and I didn't make it back to the plant for four months, and then only part time for another two months."

IF THE RYAN PEOPLE appear to have been dedicated to selling the place of recce drones in the scheme of things, the same may be said — perhaps even more so — of the handful of missionaries in the military services starting with Colonel Lloyd Ryan back in 1960.

As Ryan's top manager of drone programs, Bob Reichardt knew and worked closely with all of them.

"Way up toward the top of the list," Reichard reminisced, "you would put Ellsworth Powell because he was the man in uniform who probably knew more about drones and their details — and the hardware side of reconnaissance — than any man who ever wore a uniform. He was a remarkable man, totally committed to reconnaissance drones. I would venture his total commitment to drones may have cost him a general's star. He just lived and breathed drones. He was the only one who saw the SAC Headquarters side, then the SAC Operations side at Davis-Monthan, and finally the procurement side at AFLC.

"You'd also have to put Andy Corra high on the list of those who devoted the last eight or ten years of their military careers to the development of drone reconnaissance.

"I first ran into Andy when we was working at SAC reconnaissance operations at Omaha. Ells Powell and Dan Emrich had come out of the same shop. In June 1966 Andy moved to the Air Staff recce slot on the Pentagon and stayed with it until his retirement five years later.

"He was a very controversial fellow both within the Air Force and in his role as the 'customer' in his relations with Ryan as a contractor while he was in uniform. He caused many, many headaches but at the same time was a totally dedicated man. He used to work 12 or 14 hours a day, six days a week on the program.

"His relations within the Air Force were tough on him. There was so much security attached to the program that quite often Andy Corra — a

Lieutenant Colonel — would have to report on recce drones directly to the Assistant Secretary of the Air Force. All this without the knowledge of his superiors because they simply were not cleared on the program.

"He was placed in the peculiar position of going around or over the heads of one-, two- and sometimes even three-star generals because they weren't cleared; they didn't have the required 'need to know.' In effect he had two jobs and two bosses. His regular post was as the Air Staff's drone program manager. But then at the same time he was on special assignment to the Assistant Secretary, Dr. Alexander Flax, or the Under Secretaries — Dr. Brockway McMillen and Dr. John L. McLucas."

". . . everyone who ever got involved wanted to stay . . ."

Once the recce drone program got into operation it enjoyed broad government support "all the way from Defense Secretary McNamara to crews of the first launch plane like pilot Marv Bixby and navigator Charlie West." That was the evaluation of Andy Corra.

"Of necessity," according to Corra, "people came and went during the decade of the drones, but one has to recall particularly the commitment of men like Doug Steakley, Ells Powell, Lloyd Ryan, Dan Emrich and John Dale.

"At the Secretary and Assistant Secretary level we had fine support. One thinks, for example, of Cyrus Vance and his support of the production program for low-altitude birds. He readily saw the merit of the concept, had useful suggestions and knew short cuts to moving the program ahead quickly.

"The real leader within the Air Force of many phases of unmanned reconnaissance was Dr. Flax who had wanted to keep the program in its separate management channel. There were, of course, many others who had the foresight to see the role unmanned systems could play.

"Virtually every one who ever got involved wanted to stay with the program; it was almost impossible to pry them away from the challenge."

At another level in the Air Force were the SPO people in the Systems Projects Office, perhaps best typified by Col. Red Smith who had implemented some of the key administrative changes which got drone reconnaissance its full recognition, and who also was program manager on such projects as "Combat Angel", "Combat Dawn" and "Defense Suppression" described in later chapters.

Smith was also responsible for walking through Air Force headquarters the piece of paper establishing official missile nomenclature for the air breathing drones which had previously been known only by the company's own model designator — the 147 series of reconnaissance vehicles.

All of the recce birds were modifications of the basic BQM-34A target drone which had earlier been designated Q-2C. Thus, in Spring 1971, the nomenclature was changed to the AQM-34 series. [AQM = air launched, drone, guided missile; the 'B' in BQM indicated capability of either ground or air launch.] The high-altitude 147**H**, for example, became the AQM-34N; the low-altitude **SC** was redesignated AQM-34L. It may have been recognition for the Ryan drones but it injected a new period of confussion in keeping track of the various configurations.

FOR 37 YEARS Ryan Aeronautical Company, incorporated in 1931, had grown in the shadow of its founder-chairman T. Claude Ryan, who in fact had established his first San Diego commercial aviation business nine years earlier, in 1922.

An important milestone along the way was the year 1965 when Ryan acquired controlling interest in Continental Motors Corp. and its jet engine subsidiary, Continental Aviation and Engineering Corp. The latter's J69 engine powered Ryan Firebee target systems and the 147 series reconnaissance drones.

By late 1968, Ryan's financial and technical success, and a business volume which had grown to $430 million that year, made the company a prime target for acquisition. In response to a $128 million offer from Teledyne, Inc., of Los Angeles for all Ryan shares, Claude Ryan, Chairman, and Robert C. Jackson, President, tendered their holdings and urged other stockholders to do likewise. Thus it was that on January 2, 1969, Ryan Aeronautical Company became a subsidiary of Teledyne, Inc.

Before the month was out, Jackson was elected a member of the board of directors of the parent Teledyne company, while G. W. Rutherford, by then President of Continental Motors, and Frank G. Jameson, Ryan's Vice President-Programs and Engineering, were elected to the Ryan board of directors.

On May 14, Ryan's management information bulletin, circulated to key executives, carried another interesting announcement:

> R. R. Schwanhausser has this date accepted a special assignment with Teledyne. This appointment is effective immediately. Functions formerly reporting to Schwanhausser now report directly to F. G. Jameson and L. M. Limbach, executive vice presidents. A company organization chart defining this announcement will follow shortly.

What was the meaning of this strange document? Clearly there was more than met the eye. Was the vague announcement a corporate euphemism for putting Schwanhausser temporarily in the 'refrig' to permit a decent time period for letting some unidentified situation cool off?

The strain of managing an intelligence program of great national importance had already taken its toll. After making a presentation to Ryan's technical Advisory Board (composed of scientists and retired, high-ranking military officers) Swany went home tired and ill on December 3, 1968. That night he suffered a major heart attack.

Swany was down but not out. Although the doctors would not permit his return to work for over three months, it was only a few weeks before he was holding informal meetings with his colleagues at Ryan and in the military at an improvised 'office' at his home. By March, thin and drawn, he was back at the plant.

Nominally, the very independent Swany reported on the organization chart to Frank Jameson, a talented but very volatile and voluble extrovert who counted among his friends men in the highest levels of government and the military. He was the 'mister outside' supersalesman to the 'mister inside' administrative talent of Larry Limbach.

It was, perhaps, inevitable that Swany and Jameson would tangle. While Schwanhausser cultivated the friendship of military people at the working level, Jameson contacted their superiors in the halls of Congress and the inner suites of the Pentagon. Not infrequently Swany would have a new program sailing along smoothly at the working level only to find that Jameson had inserted a different input into a higher government command. Both were doing their job but proper coordination was lacking.

On returning to San Diego from one such confusing trip to the nation's capital, Swany was met by some of his key people. They adjourned to a nearby bar and after a rather extended discussion Swany excused himself to use the pay telephone. Calling Jameson at his home, Swany in somewhat more earthy language suggested to his boss the appropriateness of using his job to perform a proctoscopic examination. It was again the Schwanhausser of 1960 who then had made a similar suggestion to his superior of that day!

Later that evening Jameson phoned Schwanhausser for a recap of their conflicting opinions and when Swany confirmed his earlier suggestion Frank replied that it was insubordination and he would therefore have to fire him. Swany readily agreed that the punishment fit the crime. In fact he welcomed it.

The next day Bob Jackson and Bill Rutherford tried to put the pieces back together without success. After all, Swany and his team had to be rated among the most valuable assets Teledyne had bought. For his part, Swany and some of his followers began to organize a company of their own — or they could offer themselves as a package to other companies anxious to get some of the recce drone business Ryan had enjoyed for nearly a decade.

Eventually, all the kings horses and all the kings men — Jackson, Rutherford and Limbach — put humpty-dumpty back together again. Theoretically there would be no more conflict between Swany and Jameson, but corporate life just isn't like that. In any case, within six weeks of the big confrontation, Jameson was promoted to the presidency of Teledyne Ryan Aeronautical, serving to divert his attention to more pressing matters. Thereafter the combatants managed to keep a tenuous peace monitored by Limbach until Jameson departed for presumably greener pastures at North American Rockwell in November, 1971. He was succeeded as Teledyne Ryan president by Limbach.

Richard Stauss

FRANK GARD JAMESON
'mister outside'

Richard Stauss

LARRY LIMBACH
'mister inside'

21

COMBAT ANGEL

NEW REQUIREMENTS for drone operation continued to pop up in Southeast Asia, but they were not always for reconnaissance.

In late 1967, the Air Force asked Ryan to determine if it was feasible for a drone to fly a pre-strike ECM (electronic countermeasures) mission in support of manned aircraft strikes conducted by the Tactical Air Command. Too many aircraft and crews were being lost. Something was needed — some way of dispensing chaff — to jam enemy radars and dilute their defense capability.

The ECM drone requirement resulted in another rush program and a new version of the **N** bird. Developed from the basic short-wing BQM airframe with extended fuselage, the medium-altitude **NA** model was designed to carry chaff to be dispensed from two external ALE-2 pods suspended beneath the drone's wings. Flying in multiple launches, the 147**NA**s would precede manned aircraft strikes, spread thousands of tiny strands of metal foil, and thereby facilitate penetration of the manned U.S. aircraft to the target area.

To get the program going in the alloted 90 days, the Air Force again called upon Lieut. Col. Red Smith to work with the Ryan team.

"We set up the configuration," recalls Red, "and through Air Force channels assembled the assets we needed, including some 400 odd ALE-2 chaff dispensing pods. A fleet of BQMs was modified to **147NA** configuration, and a flight test program run at Eglin Air Force Base. Robbing SAC of three crews and two launch planes we were ready to deploy in the time specified."

It will be recalled that in mid-1962, Lt. Col. Lloyd Ryan, the Pentagon's recce expert, was seeking a 'home' for the drone capability. The Commanding General of the Tactical Air Command turned the project down then, so Ryan made a presentation to the Strategic Air Command at Omaha which looked on the capability with more favor. As a result, up to August 1968, SAC had flown all the missions including many in support of TAC combat operations.

Now at last, TAC was ready to get a piece of the

TACTICAL AIR COMMAND requirement for pre-strike Electronic Counter Measures *(ECM) capability resulted in development of 147**NA** model. DC-130 is up-loaded with four ECM birds carrying chaff in two pods under each drone's wings.*

Dave Gossett

operational action with the "Combat Angel" ECM capability.

The 24 **NA** vehicles were followed in production by 43 of the **NC** version, the birds differing only in their avionics packages for ECM operations. **NA**s did not have flight programmers while the **NC**s did have programming capability.

As **NA/NC**s came off the San Diego assembly lines they were sent to Davis-Monthan Air Force Base for the 4472nd Tactical Support Squadron. In August 1968, the drones were placed on a contractor-operation 72-hour alert under a 30-day contract, ready to deploy overseas on a moment's notice.

Proficiency training flights were staged out of Ft. Huachuca, Arizona, and some out of Eglin with good success devoid of serious operational problems.

By the time the squadron was qualified and ready to be moved overseas several months had passed; then, starting November 1, 1968, President Johnson called a bombing halt above the DMZ in North Vietnam. At that point the panic effort to build a drone jamming capability lost its cause. Again, as Red Smith explained, "it did show us a way to respond to a national need to build a set of hardware in 90 days that would fly and do the job."

The Ryan group was asked to continue its alert status and training flights out of Davis-Monthan under a series of 30-day contracts which continued for 17 months through the end of December 1969. For Ryan personnel with families it was no 'cup of tea.' Not knowing from one month to the next whether the program would be terminated or extended didn't make for a stable family situation.

Two veterans of Air Force operation of drones at Bien Hoa were by this time retired and working as civilians in location support for Ryan. Bill Forehand was in charge and his former deputy, Buck Lee, was Ryan's base manager for Combat Angel.

Lee was not exactly happy with the Air Force's attitude early in 1969 when he visited several TAC installations. "I am utterly amazed," he wrote Forehand, "at the lack of knowledge, lack of interest, lack of support, and lack of planning for a program that has been operational for seven months now."

Much of the problem, of course, was that they were on indefinite standby alert with no clear mission in sight since there were no bombing operations in North Vietnam requiring the decoy tactics of the Combat Angel group.

Still 52 of 53 training missions had been launched satisfactorily in the first year of standby alert, with total effectiveness after launch rated at 89 percent.

Nat Summers, one of the Ryan electronic warfare technicians who had been at Bien Hoa in the spring of 1967, monitored the **NA/NC** program.

"In January 1970, the military 'blue suit' personnel took over the program," he recalled, "although the TAC operation was not actually formalized until February 1971, when the Tactical Air Command

Bruce Engman

TWO VETERANS OF AIR FORCE operation in Vietnam, *Buck Lee, left, and Bill Forehand, worked as civilians in support of 147**NA** ECM drone project.*

began funding the activity. Up until that time the birds were Air Force assets, as were the DC-130 launch aircraft. Actually they got old beat-up '496' and '497' which were the launch planes which first deployed with 147s to Okinawa seven years earlier.

The Combat Angel squadron deployed to Pt. Mugu in June 1969 to conduct an unusual exercise. Was it feasible to have one ARCO (airborne remote control operator) direct launch of three SPAs on fully programmed missions, monitor their operation and, if necessary, assume control of the 147**NC** birds at any time? If drones were to do an effective chaff dispensing job, the more drones which could be put in the air at one time, the better.

The two DC-130s, each carrying two SPAs, flew into Pt. Mugu from Davis-Monthan. Work began shortly after midnight and by six a.m. the two launch aircraft and their birds were in the air. Ground rules were that no control corrections were to be commanded from ground stations except in the interest of safety, the ARCO being responsible for all functions before and during the corridor run.

The first drone, **NC**-4 was launched at 6:12 a.m. Within eight minutes **NC**-2 and **NC**-3 were also airborne.

Each SPA flew its designated programmed course with minimum correction from the ARCO. At the end of the corridor runs, each SPA was turned over to its respective ground station and vectored to the recovery area for MARS retreival.

After 38 minutes flight, the first drone launched, **NC**-4, was caught in mid-air by the recovery helicopter and returned to station. There the helo was rerigged and returned to catch **NC**-2 after its 80 minute flight.

Parachutes of the number three drone, **NC**-3, blossomed prematurely after an hour and three minutes flying time due to a lost carrier signal, which initiates the automatic recovery sequence. The drone was 98 nautical miles from station and search aircraft were unable to locate it.

The drone had fuel remaining for 70 minutes of flight. Had it not been for the loss of carrier, the helo would undoubtedly have recovered this bird too and established a 'three in succession' record.

Buck Lee was able to report a highly successful mission to his superiors in San Diego. Each of the three drones was turned onto the 'hot leg' of its run within 30 seconds of the planned turn point.

"As WAS TRUE in the early days at OL-8 (Okinawa) and OL-20 (South Vietnam) the blue suiters were not up to speed when they took over in January 1970," recalled Summers. Except for a few people with the SAC program who were sprinkled through the new outfit, most of the people were new and inexperienced.

"Five months after they assumed command, the TAC unit was asked to conduct an Operational Test and Evaluation at Pt. Mugu. The multiple-launch tests there had to be suspended due to drone operational losses mainly attributed to complex flight profiles and range restrictions.

"In October, TAC completed the OT&E at the Tactical Air Warfare Center (TAWC), Eglin Air Force Base, Florida. Although the drones were outstanding as far as their operation was concerned, the DC-130s were a real problem. More often than not, the primary launch aircraft would have to abort a mission and the back-up DC-130 launch the mission. Even so, all missions got off on schedule.

"Since the entire weapons system — launch planes and drones — was being rated, the OT&E was declared unsatisfactory because of poor overall reliability, maintainability and performance.

"Some minor drone modifications were suggested, but the reliability record of the **NA/NC** birds was unusually good during the three years following their assignment to Davis-Monthan. Of 258 drones launched, only 16 were lost during training and OT&E tests under both contractor and military operation.

"Although the OT&E left much to be desired, one general summed up the advantages of the **NA/NC** birds when he pointed out their value as a confusion factor. His concept was to continually congest the combat area with drones, feeling the enemy would be hesitant to expend missiles on them. Since drones could be made to look like fighters on radar screens, many actual fighter aircraft would not be fired on and could penetrate enemy defenses with much less danger.

"Had the squadron deployed on schedule as planned, the manpower and support equipment problems would have worked themselves out — as they had before — and we would have had a very creditable ECM operation going for us.

"Twice a year, TAC conducts its 'Coronet Organ' exercise. They fly everything they have and stage their own war games. General William W. Momyer, Commander of TAC, relaxes things, gives his people a free hand, and lets them plan a war, attack simulated targets, and then evaluate the whole operation.

"Our drones first participated in Coronet Organ exercises in March 1970 on the Fallon, Nevada, Naval Test Range. Two **NC**s were launched within 30 seconds of each other to fly chaff dispensing missions with a 4000 foot altitude separation. The first SPA was controlled from a ground station, the second from the launch aircraft.

"Operational results of such war games are hard to come by but we understood that neither drone was 'shot down' by the 'enemy' and that whenever the enemy radars were about to lock on the drones another burst of chaff would cause them to lose lock and have to search again.

"It was pretty substantial proof that the drones could degrade the efficiency of enemy radars and perform the ECM mission satisfactorily. In November the drones participated in Coronet Organ III, then again in Coronet Organ IV in April 1971. In ECM missions, the work of the **NA/NC**s was outstanding."

During Coronet Organ IV at Tyndall AFB in April 1971, four birds carrying chaff in external pods were launched from '497.' It was a good mission and all four SPAs were launched on time and each was successfully ground recovered.

Two days later the mission was repeated with the four drones launched at 15 minute intervals flying at altitude separations of one thousand feet while dispensing chaff.

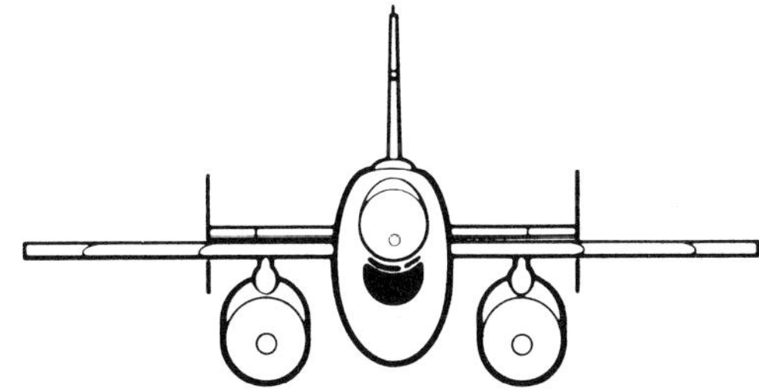

In summary, the operation was considered excellent, the drones performing as advertised. Old 497, held together by tender loving care, conducted the launch requirements with minimum problems. The effects of the material dispensed (chaff) was good. "The General who observed the operation," the company report to San Diego stated, "was pleased, and has bigger and better ideas for drone utilization.

"In July 1971, when the RF-4 recce unit from Thailand — the 11th Reconnaissance Squadron — was retired, the 4472nd unit flying the **NA/NC** drones was renamed the 11th Tactical Drone Squadron.

"Most recently they participated in Coronet Organ V, the largest aerial exercise ever conducted. They

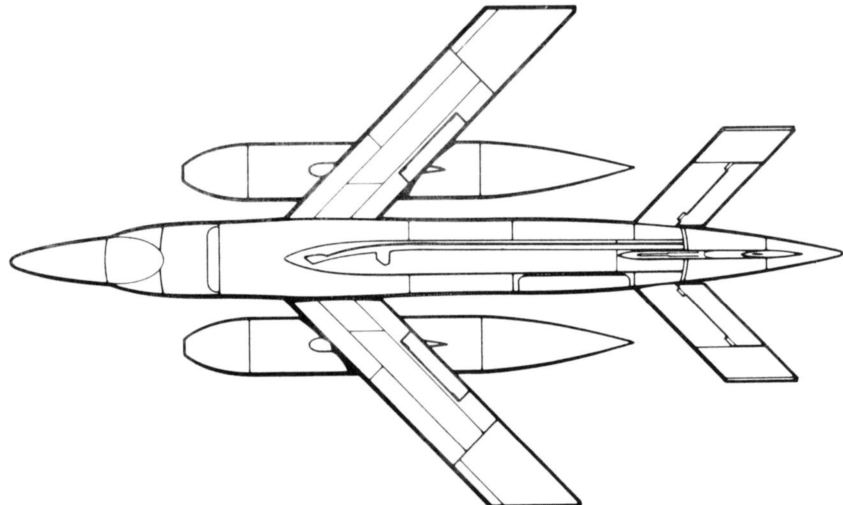

TOP PLAN VIEW OF 147NA *showing the two external ALE-2 pods suspended beneath the drone's wing.*

went a little farther this time as far as drone capability is concerned.

"We were tasked to do 22 missions in three days. Fourteen were electronic warfare (EW) sorties, four were reconnaissance and four were active jammer sorties, carrying the external pods normally flown on the F-4 Phantom. By noon of the third day we were 20 for 20, which is 100 percent. However, we had one abort on the last day and ended up with a box score of 21 out of 22.

"These flights were staged out of Davis-Monthan with launches in the Nellis Air Force Base area in Nevada and Luke Air Force Base, Arizona."

AT THE SAME TIME the **NA/NC** series for TAC were purchased, SAC placed an order for 52 units of a similar BQM-modified vehicle, the **NC** (**M**-1) [modification 1]. This version was to be a low-altitude, day-photo reconnaissance SPA ordered as an interim vehicle to fill the gap until the 147**SC** became available. The chaff-dispensing pods for the ECM mission were, of course, not included, and a new, higher-resolution Hycon camera was installed. At the drone's 1500-foot operating altitude, the new camera was designed to provide resolution of 4-inch objects taking a strip some 30 miles long. However, the camera/vehicle combination was not a good mating of capability and a different 'scorer' was considered necessary to meet mission requirements.

SAC flew the **M**-1 version only four times and, as a result, 18 of the **NC** (**M**-1) birds were transferred to TAC in February 1971 to give them, for the first time, a drone photo capability when operated on tactical mission profiles. Three 147**SC**s from the SAC inventory were also transferred to TAC to help get them up to speed on this model. The 34 **NC** (**M**-1)'s retained by SAC became training vehicles.

Dave Gossett

SUSPENDED BENEATH DC-130 LAUNCH PLANE, this 147 NA *in turn has its own pylons from which two chaff-dispensing pods are hung.*

22

BELFRY EXPRESS AT YANKEE STATION

THROUGH CONTACT with the SAC drone operations out of Bien Hoa, U. S. Navy units operating in the Tonkin Gulf knew about flights of the low-altitude Ryan drones. "In fact," Dale Weaver recalled, "they made use of the intelligence that was gathered by SAC, but they didn't feel it was timely enough.

"The Navy wanted its Task Force Commander to have the capability of committing his own photo reconnaissance drone whenever he felt it was required and to be able to react right away.

"A contract with the Navy for Operational Test and Evaluation of just such a system called for 147**SC** model drones modified for surface launch and adapted for a shipboard environment including recovery at sea in the open ocean. Designated 147**SK**, the ten birds which were committed to the evaluation for low-altitude day photo missions were the first recce drones to be ground launched from zero-length launchers rather than launched in-flight from a 'mother' plane."

Because no drones in the 147 series of reconnaissance vehicles had ever been ground launched, Bob Schwanhausser and Col. Ells Powell decided to witness the first launch in July 1969 at Pt. Mugu where the Air Force was supporting the Navy's entrance into the recce business. The weights, structure and aerodynamics for ground launch of a 147 type bird were all new.

"The first launch of a new bird always attracts a good crowd," Swany recalled. "We were in the tracking station where we could see the activity at the ground launcher and on the beach. The Admiral was just down to our right toward the beach. He had the top of his convertible down so he and his family could get a ringside view of the activity.

"We watched the JATO bottle go and the bird take off into the overcast. It had a drastic pitch-up angle as it disappeared. I turned to watch the altitude plot in an effort to get an airspeed reading real quick. By the time I turned around and looked out the window the bird had looped over onto its back and was crashing in a fireball explosion about halfway between us and the launcher.

"That, and the exposure of the Admiral's family out in the open, slowed us up from a range-safety standpoint, and I was banned as a bad omen from watching further ground launches for a while.

"The birds were put aboard the carrier USS Bennington (CVS-20) off Southern California and some time later the last launch on the final day of the training operation was scheduled. I figured the jinx had worn off by that time.

"Ray Ballweg, by then our Washington representative; Dr. Robert Cannon, a former Air Force Chief scientist and member of the Ryan Advisory Board, and I flew out from the Coast Guard Station in San Diego that morning.

MODEL SK WAS THE FIRST 147-TYPE reconnaissance vehicle ground launched. *At the Navy's Pt. Mugu facility, the Admiral and his family had a ringside seat and a too-close-up view.*

Ed Wojciechowski

"We were up on the bridge and everything was going smoothly preparatory to launch. Then the range — the Pacific Missile Range controlled by Pt. Mugu — got fouled up so we found ourselves at minus five minutes and holding. That's the countdown point at which you start the drone's jet engine.

"Just then the big speaker horns on the carrier came on announcing that the range is clear and it's 'minus five and counting'. In seconds we had a disaster on our hands.

"The launch control operator pressed the switch to start the drone's jet engine. But there was a glitch somewhere in the switching circuits — a cross coupling — and the rocket, which gives the bird its initial boost, fired instead. We had our initial thrust away from the launcher alright but no sustaining thrust from the jet engine — which was never started. The JATO booster bottle had worked just fine; so had the dye marker when the bird crashed off the starboard side. We had established a new short duration flight record! From then on no one wanted any part of me on the **SK** program.

"Despite the loss, the Navy was very cordial to us. After a fine lunch they sent us home on a COD (carrier on-deck delivery) airplane. It was a first COD flight for all of us. The skipper of the Bennington asked the pilot to be sure the engine was running before they catapulted us off. We were very grateful!"

After the initial ground launch disaster at Pt. Mugu, two good ground launches were made there, then testing had been moved to the Bennington where two more launches were made in August under seagoing operational conditions.

The Bennington had been selected because it was an anti-submarine warfare (ASW) carrier where the slower paced activity with propeller-driven planes would be compatible with the learning experience needed for initial reconnaissance drone activities. A steel deck plate was put down on the aft starboard elevator and launches made from there.

THE JATO BOOSTER BOTTLE WORKED JUST FINE
but because of a glitch in the switching circuitry the jet engine for sustained flight was not running.

Ed Wojciechowski

JEFF GRADY
Senior Field Engineer

Jeff Grady was Teledyne Ryan's senior field engineer assigned to the **SK** program and picks up the story.

"The Navy was planning to take the system overseas to Southeast Asia for use at Yankee Station in the Tonkin Gulf. A detachment of twenty personnel from VC-3, the Navy target drone operation at North Island, San Diego, was assigned to operate the **SK** drones. My job was to head up the technical support group from the company side.

"Unfortunately, right in the middle of the training period the Navy decided to mothball the Bennington. This was right after our second training flight — the one which ended in disaster because the booster rocket misfired.

"There was a lot of scrambling about what ship they would put the **SK** recon capability on, and the Navy finally selected the USS Ranger (CVA-61) because it was about to deploy. There was a lot of resistance to putting **SK**s on the Ranger because it was an attack carrier and the tempo of operations was considered much too fast for integrating and evaluating the drone system. However, once the decision was made, Captain Joseph Moorer, Commanding Officer of the Ranger, placed the necessary emphasis on the program and from that point on shipboard support was excellent.

"We boarded the Ranger at Hunter's Point, Alameda, California, October 14, 1969 and put an extra engineer on board as we had to get the control van installed and interfaced with the ship's combat information center (CIC). Too, we still had the problem of solving the premature ignition of the booster rocket.

"Before we got to Pearl Harbor we wanted to get in two more training missions. Monday October 20 we got off a fairly good flight, but had to abort the next one just before we tied up in Hawaii. One of our problems then and later was that the ship's S2-E Tracker aircraft, which were to be the airborne control stations, were having difficulty giving remote commands to the **SK** bird after it was launched from the Ranger.

"We were retrieving the birds by helicopter pickup from the ocean after they parachuted down, but the Navy originally intended to use mid-air retrievals with a MARS helicopter but they just couldn't get it going fast enough.

Ed Wojciechowski

FROM THE AFT STARBOARD ELEVATOR of the USS Bennington *the 147***SK** *is ground launched during carrier based test operations off the coast of Southern California before the drones were committed to duty at 'Yankee Station.'*

"Even with only three birds we were in very crowded quarters aboard the Ranger; after all they hadn't expected to provide us a home on the flattop. So, the operation was quite different from what was originally planned for the operational test and evaluation (OT&E). Still we got fine cooperation from Lt. Comdr. William Smith, assistant strike operations officer aboard the Ranger, and his people.

"People back in San Diego weren't at all happy with our performance to that point in time and I almost expected we'd be pulled off the program. However, I guess they understood the problems we were having of qualifying the people and complex equipment and integrating a whole new system in the tempo of an attack carrier at sea.

"The Navy's launch control operator just wasn't familiar enough with the more complicated panel for the 147 series birds. I ended up standing right behind him and trying to help him interpret the panel. On the bad operations we had out of Hawaii, I certainly goofed as much as he did. In those five minutes before launch everything's got to be right on and I've always felt if you're in doubt, shut the thing down. But we didn't.

"We sailed from Hawaii for Subic Bay in the Philippines and staged our next training mission out of there. More snafus!

"OUR TARGET SERVICE GROUP was running a regular *training operation for air-to-air missile firings for Air Force pilots in the Philippines."*

U.S. Air Force

"Our target service group was running a regular training operation for air-to-air missile firings out of Wallace Air Station for Air Force pilots and we had to dovetail the **SK** operation on the range with theirs. It took some fancy advance scheduling to be sure we got our operation over before the target people started to launch. Only trouble was the Ranger was late in sailing and we found ourselves launching just as we got out of the harbor. Because we were an hour behind schedule our flight mission coincided with their prelaunch activity causing all the control problems we had tried to avoid.

"We'd been using E-1 Tracker aircraft for airborne control when we were on the Bennington, but the Ranger had the later E-2 turbo-prop version of the Grumman aircraft with an entirely different type radar. The E-1 reciprocating engine job was used for long range anti-submarine surface search, while the turbo-prop E-2 with its huge rotating antenna was for anti-air warfare. Totally different missions, electronic equipment and crews. More problems!

"It was a hairy mission. Launch was good but the drone got way off the range. Finally we got the bird back when the E-2A got in range of the ship and passed control to CIC. The drone was recovered and the chopper picked it up out of the water. The carrier deck activity was something to behold — jets turning up on all four catapults as the SPA arrived on the elevator. It was clear we surely needed faster handling equipment on the flight deck.

"I imagine everyone was ready to scrub the **SK** project then and there — but you don't turn a carrier back when its steaming toward the Tonkin Gulf to take up line duties on Yankee Station. So it was decided to go on with the evaluation regardless and the **SK** was declared operational. 'Belfry Express' became the code name for the Tonkin Gulf photo reconnaissance evaluation.

"We still had only three birds aboard when we went on the first line period at Yankee Station but we picked the others up when we stopped in at Subic between the five line periods we were in the Tonkin Gulf. Then, while at Yankee Station, they high-lined another drone to us during an Underway Replenishment (Unrep) operation."

L. M. Limbach, Teledyne Ryan executive vice president, and an advisor, VAdm. Paul D. Stroop, retired Commander, Air Force Pacific, flew out to the Ranger from Bien Hoa in a Navy COD aircraft for the first Belfry Express operation on November 23, 1969.

"The **SK** drone was deck-launched on schedule and the operations begun without difficulty," reports Admiral Stroop. "It was planned to turn over control of the drone after launch to an airborne E-2A aircraft which would fly the drone in to the program initial point (PIP). There it would be put on a preprogrammed route for photographic reconnaissance of North Vietnam's Highway 1 which paralleled the coast a few miles inland, flying from south to north.

"Unfortunately, the airborne control E-2A could

Ed Wojciechowski

AFTER COMPLETION OF RECONNAISSANCE MISSION, a 147SK *bird is returned by Navy helicopter to the carrier deck to be readied for flight.*

not establish communication with the drone and it was necessary to conduct the entire operation from the Ranger. However, this offered no real difficulty except as regarded accuracy of navigation.

"Reconstruction of the flight indicated that the Ranger was out of geographic position about two miles to seaward of the navigator's estimated position and the drone aircraft, when it was put on program, failed to cover the desired area but instead photographed a strip about two miles to seaward of Highway 1. The photographs were of good quality but did not cover any areas of tactical importance to the Task Force Commander.

"The **SK** drone was returned to the ship and actually sighted directly overhead before being placed into the recovery mode. The drone was landed in the water about 12 miles from the carrier and recovered by helicopter as planned. It was returned to the Ranger without further incident or damage of any kind. It was noted particularly that the equipment compartment was completely dry and the photographic material was found to be in good shape."

Belfry Express flew its second mission with **SK**-5 four days later and came back with many feet of good photo material after having flown a course very close to the planned track.

Three days later **SK**-3 flew a mission and on its return was snatched in mid-air by an Air Force MARS helicopter flying out of DaNang. Retrieval was in full view of the Ranger, and the bird was set down like a feather on the carrier deck.

The Strategic Air Command was flying Air Force 147 drones out of OL-20 at Bien Hoa and, naturally, Detachment 10 at DaNang had to give priority on their two MARS helicopters to their own missions. The Navy **SK** operation wouldn't know if they were going to have an Air Force MARS helicopter until the returning bird neared the carrier. Then, if a MARS helo was in the area, he'd call the ship and let them know he was available — sort of like a taxi driver cruising around looking for a fare.

Major John Dale reported that on the Air Force's first MARS snatch of a Navy **SK** drone, the helo pilot got out of his chopper after landing on the carrier. He stepped to the deck holding a pole with the American Flag stiffly at his side and loudly proclaimed, "I claim this island for the United States Air Force!"

[The Air Force 100th Strategic Reconnaissance Wing assisted the Navy on 31 of its SK flights. — Ed.]

The Navy reciprocated to some degree. One day an Air Force mission terminated early — before a MARS helo could get to it. It was flying erratically so when it parachuted down, the Ranger's chopper went out after it and retrieved it from the water for the Air Force.

"Near the end of our last line period," Grady recalls, "we had an interesting one. All the strike aircraft had been retrieved by the Ranger and the Air Force MARS helicopter developed transmission trouble while it was towing this Navy bird around the sky. The captain of the Ranger wouldn't let him

WHEN AN AIR FORCE RECOVERY HELICOPTER came aboard *the carrier, the Navy deck crew did a real whitewash job. Later the Air Force reciprocated when their helo pilot landed on the Ranger to "claim this island for the United States Air Force!"*

Ed Wojciechowski

Christopher Kane

come aboard lest they have to take the big-bladed Air Force helo all the way to Hong Kong before it could be off-loaded. Instead the Air Force pilot MARS'ed the drone to another carrier which was going 'to be on the line forever' and the Ranger sent a Navy chopper over to bring it home.

"Some of the water retrievals were made 40 or even 50 miles from the Ranger when flights were terminated early for one reason or another. On one occasion a bird was picked up no more than two or three hundred yards off the bow. Everyone was so interested in the operation that the Admiral was tempted to have us fly one right over the ship at a thousand feet, but we never did."

THERE WERE SOME successes; some failures, but of the first five operational missions only one was considered completely successful.

After returning to Subic Bay for resupply, the Ranger headed out again on December 16 for its second line period on Yankee Station. Belfry Express No. 6 was flown five days later. It was storybook perfect. As Jeff Grady said, "We sure had this one coming."

The bird flew its mission 850 feet above the terrain it was photographing. The programmer guided the drone with such precision that the Official Mission Report noted "the SPA split at least two objectives down the middle. No deviations were apparent in any system throughout the mission." And it ended on an up note regarding the MARS retrieval with the comment, "the AF folks set her down very gently with no damage."

By January second Belfry Express 10 was flown — the sixth mission for **SK**-5 — and reports showed an excellent launch, excellent flight, excellent data.

February 10th was a day to remember. Although operational efficiency had picked up, there were still a host of problems as line period three got underway. As Jeff Grady recalls:

"When we started launching from the Ranger we were launching at a 60-degree angle across catapult No. 1. Then we moved back to what is known as the 'point' on the carrier and finally to No. 1 elevator at flight deck level where we launched 90-degrees to the ship's course.

"But this time (Belfry Express 16) we were to launch from No. 1 elevator at hangar deck level rather than at the flight deck elevation. The airborne E-2A had been having trouble anyway in locating the drone when trying to track its beacon after launch. Now it was even more difficult for the E-2A to get a confirmation of beacon performance prior to launch because the bird was poised at hangar deck level rather than on the flight deck.

"On this particular mission we'd pointed out that the beacon was the weakest of those available and shouldn't be used, but it ended up in the SPA anyway. And we were in a new electronic environment where we didn't control the radar that was going to interrogate the drone beacon — which should be capable of a 'here-I-am' response. After we in the control van handed **SK**-5 off to the E-2A, I went up to the CIC to follow the mission.

"After launch no one acquired the drone beacon, yet for unexplained reasons the E-2A continued to try and fly the SPA. They seemed to be flying it alright but just before they got to the PIP where they would have put it on the programmer they told us they were having trouble locating and tracking the drone. In reality they didn't know where it was from shortly after launch because they couldn't paint it on the radar scope. For maybe twenty minutes they flew it without knowing where it was or telling the ship of this fact. Why, I'll never know.

"At this point it would be very difficult to bring it back to the ship by dead reckoning as no one knew where to start. It was pretty futile since the bird was flying off its planned program in the hands of an unskilled operator. So the bird was flown around for a considerable time with no one knowing where it was. We had perfect telemetry information on everything except the bird's location. None of us, myself included, reacted quickly enough to suggest use of DF (direction finding) of the telemetry system.

"We just plain had a bird wandering around the sky. It was out of range of the Ranger so they couldn't pass it back to the ship and that would have been useless anyway because the ship couldn't paint the beacon with its radar. So at drone 'fuel out' the E-2A ended up in control, if you can call it that.

"Up in CIC things were tense. Communications had pretty well broken down. The voice system was 'secure' as the ship was operating under combat conditions and couldn't be used. There was some question of just who was in charge in such a situation.

"In any case, the Admiral took charge issuing the command 'Recover it; recover it!' Someone punched off the panel switch which activated the parachute system, and down floated the bird. Where we didn't know. Helicopters were sent out to where we thought the drone had come down, but they returned empty handed. The mission log reported "No retrieval as position was not known."

SEVERAL DAYS LATER more was learned about the ninth and last flight of **SK**-5. It made the headlines but without revealing that the recce birds were also being flown by a different branch of the U.S. military services.

The Honolulu Star-Bulletin carried a story by Tillman Durdin datelined Hong Kong, quoting Peking as saying that a pilotless U.S. reconnaissance plane had been downed over Hainan Island in Kwangtung Province on February 10.

"Peking," Durdin reported, "has hailed the shooting down of the aircraft as a tremendous feat, and radio stations in provincial capitals of southeastern China are still emphasizing the event.

"A broadcast from Canton describing the downing of the plane said that the craft 'cunningly' changed altitude as it veered over Hainan but 'could never escape the eyes of our radar operators.'

"Chinese Navy men were said to have 'shot down' this U.S. pirate plane at once, 'while cherishing infinite loyalty to our great leader Chairman Mao and harboring bitter hatred for the U.S. aggressors.' "

The Far Eastern Economic Review quoted the New China News Agency as saying it was the 20th such aircraft to be shot down over China since 1964. It was the last 'announcement' of its kind to be made by either the Red Chinese or North Vietnamese for well over two years.

Of course the drone had not been shot down. It had merely run out of fuel and the Red Chinese then 'captured' it or hit it with anti-aircraft artillery as it descended by parachute.

The Chinese had themselves a drone in good condition. One report, never confirmed, was that they tried to sell the **SK** back to the U.S. Navy through Communist agents in Hong Kong.

The printed media was not the only vehicle Peking used in getting across its message about 'U.S. imperialism'. Kowloon, on the mainland opposite the Hong Kong capital city of Victoria, has a multitude of Red Chinese bookstores and other outlets for goods and propaganda.

Vacationing in Hong Kong, J. L. Richardson, president of drone-engine-manufacturing Continental Motors, was surprised and not a little startled on March 8 by the window display on De Voix Road. There in the window of a book store were pictures of **SK**-5 and the Chinese Navy crew which had 'downed' it over Hainan.

AFTER THE CHINESE 'capture' of **SK**-5, fifteen more missions were flown — with varying success — before the Belfry Express project came to a close in May.

To get their own evaluation and to shore up the technical capability on the Ranger, Teledyne Ryan dispatched three of its top trouble shooters. Project manager R. A. (Pete) Petrofsky and veteran field service supervisor Gene Motter were aboard the Ranger when she sailed from Sasebo, Japan, April 12 for her fifth line period. As soon as the Ranger was again deployed in the Tonkin Gulf, Dale Weaver flew over by COD airplane from the Air Force's Detachment 10 at DaNang to help out. He got there the hard way having come from Osan, Korea, via Okinawa, the Philippines and finally South Vietnam.

Petrofsky reporting to San Diego:

April 17 — Tonight the operations briefing was gone over in detail for tomorrow's mission. It will be over familiar territory just south of parallel 19. It's a straightforward in and out mission with shallow penetration (about 300 NM round-trip). Word is that there will be three missions south of 19 and, if everything goes well, the Admiral wants to go well north. We'll be on station some time tonight and first thing

WINDOW DISPLAY IN HONG KONG featured pictures of 147SK-5 *which had run out of fuel. Legend under photo reads, in part, "Minuteman Lin Ya-shua, a witness of the air battle, describing to the local Army-men and civilians before the wreckage of the U.S. piratical plane how it was shot to pieces."*

J. L. Richardson

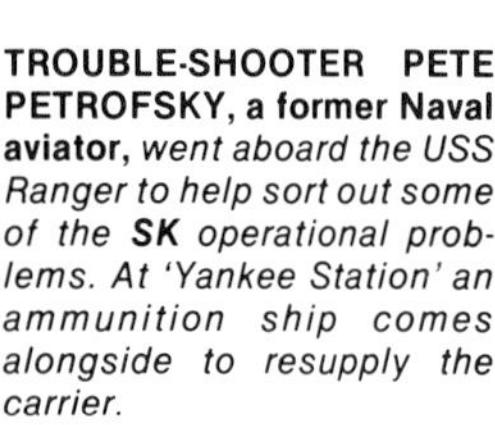
TROUBLE-SHOOTER PETE PETROFSKY, a former Naval aviator, *went aboard the USS Ranger to help sort out some of the* ***SK*** *operational problems. At 'Yankee Station' an ammunition ship comes alongside to resupply the carrier.*

Gene Motter

in the morning regular air strikes commence. This will be a very busy place for the next few weeks. So far on this deployment, ten manned aircraft have been lost.

April 18 — BE-24 (Belfry Express) mission, with **SK**-8 as the vehicle, was flown today. Launch was perfect. Bird flew entire course as planned. CIC radar plot was right on all the way. Material [photo coverage] was reported as being excellent. Recovery was in the water and returned by ship's helo. Air Force MARS helo was on station but, with bum landing gear, elected not to make the catch and returned to DaNang. Bird was in excellent shape on return and had no scars.

The Admiral followed the flight from beginning to end and treats the bird as his own little baby. Motter and I were in CIC and had access to all that was going on despite the fact that it was very busy. Dale Weaver was in the control van with Jeff Grady to observe the launch and watch telemetry. The pilot of the E-2A says that on the next mission he flys he will take Dale along.

Acceptance of the drones by pilots of the manned reconnaissance squadron flying RA-5C Vigilantes from the Ranger was somewhat better than Grady had been led to expect.

"I had anticipated a lot of hostility," he recalled, "when they invited me down to the squadron briefing room because of the pride a man develops who flies into a combat environment. We thought they'd feel their manhood was in question, but we found little of that attitude.

"They surprised me with their enthusiasm for the unmanned concept. Right in the middle of a technical discussion one pilot told me, 'Man, you can fly your drones over Vinh any day you want.' That kind of disrupted the whole meeting, but everyone pretty much agreed with him.

"Right after the Ranger's attack aircraft and manned recces would be catapulted off on a strike we would launch our drone. Then we'd run a tight mission and have to get the bird back and off the deck before the carrier began to retrieve the aircraft returning from the strike. The result was a very compressed time schedule for everyone concerned.

"Before we even got the bird off the flight deck, we had the camera out and the photo man was hauling the film magazine down to the photo processing area. About an hour after the bird got back aboard you had something you could look at.

"There was a lot of satisfaction in knowing the drone had brought back useful material. We understood the 'take' was every bit as good as what the manned recce squadron was picking up during the same period — and without risking the life of the pilot on unusually hazardous missions."

Three fine missions were flown April 18, 22 and 27, 1970, as disclosed by pictures later made available showing excellent detail from one thousand feet altitude. In addition to SAM sites and AAA sites at Vinh and Than Hoa there were clear pictures for study by photo interpreters of pipelines, railway stations and sidings, truck parks, highways, bridges, canals, transshipment points, construction, repair and storage yards, and anchorage areas.

All three missions started at the program initiate point (PIP) with deviations of less than half a mile. Reports showed the April 27 mission (BE-27) as being with a "good, controllable SPA throughout. Good MARS on the first pass. A beauty! The Navy is very grateful to USAF." Even the mission of April 24 was "excellent; but the bird died. Neither drag nor main chutes deployed!"

Of course, Teledyne Ryan tech reps never knew whether or not drone missions were integrated operationally with those of the strike aircraft. "They might have experimented with that concept" Grady said. "I hope so, but don't really know."

With only one bird left, **SK**-10, the final flight was

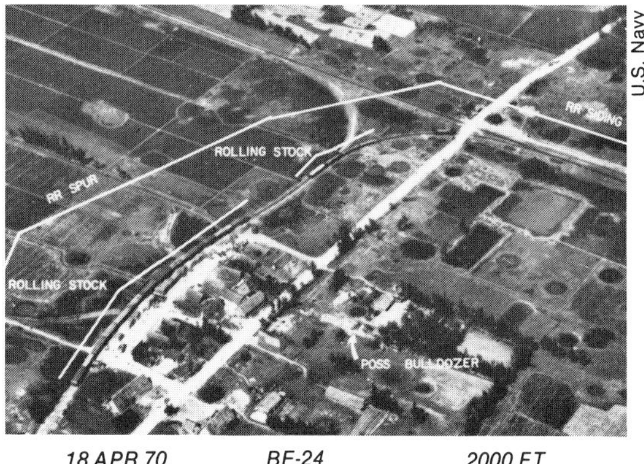

U.S. Navy

18 APR 70 BE-24 2000 FT.

RAILROAD SIDING AND SPUR at Ty My *reveals lines of freight cars near important highway. BE-24 refers to 'Belfry Express.'*

U.S. Navy

22 APR 70 BE-25 1000 FT.

PHOTO INTERPRETERS have identified *area to be analyzed in detail. Photo by drone from squadron VC-3 aboard USS Ranger (CVA-61).*

U.S. Navy

27 APR 70 BE-27 1500 FT.

TAM LU HIGHWAY BRIDGES CANAL *in this photo taken from 1500 feet by 147***SK** *reconnaissance drone launched from carrier Ranger.*

scheduled for May 10 and went off like clockwork. It returned carrying data from a near-perfect mission "up north". On command, the drag chute deployed properly but the main chute failed to blossom. **SK**-10 plunged into the water. Only a badly damaged horizontal tip was retrieved. Belfry Express ended on a sad note.

"Toward the end of the program," Adm. Stroop recalled, "a series of unfortunate recovery failures took place. These consisted of the recovery parachute for some unexplained reason being automatically detached allowing the drone to crash into the sea. This particular failure was finally analyzed by Pete Petrofsky who determined that the armored shielding cable for the parachute actuating circuit had suffered saltwater contamination from previous flights. This particular failure was corrected by using only new cables for each mission."

It was clear it would take additional time to fully integrate the drone reconnaissance capability with the fast-paced combat operations of an attack carrier strike force. A better interface of electronics equipment would also be required. Overall the drone imposed some problems that strictly attack aircraft people didn't like.

The photo intelligence the drones brought back was good. The problems were operational, integrating drones into the carrier electronics and operating pattern; not the ability of the bird to bring back useful pictures.

"The Navy," Dale Weaver said, "got what they paid for. The **SK** was a good evaluation and the Navy learned what they needed to know about the drone so they could go in and write their own unmanned reconnaissance requirement."

'P. D.' Stroop's observations were that "The Navy would have more flexibility and a better operation if the drone could be air-launched rather than surface-launched from the carrier deck. Limited funding had not permitted this type of operation in tests of the **SK** capability. And MARS is by far the best method of recovery because it reduces contamination and shortens turn-around time.

"Unfortunately what was really an R&D evaluation had to be conducted under combat conditions before the drone had been fully integrated into a new operating environment. Despite this, a good capability was demonstrated and the program served as a starting point for further Navy use of unmanned reconnaissance vehicles from aircraft carriers."

23

COMBAT DAWN

EARLY in 1967, the Air Force ordered the Model 147**T** as a successor to the **H** for the high-altitude mission. The vehicle used the proven **H** airframe and Hycon's 338A camera system, but its principal improvement was the increased altitude capability made possible by the new Continental J100-CA-100 engine. With a sea level static thrust of 2800 pounds, the new jet engine represented an increase of more than 45% over the 1920 pounds thrust available in the **H** model.

The increased thrust enabled the 147**T** to reach an altitude of 66,300 feet at 220 n.m. from launch to a fuel-out altitude of 75,000 feet. It has a flight endurance of four-and-a-half hours. Its camera equipment is capable of taking pictures of a strip 22 miles wide by nearly 800 miles along the flight path.

There were also improvements in the Doppler navigation equipment. The **T** was equipped with systems developed for the **H** to increase survivability. These included HIDE, a system to reduce radar reflectivity while flying in a hostile environment, and "Rivet Bounder," an electronic countermeasures device to jam the SA-2 missile guidance system.

Operational flights of the **T** began in the Spring of 1969 out of Bien Hoa, with the heaviest schedule of flying in the early months of 1970. **T**-17 was one bird which came to an unhappy end October 28, 1969 according to an Associated Press report from Warsaw which featured a photo of the Ryan Aeronautical Co. nameplate taken from the drone "shot down over Central South China by the Chinese Air Force."

SEA OF JAPAN, April 18, 1969 — Flying the ancient prop-driven EC-121 version of the Super Constellation transport can get pretty boring — especially on long-duration operations. Lieut. Commander James Overstreet was flying just such a course around the Sea of Japan where the plane's electronic gear could overhear the whisperings of North Korean, Chinese and Russian radars.

Things had quieted down a bit in the 15 months since the Pueblo had been captured by North Korean gunboats off Wonsan. Its electronic snooping assignment of scavenging every electronic signal for miles around had been taken over by the less vulnerable 'spy in the sky' EC-121s flying out of Atsugi Naval Air Station near Tokyo. Too, the airborne eavesdroppers could 'see' a much more distant horizon and were able to scoop up the electronic signals of potential enemies at far greater range.

The game was to see if you could be 'painted' by enemy radar whose characteristics could then be used to determine enemy intentions. But on the whole it had been a basically dull assignment until today.

The routine for Lieut. Commander Overstreet and his crew of 30 was suddenly and rudely interrupted when a South Korean ground station came on the air to warn that two North Korean MiGs were headed for the EC-121. The U.S. Navy aircraft turned east to be certain that it was at least the proscribed 50 nautical miles off the North Korean Coast.

Monitoring radars in Japan saw blips of a MiG jet and the plodding Super Constellation merge, then only one plane moved on across the screen. The

Teledyne Ryan Aeronautical

T MODEL IN THE 147 SERIES had much larger engine *than its H predecessor enabling it to reach 75,000-foot altitude. Note large nacelle for 2800 pound thrust engine.*

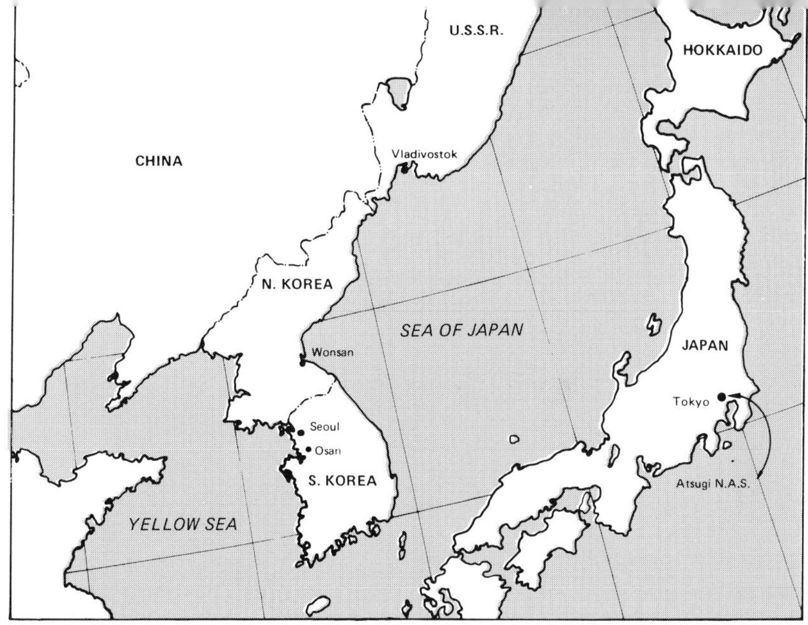

Louise M. Cram

EC-121 and the 31 Americans aboard disappeared, never to be heard from again.

Flights of the EC-121s were suspended, to be resumed as soon as they could properly be protected. With things boiling in Vietnam, President Nixon clearly could take no more drastic action lest he run the risk of opening a second front in Asia.

Had the U.S. been unwise in conducting the Comint (communications intelligence) and Elint (electronic intelligence) mission with manned aircraft?

TIME magazine wrote: "In the wake of the Pueblo incident, there was surely a legitimate question as to the prudence shown by the U.S. in sending slow, unprotected planes to spy on a jumpy Communist nation already notorious for pugnacity and unpredictability. President Nixon admitted that 190 such flights had taken place since Jan. 1."

LT. COLONEL ANDY CORRA, in charge of unmanned reconnaissance systems on the Pentagon's Air Staff, awoke restless in his room at the Islandia Hotel in San Diego. He was anxious to get to the Ryan plant for an early morning program review of the **T** model with Bob Reichardt and his management people.

As he passed the hotel clerk's desk he glanced at the pile of morning newspapers. The headline in the San Diego Union riveted his attention.

31 KILLED AS U.S. SPY PLANE
SHOT DOWN BY NORTH KOREA

So, we'd been clobbered again. First the Pueblo; now the 'Connie' electronic eavesdropper. Corra was more than a little upset.

"As soon as I got to the plant," he remembers, "I asked Bob to get hold of Dan Emrich and the three of us got right down to business. But on a new idea.

"There must be a better way, I thought, to do the Elint mission without subjecting the country to embarrassment or risking lives of pilots and crew aboard a manned aircraft.

"We all felt we could do the job, using a drone as a relay aircraft. Put a relay system aboard our newest and highest-flying bird — the **T**. Put the operators on the ground and from there control the information they wanted to hear, instead of putting them aboard an airplane as was the case with the downed EC-121.

"If Bob and Dan would get started on the problem of putting the technical package together, I'd go back to Washington and approach General Steakley on the acceptability in DOD of having the job done by a drone.

"The general thought the idea had merit and said he'd discuss it immediately with Cyrus Vance, the Deputy Secretary of Defense, who reviewed all the recce drone programs at the highest levels of government. This was one of the special channels, involving only two or three people, through which these projects got expedited treatment. Another channel was all Air Force, through the offices of the Assistant and Under Secretaries — successively held by Doctors McMillen, Flax and McLucas. In those instances the word came down direct to my office — the unmanned systems desk of the Air Staff.

"General Steakley reported back that, yes, an effort such as we proposed to replace the EC-121, would be supported.

"Another activity was involved this time — the National Security Agency — but even so the program moved ahead with virtually no delay even though there was some initial question as to whether drones or manned U-2s would get the assignment.

"In any case, the first full briefing was held a week after the EC-121 was shot down by the North Koreans. Less than two weeks later the program had been through the Air Staff, through Dr. McLucas and been presented to F. E. O'Rear, my counterpart, in the Big Safari office.

"Four prototype birds, designated **TE**, and based on the already operational 147**T** photographic model would be readied for the eavesdropping mission. The first test flight was flown November 25, 1969 — only six months after loss of the EC-121. The first operational flight was February 15, 1970 from Osan, South Korea.

"The **T** to **TE** transition is just another example of the reason for the rapid growth of the 147 program. Ryan had a basic system that could be readily adapted to meet changing requirements and the Air Force had a management technique that cut through red tape and got the job done on a compressed time schedule. The Under Secretary of Air Force and the Deputy Secretary of Defense saw to that."

As in several previous high priority projects of national importance, Col. Red Smith had the task of assembling the necessary hardware.

"In short order," Smith reports, "we had to build a new electronic collection capability with unmanned aircraft that would not risk the lives of American pilots and the 20 or 30 men sitting in the back of EC-121s.

"We literally had to rob the supply agencies of all the assets we needed because the lead time on some of the airborne radio gear and ground environment equipment was 14 months.

"We had undertaken such an apparently impossible task that the doctorate level technical people in the National Security Agency said that, physically, it could not be done. And if it could be done it wouldn't work. And if it did work it wouldn't work well.

"We did get it done on time and in budget and it did work and it did work well.

"It was a fantastic accomplishment which demonstrated what a select team of Air Force and contractor people can do. We ought not to lose the

Dave Gossett

By war's end, ***SC*** *had flown more sorties than any other 147 model, followed by* ***TE*** *and* ***TF.***

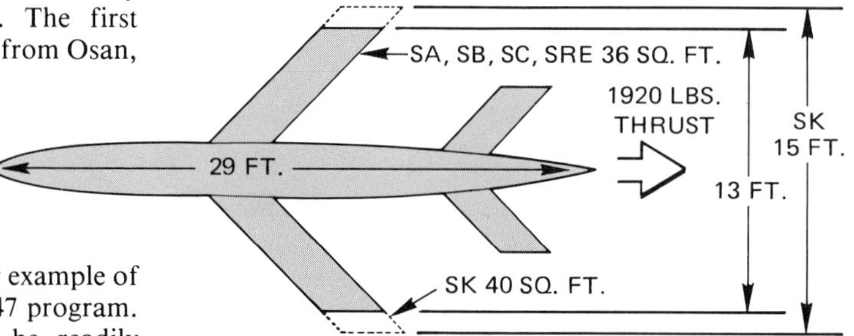

147SA, SB, SC, SRE, SK

capability to make this kind of response when the national interest is at stake."

Because of its superior high-altitude capability, the **T** airframe proved to be a fine platform for conducting real-time electronic signal intelligence (Sigint) missions. The **TE** model was able to gather signal data from enemy transmitters up to 600 miles from ground control and transmit them over FM data link.

In general, two main kinds of data are collected by Sigint aircraft:

Comint (for communications intelligence) primarily means verbal radio messages but occasionally multiplexed teletype. The plane can overhear, and transmit back to ground control, conversations between major command posts 200 miles away and thus plot troop movements and combat readiness.

Elint (for electromagnetic intelligence) measures non-verbal signals such as radar, missile guidance systems, automatic landing aids and computer traffic. This permits plotting the types and sites of radar installations and the operating channels and signature characteristics of all manner of electronic gear. By analyzing a radar signal, it can be determined what that particular radar is used for.

'Playing games' is one of the sports indulged in by members of 'Old Crows', the fraternity of electronic counter measures (ECM) specialists. As TIME magazine explained at the time of the shooting down of the EC-121 —

TESTING OF 147T during Fall of 1968 *was conducted, as were many other proving flights, at Navy's Point Mugu facility.*

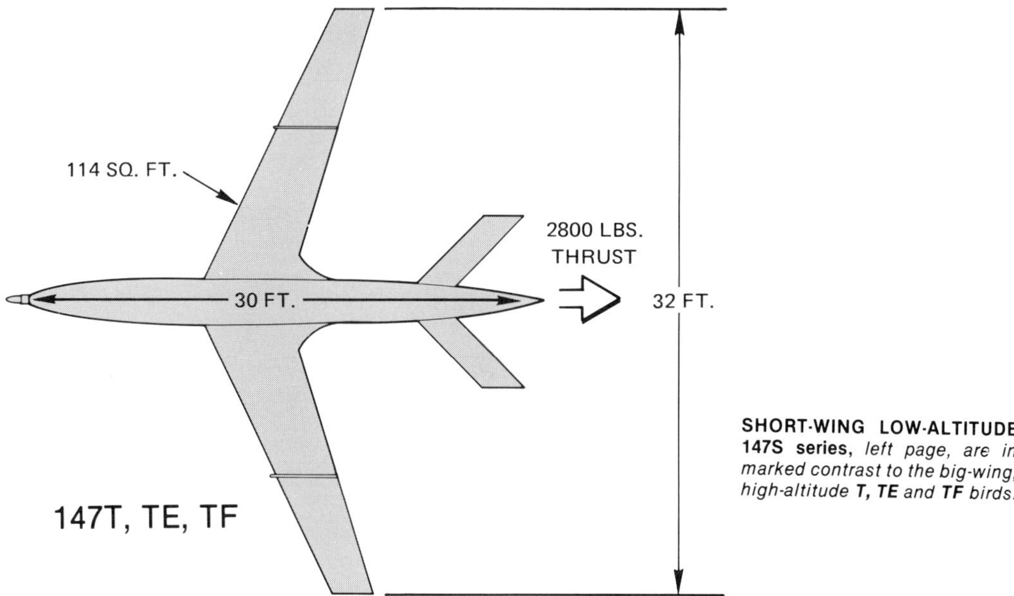

SHORT-WING LOW-ALTITUDE 147S series, *left page, are in marked contrast to the big-wing, high-altitude* ***T, TE*** *and* ***TF*** *birds.*

One ingenious way to test a potential enemy's alertness is known as "exercising." That means feeding a fake signal back to the adversary's tracking radar at precisely timed intervals to simulate an intrusion in his airspace. The defender is lured into sending his interceptors aloft and activates all his secret radar equipment to bag this fictitious intruder. Meanwhile, from a distance, the spy plane can carefully monitor everything that is done by the enemy in order to meet the electronically manufactured threat.

Schwanhausser recalls that Teledyne Ryan had already done some useful homework when the crisis brought on by the EC-121 incident showed the need for an alternate system.

"Before there was a **TE** model, the basic concept had been explored by Dan Emrich while still in the Joint Reconnaissance Center of JCS. Much of his early work was with Melpar, the company which had done so much with electronic data collection techniques. When Dan left the service he joined Ryan so that when the EC-121 went down we were in a position to push it through.

"We had the bird, Melpar had the equipment. The real problem was to take the Melpar package, install it and put in a data link. We had been working on 'Speedlink', a real-time wide-band data link, so we had a little one-upmanship there. We all felt the concept was right, but how were we going to get all of that equipment in our little bird?

"What we were trying to do was provide a real-time, remotely-controlled, peripheral collection system with the flight operation to be conducted in a politically sensitive area. It was to be a real first-of-its-kind thing."

VIC RUDD GOT INVOLVED in the **TE** program almost from the start. He, too, was a 'graduate' of the Air Force staff dealing with recce drones. He'd come from the 3205th Drone Group at Eglin AFB at a time they were flying the early Q-2A version of the Firebee training target in 1961. He moved to the Pentagon to monitor the target drone program for Headquarters, USAF, and having been involved in the early 147**A**, **C** and **D** tests inherited Lloyd Ryan's recce duties on the latter's retirement in 1963. Operational responsibility was with SAC at Omaha, where Lieut. Col. Andy Corra was deputy, with Dan Emrich and Ells Powell in the same recce group.

Rudd stayed with the Air Force recce staff through the whole alphabetical series of 147 models up to the **J** low-altitude photographic bird. Then, on retirement, he too joined Ryan. By the time of the EC-121 loss, Rudd was in San Diego with the Ryan company and Powell was at the Big Safari unit with the Air Force Logistics Command at Wright-Patterson AFB in Dayton.

"In less than two weeks after the first capability briefing," Rudd recalls, "we had been through the Air Staff, briefed Dr. McLucas, and cleared the Big Safari hurdle at AFLC. Three days later we had the first funds approved for purchase of long lead time items and had a contract for four birds in hand 64 days after the first briefing.

"It called for two 147**TE** vehicles with Melpar equipment for communications intelligence gathering and two for electronics intelligence gathering. We called these models HARC (high altitude reconnaissance Comint) and HARE (the 'E' for Elint). But that was very soon changed and the Elint versions

Dave Gossett

AT BREAK OF DAWN, DC-130 launch plane with 147TE *on right wing pylon is on its way. Note two fuel pods carried by* ***TE*** *to extend mission range.*

VIC RUDD, veteran of Air Force *target drone program, got involved in the* ***TE*** *operation almost from the start.*

were eliminated so that we built four Comint 147**TE**s.

"The first of these was delivered on November 13, 1969, quickly went to flight test, and after two months testing, was deployed, departing from Pt. Mugu in a C-141 transport for Asia. Three months after delivery the first operational mission was flown out of OL-16 at Osan. (That South Korean operating location was later renamed OL-RC.)

"We operated there for two months flying 22 sorties that were primarily an Operational Test and Evaluation of the system; literally a continuation of the flight test program. A group of about 20 Ryan types, with the ever-present Dale Weaver on tap, formed the technical support team.

"On completion of the OTE, the system was returned to Davis-Monthan, its home base. After a new series of briefings, changes in the configuration were recommended and we went under contract for an additional 15 **TE** production aircraft, the first four having been simple prototypes. Operations at Osan resumed October 10, 1970, with the production **TE**s.

"The high-altitude 'Combat Dawn' unmanned Comint system is capable of intercepting signals from target transmitters at ranges up to 600 nautical miles from the ground facility. Three hundred of these nautical miles represent the capability of the receiving units on board the drone to reach out from the bird's high operating altitude to the distant horizon. The other 300 miles is the capability of the relay system to transmit received signals back to the ground control station and to the van where they are monitored real time and recorded for later detailed analysis.

"The system utilizes a wide band data link to provide full fidelity real time transmission of intercepted data to the ground control van. A radome mounted atop the drone's vertical fin houses the downlink antenna which provides for transmission of ten channels of multiplexed Comint. Each Comint receiver is independently controlled from the ground.

"Flights from Osan are conducted for the National Security Agency at various frequencies of level of tasking in terms of hours of recorded data. We'd be in the air perhaps every third day. After equipping the **TE** with external fuel pods, flight endurance went up from about five hours per mission to eight hours, proportionately reducing the number of flights to be launched.

"With ten receivers on board, the task of interpreting some ten thousand hours of recorded data a year, is formidable.

"Usually directed by the ground control unit, the bird may also be placed on programmed flight to fly automatic mission profiles, or it may be remotely controlled manually from an airborne DC-130. The mission profiles consist basically of an orbit area — a race track type pattern, monitoring the various signals within that area. We can place the drone in an orbit of very small diameter. We need this capability because many of the signals in which we are interested are transmitted in very narrow beams, often no wider than a nautical mile.

"Though we were never informed of the reason, the operation was cut off but later resumed at a sharply reduced schedule not long after President Nixon announced in July 1971 that he would be making a summit trip to Peking to confer with Red Chinese leaders.

"The **TE** operation stays out of the news. We don't operate over land; over unfriendly territory. We operate peripherally and stay at least 50 nautical miles from any hostile land mass.

"But that doesn't mean there have been no attempts to intercept the birds. There have been. As a result of the drone monitoring certain frequencies, we are aware of unfriendly fighter aircraft being scrambled for the intercept, and can so maneuver the **TE** as to prevent the intercept and subsequent shoot-down.

"Of course, we've had operational losses, but not to hostiles. The MARS mid-air retrieval, for example, remains a specialized and somewhat tricky maneuver.

"Not long ago Dale Weaver told me he attended a briefing overseas with Dr. McLucas, the OL commander and the chief of the intelligence unit, and that they agreed the **TE** was doing work no one else could accomplish because of its outstanding high-altitude capability.

"Since then we've put the **TF** model in production as an improved version for either Elint or Comint. You have to remember that the **TE** was developed so rapidly that the follow-on — the **TF** — would have to incorporate many refinements, particularly in the subsystems."

"Three major areas of improvement went into the first ten 147**TF** models," Bob Reichardt explained, "but the basic mission remained the same.

"The later versions of the **TE** had external fuel tanks for greater endurance and we incorporated all of the fuel system improvements in the **TF**.

"The primary mission equipment — the electronic eavesdropping capability — has been upgraded to give additional frequency coverage provided by the receivers and relay equipment in the orbiting bird.

"Lastly, the Air Force has gone to great lengths and expense to produce hardware that should be even more reliable than the **TE**. We have gone through extensive environmental and other testing including — what is rare for QRC type procurement — full military specification (mil spec) qualification of some of the hardware.

Where does the **T** series go from here? We asked Dale Weaver and he identified the **TL**. "As proposed, it will have a bigger wing yet. We may eventually get out of the air launch capability simply because our drones are getting too big. Weight-wise and wing-span-wise we're running just about to the limit of the Lockheed C-130 launch plane. The **TE** with external fuel tanks — the **TF** — will go out at about 6600 pounds. We've had everything from a C-141 up to the C-5A proposed as a launch plane — even a Boeing 747, but cost effectiveness will make it pretty hard to sell."

U.S. Air Force

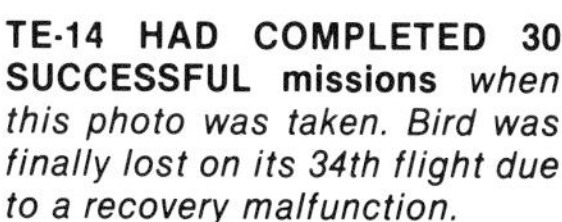

TE-14 HAD COMPLETED 30 SUCCESSFUL missions *when this photo was taken. Bird was finally lost on its 34th flight due to a recovery malfunction.*

"THIS T BIRD HAD BEEN REPORTED AWOL when all contact with it was lost. *Perhaps it was headed for Russian Vladivostok. When all else failed it was electronically instructed to head for home. After three hours incommunicado its parachute blossomed over Osan to everyone's relief."* — *Gene Timmons, Ryan tech rep. Note radome on vertical fin housing downlink antenna.*

MODEL 147 OPERATIONS
The Second Four Years

1968	1969	1970	1971
J F M A M J J A S O N D	J F M A M J J A S O N D	J F M A M J J A S O N D	J F M A M J J A S O N
← 340 Launched →	← 437 Launched →	← 365 Launched →	← 406 Launched →
← 67 →	← 21 →		
HHHHHHHHHHHHHHHH	HHHHHHH	HHHHH	HHHHH
NQ NQ NQ NQ NQ	NQ NC	NC	
SA SA SA SB SB SB SB SB SB	SK	SK SK SK SK	
	← 307 → SCSCSC SC SC SC SC SC	← 276 → SC SC SC SC SC SC SC SC	← 277 → SC SC SC SC SC SC S
SR	E SRE SRE SRE SRE SRE		
← 205 → all S models	← 392 → all S models	← 298 → all S models	
	TT TT	TTTTT T	
		← 49 → TE TE TE TE	← 120 → TE TE TE TE TE TE T

Louise M. Cr

24

SSM

SURFACE-TO-SURFACE MISSILE

SUEZ CANAL, OCTOBER 21, 1967 — The cease-fire negotiated by the United Nations Security Council was rudely interrupted off Port Said today when Egyptian patrol boats launched non-nuclear Russian-made "Styx" missiles against Israel's top warship, sinking the destroyer "Elath" with the loss of 49 lives.

All day the Elath had been virtually challenging Egyptian patrol boats, playing a cat-and-mouse game as the 2500-ton destroyer zig-zagged back and forth in the Bay of Romani at the entrance of the Suez Canal.

Obviously the Elath knew it was being tracked by Egyptian radar from Port Said because it alternately sped up and slowed down as it darted into and out of Egyptian waters.

The Six-Day War between Israel and Egypt had ended with an uneasy truce in mid-June but on July 12 the Elath had sunk two Egyptian torpedo boats in the same area. The Egyptians were hardly pleased to see her back. Now, in the late afternoon of October 21, Gamal Abdel Nasser reportedly had given orders for a strike against the Elath.

Two Egyptian patrol boats each equipped with four Russian Styx self-guiding missiles roared out of Port Said. When officers aboard the Israeli destroyer saw the white trail of the ship-launched missile streaking toward them, their only defense was a desperate but ineffectual attempt to outmaneuver the oncoming missile and to try and shoot it down with machine-gun fire. The target-seeking Styx was not to be denied and hit the Elath midship. Two more Styx followed and Elath, the biggest and best warship in the small Israeli Navy, went down two hours later with the loss of 49 lives.

The sinking of the Elath served to refresh memories in the United States of the tragedy of the electronic-intelligence-collection ship USS Liberty which had been attacked — mistakenly — four and a half months earlier by Israeli jet aircraft and motor patrol boats while in international waters off the Sinai Peninsula.

Was it a case of mistaken identity brought on by the tenseness of the fourth day — June 8 — of the Six-Day War? Did the Israelis believe they were attacking the Egyptian supply ship, El Quseir, to which it bore some resemblance?

Washington was in a real swivet when the Liberty's skipper radioed the first report. Were the unidentified jet aircraft Egyptian, or possibly Russian? Within hours the Israeli government admitted their forces had made the attack in error.

Although the Liberty did not sink, more than 25 American lives were needlessly lost and another 75 crewmen were wounded.

IT WAS NO SURPRISE to anyone that Israel retaliated three days after the sinking of the Elath with heavy raids on the oil refineries at Port Suez, destroying most of Egypt's oil refining capability. Next day seven Russian warships steamed over the horizon to visit Egyptian ports and deter further Israeli attacks.

Even before the Elath sinking, officers of the U.S. Sixth Fleet in the Mediterranean had been deeply concerned about their lack of a weapons system to counter the Soviet missile ships. As so often happens, it takes a major international event like the Elath incident to get a requirement off dead center.

Congressional interest helped the U.S. Navy, under direction of Dr. Robert A. Frosch, Assistant Secretary for Research and Development, in its effort to acquire the capability to meet the Styx threat. The ultimate answer was to be "Harpoon," a ship-to-ship missile with range two to three times that of the Styx. But, with the usual problems of technical study, development, evaluation and production, the Harpoon system would be five years from possible operational deployment. What to do in the interim?

For years, Ryan had been studying and proposing FLASH, its projected Firebee Low Altitude Ship-to-ship Homing missile which would have the capability to provide, at the very least, a quick-reaction interim system until Harpoon was ready for deployment.

John Bryson

Flight Test Engineer Berner

Unlike solid propellant missiles with a limited range of perhaps 35 miles, FLASH would be a cruise missile — one which used liquid fuel and had wings — with a range capability of better than 100 miles.

Instead of developing a system to destroy Styx in mid-flight, the Ryan-proposed Firebee weapon system would counter the Russian system with the ability to deliver a warhead at low altitude and long range, providing an effective counter threat. Its longer range would effectively reduce the chance that the Soviets would risk the retaliation which would follow their use of Styx. The Russians would be outgunned before they ever launched.

FLASH would follow a pre-programmed flight path. At about 300 feet altitude, the JATO unit would separate and the missile would be turned to a pre-selected heading, maintaining that altitude. Enroute command corrections based on radar information would be sent to adjust heading. The missile would descend to a programmed cruise altitude of 50 feet and 400 knots.

After leaving the area of friendly ships, the terminal seeker would be activated and the bombs electrically armed. While guided by the seeker toward a collision course with the target, the missile would descend to 25 feet and the proximity sensor would be turned on. At intercept, two 500-pound bombs would be detonated by the impact fuse or the proximity sensor.

That was expected to pretty well take care of an enemy destroyer.

Fortunately, Ryan and the Navy were well prepared to develop such a weapon system because of various subsystem work which had been previously accomplished. Four capabilities would be essential to convert the standard BQM-34A Firebee target system into a weapons delivery vehicle. They were (1) a demonstrated ability to carry a weapon; (2) terminal low-altitude control to point of impact with the enemy target; (3) ability to launch from a destroyer or other ship under way; and (4) real-time guidance to find and destroy the target.

USING THE FIREBEE drone for weapons delivery was by no means a new idea at Ryan. When Carroll Berner joined the company in 1953 his first assignment was on an Air Force study contract.

"We were asked to see what additional uses were practical for the Firebee target drone," Berner recalls. "We came up with two: reconnaissance — primarily side-looking radar — and weapons delivery, with the payload pylon-mounted.

"Reconnaissance got started in 1960, but it wasn't until late 1964 under Army Missile Command contract that we demonstrated the increased payload capability which would make weapons delivery practical. This had the Ryan code name 'CeeBee.' Of course the greater payload could, as an option, be used for additional fuel for extended operating range.

"At the White Sands Missile Range in New Mexico we conducted a series of ground launches using a larger rocket booster, the ASROC. Starting out with two 250-pound bombs we gradually built up to the final launch demonstration, carrying two pylon-mounted SUU-7 bomblet dispensers, each pod weighing 518 pounds. To carry the 1000-pound overload we not only had the bigger JATO bottle but also extended wing tips for greater lift."

1 ABILITY TO CARRY A WEAPON. *To carry 1000-pound overload larger ASROC booster and extended wing tips provided capability.*

U.S. Air Force

FOR THE FIREBEE'S low-altitude capability, Ryan was indebted at least in part to its competitors who were also providing target services to the Navy late in 1965.

The Australians had developed the "Jindivik," a similar jet target, which was offered in the United States by Chance Vought. A quantity had been sold to the Navy. One of the advantages of the import was its ability to provide the Navy with a target capable of making a high speed run at very low level over the ocean or terrain. The Navy needed such a target to test the capability of its defenses against very high speed aircraft coming in at mast height.

"Since both Firebees and Jindiviks were operational at Pt. Mugu," Berner recalls, "it was clear that Ryan was going to have to provide a low-altitude Firebee capability or watch the lead it had in target systems disappear.

"We got busy on a control system which would use a radar altimeter to measure altitude above the ocean and thus provide an electronic input to the control system. It was our radar altimeter low altitude control system, or RALACS, which gives real-time altitude readouts on the remote control operator's console, making precise and instantaneous control possible.

"In demonstrations we showed that Firebee targets could be flown under good control as low as 50 feet above the water at speeds of 500 miles an hour. Such a mission was flown against the USS Norton Sound in Spring 1966 off Pt. Mugu to test its 'Seaspar' missile.

"The flight began with air-launch from a Navy DP-2E aircraft. After descending to the upper altitude reference of 3500 feet, the Firebee was commanded to dive, dropping to 150 feet above the white caps. Following a remote control command to turn in for the 'hot leg' run, controllers dropped the jet-powered target to 50 feet altitude for its run on the Norton Sound, roaring in some 150 yards from the Seaspar battery aboard the ship. Subsequently the low-altitude system was applied to Air Force and Army targets operated over land.

"RALACS not only gave Ryan the low-altitude capability for converting the Firebee into a weapons system, but also effectively ended the Jindivik's threat to its use as a low-level target system by the Navy."

SOON AFTER THE ELATH sinking, Naval Ordnance Systems Command authorized development of ship-launch capabilities for the Firebee so as to evaluate the ability of U.S. radars to detect a Styx type missile being launched from a ship. Simulation of the Styx would also enable the Navy to use the Firebee as a target to practice anti-missile gunnery and evaluate weapons. Successful tests were conducted in mid-1968 with technical assistance from Ryan target systems field service teams.

"The deactivated destroyer 'Killen,' " Berner relates, "was modified with a ground launch platform on the aft gun mount base ring, with a protected launch-control station nearby.

"Richard F. Manceau, Ryan Base Manager at Roosevelt Roads, Puerto Rico, directed the contractor's technical effort in support of the Navy which sent launchers and other equipment from Pt. Mugu. The Killen was towed to sea for tests on the Atlantic Fleet Weapons Range. Six successful

2 TERMINAL LOW-ALTITUDE CONTROL, *here demonstrated by Firebee equipped with RALACS — radar altimeter low-altitude control system. Test mission was flown in 1966 at 50-foot altitude against USS Norton Sound off Southern California coast.*

3 **ABILITY TO LAUNCH FROM A SHIP UNDER WAY.** *On Pacific Missile Range a BQM-34A Firebee operating under remote control was launched from a converted aviation rescue boat separately controlled remotely from another Navy ship.*

launches from the destroyer deck were conducted in Summer 1968 for radar tracking tests with standard BQM-34As. In the three final tests the Firebees did double duty by serving as regular targets for gunnery practice by Atlantic Second Fleet units.

"On the Pacific Missile Range a similar test was conducted in March 1969 with a 104-foot converted aviation rescue boat (AVR) under way by remote control at 15 knots, used as the launching platform. From this platform, remotely guided from another vessel, the BQM-34A, also operating under its own remote control system, was successfully launched.

"Later the Navy configured two 63-foot aviation rescue boats and proved that the smaller ship could also be used as a seagoing fleet-underway launch platform. Still later AVRs were converted for Firebee launch at Roosevelt Roads.

"During the tests out of Puerto Rico on the destroyer Killen and with AVRs at both Pt. Mugu and Roosevelt Roads, we did not lose a single bird.

"While the primary purpose was to build a defense against the Styx missile, the ship-launch capability of the Firebee demonstrated the potential for development of a weapons delivery system of its own."

THE POSSIBILITY OF MOUNTING a television camera in the nose of an airplane and 'broadcasting' the image of an enemy target to a ground station had long intrigued military planners.

The Naval Ordnance Test Station, (NOTS) China Lake, California, had been an early leader in the field of airborne television monitored in real-time by ground observers. They were looking toward use of TV in a pilotless plane. The secret nature of their experiments with a Cohu camera bolted to the nose of a droned Grumman F-9F aircraft were such that only a few people were aware of its possible applications.

"Finally, in 1968," Berner recalls, "NOTS put the system in a BQM-34A Navy Firebee, making several flights staged out of Pt. Mugu, and recording the television presentations.

"The Firebee was made to respond to a proportional control system where the movement of the miniature control stick at the remote station gave the drone aerodynamic system the same proportional control inputs.

"The controller became a ground-based pilot. By simply moving the stick he could change the drone's bank angle or the pitch attitude of the bird, and see it in real-time on the TV monitor.

"In this test they flew the Firebee over a range of low hills, descending down a relatively flat desert basin where a low-level run of perhaps 20 miles was made. No warhead was carried, nor was a target impacted, but it was a very impressive demonstration.

"TV, of course, was only one way of zeroing-in on the target. It would be very effective in good visibility, but under poor light conditions or at night, a weapons-carrying Firebee could be equipped with a target-seeking radar system to more effectively do the job."

4 **REAL-TIME GUIDANCE TO FIND AND DESTROY THE TARGET** *was provided in tests which demonstrated use of nose-mounted TV camera.*

WITH ALL THE CAPABILITIES needed to convert the Firebee to a SSM (Surface-to-Surface Missile) now available, Ryan and the Navy began to work toward joint development of an interim system to counter the Styx missile. Of the many proposals studied, the one which ultimately seemed to best meet Navy requirements was to provide 80 BQM/SSM Firebee 'missiles,' 10 destroyers for launching, and an equal number of LAMPS (Light Airborne MultiPurpose System) helicopters as airborne control stations.

But before things got that far or procurement could proceed there would have to be further studies and adequate demonstrations of the ability to integrate the components into a total system.

The Naval Ordnance Center had asked the laboratory at White Oak, Maryland, to find an off-the-shelf vehicle that could be converted to an anti-ship cruise missile. Several missiles and target systems were evaluated and the final conclusion, in November 1968, was that the BQM-34A was the only vehicle with the capability of performing the mission.

Much of the Navy interest in the BQM/SSM system came from Admiral Isaac C. Kidd, Jr., of the First Fleet, based at San Diego, and from Rear Admiral Thomas D. Davies, Chief of Development in the Material Command.

Although it appeared unnecessary to develop a special warhead for the SSM — since the Firebee's JP-5 fuel could be exploded on impact with the target — Naval Ordnance wanted to have the maximum capability against many types of ships.

What China Lake was asked to — and did — develop was a warhead which could be carried internally in the Firebee so as to eliminate the need for pylon mounting of the weapon. This would reduce gross weight of the SSM, permit use of the regular JATO unit and in other ways eliminate the need for special handling equipment so it could be standardized with that of the Firebee target systems.

By the Spring of 1971 the concept was well enough along for demonstration of the whole weapons system. The Naval Ordnance Test Laboratory at China Lake had configured a BQM-34A with television camera and pseudo-proportional control. The bird would be air-launched some ten miles from San Clemente Island off the Southern California coast, fly a horseshoe pattern, descend in altitude and impact the decommissioned USS Butler, which was to serve as a target ship.

The rules for the flight on March 12, 1971 called for an abort and rerun should the drone at any time be outside a well defined operating perimeter. Remote control was from an airborne Navy helicopter. Unfortunately the Navy controller failed to keep the bird within the lateral limits set for the demonstration.

Instead of aborting the flight and coming around for another try he attempted, too late, to make a lateral heading correction requiring a banked turn.

Carroll Berner recalls that "although the bird had come around the path reasonably well, it was displaced laterally nearly a quarter of a mile on its final leg.

"They continued to descend in altitude without correcting the lateral error until they got very, very close to the water. Then, at the first attempt to alter the heading, they had to make a major correction because of the fast closing rate on the target. In the bank maneuver they lost what little altitude they had — about twenty feet — and crashed about a quarter mile short of the target.

"Except for the controller error, the bird performed beautifully. It did everything it was supposed to do. Television reception on that particular flight was very good. The TV monitor was perfect. Yet we lost the bird; we missed the target. But everyone knew the weapons system potential was there!"

NO ONE KNEW FOR SURE whether or not the normally land-based Firebee would withstand the adverse environment of operation at sea. They'd have to have the answer if the bird was to assume the surface-to-surface missile role.

In April 1971 two BQM-34As were assigned aboard the destroyer USS Anderson and placed on the aft deck. One was exposed to the elements at all times; the other enclosed in a plastic radome-type enclosure kept inflated with air from a continuously run blower.

The three-month test period included full speed runs, high speed turns and other maneuvers, simultaneous firing of all guns and operations in high sea states. The BQM inside the enclosure showed no corrosion. The bird exposed to the elements didn't fare so well but did prove that the BQM could withstand normal sea environment for as much as a year and still be airworthy.

New tests with the Cohu television camera system were also scheduled and three runs made on May 4th and 5th against the decommissioned USS Butler off Pt. Mugu. In these tests the BQM was airlaunched and controlled from a helicopter. Using a radar plot, the controller knew approximately where to go to intercept the ship. Then it was necessary to acquire the ship in television camera view projected on the monitor and maneuver the Firebee so that it flew directly over the destroyer at 150 feet altitude.

Two flights were made the first day; the third the next day. The results were reassuring, particularly to Admiral Davies who as remote controller had earlier 'flown' a droned QF-9 from a TV monitor during a China Lake test.

"It was after this test," recalls Berner, "that the Navy made the decision to go with television in the BQM/SSM rather than a target seeker. We at Ryan felt the all-weather capability of the radar seeking system would improve the chances of finding enemy ships because it could search a broad expanse of the ocean even in restricted visibility. The system would

Teledyne Ryan Aeronautical

'SPEEDLINK,' A 147S BIRD with real-time capability *could handle many kinds of data including television. Note radome atop fuselage housing antenna.*

be capable of seeking and automatically homing on a Komar (Soviet) boat-size target while flying at very low altitude over the open sea.

"About the same time that China Lake was developing its television capability, Ryan engineers were working on a new real-time data link we called Speedlink. It can handle many kinds of data, including television, and is capable of a range on the order of 200 miles compared with 50 miles for the China Lake system. It would fit nicely into the BQM/SSM capability."

"The purpose of putting the Speedlink TV into the BQM/SSM and in demonstrating it in the low altitude 147 drones," explained Bob Schwanhausser, "was to update the navigation system. For example, with real-time TV, we would have a better idea in approaching a shoreline of just where we were and could then correct and update the nav system. Originally, with Speedlink, we weren't interested specifically in terminal guidance but aimed our work at better navigation.

"The people in Washington were interested in what we could do so we made some captive flights out of Andrews Air Force Base with the bird secured on the wing pylon of a DC-130 launch plane.

"These demonstrations were witnessed by David Packard, Assistant Secretary of Defense, by Dr. Harold Brown, and others in the Air Force staff.

"We flew several cameras during the TV trials, one of them a CBS system. Later CBS gave some of the information to the New York Times and stirred up a lot of speculation about the use of drones to maintain surveillance along the Suez Canal."

"WE WERE STILL CONCERNED about the control problem during the final run of a fully configured BQM/SSM into the target," continued Berner "so proposed to the Navy that Ryan conduct a simulation study to determine the best control technique for ramming the target, and to provide controller training.

"For the final demonstration of the complete system, scheduled for September, two Ryan controllers, working as a team, would be used. One would be prime controller from the airborne helicopter command post; the other back-up controller from a ground-based MSQ control unit.

"We put the two controllers in separate rooms in our simulation laboratory — one watching the TV monitor with a command box in front of him; the other watching a radar plot and a better display of telemetry data so he could relay information to the primary controller by radio.

"The simulation was very realistic and paid off handsomely."

ALL WAS NOW READY for the pre-contract final demonstration of the BQM/SSM system with Navy participation by NOTS, China Lake; the VC-3 target drone squadron, and with Ryan personnel as control operators.

While the concept called for launch from a Navy ship, safety considerations on the Pacific Missile Range off Southern California dictated that neither ship-launch nor ground-launch from the Pt. Mugu facility be used. Instead the SSM Firebee 'missile' would have to be air launched from a Navy DC-130 for the run off the west side of San Clemente Island since there was no ground launch capability there either. Shore-based cameras would be set up, assuring complete photo coverage.

Carroll Berner reported the first demonstration, September 1, 1971:

"The mission proceeded very well. We had scheduled one flight over the target for a final check, then planned to come around and go for impact on the second approach. Everything was excellent until the terminal descent command to bring the bird down from 75 feet to 35 feet.

"The bird failed to respond immediately but before we could override the command it was too late. It flew over the ship at about 70 feet off the water, striking a wire from the mast which clipped off a wing, ruptured the fuel tank and caused the bird to explode. With a warhead we would have had a hit. Nonetheless it was an excellent demonstration of the basic capability."

"ONE COULDN'T ASK to witness a more exciting event than the demonstration of September 2nd." It was Erich Oemcke speaking. As Executive Director of Ryan Aerospace Systems he was Bob Schwanhausser's right-hand man. The top technical expert in remotely piloted vehicles, he had flown out that morning from San Diego to witness the final test.

"I chose to watch the actual flight through binoculars from my position at the command and control site 1200 feet up the side of San Clemente Island. I could always see a replay of action on the video screen, but only once would I be able to watch the actual demonstration.

"The excitement started as soon as we spotted the bird coming in on a southerly heading at about 75 feet altitude a mile off shore with an A-6 chase plane on its tail. It built to a peak as we saw the bird descend to perhaps 30 feet, skimming along the water so low we expected, from our vantage point, it might impact before getting to the target. But it kept true on course, flashed on past us, then zeroed in — impacting on the Butler in a tremendous ball of flame as it pierced the destroyer's bridge and exploded out the other side.

"There was no warhead aboard but the fire from the exploding fuel tank burned for nearly an hour. Three remotely controlled cameras aboard the Butler, and the video tape, later told the story in dramatic close-up.

"The bird had been launched from a Navy DC-130 flying 180 degrees away from the target. The destroyer was located by radar from the LAMPS command helicopter. Once the Butler was acquired by the TV camera aboard the Firebee SSM as confirmed by the real-time video link it was turned over to Ernie Moser, Ryan 'pilot' aboard the helo. In the light fog with little horizon discrimination, target acquisition took place at about five miles.

"Al Donaldson was backup controller on the ground at San Clemente in the event the helicopter lost control, but the entire mission was handled from the chopper.

"The launch was made at about 5000 feet, then the bird was brought down to 220 feet for a final run over the Butler and check of the terminal dive maneuver to see it will function properly during the last second or two of a 'hot' run.

"Satisfied he had a good bird, Moser brought it up a little as it came around the final race track pattern in a three-mile-radius turn. Then he lined the target up on the video screen, made a slight bank correction, brought it down to 75 feet, then 30 feet and at the last second dove it down still another ten feet right into a perfect target hit.

"The final run was at about 350 knots; a compromise between the Firebee's higher speed capability and the fact that we wanted a little more reaction time in order to assure positive control for the terminal phase at extremely low altitude where you could easily get into a hazardous situation as had occurred the previous day.

Teledyne Ryan Aeronautical

ERICH OEMCKE flew out *to witness the final tests of surface-to-surface missile capability.*

"During air-to-air missile firings against Firebee training targets, pilots are awarded 'kill' plaques whenever they destroy one of the fast-flying jet drones. The Navy thought Moser and Donaldson had so effectively 'killed' the SSM in flying it to a bullseye collision with the Butler that they, too, were entitled to similar recognition."

On September 2nd the technical capability of the BQM/SSM missile had been well demonstrated, but would the program go forward? Funding was, quite naturally, the pacing item but in addition there was the concern in Washington that the BQM/SSM might very possibly slow down or curtail development of the even more sophisticated Harpoon system and no one wanted to risk the future of that program.

Clearly top Navy officials wanted the Harpoon so desperately they were going to avoid anything which might jeopardize it. Although they wanted and needed BQM missiles on board destroyers of the Sixth Fleet in the Mediterranean at the earliest possible date, even the impressive demonstration would not assure the funding required.

The Navy, officials said, would take a new look at the Harpoon and the BQM/SSM in six months; until the Spring of 1972 nothing further could be done.

Schwanhausser put it succinctly. "The operation was successful, but the patient died." The Chief of Naval Operations said they weren't going to deviate from the Harpoon program. They didn't want to have anyone muddying the waters.

ON ITS FINAL RUN TO IMPACT with the decommissioned USS Butler, *the SSM Firebee was controlled by television, permitting operator viewing the scene on TV monitor to "bring it down to 75 feet, then 30 feet and at the last second dive it down another ten feet right into a perfect target hit."*

Ed Precourt

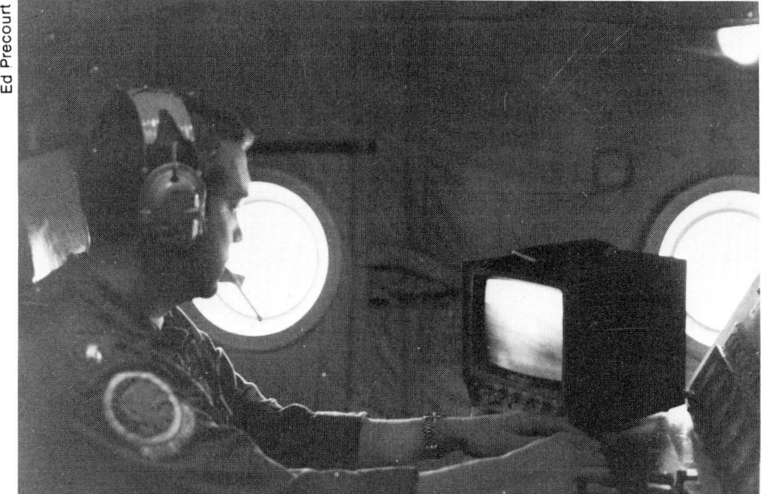

U.S. Navy

25

DEFENSE SUPPRESSION
AIR-TO-SURFACE MISSILE

THE RUSSIAN SAM and AAA batteries which the Arabs rushed into place in August 1970 along the west bank of the Suez Canal were a real thorn in Israeli Prime Minister Golda Meir's side.

With the new batteries in place, the effectiveness of Israel's air force in any renewal of hostilities would be sharply cut. Nor was Washington being very responsive on Mrs. Meir's visit a month later to her request for additional F-4 Phantom jets to help redress what Israel considered to be a weapons imbalance vis-a-vis Egypt.

What could President Nixon do to help; what equipment could Washington sell Israel that, if needed, would knock out the SAM and AAA batteries?

Inquiries in the Department of Defense in October 1970 revealed that short of close-in strafing attacks there were little other effective means of suppressing missile and anti-aircraft sites. Such attacks would, of course, be extremely hazardous to the pilots and their tremendously expensive aircraft. The attrition would be unacceptable in terms of both lives and dollars. Was some other solution possible?

What about using pilotless jet aircraft remotely directed to fire missiles from the drones to neutralize enemy surface-to-air weapons?

"Defense Suppression" began to be widely talked about. It was, as one expert said, a polite way of describing an attack system.

The Arabs had established a heavy concentration of launch sites for both SAM-2 Guideline and SAM-3 Goa missiles, in conjunction with radar-controlled anti-aircraft artillery. The Egyptian-Russian strategy was to deny Israel use of the airspace west of the Suez Canal so the Arabs could more successfully launch an invasion across the canal without worrying about Israeli strike aircraft.

In effect, then, defense suppression is an attack system to destroy the enemy's capability before he can launch an attack.

"WE HAD BEEN SERIOUSLY looking at weapons delivery," recalls Bob Schwanhausser, "for more than seven years when defense suppression came to the foreground. Our original 'CeeBee' configuration flown at White Sands in 1964 was expected to lead into this type of thing — a drone to carry external stores, fuel, bombs and bomblets and to drop them in flight.

"The Army was the first to show enough interest to let us demonstrate on a joint program, but we also talked considerably to the Air Force about what could be done with weapons delivery by drone aircraft. We were proposing a bird that would fire missiles rather than become a missile itself.

"Col. Ells Powell was one who had early envisioned a drone attack capability using a remotely guided weapon system with television link for bombing key targets.

"At a presentation of this capability some time later in San Diego, Dr. Alexander Flax, Assistant Secretary of Air Force, explained that there would not be a weapons suppression system or weapons delivery drone approved at that time; that it would be turned down mysteriously.

"He wanted us to understand why, and explained that the bombing strikes against North Vietnam were just about to halt, and that while our drones were flying on reconnaissance in Southeast Asia they were experiencing severe attrition. He just didn't want others in the service to get any madder at the drone than they were at that time, that if they thought it had a bomb carrying capability they might be even madder.

"So drone weapons delivery was turned down and top Air Force officers with whom we had been dealing never really understood why that decision was made.

"Then along came the problem highlighted by the Nixon-Meir conferences and the Department of Defense got started on the 'Have Lemon' program."

The concern was not just about how Israel might be helped. More to the point for the NATO countries was the fact that in Western Europe they might have to respond to the same threat of multiple, overlapping SAM sites co-located with extensive anti-aircraft artillery installations.

Asking for emergency funds of $14 million for a new budget line item, "Defense Suppression," the Air Force appeared before the House Appropriations Committee in April 1971.

Six 'Have Lemon' tasks were outlined to be accomplished as part of an even broader tri-service approach to accurate delivery of stand-off weapons. The program was structured toward the demonstration of capability only; not complete systems. Task 05 assigned to Teledyne Ryan Aeronautical appropriated $3 million for four Model 234 drones, bearing military designation BGM-34A. [The 'G' stood for 'Surface Attack.']

There were, of course, a stable of air-to-surface tactical guided weapons already in the active Air Force inventory, including the powered "Shrike" and "Bullpup" missiles as well as various glide bombs with electro-optical guidance. But, as Lt. General O. J. Glasser, Air Force Deputy Chief of Staff, Research and Development, testified, "It is an extraordinarily complex and dynamic task. We have had a number of programs that appeared at the time to be the answer, only to have the response on the other side negate their utility."

The AGM-45 Shrike anti-radiation missile, for example, does home in on a radiating site but the minute the enemy can 'see' an airplane coming in they shut the SAM site down, so that Shrike will lose its guidance to the target.

In the Task 05 program, Col. Gerald Hendricks of the Air Force Systems Command explained, "We are going to use the drone to launch a guided weapon such as the 'Maverick,' the electro-optically guided bomb, and return the drone to our side. We have experience which indicates we can reuse the drone quite extensively, and it should be a reasonably cost/effective system to get into the heavily defended areas, and to strike targets very accurately."

"Not only would we demonstrate Maverick — a smart weapon —" Swany recalled, "but we were also tasked to launch 'Stubby Hobo' — a bomb that had been converted as part of Task 03 to have some 'smarts' of its own.

"There was open competition for award of each of the task contracts but we were, I feel, about the only choice for Task 05 because you have to build the rest of the system capability about our basic bird. But to make sure it was on the up-and-up it was competed and we won that one fair and square."

Teledyne Ryan got the go ahead contract from AFSC on March 4, 1971 and William F. Helmich, Jr., became program manager for the Model 234, the company's in-house designation. Again, outside the regular drone administration office, Col. Red Smith served as the Air Force's special project head.

"We actually hit the target," Helmich related, "nine months and 10 days after go ahead. When I say 'hit the target' I'm not using a figure of speech but referring to an actual demonstration of the weapons system against a simulated SAM radar control van. And that flight was accomplished four weeks ahead of schedule.

"The Air Force wanted these birds developed as rapidly as possible so established a Safari-type system to shortcut many formal procedures. We minimized the release cycle time by getting drawings off the engineers' boards directly to the manufacturing planners. We physically relocated all key members of support groups — engineering, quality assurance, manufacturing planning, etc. — in a quick reaction shop where the hardware and people would meet on the factory floor.

"There was no design review or final acceptance until after the bird had accomplished final checkout. It was a quick response, skunk works approach; bare bones dollarwise and schedulewise. We had to.

Ed Precourt

"WE WERE ABLE TO TINKER-TOY the Model 234 *more than any drone we'd previously built," says Bill Helmich, center, Ryan's program manager on the air-to-surface missile project.*

"Over the years we'd developed such a variety of vehicle configurations, subassemblies and equipments that we were able to tinker-toy the Model 234 more than any drone we'd previously built. To start with, the Air Force bailed us four stored, mothballed 147s developed in 1965 for SAC training. Several of them had better than 20 flights already; all were essentially the basic BQM training targets with microwave command guidance (MCGS) and mid-air retrieval (MARS) systems.

"We combined parts and pieces from six different SPAs after we'd gutted and refurbished the basic vehicles. We used **NA** wings with bomb shackles for the hard points to support the missiles. This was a 40-square-foot-wing configuration so we turned the 36-foot area wings of the basic target model back into stock for the assembly line. We used the football-shaped antenna system from the **TE** model for the data link and the MCGS. We used **SD** horizontal tips, **NC** end plates, an **S** nose and a standard model 124 BQM nacelle.

"Preceding our first free flight on October 5 we'd had five captive flights to resolve interface problems between airborne subsystems. Ten free flights, during which two birds were lost, were made to verify the entire system before we were ready on December 14. That day we'd have the first full demonstration of the defense suppression capability of a drone firing a powered, guided air-to-surface missile against a simulated SAM site.

"The flight work was being done by the 6514th Test Squadron at Edwards Air Force Base. That desert test range may seem large but range and safety requirements, because of nearby population centers, were so restrictive as to make flying difficult. We were pulling a lot of left-hand turns all the time to meet range restrictions and that is considerably more difficult than any real operational scenario would be.

"IN THE NOSE WAS A TV CAMERA with a zoom lens *to transmit an image of the terrain ahead. On the wing was a Maverick electro-optical seeking missile."*

Ed Wojciechowski

"The '234' was launched from a DC-130 at 9000 feet and then descended immediately to about 3500 feet over the desert floor until we got to the final leg where we had to make a descending left hand turn down to 800 feet. That meant we had to do more maneuvering to line up the target which would ordinarily be approached on a long, straight-in run.

"In the nose of the drone was a TV camera, equipped with a zoom lens, which in real time transmitted an image of the terrain ahead to the screen in the remote control van. On the drone wing was an AGM-65 Maverick electro-optical seeking missile, also capable of telemetering back to control the actual video of the seeker head as it locked on the target. In this case the target was an obsolete radar control van located on the desert to simulate the heart of a SAM site.

"The remote control operator on the ground was able to see the target on his TV screen at about five miles out without using the zoom capability. At 360 knots airspeed three miles out he switched over to the Maverick's optical seeker and then he was looking at what the weapon was seeing. At about 2½ miles Maverick locked on the target and at two miles the Maverick was fired under its own power, hitting the target squarely in the center about nine seconds after firing. It was just as if the ground controller had guided the missile to a direct hit while riding astride the speeding weapon.

"It was the first missile launching from an RPV to score a direct hit. The first hit had been about eight inches off dead center of the van and the shot on the next flight was essentially through the same hole as the first.

"On that flight, a week later, the mission was duplicated. This time the RPV's own TV camera continued to operate after separation of the missile so that the remote controller could visually follow the weapon's trajectory to the point of impact as seen from the drone and assess the accuracy of the hit and subsequent bomb damage.

"In actual combat conditions, of course, the remote control operator would be in the launch plane or other director aircraft, because of the radar's line-of-sight capability. Thus a control aircraft could be over friendly territory with the attack going on some 200 miles away.

"In the demonstrations we simultaneously dropped a counterbalancing dummy from the other wing when the Maverick was salvoed, but we can provide the capability of firing one Maverick, then reattacking the same target or choosing another with the second Maverick.

"About seven weeks later, on February 10th and 15th, 1972 we hit the target twice more, this time with the 'Stubby Hobo' which was developed as Task 03 in the Defense Suppression program. Stubby is an electro-optical glide bomb with an autopilot which drives the vaned control surfaces to give it guidance.

"In the proposed follow-on system we'd use a 147**NA** bird with extended fuselage and fuel capacity

Harold Wolford

U.S. Air Force

"THE REMOTE CONTROL OPERATOR on the ground was able to see the target on his TV screen. *At three miles out he switched to the Maverick's optical seeker and saw what the weapon was seeing. When Maverick locked on the target it was fired under its own power."*

Teledyne Ryan Aeronautical

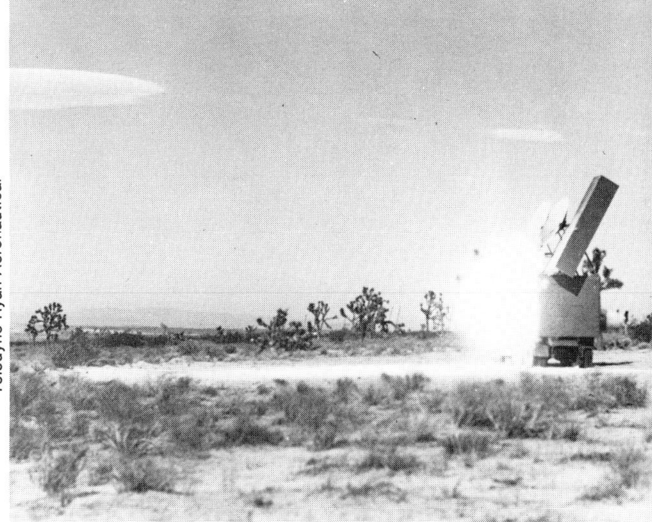

"THE TARGET WAS AN OBSOLETE RADAR CONTROL VAN located to simulate the heart of a SAM site. *Maverick hit the target squarely in the center nine seconds after firing. It was as if the ground controller had guided the missile while riding astride the speeding weapon."*

for longer range. We'll have larger control surfaces so we can launch one weapon and still do the maneuvering required with an asymmetrical loading to reattack the same target or go after a new one."

Again the Air Force-Ryan team had done the impossible, as related by Col. Red. Smith.

"Fortunately they chose the old, established Air Force-contractor group we had built up from the early drone years and we used the 'Big Safari' method of management and acquisition of assets.

"In less than one year we had devised, put together and integrated a system, flown the vehicle and made it operate. Normally it would have taken three years at a very minimum.

"If there is one lesson that needs to be told repeatedly over and over again it is that the crisis jobs can be done if you have the people with the right skills and the high priority management system that solves the problem of long leadtimes in acquiring the hardware you need. The 'skunk works' is a proven system in time of national emergency. We need to retain it."

JUST AS THE FIRST full demonstration of the new defense suppression system was being made in December, 1971 renewed activity in the air war in Vietnam highlighted the attractiveness of unmanned aircraft as a means of saving aircrew lives and reversing escalating aircraft costs.

As President Nixon's plan to speed up the withdrawal of American ground forces from Vietnam moved forward, North Vietnam increased

AND HERE IS 'STUBBY HOBO,' an electro-optical glide bomb *with an auto-pilot to give it guidance. Note vertical fin with football-shaped antenna for the drone data link.*

Ed Precourt

the movement of supplies, weapons and men down the Ho Chi Minh trail.

Washington felt that for the protection of the remaining American troops against another buildup which might duplicate the Tet offensive of February 1968, concentrated air strikes must be undertaken. Although prisoners of war held by North Vietnam continued to be a matter of grave concern and a political liability to the Nixon administration, the need for stepped-up air war outweighed the obvious disadvantages.

Intense, widespread American bombing of North Vietnam — the sharpest escalation of the air war since saturation bombing had been halted three years earlier — started on December 26. Hundreds of U.S. fighter-bombers hit North Vietnam for five straight days.

For weeks the air strikes continued. Thus for the first time in many months a significant number of U.S. planes and pilots were being shot down during 'protective reaction' raids.

This concern added new fuel to the need to develop the unmanned defense suppression capability.

"In the latter part of January," Helmich recalls, "we were specifically requested by the Air Force to tell them, using primarily the 147**SC** and **SD** models SPAs, how many birds and how fast we could deploy to Southeast Asia.

"The philosophy of Tactical Air Command was to use an RPV attack system to go in on the first wave and soften up the target so that the manned aircraft, F-4 Phantoms and F-105s, can go in and finish the job with the human eye. We wouldn't expect to replace the manned aircraft or the pilot; what we

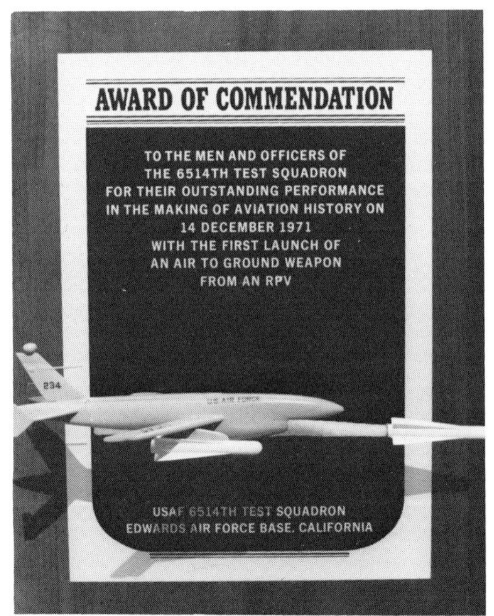

Ed Wojciechowski

'STUBBY HOBO' on the 234 *which, in turn, is carried on pylon of the DC-130 before launch of the drone and weapon the latter carries.*

Teledyne Ryan Aeronautical

really want is to go in and soften up the targets and give the pilot a fighting chance.

"The drone runs about one-tenth of the cost of modern manned jet fighters, which carry one or two pilots each. And, everyone wanted to cut down the number of guests in the Hanoi Hilton, and this is one way to do it.

"Unfortunately the drones were not deployed early in 1972 for a very good reason. The SAM sites in North Vietnam are very well camouflaged; pilots of the F-4s can't see them now. And if the human eye can't see them, neither can the TV camera in the nose of a drone or the electro-optical acquisition and lock-on system in the missile.

"So now there's a new Air Force Program, 'Have Onyx,' to develop a system which will use some type of IR (infra-red) weapon that will see through the foliage and lock on the radiation of the IR characteristics of a SAM site. IR also gives you day and night operational capability and has the added advantage of seeing through fog and clouds.

"Whatever weapons are finally developed for defense suppression can ultimately be carried by the pilotless birds. We still have the man — the 'pilot' — in the loop, but we've taken him out of the cockpit of an aircraft flying in hostile environment and placed him where he can control the missile-carrying drone from a remote ground or airborne station.

"The possibility of weapons delivery by drones can go far beyond the defense suppression mission. For example, a SAM site is usually guarding something of value to the enemy so there's increased acceptance for the concept of flying right on past the SAM site to find the POLs (petroleum, oil, lubricant storage), railroad marshalling areas, bridges and similar targets they'd be protecting. It is anything that is heavily defended where high attrition rates with manned aircraft can be expected."

Bob Schwanhausser probably best summed up the potential of the 234 type of defense suppression system. "The 234," he said, "doesn't give a damn for its own safety. Thus every unmanned bird is a potential Medal of Honor winner!"

The somewhat cynical headline writer for the Hong Kong Standard had the right idea, too, when he borrowed as a sub-head for a 'robot air force' article a quotation from The New Republic issue of April 29, 1972. It read ". . . machines do not bleed, get addicted to drugs, shoot their officers or refuse to fight."

AIR LAUNCHED FROM 234 DRONE, Hobo missile *hits the mark, demonstrating how RPV when employed in strikes against enemy targets could eliminate hazards faced by manned aircraft. "In less than a year we flew the vehicle and made it operate." — Col. Red Smith*

Teledyne Ryan Aeronautical

26

AIR-TO-AIR 'COMBAT'

AS ATTENTION CONTINUED to focus on the inherent capability of RPVs, experts tried to realistically evaluate their future role.

Would the air superiority fighter of the future be under the real-time command of a remotely situated pilot in a launch/director aircraft or on the ground hundreds of miles from the scene of action? Was push-button warfare with robot planes engaged in aerial dogfights just around the corner? Could the trend toward ever more costly and complex manned aircraft be reversed?

The advantages of the remotely piloted fighter aircraft were obvious. With the pilot removed from his cockpit, the need for complicated, expensive, man-rated equipment would be eliminated. The engine could be a short-life turbojet. Life support and human safety features could be virtually forgotten. And, with no man aboard, the pilotless jet could engage in deceptive aerial maneuvers far beyond the ability of any pilot to survive the higher G forces.

While waiting for the definitive answer, technicians were busy developing new maneuvering systems for the aerial training targets used in sharpening the skills of gun crews and pilots who fire ground-launched and air-to-air missiles against Firebee drones simulating 'enemy' aircraft.

IN THE MID-SIXTIES the military services requested a new capability in the Firebee — a more sophisticated system to better simulate the evasive tactics an enemy interceptor would use in combat. Such a system would also be the building block on which later aerial tactics could be based.

The requirement resulted in Ryan developing an Improved Maneuverability Kit (IMK) so the drone could make turns so tight the plane would be under stress five times that of gravity (5G). Both roll and pitch circuits of the flight control system were modified to enable the training targets to make short radius turns at 75 degrees bank angle with minimum loss of airspeed and altitude.

IMK, however, was not quite as good as its press notices, according to engineer Carroll Berner. "Initially we could pull only 3Gs. With later modifications we got to 4Gs and then to 5Gs, but it was a 'brute force' type of approach.

"We just didn't achieve a good, steady, tight bank. It was sloppy in the turns, gaining and losing altitude as G forces wandered around during the 12 to 15 seconds it took to stabilize the bird at one particular value. We seldom pulled more than 4Gs and 75 degree bank angle.

"What the Air Force and Navy wanted was a target simulating a threat aircraft that could roll into tight turns in a matter of seconds and hold them. They were calling for 6G turns, not 4 or 5Gs. So we went to work on the problem.

"It was readily apparent that with a few straightforward applications we could provide a maneuvering system that would indeed roll the target drone into an 81 degree bank angle in three or four seconds and hold G forces constant up to a value of about 6Gs. With little effort we could also give them climbing and diving turns. Finally we built and offered to the services for test three of the new MASTACS (Maneuverability Augmentation System for Tactical Air Combat Simulation) systems."

The Navy provided several BQM-34A training targets which were easily modified to accept MASTACS since the vehicles were already equipped for the earlier IMK system. The test range at Pt. Mugu was made available and the Navy provided the usual scheduling and coordination of range time.

Nine MASTACS proving flights were flown on the Pacific Missile Range between January 25 and April 28, 1971 to evaluate the second generation improvement in maneuvering capability.

The Navy's Fighter Weapons School at Miramar Naval Air Station, San Diego, was greatly interested in the potential of MASTACS because it was their

Teledyne Ryan Aeronautical

PILOTS OF TWO NAVY F-4s went out to challenge a Firebee *equipped with a maneuverability augmentation system for tactical air combat simulation (MASTACS). The shoot-out demonstrated potential of RPVs in air-to-air combat situation if one takes a step beyond the requirement of merely providing a training target.*

assignment to provide air-to-air combat training for Navy pilots assigned to operations off Vietnam. With a record of 21-to-1 against MiG fighters over North Vietnam they had a reputation to uphold.

Midway in the MASTACS tests at Pt. Mugu, Bruce Jackson, a Teledyne Ryan requirements engineer, invited Cmdr. John C. Smith, commanding officer of the "Top Gun" School, to visit the operation. Seeing how impressed Cmdr. Smith was with the drone's improved evasive tactics, Jackson baited him with an "I'll bet you can't shoot it down" dare. Smith accepted the challenge.

At the end of the test period Cmdr. Smith was ready to make good. A MASTACS graduation exercise was scheduled for May 10.

Two F-4 Phantom fighters flown by Smith and three Vietnam combat veterans as students 'scrambled' from Miramar. The fighters were equipped with mixed loads of "Sidewinder" infrared and "Sparrow" radar-guided missiles.

As the F-4s approached Santa Catalina Island off the coast, a MASTACS Firebee was ground launched from Pt. Mugu. Ground control intercept vectored the F-4s to the drone test range, and the 'battle' was on as described by Al Donaldson, veteran Ryan controller:

"Looking over my shoulder at ground control was Cmdr. John Pitzen, a 'Top Gun' combat instructor who helped direct the aerial tactics against the F-4s.

"Commander Smith was flying as radar operator, and chief tactician, in the back seat of the lead F-4. It was a no-holds-barred contest. No constraints had been placed on me relative to maneuvering the drone. The F-4s were on their own in a 'combat' situation and would have to look after themselves to see they weren't rammed by the Firebee as it took evasive action.

"After a short period of familiarization for the pilot-radar operator crews aloft to see the behavior of the target, and those of us at ground control to learn something of their tactics, we were ready to take them on.

"Initially we set the stage for a head-on approach from which they would break off into a dog fight situation. Remember, that the radar's good for weapons control, not for keeping track of the fight. The pilot still has to position his plane to deliver the weapon and that's where the tactics and maneuvering take place.

"On the open radio circuit we could hear the chatter between the two F-4s.

"'Tally ho, off the left wing' called Smith as he tried to line up for the kill, but the drone was able to pull such a high-G turn that the F-4 could not follow the maneuver. 'It's turning like a mother.'

"After a hard turn, Smith was back on the radio with 'it's going over the top of my canopy.' In getting the F-4 off the tail of the maneuvering drone we would end up with the Firebee on *his* tail.

"Smith was learning the hard way that we could rack the Firebee into a hundred degree bank and make a 180 degree turn reversal in only 12 seconds, permitting the drone to get in behind the now vulnerable F-4. In that position the drone was not a target but an attack aircraft.

"The F-4 was simply unable to turn laterally with

Ed Wojciechowski

MONITORING ACTION on the Pacific Missile Range *off Southern California from Alpha Station at the Navy's Point Mugu facility.*

Ed Hayes.

RUGGED NAVY BQM-34A training target *which, in 1964, had already flown 36 missions as a 'clay pigeon' for pilots firing air-to-air missiles.*

the target which was demonstrating the ability to pull and hold a 6G turn three seconds after the command was transmitted, and do so while maintaining altitude.

"Neither Smith nor his wingman could keep their F-4s in turns tight enought to hold the drone in firing position long enough to get off a solid shot. Two Sparrows and two Sidewinders were fired and although one 'he-just-spliced-it' claim was heard over the air, the Firebee was not hit."

Back on the ground at Pt. Mugu, Cmdr. Smith was the first to admit that "You guys build a good drone!"

It was a pretty convincing demonstration of both defensive and offensive maneuvering by the drone. It demonstrated the potential that can be realized with an RPV in an air-to-air combat situation if you want to take the capability a step beyond the requirements for just a training target.

After the Pt. Mugu demonstration, the MASTACS system was taken to Roosevelt Roads in Puerto Rico and flown against an unseasoned Marine Corps fighter unit. It was too sophisticated an exercise for the student wing down there for their first live shots.

Later MASTACS was taken to Tyndall Air Force Base for more flights. These too were in support of high maneuverability training rather than in an air-to-air combat atmosphere but still with the same learning potential for future robot warfare.

AS WEAPONS USED against high-flying planes have become more and more sophisticated, and as tactics have changed to meet the increased performance of potential enemy aircraft, target drone systems have had to become ever more versatile.

The Navy had indicated need for a serpentine maneuvering capability in order to evaluate the Standard missile. This would require pulling 5Gs to the left, then reverse drone direction to pull 5Gs to the right, then left again, back to the right and so on. "Just give us a course reversal every six seconds and hold a constant peak of 5Gs," said the Navy.

Easier said than done, but Schwanhausser's people tackled that one, too. An old IMK kit was modified by speeding up the roll rate; it was sent to White Sands Missile Range for flight evaluation.

The modified IMK provided the target drone with the capability needed for the test but the drone was constantly changing altitude and airspeed. Although the Navy was marginally satisfied, Teledyne Ryan was not. Paul Bunner, the company's man on the White Sands scene, took it upon himself to study the data and gradually improve the system.

Eventually Bunner tied an accelerometer into the system and, using techniques similar to MASTACS, was so successful that the Army (which operates White Sands) gained enough confidence to ask him for still greater capability. They wanted a very steep, diving turn, so Bunner added additional control devices and tailored the system before launch to achieve this maneuver.

Another maneuver requested — and delivered — was a sudden, steep pull-up at high Gs, then a dive and pull-out near the ground followed by straight and level flight — all in one continuous, smooth maneuver. Bunner did it by pulling the drone up sharply, rolling it over into inverted flight, pulling positive Gs going over the top, and as it's diving down, rolling back to a conventional attitude. There the bird flattens out and flies straight ahead. That one surprised everybody!

"The human pilot with a G suit," Carroll Berner observed, "can pull 6 or 7Gs for a short time and live. He can't go much farther than that. But we've already demonstrated comparable capability with pilotless aircraft, and we've really just started to exploit the potential of the RPV.

"With MASTACS we have a good capability, but one weakness is that airspeed degrades by as much as 50 knots in some turns. The true RPV is going to need more thrust than the 1700 pounds we now have in the target drone's jet engine. So, we're thinking of installing a 3250-pound thrust General Electric J-85 jet engine which will take us up to 8Gs and assure us that we can hold airspeed in these more strenuous maneuvers.

"In fact we'd have thrust in excess of the drone's weight, and that would make drone VTO (vertical takeoff) possible — but that's another subject, for another day."

Ever improved maneuvering capability will be required to provide the most realistic training possible but out of it will certainly develop the air-to-air combat drone of the future. Realistically, though, other RPV combat missions — particularly defense suppression — will undoubtedly be flown operationally before robot aerial dog fights become commonplace.

27

THAI BASE

ALTHOUGH DRONE RECONNAISSANCE flights over China and North Vietnam had been common knowledge for nearly seven years, at no time had the United States officially confirmed their use. But they came very close to it in July 1971 right after President Nixon startled the world with the announcement he would visit Red China.

The cancellation of the scheduled Eisenhower-Khruschev conference at Paris in 1960 following the Francis Gary Powers U-2 incident, was certainly on everyone's mind. A similar incident could interfere with President Nixon's trip to Peking.

Thus it was that William Beecher, Washington correspondent of The New York Times, reported on July 28 that *"administration officials"* said the United States had suspended flights over Communist China by manned SR-71 spy planes and *unmanned reconnaissance drones.*

Continuing, Beecher wrote, "Informants said the political reasons for the decision to halt American flights were regarded as much more compelling than continued intelligence from an occasional SR-71 or drone mission. Some sources also noted that the suspension conceivably might be lifted after President Nixon's visit to China, although a similar suspension of flights over the Soviet Union, instituted after the 1960 U-2 incident, remains in effect.

"Peking has publicly protested nearly 500 incursions of its air space by United States aircraft.

"The United States also uses SR-71s and drones over North Vietnam and North Korea. Besides cameras, the SR-71s also carry equipment to monitor and record radar and radio transmissions."

DESPITE THE SOMEWHAT reduced schedule of **TE** Combat Dawn electronic intelligence missions after the announcement of President Nixon's planned visit to Peking, operations were conducted out of Osan throughout 1971.

Photo reconnaissance flights had also continued from OL-20 during 1969 and the first half of 1970, in support of the Vietnamese war in Southeast Asia.

After July 4, 1970 the 100th Strategic Reconnaissance Wing operation, which had been at Bien Hoa for nearly six years, was moved to a new location at U-Tapao Royal Thai Airfield, Thailand, 90 miles southeast of Bangkok on the Gulf of Siam. **(See map, page 75)**

Reconnaissance drone activity had reached a new peak at Bien Hoa in 1969. Including all types of vehicles and sorties, 437 missions were generated. Of these, the 147**S** group of low-level birds accounted for 392 missions. July set a new high in monthly activity with 52 missions.

In January, **SC**-11 had been the first of its type to be launched. Ten months later it was lost but not until it had set a new record of 28 missions for a single operational SPA.

Only a few high-altitude missions were flown with the remaining 147**H** drones. Seven of **H**-58's thirteen missions were flown in 1969 and on two of these the bird sustained in-flight damage. The 147**T** model had been fielded but was not extensively used at that time.

After President Johnson called off bombing raids above the 20th parallel the end of March 1968, the

U-TAPAO ROYAL THAI AIRFIELD *in mid-1970 became operational location for 100th SRW recce drone activity after six years at Bien Hoa, South Vietnam.*

Dave Gossett

Dave Gossett

North Vietnamese were able to concentrate more of their fire power against the recce drones. Flying at 1000 to 1200 feet altitude in a very hostile atmosphere the drones were taking unacceptable losses. To counter the concentrated firepower, mission profiles were changed so that after launch at 3000 feet the **S** birds were flown down to 500 feet above enemy terrain at 500 knots. With this change the low-level mission again began to provide usable data at acceptable SPA attrition rates.

Jet engines have a bad habit of gobbling up fuel at low altitude. Installing external wing-mounted fuel tanks would solve the problem, but none suitable for installation on the 147S could be located. Specially configured 'scorer' tanks which had been developed to house camera equipment were modified to carry fuel and proved adaptable. Test flights at Pt. Mugu in **SB**-17 demonstrated an approximate 100% increase in low level range. Later the fuel pod system would also be used on the **T** series.

Occasionally an **S** bird performed beyond the call of normal duty and was suitably recognized. **SC**-75 was awarded a Purple Heart for its mission of August 19, 1969.

Carrying the Oriental nomenclature "Myassis Dragon", **SC**-75 flew off on its eighth combat flight. According to the citation, "It flew through a veritable hail of bullets and shell fragments, sustaining seven hits from enemy fire. Although severely wounded it forged through to waiting friendly forces who guided it back to safety. For heroism under fire, Myassis Dragon is hereby awarded the Order of the Purple Heart."

Myassis Dragon flew a ninth mission a few days later, then on August 31st was killed in action over hostile territory on its tenth mission.

"WE WENT INTO BIEN HOA originally," Schwanhausser recalls, "because it was a secure area, since no one then wanted to take a brand new operation like that into another country. But as the war began winding down with the United States pulling its forces out of South Vietnam, it was the kind of operation that could easily be moved.

"All the way around, Thailand is probably a better place to operate than at Bien Hoa where it was sure to cause some problems with the heavy air traffic there. And, it's closer to the area where the birds are launched on their missions."

At the new location, designated OL-RU, operations continued to be primarily **SC** low altitude day photo missions although some flights during winter 1970-71 were flown with the few remaining high-altitude **H** and the new **T** birds. A total of 365 missions were generated in 1970 at the overseas bases in Bien Hoa and U-Tapao. Of these, 298 were flown with the **S** series SPA. Successful recovery of drones returning from operational missions improved from 76 percent in 1969 to 86 percent in 1970.

By the following summer — 1971 — the **SC** was conducting all missions from U-Tapao, usually on a daily schedule 'up north.' Overall, the **SC** was probably the most successful of the drone recce birds

U.S. Navy

RANGE OF 147S SERIES BIRDS was greatly extended *by use of fuel carried in external tanks. In tests, an* ***SD*** *model drops its tanks after fuel out.*

because of the stable utilization by the Air Force. In fact the Air Force had learned to operate and maintain the birds so well that Teledyne Ryan support by civilian technicians was cut to a minimum.

One of the heroic, yet tragic, expressions of concern for prisoners of war was the November 21-22 commando raid in 1970 on the Son Tay prison camp 23 miles west of Hanoi.

An estimated 400 Air Force and Navy planes hit North Vietnam in the heaviest raids since the 1968 bombing halt to act as a diversion for the raid by a 50-man, 10-helicopter commando team. But they returned empty-handed because the American prisoners had been removed some time before the raid.

Ed Sly

MANNED U-2 RECONNAISSANCE PLANES and 147 drones were teamed *in Southeast Asia for maximum results. Ski-nosed* ***SDL*** *model, in both pictures, had Loran navigational capability.*

Where had American intelligence gone astray? A check of flight records for the recce drones during November operations reportedly shows 19 sorties flown, and all birds recovered. None appear to have been scheduled for flights as far north as Hanoi. Two missions on the 20th and 21st were cancelled because of weather. Whether or not they were scheduled to have been routed over Son Tay is not clear. On other occasions, however, the drones did bring back good photos of the downtown 'Hanoi Hilton.'

The success of the low-altitude **S** series extended their production life through further design improvements in the ski-nosed **SD** model, 78 of which were contracted for with deliveries starting early in 1972.

"The **SD** was occasioned more than anything else by a need to have an improved navigation capability to assure even better, more accurate coverage and mapping of the targets," explained Bob Reichardt.

"While the **SC** spec nav accuracy was 3% of the distance traveled, the **SD** nav system has a 1.1 percentage which means that at 100 miles it should never be more than 1.1 miles off target.

"This has been accomplished with an upgraded Doppler navigator, a completely new flight control system designed and built by Teledyne Ryan and a better heading reference through replacement of the MA-1 compass with the more modern SR-3 unit.

"Other improved capabilities include radar altitude control equipment (RACE) and external fuel tanks to extend the operating range of the **SD** at low altitude. Also we have a new cooling system to compensate for the increased heat generated in the equipment compartment by extended low-altitude operation in a tropical environment of high ambient temperature."

Dave Gossett

28

1972 — YEAR OF DECISION

WITH EMPHASIS on Vietnamization and the pull-out of American ground forces reaching a climax, 1972 saw an offsetting build-up in aerial bombing and an accompanying need for increased drone reconnaissance as the long, tragic war slowly but surely ground toward a cease-fire.

The story of the final phase really begins with Christmas 1971. Starting on December 26, hundreds of U.S. fighter-bombers hit North Vietnam for five straight days. The strikes were the sharpest escalation of the war since bombing North of the DMZ was halted by President Johnson more than three years earlier on October 31, 1968.

In explanation of the raids, Defense Secretary Melvin Laird, pointed out the recent upsurge in North Vietnamese military activity and that "We are down below 160,000 Americans today in Vietnam . . . and it is very important we protect those Americans."

Barely a month after President Nixon's historic visit to Peking in late February, and seven weeks in advance of his scheduled Moscow trip, the Communists on March 20 unleashed their strongest attack since the Tet offensive of 1968 on the northern provinces across the Demilitarized Zone. Additional MiG-21s also started showing up at Vinh and other bases.

Clearly Hanoi was determined to test the effectiveness of President Nixon's policy of Vietnamization at the very time U.S. ground forces were being withdrawn. And, as in the 1968 Tet offensive, there would be a bonus for the Communists if they could again have an influence on the upcoming presidential election.

In response to the Communist pressure American pilots were ordered to stem the southward flow of enemy supplies and immediately tripled the number of strikes including those against the increasing number of SAM missile sites in the southern half of North Vietnam. Pilots reported 'spectacular results' on April 6 and 7 including heavy destruction of Communist armored units in the South.

Then, on April 16, Haiphong got its first taste of B-52 raids as the giant bombers and smaller fighter bombers hit fuel dumps and supply areas. It was the first time in four years the B-52s had joined the air war above the 20th parallel. Pilots also attacked MiG bases and POL (petroleum-oil-lubricants) storage areas in the Hanoi area.

The next day, Hanoi asked for a halt in the bombing raids and a return to the bargaining table at Paris. Ten days later President Nixon reopened the talks and also commenced a fresh round of secret meetings conducted by Henry Kissinger.

Stepping up the pressure, President Nixon on May 8 ordered the mining of Haiphong Harbor risking the possibility that his Moscow visit scheduled for a fortnight later might be cancelled or postponed, but that eventually did not happen. Beside sowing hundreds of delayed-action mines into Communist shipping channels, U.S. aircraft struck heavily at bridges, barracks, trucks, barges, rail junctions and other military targets in the Red River Valley heartland.

Never before had American air raids been so successful. What made the difference was a new generation of 'smart' bombs with highly sophisticated electronic guidance systems to fly missiles directly to the target while the launching aircraft 'stands off' at a relatively safe distance.

The smart bombs like Walleye or the electro-optical Maverick can be guided by the pilot as he monitors a television receiver or they can be led by a laser beam.

Laser-directed bombs require the coordinated use of two aircraft. One locates and circles above the target, pin-pointing it with a laser beam, while the other plane drops the bomb which rides the beam in a long glide pattern to the target.

IT WAS AGAINST this background that we asked Bob Reichardt in May 1972 to give us an update on the role of Ryan reconnaissance drones in the stepped-up air war.

"Beginning in late December our sortie rate of SC

Dave Gossett

RYAN RECCE EXPERT BOB REICHARDT *at U-Tapao with 'Baby Buck' which flew 46 missions, fourth highest of any reconnaissance drone.*

vehicles used in the "Buffalo Hunter" project was increased to at least double what it had been running. As a matter of fact right now we are flying sorties at a higher rate than at any time in the eight years we've been deployed — higher even than during the "Rolling Thunder" bombing of North Vietnam from 1966 through October 1968.

"We have been operating about 1.2 flights per day on the average since the first of January. More recently, since the North Vietnamese crossed the DMZ, we have probably been operating at a rate of almost two a day.

"The drones have been operating in areas that are normally denied to manned reconnaissance airplanes because of the high threat environment. Routes typically covered are Haiphong and Hanoi; in fact all of North Vietnam and even some flights over South Vietnam in areas that are now occupied by the North Vietnamese Army. They are bringing back fantastic results. They are actually planning B-52 strikes on the basis of the information the drone brings back.

"A specific example of this occurred three weeks ago where B-52s bombed railroad yards in North Vietnam but they missed the target. They sent a drone out the next day to get bomb damage assessment (BDA) and the drone brought back the information that they had missed the targets. But it also indicated that the North Vietnamese had moved in two mobile SAM sites anticipating that when the Americans knew they had missed they would send the B-52s back again. So the drone's information indicated that they shouldn't do that and therefore the B-52 strike scheduled for the next day was cancelled.

"The drone flights are usually launched over the Gulf of Tonkin and occasionally from Northern Laos, but I'd say at least 90% are from the Gulf of Tonkin. So far this year we have lost a total of 19 drones out of approximately 130-140 missions flown and I would estimate probably two-thirds of those have been due to enemy action and the other third to system malfunctions.

"These low altitude Buffalo Hunter missions are usually flown between 500 and 800 feet. This is where the drone brings back the best technical intelligence. The **SC** doesn't have the added navigational capability that the **SD** does. It has to be updated by remote control on occasions to be sure that the targets are covered. But with the deployment of the **SD** sometime in June they will have a system that will be much more accurate; not only the basic nav system in the **SD** but there will be a Loran capability also that will provide accuracies up to ± 200-250 feet.

"We have also been at work over at Davis-Monthan for the last week modifying an **SC** with a TV camera that should be deployed a week from today.

"Currently there is no high altitude drone activity going on in or over SEA (Southeast Asia). Of course we have the operation at Osan with the **TE**. That's an Elint type operation. There is an indication they will shortly deploy four or five new capabilities in response to stepped up activity.

"In addition to the Loran equipped **SD** and the TV equipped **SC** out of Thailand, there is a possibility that we will deploy about 20 **NC**s to perform a leaflet dropping mission over North Vietnam and some quantity up to 30 **SC**s for chaff dispensing to assist the penetration of the manned bombers. There is also talk of renewal of the 147**E** or United Effort program to obtain electronic guidance information on some new threats that have been installed in North Vietnam by the Russians.

"Of course the SR-71 is operated over North Vietnam but at extremely high altitude and generally in a peripheral mode to avoid the threat of the SA-2 missiles. So their photography, although it does bring back order-of-battle type information, does not develop a technical intelligence photography because the resolution isn't nearly what we can get in the **SC**. The **SC** can identify the exact type of a tank. The SR-71 can only tell you that a tank is there. But photo interpreters can actually name the model of the tank photographed by the **SC**.

AN SDL OUT OF U-TAPAO down in a rice paddy *after returning from a successful mission.*

U.S. Air Force

"We've had as many as five missions scheduled in a single day. Last weekend in a three day period, Friday through Sunday, there were nine missions flown out of U-Tapao.

"There have been many missions flown over Haiphong. I don't know if they were specifically to count the number of ships in the harbor or to survey bomb damage in the Haiphong area. But I am sure a fallout of those missions would be intelligence on the numbers and nationalities of the neutral shipping in the harbor.

"To my knowledge there is still very limited if any manned reconnaissance being done north of the 19th parallel. It is too hazardous. The Navy lost an $8 million RA-5C Vigilante the week before last over there and they just can't risk two men and an airplane that costs that much under these conditions, particularly if we can do the job. The weather is another argument in favor of the drone. The RA-5C for instance isn't even launched on a recce mission if there is less than a 2000 foot ceiling. And this is where the drone comes into its best area — down on the deck.

"I think we will be called upon to do a lot of things that we have been working with the Air Force on over the years that have not been picked up because of funding problems or the fact that there just wasn't an urgency attached to them as there is at this time. I look for the level of drone activity in SEA to climb rapidly in the weeks ahead."

AN AIR FORCE 'targeting officer', through whom orders for air strikes and follow-up reconnaissance flights were scheduled, confirmed Reichardt's assessment.

The low-level 147**SC**s, he reported, frequently went in far deeper northwest of Hanoi than ever before, requiring terminating the flights much farther north in the Gulf of Tonkin. On those occasions, the Air Force arranged to have the Navy pick up the birds; then the Air Force would immediately fly the intelligence 'take' back for processing and interpretation.

Even though the manned SR-71 blackbirds were operating in the same area, obtaining an overall picture, the **SC** had to go back in for low-level close-ups for bomb damage assessment, since its optics were capable of getting 3- to 5-inch resolution. Also, the **SC**s were capable of being routed so as to obtain information on a number of targets, reducing the requirement for going after just a single target.

Despite the heavy aerial interdiction of the Ho Chi Minh trail, the three-layer jungle canopy made it possible for North Vietnam to move up to 80 tanks south for their offensive thrust below the DMZ without being observed.

Targeting officers were also amazed at the ability of the North Vietnamese in bridge building, both conventional and pontoon construction.

As one officer commented, "They must have had

Dave Gossett

THE BIG-WING, EXTENDED RANGE TE operating out of Osan, *Korea, could run missions of eight hours duration while collecting enemy electronic data.*

tremendous morale for it was certainly evidenced by their ability to replace bridges virtually overnight. One technique was to use a rock fill in shallow rivers so that trucks could very soon ford these waterways. Another great advantage this technique had for NVN was that there were almost no tell-tail sign on the reconnaissance photos — except where the picture showed the white water of a new 'rapids' in the river."

Another surprise for the U.S. was the relative ease with which the mobile SAM sites could be relocated and set-up as Hanoi began to bring the SAMs back to the industrial centers after their earlier deployment just north of the DMZ. However, this was a bonus for the recce drones which no longer had to face the concentrated SAM fire just above the DMZ.

Monitoring shipping activities, or rather the lack of activity, in Haiphong Harbor was a special concern of the 100th Strategic Reconnaissance Wing's "Buffalo Hunter" missions during May. Some of the finest, most detailed aerial photos of the war showed excellent close-ups of Russian ships anchored in the roadstead and tied up along the embarcadero of Haiphong.

In early summer Dale Weaver, the tireless trans-Pacific commuter, returned briefly to home base in San Diego after yet another technical assignment at the Overseas Location.

"Things have really been looking up," Dale reported. "By the time the operation was moved from Bien Hoa to U-Tapao, the 147**SC** had become a matured weapon system. The logistics was good; the training was good, and we had just the one model bird to worry about. Because of increased Air Force know-how we were down to just two contractor technical personnel. The operation became routine and increasingly reliable.

AIR FORCE MAJOR JOHN DALE and his stellar *SC* *performer 'Tom Cat,' the all-time record setter with 68 successful missions to its credit.*

"This is largely due to the other Dale — Major John Dale who, after a great deal of research, carefully worked out the strategy and tactics which fully exploit the real potential of unmanned reconnaissance under combat conditions. As much as anyone, John Dale has kept the program going.

"The sortie rate compared with our early days at Bien Hoa is roughly four times as great. Now we've got two C-130s available full-time, compared with the one we could formerly depend on. The sortie rate in the first half of 1972 was about 40 per month, against half that in 1971. The **SC** is providing the Buffalo Hunter program with the majority of usable photo intelligence that is now coming out of North Vietnam.

"When the move was first made to U-Tapao, the **H** and **T** models were still operational but requirements for high-altitude reconnaissance diminished with the operational capability of the SR-71. We take the low level stuff because at certain times of the year that's all you have available to get under the clouds.

"One new project we got going while I was over there this last time was the **SC** fitted out with a TV camera in the nose so the controller aboard the C-130 director aircraft can guide the bird right over the target with pin-point accuracy — once the television screen displays the general area.

"There is a lot of enthusiasm for it both as a navigation aid and for what we were shooting for even more — the ability to pick out a target by eyeball. For example, we 'target' an enemy airfield and the bird may fly over one end of it — pretty good navigation — but it's not the end the customer wanted. So this way they can line up on the airfield and fly over the whole thing or any part of it if they want to.

"But we've had some tough luck in getting the TV bird started. The problem has not been electronics but getting the vehicle to fly properly."

Dave Gossett

Ed Sly

THE 147SC was fitted out with a TV camera in the nose *so the controller aboard the C-130 director aircraft, above, can guide the bird right over the target after the video screen displays the general area.*

Running down the bugs in any bird carrying new equipment, or of a slightly different configuration, is frequently a long, tiresome often frustrating task. That was the case with the **SC/TV** bird. It had a habit of literally falling out of the sky out of control. But why? The aerodynamics detectives finally found the gremlin. A small finned antenna had been installed on the forward fuselage to transmit the TV image signals to the accompanying C-130. It was discovered that this small protrudence had a canard effect which made the drone directionally unstable. When the 'fin' antenna was replaced by a flush type, the aerodynamic problem was solved.

The 147**SDL**, an **SD** with Loran navigation capability added, also ran into aerodynamic control problems. The bird flew fine as a standard **SD** model, but whenever the Loran capability was added it became uncontrollable. Two missions flown in August were non-productive. Some electrical anomaly was suspected but weeks passed without a definitive answer.

Normally the drone can be banked to a maximum angle after which it will not accept a further roll command. Somehow the Loran equipment was inserting an overriding signal which permitted the bank angle to go beyond the danger point with resultant loss of the drone. Once identified, the problem was corrected.

Teledyne Ryan Aeronautical

147SDL (Loran) deployment team *at U-Tapao. Left to right, rear: Muklebust, Lee, Boyd, Grady, Riley, Wilson, Capt. Silliman. Front: O'Hara, Akashi, Smith, Sly, Allen.*

DRONES WERE CALLED ON in July 1972 to play a role in a stepped-up propaganda war against North Vietnam. The 147**NC** drones of the Tactical Air Command came equipped with external pods from which chaff could be dispensed to confuse enemy radar and neutralize their electronic capability. Why not use the **NC**s to drop propaganda leaflets over the North?

Rather than set up a new unit at U-Tapao to be operated by TAC, the better part of discretion was to add the 'litterbug' assignment to the task already being done by the Strategic Air Command reconnaissance unit.

"They had some start-up problems," Weaver explained, "but they were solved after a couple of sorties. For three years the TAC people had been operating the **NC**s successfully; then they were turned over to another group which had to learn the ropes in a week.

"The biggest problem with the leaflet drops was trying to predict the winds which would be encountered by the time the bird was over the target to be showered with leaflets. In some cases the missions were only marginally effective because of wind conditions which had been impossible to predict."

In all, 28 missions were flown between July and December by the NCs with loss of three birds. It should come as no great surprise that Project Litterbug's birds were more widely — and perhaps aptly — known as the "Bullshit Bombers."

Tổng Thống Hoa Kỳ
Richard Nixon

Tổng Thống Hoa Kỳ đã nhắn nhủ các nhà lãnh đạo Hà Nội như sau : « Nhân dân quý quốc đã quá đau khổ vì quý vị theo đuổi cuộc chinh phục. Xin đừng gia tăng nỗi thống khổ của họ với sự tiếp tục kiêu căng của quý vị. Thay vì thế, quý vị hãy chọn con đường hòa bình để đền bù những sự hy sinh của quý vị, đảm bảo nền độc lập thực sự cho quý quốc, và khai sinh một kỷ nguyên hòa giải».

4505

NGƯNG BẮN

rong bài diễn văn
9-5-1972 Tổng Thống
Kỳ nói rằng những
động quân sự gần
ại Bắc Việt là để
ng lại cuộc xâm
ạt vào Việt Nam
a do các nhà lãnh
ng chủ trương.
nói rằng Hoa
ông bao giờ bỏ
ều dân miền
Nam vào bàn
, khủng bố
ản. Nếu các
Đảng muốn
động quân
ấm dứt thì
lòng thả
Hoa Kỳ
c ngưng
giám sát
Đông
hứa sẽ
quân đội Hoa Kỳ
ra khỏi Việt Nam trong
vòng 4 tháng sau khi
cuộc ngưng bắn nói trên
được thực hiện.

4505

MUCH OF THE SUCCESS of the electronic counter measures which provided U.S. B-52 and fighter-bomber aircraft with a protective shield against SAM missiles was based on the probing flight of the 147**E** bird in the United Effort project of 1965-66 which was used to 'ferret' out the original electronic intelligence data on SAM systems.

To reassess the enemy threat, Dale Weaver was sent back to U-Tapao in September to re-run the eavesdropping mission against the Russian SA-2 Guideline missile. Four "Compass Cookie" missions were flown with the last of the 147**H** birds, specially equipped for the task. The **H** bird flown September 28 transmitted back to the '130' the needed electronic data on three SA-2 missiles.

By Fall, Dr. Henry Kissinger and North Vietnam's Le Doc Tho appeared to have peace so nearly at hand that President Nixon on October 24 ordered a bombing halt above the 20th parallel as a good-will gesture. Then the fragile thread of an expected peace was broken and massive bombing of Hanoi and Haiphong by B-52 bombers was conducted for two weeks starting in mid-December. For the first time in the war, B-52s began to be shot down — an average of more than one a day.

Had the signatures of radars on the SAM missile sites been changed; had the enemy deliberately fed false information to the 147**H** "Compass Cookie" bird? Probably not. More likely the North Vietnamese so saturated the air over Hanoi with SAM missiles that there was virtually no way to thwart them.

The B-52 strikes were being flown not only out of Guam but also from U-Tapao, the same base from which the drones operated. On one occasion, a B-52 from U-Tapao, was hit by SAMs over North Vietnam and the crew bailed out. On a follow-up drone mission, the unmanned recce bird came back with photos taken at low level which showed the actual capture of the crew.

After a brief New Year's respite, bombing resumed again but only below the 20th parallel. Then on January 15 there was a complete suspension of bombing north of the 17th parallel separating the two Vietnams. Of the many off-again, on-again bombing pauses and starts, it was to be the last switch in tactics before the cease-fire was signed on January 27, 1973.

In suspending bombing on January 15 it was also announced that reconnaissance flights over North Vietnam would be limited to low-level surveillance drones [AQM-34L, model 147**SC**] and manned SR-71 Blackbirds flying at high altitudes and slant ranges outside anti-aircraft and SAM ranges.

"The use of pilotless drones is no change and is one method we have used whenever bombing missions over North Vietnam have been halted," one Pentagon official said.

The success of the **SC** low-level missions over North Vietnam and of the intelligence gathering

Dave Gossett

147TF CARRYING TWO EXTERNAL FUEL TANKS for extended range *missions is launched on a mission out of Osan to monitor electronic activity along the DMZ.*

AFTER A MISSION OVER THE YELLOW SEA *between the Korean peninsula and the mainland of China, a TF is returned by helicopter.*

Dave Gossett

capability of the **TE** over the Sea of Japan made 1972 the top operational year for the 147 birds.

During the year 466 **SC** missions were flown out of U-Tapao, Thailand, with a loss of 52 vehicles. In 1971, by contrast, there were 277 **SC** missions with 29 losses. The peak month operationally was December 1972 when 75 **SC**s were launched — two-thirds of them on bomb damage assessment missions in support of the heavy B-52 bombing strikes. This was the highest level of activity at any OL operation, surpassing that of July 1969 when 52 sorties were flown.

In the 30 days between December 20, 1972 and January 19, 1973 when BDA flights were at their peak, over 100 sorties were flown. In support of "Linebacker II," the 100th SRW flew 27 missions in the third week of December. And, on December 22, Major Regal DuBose and crew became the first CH-3 helicopter unit to make four successful MARS operational drone 'catches' in one day.

A new turn-around record was set when a single **SC** flew missions on four days in a row. Three or four missions were being flown daily and reports were that post-cease-fire it might go to 8 per day to monitor the peace.

With shut-down of air raids above the 20th parallel on January 2 and later cut-off of all aggressive activity above the DMZ (17th parallel), North Vietnamese MiGs and SAMs had no targets to work against except drone flights — and this increased operational losses in the closing days of the war.

At least one TV mission, reportedly, was flown after the start of the heavy B-52 raids. Guided from an image on the TV screen aboard the C-130 the bird covered 8 of 9 assigned targets, despite visibility restricted to 2 miles, and also picked up 3 bonus targets. The video tape could easily be duplicated and in this instance, because of the sensitivity of the information obtained, the Joint Chiefs of Staff instructed that the tape be destroyed. One report was that there was concern that the communications data link was not secure and that any TV receiver in the area could acquire and display the picture. Another report had it that the AQM designation of the vehicle misled Washington into believing a drone had been used to launch a missile against enemy targets, something they would not want publicized.

The last **SC** to fly before the cessation of hostilities was a TV-equipped bird. The final sortie was appropriately dubbed "The Last Picture Show."

When the cease fire finally came at 7 pm Washington time January 27, 1973, the recce drone operation was placed on a "hold/standby" basis awaiting further instruction.

But the pilotless birds were out of the barn again five days later for two flights on February first. The next day a series of monitoring flights in TV-equipped **SC**s were resumed.

The **TE** operated all during 1972 with a total of 69 missions — about 6 per month on the average — with loss of 5 birds (none due to enemy action. If the enemy showed up, the **TE** pulled back).

On December 26 the follow-on **TF** deployed to Osan, but did not fly any mission until February.

Two types of missions were flown out of Osan: (1) those over the Yellow Sea between the Korean peninsula and the mainland of China; and (2) flights to monitor activity along the 38th parallel, the demilitarized zone between the two Koreas.

In May, **SC**s and Loran-equipped **SDL**s were still operational out of U-Tapao as were the **TE** and **TF** electronic eavesdropping birds out of Osan, Korea.

99th CONSECUTIVE MISSION without a loss *was flown by 99th SRS in November 1973 at U-Tapao with an* ***SD****(Loran) bird. An* ***SC*** *with TV (LTV 250 'Buffalo Chip'), in background, flew the 100th mission. (The string ended on 102nd mission.)*

"TOM CAT" — THE RECORD HOLDER

Dave Gossett

CHAMPION OF CHAMPIONS, 'Tom Cat,' the record-setting 147SC *(Air Force nomenclature, AQM-34L). Operated by the 99th Strategic Reconnaissance Squadron of the 100th SRWing, its record of 68 sorties and an averge of 12 targets per mission was unparalleled. 'Tom Cat' failed to return from its mission of 25 September 1974.*

BOX SCORE

The **SC** was the real 'workhorse' of the 147 family of recce birds, with a total of 1651 missions flown.

Purchased with a life expectancy of 2.5 missions each, the 147**SC** drones actually averaged 7.3 missions in the combat environment of Southeast Asia.

''Tom Cat'' flew 68 missions before being lost; followed by ''Budweiser'' with 63, ''Ryan's Daughter'' with 52 and ''Baby Buck'' with 46 missions.

Next to the **SC** in total missions flown was the 147**TE** with 268 flights and the **TF** with 216.

The longest mission ever flown was by a **TF** electronic snooper which logged 7.8 hours. Operations continued out of U-Tapao with **S**-series birds and Osan with the **TF** right up to the very day that Saigon finally fell to the North Vietnamese in Summer 1975.

The last flight out of U-Tapao, April 30, 1975, was on a mission over Saigon; the last overseas mission was flown out of Osan by a **TF** on June 3, 1975.

In all, the 100th Strategic Reconnaissance Wing flew 3435 operational sorties in Southeast Asia.

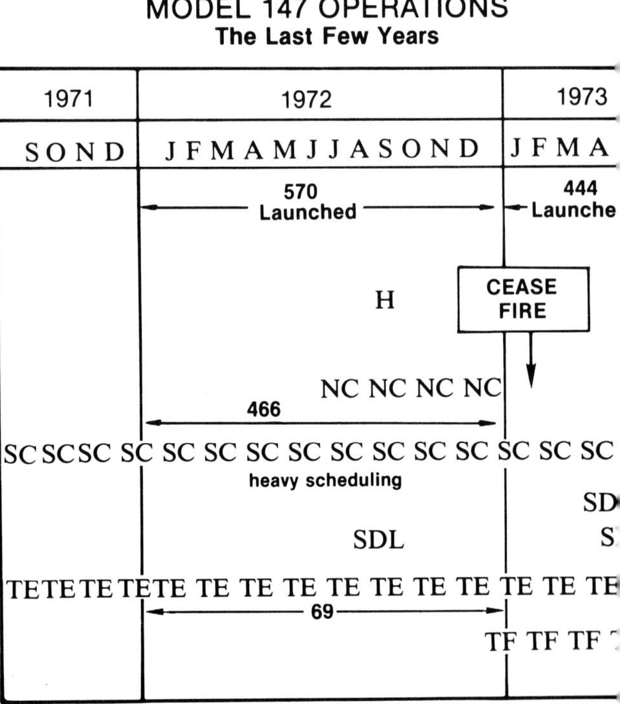

Louise M. Cram

29

BDA and POWs

Reflecting the concern of all Americans, a subcommittee of the House Appropriations Committee on January 9 and 18, 1973 conducted a closed hearing on the 'Bombings of North Vietnam' with its principal witness Adm. Thomas H. Moorer, Chairman of the Joint Chiefs of Staff.

Rep. George H. Mahon, (D), Texas, as subcommittee chairman opened the hearing:

> "Admiral Moorer, we are all very much concerned about the war in Vietnam. I think most of us are somewhat skeptical about the productivity of the acceleration of the bombing. None of the things we have tried have seemed to bring about peace."

Subsequently Admiral Moorer gave an extremely thorough presentation on bomb damage assessment (BDA), supplemented by slides and photos detailing results of the concentrated bombings conducted in the eleven days December 18 to 29, except for a 36-hour standdown over Christmas.

"The weather in North Vietnam," the JCS Chief reported, "because of the northeast monsoon, is such that it is mandatory that one use all-weather aircraft in order to maintain continuous attacks. So we used the B-52s to permit continuous heavy attack against the military targets; that is, the logistics facilities that were being used to support the war in the south.

"We did use a very integrated effort involving the use of chaff. That is simply a radar cloud. We used electronic countermeasures which are designed to jam the various frequencies used by the [Russian-built] missile.

"There were actually only about 12 hours [in eleven days] which were suitable for visual bombing, including use of the so-called 'smart' bombs . . . for those targets which were immediately adjacent to heavily populated areas.

"Of the 15 B-52s lost, ten actually went down in North Vietnamese territory . . . in the immediate vicinity of Hanoi . . . where the concentration of surface-to-air missiles was found.'"

Admiral Moorer went on with specifics concerning each of the major types of targets attacked:

- Railroad marshalling yards including that in downtown Hanoi "struck by laser-guided bombs," and railroad/highway bridges also dropped by 'smart' bombs.
- Nine major storage and distribution areas to which supplies were brought in to Hanoi and Haiphong, generally by rail from China.
- Transportation, equipment and repair facilities including vehicle depots for Russian trucks and other transports which carry equipment down into the battle areas of South Vietnam.
- Port and waterway targets including the Haiphong waterfront.
- Key hydro-electric powerplants and the grid of transformer stations.
- Communications centers including the main control buildings of the Hanoi radio communications complex.
- POL (petroleum, oil, lubricants) storage parks. "They like to take the 55-gallon drums out and disperse them over the countryside, including right on the dikes."
- Airfields and their aircraft including the Hanoi Gia Lam 'commercial' field "where they have stationed all of their best MiGs, the MiG-21M." Only 32 MiGs were launched during this period and eight of them were lost.
- The SAM surface-to-air missile sites. "Over 1000 SAMs were fired during this period."

"This was not indiscriminate bombing in any sense," continued Admiral Moorer. "This was a very selective bombing against limited military targets. I think the military targets that were attacked were essentially destroyed. If you are asking me why is anything left in Haiphong and Hanoi, we made a major effort to prevent damaging other than military targets.

"I would like to show the committee now some

pictures of the POW camps in Hanoi, because there was quite a lot of publicity to the effect that they had been attacked. This is not the case.

"This one is at Cu Loc. I think a close study of this picture shows there is no damage on this prison camp.

"The next [slide] is the one they called the Hanoi Hilton. I have already showed you some pictures of this railroad station. This is where the prison camp is. Our photo interpreters can find no bomb damage to that prison.

"The next one is the final one, which is the detention installation they call the Citadel. Here again, you can see in none of these buildings do we have bomb craters."

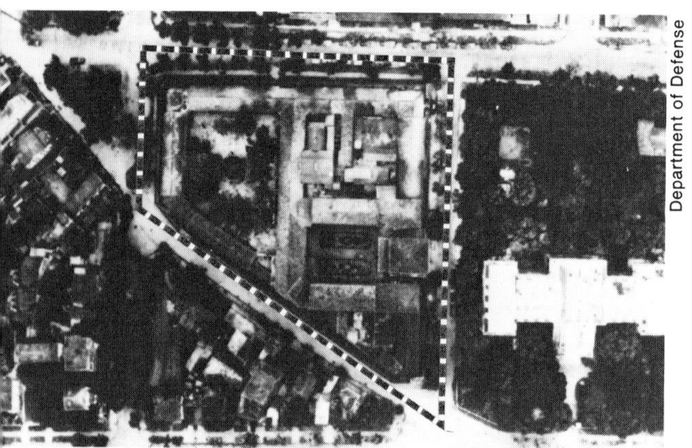

Department of Defense

19 **HANOI HILTON (Hoa Lo POW camp),** *location 19 in aerial photo opposite page. Photo taken 23 December 1972.*

What did residents of the Hanoi Hilton think about the B-52 bombing raids and the flights of the pilotless drones and manned SR-71 Blackbird reconnaissance planes over their prison camp?

When the POWs, mostly captured pilots, began to return in March, their impressions proved interesting.

Navy Captain James A. Mulligan, a prisoner for seven years, referring to the December bombings in a TIME interview, said, "It was spectacular. We saw explosions and realized they were working hard to wind things up. I knew the war would end when the B-52s came. I said it was just a matter of time and I'd be going home."

As for the 147 reconnaissance drones, one POW reported, "Sometimes we heard the drone. Sometimes we saw it. After a while, the usual comment was 'there goes the little guy! On Christmas Day, I was standing out in the open in the middle of the compound when a drone approached overhead. I figured it was taking pictures, so I just stood and smiled up at it. I figured somebody looking at the picture back there just might recognize me!"

Responding to a question from a House Appropriations Committee member as to "whether any foreign embassies were hit and whether a large hospital had been damaged," Admiral Moorer responded that "The Bac Mai Hospital was inadvertently hit.

"This was an attack which was designed to strike the Bac Mai storage center and airfield. So far as the embassies are concerned . . . the only 'embassy' that I am aware of is the Cuban Embassy and this was not the embassy itself, but a support building in the compound over on one corner."

Joseph P. Addabbo, (D), New York, commenting on the clarity of the photos shown in the presentation asked "Were the photos taken during the bombing runs or at a later period?"

Admiral Moorer: "Most of them were taken at a later period at low altitude at ____ feet. The ceilings [cloud cover] about which I am talking are usually about 2,000 or 3,000 feet. Therefore, it is impossible for a plane overhead to see the target. If he would come below that, he would probably be destroyed by his own bomb. We are using drones. If you noticed, every picture I showed you had the word "drone" on it and most of those pictures are taken at ____ feet, far too low to conduct bombing. That was the reason I showed you more than one picture of the same target because the drones are so close to it that they cannot get all the target in one photograph."

When the testimony before the House Appropriations Committee was finally released on February 26, 1973, after being reviewed for security considerations, it was the first time that a U.S. official had confirmed the use of unmanned aircraft for reconnaissance in Southeast Asia. The acknowledgement was eight years in coming.

12 **BAC MAI AIRFIELD military target area** *near which was POW camp known as 'The Zoo.' Photo taken 6 January 1973.*

Department of Defense

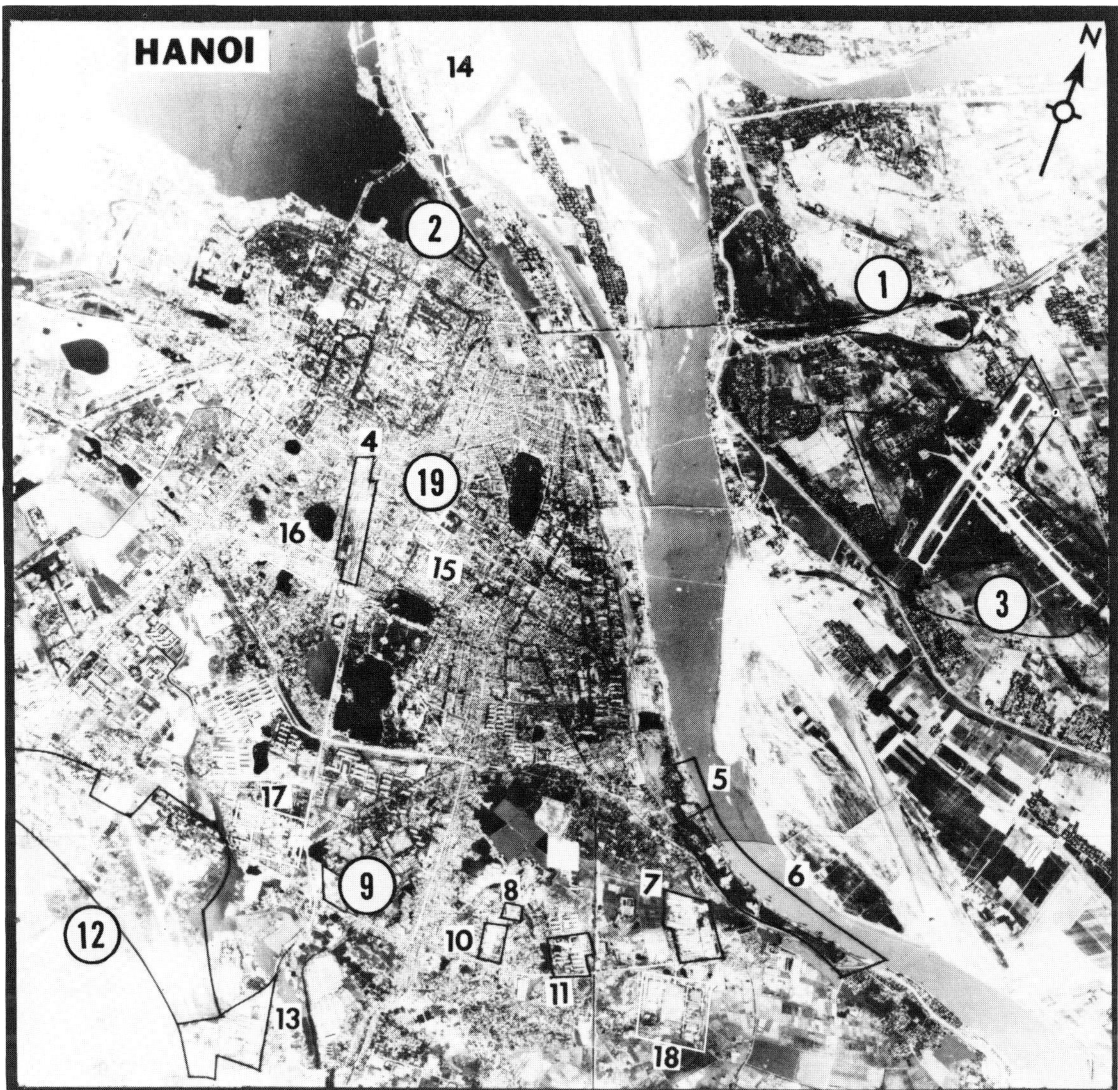

Department of Defense

COMPOSITE PHOTOGRAPH OF HANOI AREA from photo reconnaissance film *taken in January 1973 on completion of 'Linebacker' operations. Detailed study shows that areas targeted for strike during B-52 raids in December were military targets (outlined in black) and that there was no indiscriminate carpet bombing of Hanoi as had been alleged.*

Detailed photos made from Ryan 147*SC* low-altitude reconnaissance drones are found on prior page and two following pages. Large number with each photo corresponds to similar location number on this Hanoi aerial view.

2 HANOI'S IMPORTANT THERMAL POWER PLANT. *'Before' photo was taken 16 November 1972. Five weeks later a 147***SC** *returned at low altitude to assess the bomb damage from pre-Christmas B-52 bomb attacks.*

WE FIRST MET Cmdr. Edward H. Martin, a return POW, beside a waterfall in the Tijuca Forest outside Rio de Janeiro in mid-April 1973 as he and his wife, Sherry, vacationed together while rebuilding the threads of a relationship tattered by six years of forced separation. He was anxious to 'meet that fellow from Ryan' and tell him what a great morale booster the recce drones were to the 'guests' at the Hanoi Hilton. But we put him off until our return a week later to San Diego.

Meantime, a day before our departure, Rio's leading newspaper, O GLOBO, 21 de Abril de 1973, headlined

AVIOES DE RECONHECIMENTO VOLTAM A SOBREVOR HANOI

> "For the first time, since inception of the cease-fire, planes of reconnaissance without pilots of the United States flew over Vietnam of the North, including the capital, Hanoi, bringing a protest of the Governo norte-vietnamita . . ."

We discussed the Brazilian newspaper story briefly with Ed after he had gone forward to the flight deck of the Varig 707 charter to fly the right hand seat for a period on the leg between Rio and Lima, Peru.

A week later Ed visited the Teledyne Ryan plant in San Diego to share his experiences with a group of management officials and drone program personnel.

"Within a week of being shot down on July 9, 1967 I was aware of the overflights of the Firebee reece birds despite the fact I was a crumbling heap of humanity tied up in ropes and lying near unconsciousness on the floor of my cell in the "New Guy" Village of Hoa Lo Prison in Hanoi.

"As executive officer of VA-34 attack squadron from the carrier 'Intrepid', I was approaching Hanoi in an A-4C from the southwest when, about 15 miles from the city center, the missiles began coming. I managed to evade most of them but an SA-2 I didn't see detonated about 250 feet in front of me. When I flew into the burst, that was the start of my five and a half years as an unwilling guest of the North Vietnamese.

"I was well aware of the Firebee recce drones because I'd been operations officer of the squadron for two years and it was my business to keep informed. Also, I knew of the Firebee target drones which I first encountered as a participant in the Navy's 'Top Gun' Weapons Meet at Yuma, Arizona, in October 1959.

"Earlier, over the Tonkin Gulf, as I was in-bound one day to the coast of North Vietnam we were advised of, and saw, reconnaissance activity to our south. It appeared to be Firebee, although we were not specifically advised the recce birds flying in that area were pilotless.

"My first week in prison was an extremely traumatic one. I was in Room 18 — the infamous 'blue room' — under terrific pressure [torture] but not about to give in. Any sense of time was a very difficult thing at this stage of interrogation.

"An alert sounded. There was a raid. And an enormous quantity of Triple-A artillery, almost beyond belief. The guards and interrogators had vacated to their shelters nearby.

"The raid was over in about 20 minutes. Soon my friends returned. They were more than a little angry as they resumed their work, so that time for me was pretty hazy. You understand I can only give you the date of this raid plus or minus four or five days as I had no track of time. But suddenly, without an alert being sounded, there was the noise of a jet engine — light type — and the unmistakable swish of a single aircraft in high speed flight, followed by a lot of anti-aircraft activity.

"My interrogation officer, who did not speak English very well, was extremely angry when he told me 'we just shot down another of your spy planes.' But I remember for that short time it gave me a great sense of elation at what was the most trying period of my life.

"One thing that impressed me most about the pilotless recce aircraft was the relative degree of impunity with which they intruded upon North Vietnamese air space. When a strike force of bombers and attack planes came in there was always an alert, but when a single 147 Firebee (we didn't know their nomenclature then) came in fast and low they wouldn't draw an alert.

"Thus, on several occasions when we were outside for ten or fifteen minutes to bathe, wash our clothes and plates, and empty toilet buckets, we'd see the 'spy plane' drones. I'd been immobile and so critically ill for three months I didn't think I'd live so the first time I actually saw one going right over the camp was not until October or November, 1967. The guards got very excited and herded us back inside. By the time they started firing their small arms at it, the bird was well out of range.

"The next spring — it was betweeen April 27 and May 7 after I'd been moved to a camp known as 'The Zoo' near Bac Mai air field, missile storage area and hospital — a drone came down during the period we were getting outside for up to thirty minutes. I'd guess it was flying at .9 Mach and they were firing at it all the way with AAA radar control aimed fire.

1 **RAILROAD MARSHALLING YARDS at Gia Lam** *were struck by laser-guided bombs 27 December 1972.*

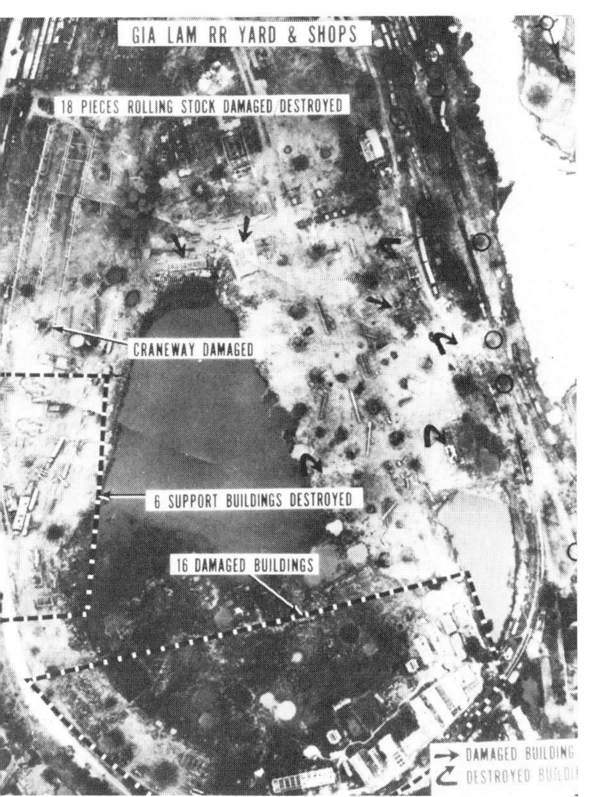

Department of Defense

3 **ADJACENT GIA LAM AIRFIELD** *had been severely damaged six days earlier, 21 December 1972.*

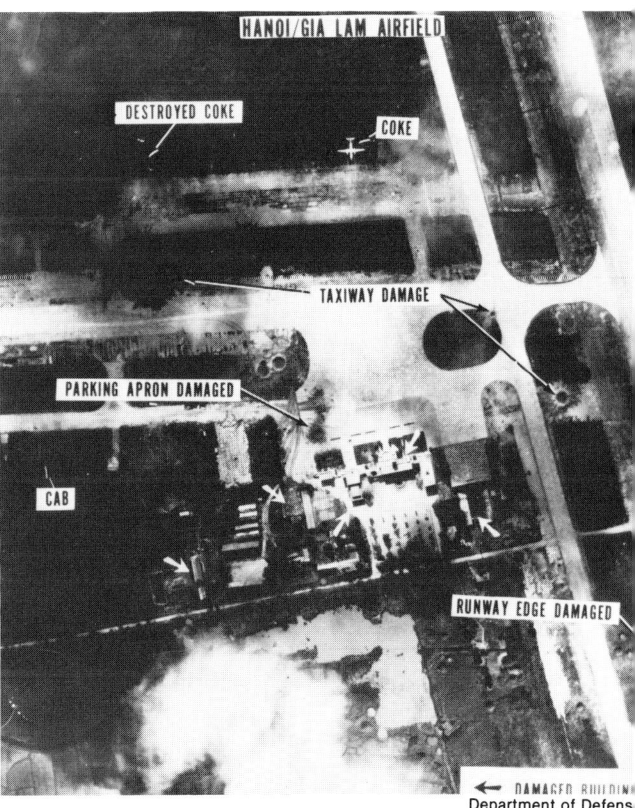

Department of Defens

"They got quite a few hits and I saw pieces flying off that aircraft. We had a very good view of it — it was a very beautiful spring day, unusual for Hanoi — but the Firebee, which appeared to be jinking, kept right on going.

"The guard was absolutely horrified and tried to run us back in but we refused to go — it was only a matter of seconds — until the drone was out of sight. I remember we were all elated; so much so that they dragged me out for special treatment as I was the senior officer at the 'zoo.' They reprimanded me for my bad attitude because I had smiled when one of the spy planes, as they called them, intruded upon the Vietnamese people.

"From then, April 1968, until November of that year when the bombing halt above the 20th parallel was extended south to the DMZ at the 17th parallel, the drones continued their intelligence-gathering flights over the Hanoi-Haiphong area. We saw many of them. The drones and manned reconnaissance planes were the only aircraft we heard for a long, long time [until bombing was resumed April 16, 1972]. They were about the only thing that did lift our morale during those years.

"When we heard about the resumption of bombing after a lapse of four frustrating years, our high-spirited group couldn't hold back their emotions in front of our Vietnamese friends. But that brought a young lieutenant j.g. who worked for me in our prison camp organization a brutal beating just outside our door. The beating was for our benefit since we had displayed an incorrect attitude, and because the guards had also found out that the lieutenant was wearing on the reverse side of his skivvy shirt the hand-made American flag to which we pledged allegiance each evening after things had quieted down.

"The big event for all of us was, of course, the B-52 bomber raids. When they started their awesome, devastating strikes in mid-December 1972 we knew we were coming home.

"By then I was back in Hoa Lo Prison downtown, the Hanoi Hilton, and your 147 drones were flying their low-level daylight bomb damage assessment sorties.

"The last flight we saw was about January 20, and it was indeed impressive as it virtually duplicated one we had seen in May. This drone flew directly over the camp at an unusually low altitude. Again it split the prison compound right down the center and flew off to the southwest. We believe it did a 180 degree turn, because shortly a drone returned from that direction and came back over, again splitting the camp right down the groove. We were waving and shouting to it as was customary because we always did what we could to let our presence there be known.

"We'd soon be going home and the guards knew it. By then we knew just how far we could push them. It was then we told 'Boris' that he was on candid camera and had better smile the next time so we'd know what he looks like for future reference!"

Department of Defense

INFAMOUS HANOI HILTON, the Hoa Lo Prison *where Cmdr. Ed Martin spent most of his 5½ years as a POW. "Reconnaissance drones overhead were about the only thing that lifted our morale during those years."*

Harold Wolford

CMDR. ED MARTIN ON A VISIT to Teledyne Ryan *after the return of American POWs meets with Admiral Ulysses S. Grant Sharp (USN, Ret.) and Robert C. Jackson, Teledyne Ryan chairman of the board.*

Admiral Sharp is the author of "STRATEGY FOR DEFEAT — Vietnam in Retrospect," an account of how civilian coaches LBJ and Defense Secretary McNamara sent in plays from the side-lines in Washington instead of permitting military experts in the field to effectively use American power in Vietnam.

As Commander in Chief Pacific (CINCPAC), Admiral Sharp was America's top commander in Southeast Asia from the Gulf of Tonkin incident of 1964 to his retirement in August 1968.

OPINION

FOR THE RECORD

THE INTERNATIONAL INTELLIGENCE community operates under its own unique ground rules and code of ethics. Its cardinal rule is "never admit anything." Everyone may know pretty well what everyone else is doing and knowledge of covert operations may be widely held and publicized. But that is not sufficient reason for any government to make an open admission of its methods. So goes the rationale.

When Francis Gary Powers floated down over Russia after his U-2 spy plane was knocked out of the sky in May 1960, the United States government tried to pass off as accurate a number of not very ingenious 'cover' stories. Not until pushed in the corner did the government, in the person of President Eisenhower, confirm the U-2 flights of which Russia had long been aware.

When the first Ryan 147**B** unmanned reconnaissance drone was shot down over South China on November 15, 1964, and so announced by the Red Chinese at Peking, Washington became tongue tied, relying on the traditional "no comment."

In Southeast Asia, however, some partial truth in the matter was disclosed two days later in press reports out of Saigon which stated that 'American military sources' admitted drones were being operated on intelligence missions. But, it was pointed out, the U.S. Air Force refused to comment 'officially' on the drones.

Officially seemed to be the key word.

If there was still any doubt that the drones were being used it was dispelled April 2, 1965 when a 147**B** was put on display in Peking and photographs sent by wirephone to the world press.

This was further fortified 16 days later when photos appeared of not one but three downed 147**B** Firefly drones. Even with this evidence, and the all too obvious knowledge that China and North Vietnam knew what we were up to, there was still no 'official' confirmation from Washington.

Thus for eight years the Communists continued to publicize operation of American reconnaissance drones in Southeast Asia while the U.S. government held to its 'Maginot Line' no-comment strategy. No loss of U.S. drones was ever reported because, officially, they didn't exist.

Who was fooling whom? No one, actually.

Pictures began appearing in American aviation and other magazines showing exceptionally good reconnaissance photographs of bombed bridges, POL (petroleum, oil, lubricant) storage areas, railroad marshalling yards and similar military targets in North Vietnam. Often the pictures were credited as having been taken by unmanned reconnaissance drones. Still no 'official' admission from Washington.

Eyebrows were really raised, however, when the November 9, 1970 issue of Aviation Week was distributed. There, big as life, was a very complete, very accurate disclosure of drone operations and drone designs. Written by staffer Barry Miller, it was obvious he had been given access to much classified information and had tacit understanding that the material could be used so long as no source was identified or no impression given that the release constituted an 'official' confirmation.

Could it have been that Department of Defense officials were anxious to broaden knowledge of the existence of the drones? They had every reason to do so because, with Israel buying a quantity of Ryan 124**I** model vehicles, it was entirely possible that one would be shot down in the Middle East, perhaps over Egypt.

Should that unlikely event happen its propaganda advantage to the Egyptian government would be greatly minimized. After all it would be common knowledge that American-built drones had such capability. 'What's the fuss all about?' might well be the response in such a circumstance. At least it would be better than the handling of the U-2 incident in 1960.

The writer, busy compiling this documented

record of the covert drone activity, found himself standing helplessly on the sidelines as bit by bit the key information got wider and wider coinage. How long would the government maintain its posture of officially ignoring the existence of the program?

In the spring of 1971 official Air Force classification documents were revised to permit release of external views of the 147 family of drones. A general statement that the U.S. Air Force had developed drones which could be used for reconnaissance was permitted, so long as there was no use of program code names, technical details or reference to operational missions.

When, in July 1971, it was announced that President Nixon would visit Peking, 'administration officials' in Washington indicated that drone reconnaissance flights over China would be curtailed to avoid a possible U-2 type incident. Still no official admission that such flights had been taking place.

By the Spring of 1972 official Washington was getting very close to a full disclosure. Officials began referring to 'drone reconnaissance operations in Southeast Asia' but stopped short of specific mention of the activity based out of U-Tapao Thailand, which was then providing unmanned reconnaissance over North Vietnam and South China, or of electronic intelligence gathering flights out of Osan, South Korea.

In an interview in April, 1972, which appeared in Air Force Magazine the following month, General George S. Brown, Commander, Air Force Systems Command, was quoted as saying, "We are using some of these devices (RPVs) in Southeast Asia in an operational role.

"The only reason that we need RPVs is that we don't want to expose the man in the cockpit needlessly or expend our resources in getting him to the target."

Dr. John L. McLucas, Under Secretary of the Air Force, presented a paper on "Some Air Force Views on Remotely Piloted Vehicles" before the Electronic Industries Association on May 31, 1972. He further lifted the veil of secrecy. Here are excerpts:

> ". . . we used drones . . . more recently for certain reconnaissance functions.
>
> "Most of our attention was directed toward satisfying immediate requirements in Southeast Asia . . . as requirements increased . . . we accumulated more experience in high and low altitude drones.
>
> "The successful development of drones for aerial photography had added significantly to our reconnaissance and surveillance capability."

Could anyone reasonably doubt that the United States had confirmed its use of unmanned vehicles for reconnaissance in Southeast Asia? Yet any reference by the contractor to mission capability remained classified.

HOW TELEDYNE RYAN knowledge about its military customer could be so lax is unclear, but management of the reconnaissance programs awoke on the morning of Friday, November 3, 1972 to read a startling article in the San Diego Union.

General John C. Meyer, Commander in Chief, Strategic Air Command, had flown into San Diego the previous day and had delivered an address before the San Diego Rotary Club which included significant information about Ryan's hush-hush programs. No one from Ryan knew he was coming to town; no one was present at the luncheon where his remarks included —

> "We (SAC) are in the drone reconnaissance business. I think San Diego is probably the drone capital of the world and certainly our major supplier.
>
> "We have our people in the system as much as possible but we let the drone do the 'high risk' flying. They have been doing a great job in Southeast Asia."

In a later interview with Kip Cooper, Military Affairs Editor of the San Diego Union, General Meyer was quoted in greater detail:

> ". . . drones . . . have been doing low altitude reconnaissance flying over heavily defended areas of North Vietnam.
>
> "The disadvantage of using drones this way is that we lose a lot of them. The loss rate is higher but we are willing to risk more of them, and they save lives."

The afternoon paper of the same day continued to quote General Meyer:

> "The remote-controlled drones are replacing photo planes on what we call high-risk missions. They can assess bombing damage and see what else is going on. They bring back film and we get very accurate electronic transmissions on the exact locations they are covering."

Why all the secrecy and mystery in withholding from the American public information we know the enemy already has? People who have long been in the military and intelligence structure say that civilians just don't understand. One key contention is that we simply don't want the enemy to know how much we really know about him . . . how sophisticated our intelligence-gathering capability has become.

As Rep. Joseph P. Addabbo, (D), New York, phrased it in directing his remarks to Admiral Moorer during his January appearance before the House Appropriations Committee:

> The pictures you have shown us and the charts you have shown us this morning have been marked secret, classified, etcetera. What is secret and classified in those pictures as to

> the sorties? Why can't these pictures be made known to the public so we can stop the question of whether we are bombing hospitals or not; we are sending over 1,000 planes; we are losing 300 planes, 30 men. Why must these pictures and this information be classified and secret? North Vietnam knows where you have hit and how many planes you have sent over, so why must this information remain secret?

Two months after the January 1973 cease-fire a Teledyne Ryan representative hand-carried a copy of the manuscript for this book to Department of Defense Security Review officers to have it blessed with 'holy water.' Several days later the company representative was told that while the material was extremely interesting, it would have to be so sanitized for public release that it would hardly be recognizable.

"Maybe in six months or a year, you'd have a better chance of having it cleared," was the best advice offered.

Coming as a refreshing breeze after Watergate and just prior to the Pentagon Papers mistrial was an editorial, "Fumbling the Facts," by Robert Hotz, veteran editor of highly regarded Aviation Week and Space Technology. Its April 23 issue featured ten pages of the much-delayed drone reconnaissance photos used by Admiral Moorer in his January briefing.

> "As in the Watergate affair, the White House has been several months late in making these pertinent facts available to the American people and has lost a large measure of credibility as a result.
>
> "The tardy release of these pictures and the information about the bombing campaign provide another example of official fumbling with the facts in a manner that does discredit to U.S. policy at home and abroad. This is particularly stupid when revelation of the facts would generate support for the policy and take most of the wind out of the critics' wails. **It also generates an aura of suspicion and mistrust when facts that are no secret to the enemy are deliberately withheld from the American people.** *[Emphasis added — Ed.]*
>
> "In mid-April when few media still had any interest in the matter, these pictures slithered out of the Pentagon.
>
> "The fumbling of these facts through three crucial months by the highest levels of the Nixon Administration is another demonstration of the shoddy treatment accorded the citizens of this country about their nation's business."

APPENDIX

The TELEDYNE RYAN FAMILY of RPVs
at Edwards Air Force Base 1971

Dave Gossett

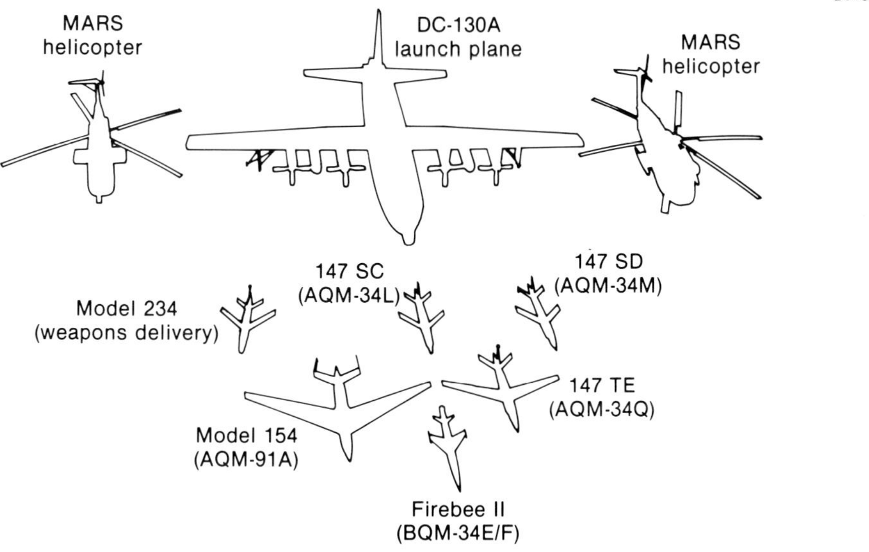

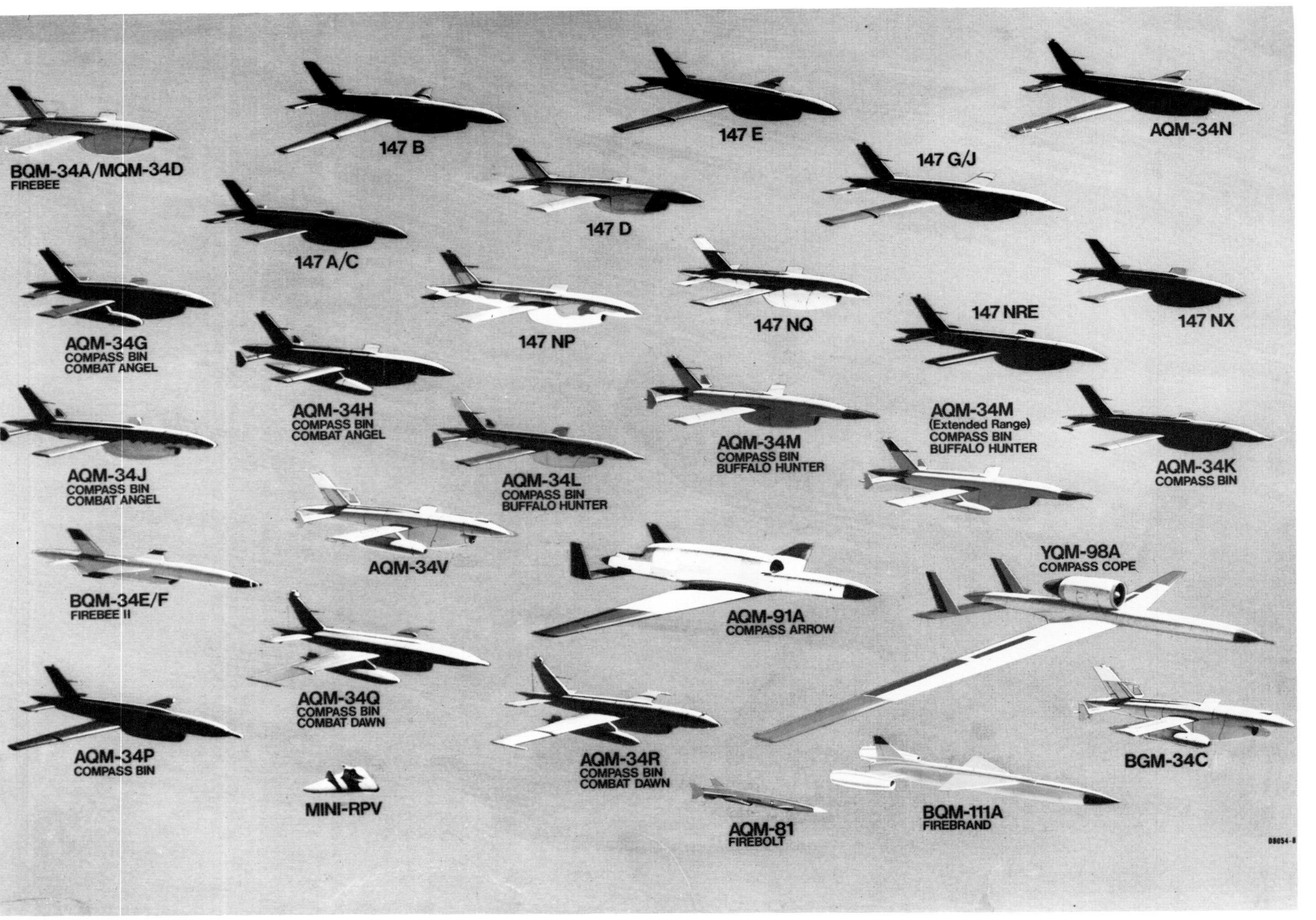
147 B
147 E
AQM-34N
BQM-34A/MQM-34D
FIREBEE
147 G/J
147 D
147 A/C
147 NRE
147 NX
147 NQ
147 NP
AQM-34G
COMPASS BIN
COMBAT ANGEL
AQM-34H
COMPASS BIN
COMBAT ANGEL
AQM-34M
(Extended Range)
COMPASS BIN
BUFFALO HUNTER
AQM-34M
COMPASS BIN
BUFFALO HUNTER
AQM-34K
COMPASS BIN
AQM-34J
COMPASS BIN
COMBAT ANGEL
AQM-34L
COMPASS BIN
BUFFALO HUNTER
AQM-34V
YQM-98A
COMPASS COPE
BQM-34E/F
FIREBEE II
AQM-91A
COMPASS ARROW
AQM-34Q
COMPASS BIN
COMBAT DAWN
AQM-34P
COMPASS BIN
AQM-34R
COMPASS BIN
COMBAT DAWN
BGM-34C
MINI-RPV
BQM-111A
FIREBRAND
AQM-81
FIREBOLT

RYAN RECONNAISSANCE MODEL DIRECTORY

Ryan 147 Model	*Military Model*	*Length '*	*Span '*	*Area □ '*	*Thrust (lbs.)*	**Mission**	*Month/Year Operated*	*Number Launched*	*% Return*	*Most Flights by a Bird*
A		27	13	36	1700	Fire Fly — first recce demo drone	4/62-8/62			
B		27	27	80	1700	Lightning Bug — first big-wing high-altitude day photo bird	8/64-12/65	78	61.5%	8
C		27	15	40	1700	Training, and low-altitude tests	10/65			
D		27	15	40	1700	From C for electronic intelligence	8/65	2		
E		27	27	80	1700	From B for hi-altitude electronic intelligence	10/65-2/66	4		
F		27	27	80	1700	From B — electronic countermeasures	7/66			
G		29	27	80	1920	Longer B with larger engine	10/65-8/67	83	54.2%	11
H	AQM-34N	30	32	114	1920	Hi-alt. photo; more range	3/67-7/71	138	63.8%	13
J		29	27	80	1920	First low-alt. day photo (BLACS)	3/66-11/67	94	64.9%	9
N		23	13	36	1700	Expendable decoy (from BQM-34A)	3/66-6/66	9	0	
NX		23	13	36	1700	Decoy and medium-alt. day photo	11/66-6/67	13	46.2%	6
NP		28	15	40	1700	Interim low-alt. day photo	6/67-9/67	19	63.2%	5
NRE		28	13	40	1700	First night photo (from NP)	5/67-9/67	7	42.9%	4
NQ		23	13	36	1700	Low-alt. NX; hand controlled	5/68-12/68	66	86.4%	20
*NA/NC	AQM-34G	26	15	40	1700	By TAC for chaff and ECM	8/68-9/71			
NC	AQM-34H	26	15	40	1700	Leaflet dropping (Bullshit Bombers)	7/72-12/72	29	89.7%	8
NC(M1)	AQM-34J	26	15	40	1700	Interim low-alt. day photo and for training				
S/SA		29	13	36	1920	Low-altitude day photo	12/67-5/68	90	63.3%	11
SB		29	13	36	1920	Improved SA low-altitude bird	3/68-1/69	159	76.1%	14
SRE	AQM-34K	29	13	36	1920	Night photo version of SB	11/68-10/69	44	72.7%	9
SC	AQM-34L	29	13	36	1920	The low-altitude workhorse	1/69-6/73	1651	87.2%	68**
SC/TV	– 34L/TV	29	13	36	1920	SC model with real-time TV	6/72-	121	93.4%	42
SD	AQM-34M	29	13	36	1920	Low-altitude photo; real-time data	6/74-4/75	183	97.3%	39
SDL	– 34M(L)	29	13	36	1920	SD bird with Loran navigation	8/72	121	90.9%	36
SK		29	15	40		Navy operation from aircraft carrier	11/69-6/70			
T	AQM-34P	30	32	114	2800	Larger engine; high-alt. day photo	4/69-9/70	28	78.6%	
TE	AQM-34Q	30	32	114	2800	High-altitude; real time Comint	2/70-6/73	268	91.4%	34
TF	AQM-34R	30	32	114	2800	Improved long-range TE	2/73-6/75	216	96.8%	37
								3435 operational sorties by 100th SRW		

*Note: *NA/NC Combat Angel birds were operated on standby in U.S. by Tactical Air Command for possible pre-strike ECM chaff-dispensing missions.*

***68 missions by Tom Cat*
63 missions by Budweiser
52 missions by Ryan's Daughter
46 missions by Baby Buck

INDEX

A

B

C

D

E

F

G

H

I

J

K

L

M

N

O

P

Q

R

S

T

U

V

W

X

Y

Z